TRIANGLE CLASSICS

ILLUMINATING THE GAY AND LESBIAN EXPERIENCE

And the Band Played On
by Randy Shilts

The Autobiography of Alice B. Toklas
by Gertrude Stein

The Beebo Brinker Chronicles
by Ann Bannon

A Boy's Own Story/
The Beautiful Room Is Empty
by Edmund White

Brideshead Revisited
by Evelyn Waugh

The Celluloid Closet
by Vito Russo

City of Night
by John Rechy

Dancer from the Dance
by Andrew Holleran

Death in Venice and Seven
Other Stories
by Thomas Mann

The Family of Max Desir
by Robert Ferro

Giovanni's Room
by James Baldwin

The Lure
by Felice Picano

Olivia
by Olivia

Oranges Are Not the Only Fruit
by Jeanette Winterson

Orlando
by Virginia Woolf

The Picture of Dorian Gray
by Oscar Wilde

The Price of Salt
by Patricia Highsmith

Rubyfruit Jungle
by Rita Mae Brown

A Single Man
by Christopher Isherwood

The Sophie Horowitz Story/Girls, Visions and Everything/
After Delores
by Sarah Schulman

Surpassing the Love of Men
by Lillian Faderman

The Well of Loneliness
by Radclyffe Hall

What Is Found There/An Atlas of the Difficult World/
The Fact of a Doorframe
by Adrienne Rich

Zami/Sister Outsider/Undersong
by Audre Lorde

THE SOPHIE HOROWITZ STORY

GIRLS, VISIONS AND EVERYTHING

AFTER DELORES

THE SOPHIE HOROWITZ STORY

GIRLS, VISIONS AND EVERYTHING

AFTER DELORES

SARAH SCHULMAN

QUALITY PAPERBACK BOOK CLUB
NEW YORK

Contents

Introduction by Sarah Schulman ix

The Sophie Horowitz Story 1

Girls, Visions and Everything 197

After Delores 381

INTRODUCTION

I t is wonderful and weird, at thirty-eight, to have
lived long enough to have a compendium of "early
novels." But I think it is really more of an acknowl-
edgment of how quickly gay life has changed. Some of these
books have already become outdated, and then had historical significance, and then acquired nostalgic value, all in a
very short period of time. A professor recently told me that
she teaches *The Sophie Horowitz Story* because her students
don't know what a collective is.

Of course, it is somewhat painful to reread these books.
I've learned a lot more about writing and some of the awk-
wardnesses are now embarrassing. Also, I've lost a certain
innocence that I find enjoyable in these first novels. In them
I can see the origins of themes that have transformed and
dominated my writing over the years. For example, familial
homophobia is treated in *Sophie Horowitz* as comic relief. I
abandoned it as a subject until 1992 when, with the publi-
cation of *Empathy*, it reemerged as the revelation at the core
of the book's formal structure. Another consistent theme is
the destruction of my neighborhood through yuppification
and the collapse of low-income housing. In the early books,
again it is a source of humor and sarcasm. But, over the
years, the transformation of the East Village from a center
for the production of global ideas to a place of consump-
tion by the wealthy has become morbid, annihilating, and
ultimately just sad.

Of course, the documentation of gay life before AIDS

seems stark when looking back on these manuscripts from the vantage point of 1997. In *Sophie Horowitz*, there are unknowing descriptions of the gay-male public-sex scene and the exclusion of women from gay men's bars, as well as prophetic sarcasm about the kitsch of S/M and cross-dressing. In *Girls, Visions and Everything*, there is a world of women only. The underground quality of lesbian cultural life at that time could never be experienced in the contemporary context of gay consumerism and niche marketing. Today we are blatantly misrepresented in the popular culture, then we were not represented except in arcane code. To be a lesbian artist in a time when such a concept was unfathomable removed any real possibility of career (although delusions abounded) and so left a kind of pure, longing, passionate love of art coexisting with daily but unanalyzed wounds from the brutal homophobia we experienced. I don't think we ever understood how deeply we had been affected by that injustice. Simultaneously, there was the revelatory necessity of making of a new worldview out of both creative energy and deep, misunderstood deprivation. Writing *After Delores*, I think, was a moment when the life I had been trying on for a few years became my real life. That cast of outcasts became my normative environment, and I was forever one of them, a product of them. The really frightening, dangerous, cold-blooded experiences of young women totally alone became more than just a story but the facts of the matter. Even though imitators have created kitsch out of this life, rereading these books reveals the authentic experience at its root.

I'd just like to say a few things about the historiography of these books.

Sophie Horowitz was, I believe, the third lesbian detective novel on the face of the earth. As a journalist, I had covered the arrest of some Weather Underground people after they attempted to rob an armored car. Their resurfacing gave me the opportunity to try to articulate a new view of sixties radicals from the perspective of the next generation. I was twenty-four at the time and simultaneously trying to articulate a new lesbian generation, one with a foot in the underground lesbian culture and a foot in popular culture. I falsely believed that inserting such unknown and forbidden content (as you must remember it was) into such a popular form as a detective novel would have long-range radical results. However, now I see that the project ultimately became co-opted. For now, literary agents tell lesbian writers to "throw in a murder" since, in 1997, lesbian life is still not considered to be a literary life but rather a life suitable for genre fiction only.

Sophie Horowitz, by the way, was turned down by twenty-five publishers, many of whom claimed to like it but either suggested it would be offensive to someone else (notably "conservative librarians") or suggested I change the protagonists' sexuality.

Girls, Visions and Everything was for many years my favorite of my books, only recently superseded by *Empathy*. It was the beginning of my ongoing efforts to take a life that defies conventional narrative (Romance, Marriage, Motherhood) and build its own formal inventions motivated completely by the emotional revelations at the core of the book. This novel really affected people. I have met women who moved to New York because they read it, and others who used it as a way to imagine their lives, to situate themselves, to model their own cultural aesthetics. All of this was possible only because it was written for a generation that was denied a context. And, like all my books, it has many cameo appearances by minor cultural icons and long-forgotten girls on the scene. For me, it was the beginning of trying to understand what lesbian friendship and romance really meant and to situate it as an essential heartbeat of a city on the brink of enormous changes. It also is a document of artists with integrity about their homosexuality in the middle of a huge moral void. I was very typical of the other lesbian artists of that time in that I had no training, no connections, and no institutional support. I learned how to write by writing in my apartment, not by taking classes; I was influenced by an eclectic array of work that fell into my hands through many avenues, and I clawed my way into an unwelcoming profession through the support of underground presses and a will of steel.

By writing *Girls, Visions and Everything* in response to Jack Kerouac (just as *After Delores* was in response to Jean Genet), I was insisting on my experience as an organic part of American life and therefore asserting that fiction with primary lesbian content should be recognized as an integral part of American literature. If I could stretch to universalize to Jack Kerouac, then the dominant-culture reader must be able to reciprocate by universalizing to me. This last goal has not yet been realized. Yet over the years, it has become clearer to me what that shift in subjectivity would require. And, of course, being able to imagine a cultural progression is the first step towards achieving it. Which all goes to say that winning respect and recognition for fiction that does not obscure the lesbian content of the author's life is a difficult, frustrating, unabandonable project, rooted in problems of caste, not quality.

After Delores was, for many years, my best-selling novel

(until *Rat Bohemia* in 1995). I wrote it against the grain of the tyranny of positive images. I longed for a lesbian fiction that depicted us in the totality of our humanity. And yet, at the same time, when I was writing it, I worried that I was showing too much of myself. We were so punished by exterior lies that lesbians had had no opportunity to see ourselves complexly. I feared showing that I had violent fantasies, that I was jealous, that I experienced anger. I was sure I would be looked upon as a freak. Ironically, over ten years later, I still get letters from across America and as far away as Japan, Greece, and Germany saying how much readers identified with the novel. That experience taught me to always write from a place of personal truth no matter what disapproval I feared in the moment.

Time passes, and the three novels collected here are both evidence and a testament. The world they describe no longer exists. It has been destroyed by AIDS, gentrification, and marketing. But it did exist, and that can never be denied. And I am very grateful to have these books presented together in this volume.

—Sarah Schulman
May 1997

THE SOPHIE HOROWITZ STORY

ACKNOWLEDGMENTS

I'd like to acknowledge all of the people who gave me their time and encouragement during the completion of this work. Peg Byron, Robin Epstein, Charlie Schulman, Lydia Pilcher, Susan Seizer, Susan LaVallee, Marie Dagata, Steve Berman, Jaime Horwitz, Beryl Satter, Julia Scher, Shirley Arriker, Maxine Wolfe, Sam, Frederique Delacoste, Danielle Frank, Joan Jubela, Bettina Berch, Deb Sherman, Suzanne Seay, Harriet Hirschorn, Stephanie Skura, Stephanie Doba, and Stephanie Roth.

I am especially grateful for the efforts and support of Rebecca Sperling, without whom this work never would have been published, and Barbara Barracks, without whom Sophie Horowitz would never have come to life.

For Ethel Stevens

CHAPTER ONE

I wanted to feed Lillian something delicious because I knew that's what she was going to feed me. Glancing over the meat and poultry case at Key Food, nothing spoke to the sweetness of that woman. Maybe fresh pears stewed in brandy with orange chocolate sauce. "Mmmm," I sighed out loud. "You too baby," winked the stock boy over by the Campbell's soup. Every other weekend for ten months now, she's been coming down on the Friday night express from Boston to wrap her legs around me.

"*WHUL, its four o'clock. You give us a minute, we'll give you the word.*"

I glanced at the No Smoking sign and lit a Parliament.

"*Taxi strike at midnight. Yanks drop to third place. Germaine Covington arrested in bank robbery. Mayor announces plans for Times Square shopping mall, 'Just like Albany' he predicts. All this and more after a word from Mighty-Fine.*"

My eyes glazed over. My cheeks flushed. My skin turned cold. My palms began to sweat. *Germaine Covington*. It must be twelve years.

Twelve years ago my grandmother and I sat at the kitchen table breaking the ends off string beans and singing Yiddish songs. Suddenly the sky cracked in a giant crash of sound and power. I thought it was the war come home, but nothing followed that first explosion. For minute one large silence reverberated through the neighborhood, but it was quickly broken by screams and sirens and street sounds as children rushed to the remnants of a recently opened recruiting station two blocks away. We heard the story on the news that night. The bomb had gone off too soon. All the conspirators were killed. All except one. They showed her picture on TV. Germaine Covington looked out at America and her face has stayed with me all these years.

All these years she's been an integral part of my childhood and adolescence. The backdrop of my teenage crisis was her face plastered on post office walls. Six years on the Ten Most Wanted List. Four years as Public Enemy Number One. Around the dinner table my mother would thank her stars I hadn't been born ten years earlier. "You would have ended up just like that girl, throwing away the best things in life." She never said what those things were.

The story came out. She was from a rich family. "The richest," my grandmother said. Her father was vice-president of American Express. She went to a good small liberal college like other young women of her time and caliber. One day she joined a picket line. The next day, a demonstration. Soon she was throwing bombs and killing people. At least that's what the newspapers said. The years passed and the world changed. Most people forgot about Germaine Covington. But not me.

Later that night Lillian and I were hanging out in the tub eating blintzes with sour cream, sucking on Lowenbrau darks. I watched the beer dribble down her chin.

She's a strong woman with a tight body. Her skin and hair are henna-colored except for a patch of bright orange over her left ear. I never know how I feel about her visually. She's got a particular look that speaks to a particular taste like French cigarettes or a Budweiser. She's ten years older than me and likes to fight.

"I remember Germaine from Ann Arbor, '67, '68," she reminisced. "She was the leader of our cell—The Center City Six. We ran into the cafeteria of Dwight D. Eisenhower Intermediate School sticking our fingers in the kids' food chanting 'something's rumbling.' The line then was that elementary school kids were the revolutionaries of the future. By the time they got to senior high school they were already just like their parents so we had to get them early. We occupied the cafeteria, all women wearing football helmets. Mine said 'Philadelphia Eagles.'"

A dollop of sour cream fell into the bathwater. "Later that afternoon when we were in jail, Germaine said we had to be willing to risk getting killed by the police. She said we had to give everything to *the struggle*. We had to *smash monogamy,* we had to *break with our parents,* we had to give up our *white skin privilege* and we had to *fight the pigs*. I was scared. I was young. I took out a pen and started scribbling on this roll of toilet paper about how things were getting too heavy for me. I admitted my fears and doubts. I wasn't sure I wanted to *struggle* for the rest of my life. At first it was really exciting. We were trying so many different things. I felt powerful, turning over the world. But the situation was getting tenser, tighter. I wasn't having any fun, just being heavy. I decided I just didn't agree with a small group of people from New York telling me what to do all the time, telling me how to live."

I glared at her.

"Soph—you know what I mean. I felt they were controlling me. I wasn't making decisions for myself. Three weeks later I was summoned to the revolutionary council.

Germaine was standing in front of the room in a leather mini-dress and thigh-high leather boots. Rumor was she'd lifted them from Bergdorf's. She pulled out my roll of toilet paper and flung it across the room where I sat stunned. 'This isn't for the revolution,' she said. 'This is for *The New Yorker.*'"

Lillian took a reflective drag off her Marlboro Light.

CHAPTER TWO

Saturday morning the *Feminist News* office was buzzing with activity. When you work sixty hours for ninety dollars you often ask yourself why. Days like this, however, made it all seem glorious and electric. Something very heavy had happened and women were looking to us for an explanation. Calls came in from all over the country and even Paris. They wanted information about Germaine Covington. We had nothing about her on file. Most of us were too young to ever have seen her. We didn't even know if she was a feminist.

"I think it's a clear case of male ejaculatory violence," Chris said. "Just look at the dailies."

The New York Times features her Wanted photo on the front page. According to the article, the robbery had been a very sloppy job. They didn't get much money, just a few ten-dollar bills and a handful of papers and microfiche. Then the getaway car ran out of gas. Smelled like a setup to me. Everything was recovered including Germaine, but one other woman was seen fleeing into the shopping mall. The police had put up roadblocks all around White Plains but so far she'd eluded them. What was Germaine doing in a mess like this?

"I think Sophie should take this beat."

"Why me?" My instinct said *no.*

"Face it Sophie, you know more about her than any of us. How many times have I heard you wonder out loud what your life would have been like if you were Germaine Covington? You've always nursed revolutionary fantasies, so I know you'll put your blood and guts into it and write a really good piece."

It's true that I occasionally allow myself to dream of something more romantic than a low-budget women's monthly but I still felt nervous. "I'm so busy already. I'm doing a twelve-part story on women and botany and I have an interview on Tuesday with a group of go-go dancers from New Jersey who want to take over the sex industry. I just don't have time for a new project." My phone rang.

"Soph." It was Lillian. "The police just identified the woman who escaped from the scene of the crime. I heard it on the radio. Her name is Laura Wolfe."

My heart sank. I knew Laura Wolfe. We all knew Laura Wolfe. We've all known her for years as the biggest pain in the ass around. She was part of a group known as Women Against Bad Things. They had some kind of politics which none of us understood. Whatever we did, they didn't like it and usually picketed feminist events with very long leaflets. I'd never dream that she would be involved in something as heavy as a bank robbery. I guess I never really took her very seriously.

On the way home I grabbed an order of fried sauerkraut pirogies to go and copies of all the afternoon editions. There were pictures of Laura and Germaine all over the place. The *New York Post* headline read ANTI-AMERICAN, COMMIE, LEZZIE BLOOD-THIRSTY PIG over a copy of Laura's high school graduation picture. I cleared a place on my desk and tacked her photo to the wall.

CHAPTER THREE

Lillian left at three Monday morning to catch the Nightrider back to Boston. I stayed up working on Laura Wolfe until noon. The girls at the office think I can write any story in fifteen minutes, but this was going to be a tough one. Besides, Lillian's smell on my fingers was becoming a serious distraction. By noon I had the itch and decided to grab a piece of cheesecake at Junior's on Flatbush Avenue. I bought all the papers and hopped on the D train. *The Village Voice* cover story caught my eye. I FUCKED GERMAINE COVINGTON by Seymour Epstein. He didn't mention if she came or not.

Junior's is far, but it's worth the trip. Nothing beats that light lemony cheesecake and those lox-orange walls. The waitress was dressed like the world's last dyke. If there was one lesbian left in the world you'd know it was her. She's the kind that pats your ass every time she passes in the bar. She was giving me the once-over when her eye caught Laura's picture in the *Daily News*.

"That bitch."

"You know her?"

"I know her and I wish I never did know her."

"What time do you get off?" I smelled a scoop.

She glanced at my I LIKE GIRLS lapel pin. "Three."

"I'll have another piece of cheesecake. Cherry."

We walked slowly down De Kalb Avenue. Her name was Fran Marino. She was from Canarsie. A couple of years ago she started working in a sleazy Wall Street restaurant. "You just throw the food down and they leave you a buck. The gimme-a-Courvoisier-and-Coke crowd. Real animals." She lit a joint.

"So I see this other girl working there and I could see right away she was gay, but also she had something different about her. Sort of refined or smart or something like that. Not like the other waitresses. All they talk about is taking ups and giving head. So I started to do her favors, little ones, like refilling her water glasses, condensing her ketchups. She was always behind, a terrible waitress. I really covered her ass, even cleaned her ashtrays. We started getting it on once in a while."

The joint was played. She ran her fingers nervously through her butch cut. "One night we were coming out of the movies, this Cuban flick. She picked it. I didn't understand a thing. So we're walking along and she turns to me and says, 'I went to a movie with you, now you have to go to an educational with me.' That was the beginning of the end."

We got into her red Rabbit. She shouted over the radio as we sped across the Brooklyn Bridge. "From then on, every time we did anything normal, I had to go to an educational. The next thing I knew they had me standing on street corners selling their paper, *The Young Sectarian*. Then it wasn't good enough that I went to their meetings. I had to bring my friends to their meetings. Then they told me I wasn't going to enough meetings. Then, every time they saw me they told me what I was doing wrong. I shouldn't play ball. I shouldn't go to the bars, except to *organize*. I shouldn't see my friends. I wasn't getting much out of it either. Laura made me do a whole song and dance just to get a little feel."

We turned off the bridge and drove up through the Lower East Side. I thought about stopping off at the Garden Cafeteria for a little borscht all-the-way. They do a great job with chopped-up cucumber, radishes and fresh dill, a hard-boiled egg and a boiled potato. By the time I thought twice, we'd pulled up to the Dutchess.

"So one day," Fran continued, "they were having another one of their piddly-shit demonstrations where no one goes but them. I finally put my foot down and told her I wasn't going to go."

She ordered a Seven and Seven at the bar. The bartender sneered at me. Her name was Barbie. More than once she had threatened to punch my teeth in for handing out leaflets in that joint. Lesbian liberation and the mafia mix like scotch and prune juice. You don't try it if you don't have to.

"So you know what she had the balls to say to me, that bitch? She turns to me and says 'Sister, I care about you, but if you do not march, we are through. Sister, you are unprincipled.' If the fucking FBI ever came to my door, I'd tell them everything. I hope she fries."

That was my cue to go. You never know who's listening to your conversations. I understood why Fran was pissed off but I hoped she'd change her mind about the FBI. It just wasn't right.

"Look Fran, here's my name and address. If the FBI comes knocking at your door, call me. Don't tell them anything before you call me. They're not nice. They're no good, you know, they're like cops."

"What's wrong with cops, my brother's a cop."

Even my grandmother knows what's wrong with cops. I know they're just little working-class guys who want to have somebody to push around but they're not my friends. This Fran Marino could be trouble.

I walked home along Eighth Street back to the East Village. This street and I have gone through so much together. It used to be a quiet place when I was little. My family would go out for Chinese food on Sundays. Now music blares from the cheap clothing stores run by Sephardic Israelis. Grease smells emanate from fast-food pizza, hot dogs, Orange Julius and croissants.

So, Laura Wolfe uses sex as a tease to recruit for her group. Funny, I thought it would be more important to her than that. Maybe she has real lovers and then she has recruits who she keeps hungrily salivating on street corners selling newspapers hoping that if they're good they'll get a little piece. Even if she's not a good waitress, she's got a strong will. I'd like to know more about this Laura Wolfe.

CHAPTER FOUR

"**W**here the fuck am I?"

The streets were empty of people and full of boxes and scraps of polyester. By day the neighborhood bustled with Chinese and Latina women working the sweatshops for ninety dollars a week. Same salary as *Feminist News* but a whole different ball game. At five o'clock they start smashing into the subways heading for Elmhurst, Queens, shopping bags full of take-home sewing, paid for by the piece. Just like grandma used to do. At night the area is deserted except for a few lock-outs from the men's shelter huddling around a burning garbage can.

There were two greasers coming towards me in leather jackets and Mohawk haircuts.

Shit, I thought.

I was about to jump into my karate stance when it occurred to me that they were females. This was the place. The Dinette Sette, a new nightspot featuring ambi-sexual rock and roll. Melonie was appearing there with her new band.

Melonie Chaing was an old acquaintance. It never got to be more than that. When we first met, she was a psychologist at Payne-Whitney married to a psychiatrist at Bellevue and living on the Upper West Side. She walked out of her marriage and her career on the same day. First she went to Hong Kong, spending her nights walking the streets talking to prostitutes and taking their pictures. She published a photo-essay with a new age press. The called it *Nationalist Cunt: Cash, Charge or Check*. Then she came back to New York and started playing the electric guitar. When the punk scene opened up, Melonie jumped right in, dyed her long hair green and started to "develop an electric Asian aesthetic." She moved back to Chinatown, converting an old sweatshop into a luxurious loft. It was about two blocks from where she grew up. "I've forgotten about my genitals for thirty years," she told her stunned family. And now she just wanted to have fun and carry on in the tradition of the "great and powerful dragon lady." She tours with her band, The Dogmatics. There was a message on my tape that she had some information.

I looked for a corner to squeeze into but the whole place was the size of a corner. It was two bucks for a Schlitz. I smiled at the waitress and leaned against the back wall. The first act, Charlie and the Lesbians, featured a sixteen-year-old boy in a paisley tuxedo with a backup band of three bull dykes in overalls. They did a reggae version of "Youngblood." Five or six bands followed that one, all mushing into one endless pink and green sound-check except for this girl group called Beverly Hell and the Five Towns. The drummer could have been a drag queen but I especially liked Beverly with black lipstick on her teeth. It was different. They did sort of a samba rendition of "Bei Mir Bis Du Shayn." The Dogmatics came on around four and played a fifteen-minute set. They did ten songs including their underground hits "Jenny Was a Fag Hag" and "Looking for a Chinese Dyke."

I'm looking for a Chinese Dyke.
I'm looking for a Chinese Dyke.
I went to a Black bar
They told me I was white.
I went to a white club
They told me to do outreach.
I'm going home to cry in my tea
Yeah, yeah, yeah.

Melonie wore Saran Wrap, a dog collar and leather cutouts. As the band reached a rock and roll crescendo, she ran into the audience and emptied out a large mailbag full of Chinese Restaurant take-out menus. In the flashing red light, she set them on fire and doused the flame with Dr. Pepper.

After the show, Melonie told me what I wanted to hear. "I know a woman who has information. Her name is Vivian Beck. We were once in the same place. She knows Laura and Germaine from way back. At least she knew them then. When this whole robbery exploded, Vivian called up the old comrades from ten years ago to organize a response from the academic community. Poor girl, I'm not very academic any more, thank God. Anyway, she's very concerned, and since I heard you were investigating this story, I thought you'd like to talk with her."

Melonie laid out her coke lines like a pro. Now that her ex-husband had finally come out as a faggot, he wrote her prescriptions for pharmaceutical cocaine. The best. At only $14 a gram, she could re-sell it for $200 and keep herself in leather.

"Vivian's sort of a lost soul but a good woman. She teaches Italian. Her thesis was on the gourmet cooking utensils of the Italian bourgeoisie. Did you see her book *Knife and Fork as Metaphor?* Here's her number."

I almost asked Melonie for her number. I took another look at the studded dog collar. No, I like adventure in my relationships but only if it's my adventure.

"Thanks pal, see you later."

"Hey Sophie." She grinned. "Keep on rocking."

"Yeah."

CHAPTER FIVE

Vivian wanted to meet at the Prince Street Bar. Being compulsively early I had already cruised all the bookstores and bakeries in the area and still had fifteen minutes. A beer was out of the question. Probably costs $3.50. SoHo is the worst New York City has to offer. Built in a chic shopping mall motif, its inhabitants resemble victims of the body snatchers, pod people with a vague voidoid quality. A chill ran through my spine. This was really dangerous territory.

I spotted Vivian by the bar. I recognized her by her earrings in the shape of miniature serving spoons. She had so many strange and expensive looking trinkets, sashes, necklaces and bracelets, that she closely resembled a tie rack. Anyone who pays that much attention to detail spent an hour getting ready, which means they had an hour and decided to spend it getting ready. Scary business. Still, on closer examination, I sensed that somehow her heart wasn't in it. The makeup on her face was applied by habit, not passion, and sat on her features like a fly.

"Laura was my roommate and my best friend from '65 to '69 at Sarah Lawrence. I know it's a classically bourgeois place to have gone to school but I didn't have much choice. I grew up in Connecticut after all. My father worked for Nabisco."

Her serving spoons tinkled as she talked. "We had a great time together. I was an Italian major, comp lit minor, I always knew what I wanted to study. But Laura, first it was psychology, then philosophy, then history, then political science, she couldn't get focused. She was always flunking everything and I ended up writing most of her papers for her. We smoked cigars in our room and went to bars with fake ID's and planned on going to Florida over winter break. Then I took a year abroad and Laura spent that time in a new program where college students went into the city to tutor ghetto kids. When I came back she was all excited about some books she had read and new people she met at Columbia. We got into politics together, formed one of the first consciousness-raising groups and read Mao together. We shared out money and our secrets."

Vivian's mauve lipstick stained the cigarette. It burned next to her lipstick-stained glass. Tanqueray and tonic.

"What brand are you smoking, Vivian?"

"Marlboro Light. I don't even have to ask. They just look me in the eye and know that I smoke Marlboro Light. Spacy but smart, a little worried about growing older. Not ready to quit smoking yet though."

I slipped one out of her pack.

"Laura knew the rhetoric better than I did but we were both overcome with the feeling of the moment. Every day was a revelation, not only about how little of what we knew was worth anything, but also that none of us were prepared in any of the important ways to be anyone purposeful in this world. Sometimes the insights gave you elation and power, other times they turned your stomach. I remember one day sitting with Laura over a tuna fish sandwich realizing that every bite we took, every cigarette we smoked, every step we made was off the backs of most of the people in the world. It could make you lose your mind. It could also keep you glued to your chair."

"Sort of a *Naked Lunch?*"

"What?"

"Never mind." Vivian felt so familiar, like every character in every Marge Piercy novel.

"My boyfriend, Jerry Silverman, was a big shot in SDS at the time. He was rising into leadership and editing a newspaper out of a communal apartment on the Upper West Side. He didn't like Laura and encouraged me to get away from her and move into his place. There were always nameless, faceless people coming through. It was never clean, there was never any food in the refrigerator. There were always discussions and loud fights and secret plans and people fucking on the living room floor."

"What about you?"

"Oh, I fucked Jerry and sometimes he'd tell me to fuck some guy who was getting alienated from SDS."

"Sounds pretty alienating."

Vivian fit in here. Other women were dressed like her and holding their cigarettes in the same way but I could also see her with long straight hair and jeans and her old man's army jacket, ink all over her hands, putting out Jerry's newspaper.

"Then of course, I got pregnant and went home to Connecticut where my parents paid for the abortion. My sister had just married a young man from Nabisco and was about to move down to Westchester. I gave her a copy of *The Politics of Experience*. We had nothing to say to each other. When I came back Laura was busy working in groups that were woman-only. We decided to officially withdraw from school and moved in together to a woman-only communal apartment, also on the Upper West Side. We spent a lot of time together. Even slept in the same bed. I started fucking Jerry again, got pregnant again and married him."

Vivian talked so fast. Like someone who would tell you anything if you only asked. "Then she came out of the hospital."

"When was that?"

"I think it was around 1969. It was awful. When Laura signed her trust fund away to the Black Panther party, her parents were very upset. They owned some nonunion company in New Jersey that made artificial lawns for stadiums and indoor swimming pools. So that's when they finally interceded. They committed her and put her through electric shock and aversion therapy."

She gulped down the rest of her drink. A little piece of lime was caught between her teeth. "Just like in *A Clockwork Orange*. They gave her drugs that put her in convulsions, and showed her pictures of women making love. It was a very expensive private clinic off in the woods somewhere. When she came out she was never the same again. She never had friends after that and believe me I tried. Only her comrades were important to her. The rest of us were simply *unprincipled*."

"Did you try to talk to her about what had happened?"

"I did try Sophie, I did, but I had my own life too. I miscarried. The whole thing miscarried. The revolution wasn't around the corner anymore. I had to go on with my life. I finished my B.A. at City College and by '73 I decided to go on to graduate school. I divorced Jerry and I moved to Philadelphia to get my M.A. in Italian."

"Did you try to contact Laura again?"

"I thought about her every once in a while. When I got married again I tried to contact her. I left a message but she never got back to me."

I was getting hungry. Glanced at the menu. Forget it. "Vivian, do you think she felt let down by her friends?"

"If she did, she never said so. She told each of us about her experience in the hospital and then she never mentioned it again. There were no personal accusations or recriminations. Everything was politics. Either you were *principled* or *unprincipled*. It didn't matter if you wet your bed, talked to the dead, only ate Jell-O on Sundays. As long as you could regurgitate the political line, well, that was all that mattered." Tears welled up in Vivian's eyes but she must have been wearing drip-proof mascara because nothing ran down her cheeks.

"Vivian, I know this must be painful for you but please, try and remember what her politics were. I don't really understand it. Were they feminist? Marxist? Can you put your finger on it, so to speak?"

"She called it the theory of the big lie. It was based on the idea that everyone lies to themself and abuses others to justify their lies. The goal of the revolution is to cut through that. Like the etymology of the word radical is "to get to the root." They called themselves "Women of the Roots." At least that's what they called themselves in '71. There's been a million splits and new formations since then."

I speared an olive out of the bartender's setup and munched thoughtfully. "What kind of women did Laura work with?"

"A lot of them had been friends of ours at one time or another. But when most of us started readjusting our lives to match a different reality, going back to school, raising families, these women kept at it. They kept at the tiny demonstrations, the long, boring leaflets, educational after educational. They were afraid to go on with their lives."

She paused. "Or maybe we were afraid not to."

Her candor surprised me and it showed.

"I know what you're thinking, Sophie. That all the conditions in the world that motivated our commitments to change were still just as pressing, only our commitments changed. It's true. Most of the women in her group didn't have the same choices I did. They didn't do well by New Left standards. You know, a woman's power depended on the man she slept with. It was a sexist but historically consistent practice. Not that fucking Jerry actually ever did me any good."

Having finished off the olives I started in on the onions.

"Their politics," continued Vivian, "last I understood, went something like this. They argued that if you really want a better world then every institution has to be thrown out or re-evaluated. We have to restructure all of the ways that we relate to each other."

"I'm with you so far."

"If you really want a new culture and a new system, you have to be willing to fight for it. Your personal desire to fit it, in case the revolution doesn't happen, is precisely what keeps it from happening."

"Vivian, its intriguing. You're so clear about what you do and how you feel about it, and at the same time you accept it as given and unchanging."

Vivian looked at her third Tanqueray. Straight this time. "Look, I know that on some level Laura's right. I've always known it. But I just don't want to live that way. I'm happy with my life and I wouldn't want to change it. I've finally found a man that I don't have any illusions about. He's not what I imagined when I was twenty, but after a few reality checks I realized that just as I'm not living in the world I'd like to be living in, I'm not going to find the ideal man either. It's just not going to happen that way. Anyhow, I'm 34 years old now. I can't get up at four in the morning and leaflet factories. I won't stand on street corners talking to people who don't care or don't even know where they are. I don't want to end up like little old ladies from the Communist party who are still trying to get winos to buy copies of *The Daily World,* and won't accept that their dream has crashed. But I do know one thing. When change finally comes, and it will come, history will remember Germaine Covington and Laura Wolfe as the real revolutionaries. And I hope the day comes when I can tell Laura that to her face."

The bar was filling up. Vivian staggered out the door. I watched her slide into a cab. I was getting to know Laura Wolfe very well.

CHAPTER SIX

I sat in my apartment. Just sat. The public radio station was droning on and on, a marathon fund-raiser. *"Please give us money. Please give us money. Please, please, please."* The new *Village Voice*, covered in cherry babka crumbs, lay limply in my lap. Seymour Epstein had a first-page exclusive interview with Germaine Covington from inside Metropolitan Correctional Center. I reread the story for the third time:

> Sunlight streaming through a slit in the wall illuminated the courageous features of Germaine Covington. Her strong and slightly greying temples. Her sharp jaw. She pointed to a stack of books. "I've been reading Fidel," she said, her clear eyes blazing with revolutionary fervor.

How the fuck did such a fat slob, fake-intellectual dog like Seymour Epstein get that interview? Where was I? The doorbell rang.

"It's Henry." The voice came up through the intercom.

Henry Tsang was Melonie Chaing's ex-husband. We'd had a brief affair before either of us decided to be gay full time and it was pleasant. We murmured "You're not like all the others" and it didn't take long to figure out that we were right. Henry's real different from Melonie. Comes from a rich family in the burbs. His father's a Chinese scientist and his mother's a Lithuanian refugee from communism. He was a regular suburban kid, played ball, marched in the high school band and went to medical school just like his parents told him to. But during his first year at Mount Sinai the world started to change and Henry took a leave of absence to find out what it was all about. He began reading those dangerous Chinese communists he'd heard maligned around the dinner table. Henry joined a pro-China group and firmly believed that in order to organize the workers, he had to live like the workers. The group he belonged to, The February Twentieth League, claimed that workers had short hair, didn't smoke dope, ate white bread with creamy peanut butter. They also lived in stable, monogamous, heterosexual marriages and didn't have oral sex. He tried to be more of a man for the revolution but he always remained lithe and slight, almost like a fairy. Then China began to change and so did his wife. The League split into those who supported Mao and the Gang of Four and those who went with the new China and their neo-capitalist ways.

Henry got depressed and stopped going to meetings. He started working harder at the hospital and reading jogging magazines. Sometimes after work he would go down to the West Village and have a man suck him off in the bathroom. He didn't really think about it when he wasn't doing it and wasn't really sure later that it was him at all. When Melonie left him he was relieved and didn't take it as a personal affront, which it wasn't. Soon he fell in love with Harold, the piano player at Marie's Crisis Piano Bar and moved into his apartment in Chelsea. Henry realized that Melonie was smarter than he and that he had deceived them both in their early years together. Now he didn't understand why she needed to do what she needed to do but he had faith in its value and did his part when told to.

"Henry, you look great," I said. "Sit down, have some food. I've got bagels, smoked herring, schmaltz herring or herring in cream sauce. How's Harold?"

"Soph, listen, I came here to tell you something important."

His eyes caught the walls of my apartment. They were covered from floor to ceiling with pictures, clippings, leaflets and posters depicting Laura and Germaine. Notes overflowed onto the floor. "That's what I want to talk to you about."

He leaned forward on his skinny hips and wiggled his mustache. "I've been on rotation at Bellevue emergency, psychiatric emergency that is, you know, supervising interns so that the experience doesn't make them throw away medicine for a more sane business like . . ."

"Investigative reporting?"

"I don't know." Henry has always been absentminded. "Last night, around four-thirty in the morning, they brought in an important prisoner from MCC. I knew something big was happening because the Westchester D.A. was right there with her."

"Her?"

"Yeah, a woman in very bad shape. She was having a violent psychotic episode, but if you ask me, they encouraged it. She was screaming at the top of her lungs and attacking all the orderlies and doctors. They put her in handcuffs, leg irons, waist chains and a straightjacket."

"Sounds like you guys weren't kidding around. What was she saying?"

"I don't know. She wasn't speaking English—or Chinese for that matter. It was some kind of Mediterranean language like Greek or maybe Armenian, but that's just a guess. Anyway, one thing I do know is you don't take a foreigner who's that upset and wrap them up in restraints. It's ridiculous. It's like asking someone to crack up, they used such poor judgment."

"They?"

"Yeah, the Westchester D.A. was there bossing everyone around. He insisted we shoot her full of Thorazine. A lot of Thorazine. Enough to sedate the Dogmatics and all their friends."

He took a gulp of Dr. Brown's Cel-Ray tonic. "So, I looked at her record. Sophie, guess what her name was."

"Frances Farmer."

"Germaine Covington."

"What?" Inside, my heart skipped three beats. A scoop. I got a scoop. Oh God, please give me this, I'll never ask for anything again.

"Soph, it wasn't her. No way. I haven't seen Germaine since my days with The Yellow Panthers, but still, there is no way on earth this woman was Germaine Covington. That's why I came to see you, Soph. Whoever she was, she was old and had scabs, ulcerated legs. She looked like someone who'd been having a hard time for a long time. I've been thinking it over pretty carefully. You know, I'm not a very impetuous guy, but really, don't you think it's possible that the government got her?"

"Who?" I was thinking about my Pulitzer.

"Germaine. It sounds to me like they're hiding her somewhere and maybe torturing her or who knows what—you know, to get information."

Henry's theory had a high probability rate. The government was known for pulling neat tricks like that.

"Henry, they may have been able to kill Allende but they can't pawn off a Cypriot bag lady as Germaine Covington."

"They can if she's in a box."

"*No entiendo.*"

"She never made it out of emergency. They shot her so full of Thorazine she choked on her own vomit. I was really worried but the D.A. didn't care. He said he took full responsibility."

"Henry, what do you know about Seymour Epstein?"

"Well, I don't know him personally but he doesn't have a very good reputation on the grapevine. He writes pieces for liberal publications about what a stud he is with the ladies and then at night he cruises heavy men's bars like the Mine Shaft."

My mind was racing. If only I could get it together, solve the puzzle, publish the story, sell the film rights and have a bestseller before the rent comes due. Only one person held the key.

"I've got to find Laura Wolfe."

CHAPTER SEVEN

Friday night I sat waiting for Lillian to come in off the 6:30 Colonial. The place was a disaster. Cartons of fruit soup and an empty bottle of Krakus beer sat in the bathtub. Everywhere there were packs and packs of cigarettes: Newports, Marlboros, Drum (roll your own), and rolling papers. I even had Pall Malls for those really difficult moments. Copies of the day's *Times*, *Post* and *News* were spread out on the floor. There was a knock at the door.

"Come in," I yelled but nothing happened.

Ten minutes later another knock. I opened the door to a tall young boy. About six feet tall in a little kid's striped T-shirt and torn jeans. He had glasses that looked like his mother picked them out—large black frames held together by a Band-Aid, and straight brown hair cut into bangs. On closer examination I realized he was older than his appearance suggested, much older. His full yet clean-shaven beard indicated middle to late twenties.

"Yes?"

"Uh." He rocked back and forth on his Pro-Keds pulling out the hairs in the middle of his head. Obviously an unfortunate habit. "I'm a friend of Rita's."

"Who?" I asked blankly, trying to decide if it was worth being polite.

"Rita from Missoula."

"Oh." Then I realized I was in trouble. Two years ago my old girlfriend and I had decided to hitchhike cross-country. Being city girls we didn't realize that you just don't hitchhike through Montana in the winter. We never thought it would take us so goddamn long to get from one town to another. Rita found us half frozen between Billings and Butte and took us to her place in Missoula. It's a small town with a large lesbian underground. We stayed there a week. She was so wonderful, I promised her that if she ever had any friends passing through New York, I would be glad to . . . oh, well.

"Actually, I'm not her friend. I'm her brother."

"Oh well, come in."

That's how Evan came to my house. The beginning was quite simple in comparison with the end. He took up residence in the corner of the kitchen and laid in for the long haul.

"What are your plans, Evan?"

"Well, I'm not sure exactly but I'm sure I won't have any problems. I started college when I was fifteen you know, the University of Chicago. I was sort of a child prodigy."

"How old are you now?"

"Twenty-six."

"So why are you here in New York?"

"I'm going to make it in music. I play the guitar and write my own songs. They're pretty good. Here's one."

Before I learned to refuse, Evan sang at the top of his nose:

> With blood dripping out of the mouth of the
> vultures
> The lightning and fire destroying all cultures

36

He stabbed her and mauled her and threw her
in the creek
And hitchhiked to Reno and got high with some
Greeks.

He looked at me sheepishly. I was beginning to understand that that was his only expression.

"Nice cadence."

He rocked back and forth, pulling out hairs again. "Do you have any food?"

I watched him wreak havoc in my refrigerator in a way I never thought possible.

"Don't you have any white bread? I only like white bread."

He made himself a dinner of instant coffee and looked very unhappy. "Don't you have any meat? I need meat."

"There's vegetables. They're nice."

"I don't like vegetables, I only like meat. How about rice. White rice?"

He ate some white rice with margarine, not butter, and curled up in a corner with a copy of Hunter S. Thompson's *Fear and Loathing in Las Vegas*.

This was going to be a long, hard winter.

CHAPTER EIGHT

An hour later Lillian walked in.

"Soph." She came and sat on my lap, bringing me into her beautiful softness.

"Hi gorgeous, I'm having a terrible life."

"I saw the papers. I'm sorry."

"Yeah."

"Sophie, you know you deserved that interview. You're a better and more delicious journalist than Epstein any day."

"Thanks Lil, but we've got new problems now."

I showed her the headlines: COP KILLER ODs IN JAILHOUSE ORGY.

We stood in quiet reverence for a minute. I filled her in. Then she filled me in. An hour later I was relaxing in the tub sucking on a Guinness Stout while Lily talked to Evan in the kitchen.

"Who's the Boy Scout?"

"Evan's staying here for a while. Uptight, isn't he?"

"His personality reminds me of a fourth grader with a perpetual hard-on. Sophie, you're awful, always feeling sorry for losers. No matter what you say, I know your mother did a good job on you."

"Now don't go blaming everything on Mom."

She smiled her big smile at me. Lillian has big teeth. She says that one of them is false but I don't know which one.

"Lil?"

"Hmmm?"

"Why do you taste so good? Why do you feel so good? Why are you so exciting, adventurous, aggressive and satisfying?"

"Skin texture," she said, almost absentmindedly.

"What do you mean by that?"

"Skin texture is the key to good old-fashioned, unromantic but sufficiently affectionate nitty-gritty sex for pleasure. Some people, you like the way they look. You like the way they smell. But when you get next to them, something just doesn't feel right. You know, you can't get comfortable, like it doesn't fit. The key is skin texture and honey, you've got it."

"So that's the key?"

Sometimes I wonder what Lillian sees when she looks at me. I put out my usual old gruff, tough, smooth-operator image and she keeps giving me puppets and underwear with strawberries on them. She's just invented a Sophie Horowitz who is vulnerable and childlike and that's who she relates to. No, not all the time, sometimes she likes me to be strong and sweet.

"Yes Soph, Seymour Epstein is definitely the key." She rubbed her toe on my pubic hair. "He made up this interview, that much is clear. So now Germaine is dead, not the real Germaine but some poor Mediterranean bum or revolutionary or whatever she is. While our heroine sits in the clutches of the FBI, we sit in a sagging tenement knowing that Seymour is, undoubtedly, the key."

Lillian is so smart. Sometimes I feel like suggesting that she give up her nice boring, fair-paying job in Boston and get into the swing of things down here. But I know she's not that way. She likes to have her cake and eat it too, and I'm dessert, so to speak. Besides, I wouldn't be happy with a girlfriend I could see every day. I know that much from experience. After enough years of good starts and bad endings I've learned that a weekend lover and confidante is the most I would ever want. Well, maybe three days by the beach thrown in for romance's sake, but that's it.

"Sophie, you know you're really special."

"No I'm not, I'm really not. You just think I am, that's all."

"Well, maybe not special, maybe unique is more like it."

"Look Lillian, I admit I'm not exactly what you'd call run of the mill but don't get carried away. I'm typical of a kind of person who just doesn't get much publicity, so it looks like I'm special. Anyway, listen, here's what I found out about Seymour. He's egotistical, a braggart, fat and disgusting."

"Fat people are not disgusting." Lillian is a former member of the Fat Dykes Liberation skinny support group.

"True, but he happens to be both those things. Plus, he's a closet case and a masochist, you know, a bottom. He cruises fuck bars, gets fucked up and then he gets fucked." I swam over to Lillian's side of the tub and put my arms around her neck. She thoughtfully ran her fingers down the crack in my ass.

"Sophie, I think I've got an idea."

41

CHAPTER NINE

I was thankful for the cool October air. Lillian and I sat in Chris's cab chain-smoking Camel straights. Chris let us use it on the condition that I put in extra hours pasting up the newspaper this month. The wind cooled the sweat on my forehead but not the rest that slowly dripped over my body from a combination of leather and fear.

I have to admit we did look kind of cool. Lillian dressed as a cabby with a newsboy hat and a big cigar. Her hennaed hair tucked away with bobby pins. She's a big woman with strong muscles. I like that.

I glanced at myself in the rearview mirror. "Lil, you know, I don't think Melonie believed me when I told her I needed her leather getup for a story. She had that look in her eye like 'Sure Soph, your girlfriend comes into town and the next thing I know you're sauntering around in here wanting to borrow a leather jacket and pants for work.'"

"Well, I wouldn't believe you either. Are you sure you're not getting some kind of thrill from wearing those clothes? I'm getting one from watching you."

The leather was strong and soft. Like Lillian. It was good protection. "I'm glad you're here Lily, it makes me feel safer."

"My pleasure."

"That haircut is a little too butch for me, though, don't

you think?" I examined my clone cut. Between the clothes, hair, fake beard and padded crotch, I was convincing if not ravishing.

"Don't worry Sophie, I know the real you. Butch in the streets, femme in the sheets."

The radio played Sarah Vaughn singing "Stairway to the Stars." We were quiet for a moment, letting her take us along.

It was 2:30 on a Saturday night. We parked outside Epstein's apartment on Central Park West and 95th Street, number 350. It had been an hour since I called his number asking for Beverly Hell. She really stuck in my mind. So, we knew he was home and hoped he wouldn't spend his Saturday night in front of the TV. Even though it probably was cable. We'd been waiting since eleven swapping stories, singing songs. I kept readjusting the lump of foam rubber between my legs until Lillian volunteered a blow job. I took a rain check.

Just then Seymour stepped out into the night. He was smiling, in full leather, cap and all. We followed his taxi down Broadway. The city was completely alive, the way it looks from an airplane coming into Kennedy airport on a summer night. A one-celled organism. A paramecium with fluorescent protoplasm.

He got out at Sheridan Square. As usual the streets were packed with gay people and the cafes were packed with straights. He stopped in at Ty's for a drink. It's a nice place—flannel shirts. People know each other and come to meet their friends. I noticed Seymour ordered a Jack Daniels. That was the first good thing I could say about him.

We followed west along Christopher Street. Me on foot and Lillian behind the wheel. Then it was Boots and Saddles. After that, Christophers. Each time I followed him into a bar, he'd order a shot of Jack. Seymour never tried to connect with any of the men. Not even a smile. He just watched and so did I. Most of them were really beautiful. Thin and tan, well dressed. They laughed and smoked and talked with each other. Sometimes in the corner there'd be a guy dressed in cowboy clothes just holding on to his beer and staring out from behind his large mustache. But most of these men were friendly and relaxed. It's funny, but it occurred to me that none of the straight men I'd ever hung out with were so good-looking. They certainly didn't know how to talk to other men, except about avant-garde jazz or Jack Kerouac. Faggots aren't bad really. They know how to have a nice time and I bet every man in that bar could iron his own shirts.

By the time we crossed Hudson Street Seymour must have been a little tipsy. Then I realized that the scenery was changing. No more nice little cutesy bars. There seemed to be more street action. Some young Puerto Rican boys were hanging out by the entrance to the PATH train. A few had pink and yellow streaks in their feathered hair. I watched an all-American blonde type cruise a Black transvestite prostitute from his Toyota with New Jersey plates. She wouldn't have a thing to do with him. I've always admired drag queens—they have style and courage, and they're very tough. After all, it was drag queens, Black drag queens, who fought the police at the famous Stonewall Inn rebellion in 1969. Years later, a group of nouveau-respectable gays tried to construct a memorial to Stonewall in the park across from the old bar. The piece consisted of two white clonelike thin gay men and two white, young lesbians with perfect noses. They were made of a plasterlike substance, pasty and white as the people who paid for it. Some of us were furious. Chris called together all of the Black gay and lesbian groups in the city and *Feminist News* got involved in the fight for a full color statue of a Black drag queen throwing a brick at a cop. We didn't get it, and frankly, I'd rather have nothing. At least that way you know what you've got.

I recognized one of the queens, my neighbor Rick. He was a nice guy, always lending me stockings, dresses and heels when I needed to infiltrate right-wing conferences or go to court. I didn't want to let him spot me. He'd feel bad that I left him out of the fun. Anyway, my instinct said to keep the whole affair hush-hush. It could get sticky.

At West Street I followed Seymour out to the docks. It's a beautiful view of New Jersey at night, all lit up over the Hudson, but I think the men are drawn there by the seclusion and element of danger. There are large holes in the rotting wood and rats openly scamper around the exposed bodies. All around me was the sound of men having orgasms. It was definitely weird, but sort of exciting—you know, different. Men's sex sounds and the smelly breeze from New Jersey. Still Seymour didn't approach anyone. He just stood and watched and smoked a joint and then a cigarette.

Leaving the dock, we headed towards the Ramrod, the famous fuck bar. A few years ago some gay men were hanging out in front, on the street, and a car drove by and opened up with a submachine gun. The killer got off on an insanity plea. Claimed they were trying to make him be a homosexual. Just by standing there. Some people said that if he had shot Wall Street executives, he never would have gotten away with it. Chris says there are plenty of Wall Street executives at the Ramrod. They just wear different clothes.

By this time Seymour was really high. He started a fight with the bouncer about the $10 cover. I was glad he did because Lily and I only brought $15 and I didn't want to start spending it just to get into places. Before it went too far, Seymour cursed out the bouncer and moved up West Street past the leather store, the bikers' bar, past the car cruisers and the trucks, through the meat-packing district. He was looking for something. The sidewalk was covered with blood and the garbage cans overflowed with dead meat parts rotting and filling the air with a nauseating stench. Then he disappeared down a narrow staircase. The sign said ASS*TRICK. A porcelain cast of some man's ass hung over the entry way. Cover was only $5, one drink included. I followed him in.

The place was pretty crowded. It had an air of intentional sleaze. All these big men in leather suits, caps, some with whips or spurs. It wasn't scary at all, everything seemed so artificial. Maybe in the early days when leather was starting to get so popular, there was more of a thrill of danger about it. But now, anyone can wear leather. I wondered what the next fad was going to be. Maybe paper? These men were dancers and CPAs and graduate students in Marxist political economy. So, they dress like Hell's Angels once in a while, big deal. I'd suspect it would get boring after a few months. I noticed the walls covered with photos, drawings, replicas and representations of penises. Enormous, swollen and grotesque penises, as if they were Betty Grable pinups or other graven images.

"Gross," I said to myself. Clearly, I didn't want to stay there longer than I had to.

I waved to the bartender. "You see that guy over there? When he orders a drink, make it a triple." I put my ten on the bar. Didn't get any change.

By four o'clock the moment had come. Seymour was literally on his knees sliding even further down along the side of the bar. Men were disco-ing over him. I knew it was time to act. The trick was to keep him away from my fly. Fortunately, Lillian had thought of this in advance. I grabbed his wrists and handcuffed them behind his back.

"Drink," I commanded and poured the triple shot down his throat.

"Come on you little scum, I'm taking you home." I had worried a little about the humiliation part, but it wasn't hard at all. I pushed him into a conveniently waiting cab.

"Tell me more," he drooled.

"You disgusting shit. You don't deserve the leather on your back."

I pulled his cap over his eyes. "Just sit there and don't say a word."

Lillian drove us home. Just as we expected, he was passed out by the time we got there. The doorman was rather large. His nameplate said Mukul Garg. He seemed to be used to Seymour's behavior and pretended not to notice the cuffs. We carried the dead weight up to Seymour's apartment.

I opened the door with Seymour's keys and threw him on the bed. He had a pretty nice place for a sometimes-employed freelance writer. I found a leather mask on his night table and tugged it over his head, leaving the eye and mouth zippers open for air. I knew I didn't have much time. I grabbed whatever a good detective would grab—papers, bills and a little metal box locked to the desk. It was easy to pick. One of the skills I learned from watching television. I noticed a copy of *Feminist News* opened to my article "A Wolfe in Wolf's Clothing." Chris always picked out the titles.

"Well, what do you know about that." I smiled to myself. It was nice to be noticed, but this wasn't the moment to dwell on it. I dashed out the door leaving Seymour snoring like a baby.

CHAPTER TEN

Sunday we slept till three. First I was groggy and then jubilant. What a coup! We celebrated our success over breakfast. I noticed that Evan had done a little shopping. The fridge was filled with white bread, Kraft macaroni and cheese in a box, cans of corned beef hash and a bottle of ketchup. I felt a little queasy when I noticed the ketchup stains on the mouth of the milk carton.

"Watch out Lil, I think the milk has cooties."

"That boy really is unpleasant, isn't he?"

"Yeah, you know what drives me mad? How he sleeps in his clothes and never changes them and smells bad all the time and walks into a room like he's the only one in it and relates to the world as if nothing happens when he's not there."

"Well, Sophie, you know what happens when you eat all those nitrates and nitrites, it stimulates the testosterone."

We cleaned up the greasy bags and remnants of Chinese take-out and tried and tried to pick up the grains of white rice that had fallen between the floorboards.

"I couldn't believe the expression on Seymour's face when you brought him to the cab," Lillian said between mouthfuls of scrambled egg.

"He looked almost thankful. You know Soph, in a weird way I think we made him happy."

"Well," I replied, slurping some cold cucumber soup, "he's not going to stay happy when we figure out how he's involved in all this. I think we got some good information in those papers we swiped from his desk."

"Sophie, don't they ever eat eggs on the Lower East Side?"

"No, we eat cold cucumber soup," I replied a bit sharply. We'd been through all this before.

Sometimes I don't really understand why Lillian and I get along so well. There have definitely been some rocky moments since we first met.

I gave a talk in Boston at the invitation of a local lesbian group, one of those coalition efforts where people with nothing in common except their opposition to something pretend to work together. They close their eyes temporarily to the fact that if any of them ever got power, they would quickly obliterate the others. After weeks of *struggle*—caucuses, manipulations and purges—they plan a program where each group has one speaker and three minutes to talk about their issue and ignore everybody else: "One of you and one of you and one of you." It's pretty undialectical if you ask me.

On the platform was Mark Wilson, a Marxist economist from the New School for Social Research. He wore a brown corduroy jacket with leather elbow patches. He used indecipherable economistic lingo to talk about the crucial role of intellectuals in the leadership of the working class. The second speaker was Richard Gordon, associate professor of Latin American intellectual and political history at Yale University. He wore a grey corduroy jacket with leather elbow patches and used indecipherable historical and political lingo to talk about the crucial role of intellectuals in the leadership of the working class. I wore my Patti Smith T-shirt with cutoff sleeves and called my talk "Heterosexuality: What Is to Be Done?" There were 400 people in the room. Afterwards there was a three-hour question and answer period. No one asked me a single question. *The Boston Globe* did a short piece on page thirty-six. They spent a paragraph on each of the two gentlemen. The last line said, "Susan Horowitz, a feminist, was angry."

After the talk, a bunch of us went out to a local bar called The Saints. I was tired and cranky and let the chitchat circle around me like cigarette smoke. Out of boredom I started a bit of girl-watching and noticed that one girl was watching me. Every ten minutes or so we would check in with each other. Our eyes would meet and we would both look away. Hours passed. Finally the place was empty and quiet. I turned down a few rides back to where I was staying and ended up sitting alone with a glass of flat tonic water and an overflowing ashtray. Besides the bartender cleaning up, we were the only ones left in the place. Finally, feeling a bit dizzy, and for drama's sake, I got up to wait outside. Standing in the early morning air, one foot flat against the wall, like the narcs posing as gay men on the cruise in Washington Square Park, I waited. I waited like Humphrey Bogart. I swung my jacket over my shoulder and waited. I smoked a cigarette and waited. Then another. Fifteen more minutes passed but no sign of Madame X. I practiced what I would say. I tried out, "Hi." No, too wimpy. "Are you look-ing for me?" No, too moronic.

At that moment the door opened and out she walked, on the arm of her girlfriend, the bartender. Oh well. Feeling like a fool I took a cab back to the Cambridge house where I was assigned to sleep. I walked in at four A.M. to the sight of a woman on all fours scrubbing the kitchen floor.

"It's for my nerves," she said. That was Lillian.

She offered me a cup of tea. "Chamomile, Red Zinger, Rose Hip, Purple Haze?"

"Don't you have real tea? Like Lipton?"

She did. We sat down together and talked. She was from a small town in Michigan. Her father was a mechanic and her mother sewed for the Woolco chain. She worked hard all through high school to be able to go to college and ended up at the University of Michigan at Ann Arbor in the fall of 1967. All around her, middle- and upper-class kids, kids from New York and California, Jews and Communists and Hippies and even some Blacks, were running around campus changing the world. At least that's what they said. She lived in collective houses and did street theatre, worked the people's clinic and did a radio show called "Free Waves." But, when the revolution was over, they went back to school and Lillian went back where she came from. She married a local boy and after a year started an affair with a married woman who lived on the same street. They had gone to high school together, although they never hung out with the same crowd. When her old man found out, the two women fled in the middle of the night and hitched on the interstate to New York City. A month later, Lily realized that she was pregnant and knew she had to get an abortion. The two of them scraped together every possible penny and Lillian hitched with truckers down to the famous abortion doctor in Pennsylvania. The story was that he had turned his back on his own daughter when she was pregnant. She died on a kitchen table. From then on, he did as many as he could do with a minimum of contact with the women. He didn't speak with them or look them in the eye. He just took the cash, did the job and left the room. By the time Lillian got back to New York, her girlfriend was gone. She had returned to her husband in Michigan. Lily has called her a few times over the years. It's sort of a tradition. Lily calls and the woman hangs up. Sometimes a child answers, though she's not sure yet if it's a boy or a girl, the voice is so high. After a few months Lillian moved to Boston and started working as a typist for a publishing company. She's been there ever since. Every other weekend she counsels rape victims from the Women's Center Hot Line.

I felt shy around her age and experience. I hoped she'd overlook my lack of sophistication for the thrill of having a young lover full to the brim with cute bravado. That night, wearing a sleeveless T-shirt that showed off her long neck and throat, she looked like someone I wanted to throw my arms around and climb into.

"Let me taste some of that cucumber soup." She smiled. "Well, it's not too bad." That was an apology.

"Oh Lillian . . . Let's take a look at Seymour's papers."

CHAPTER ELEVEN

Evan sat staring into space in the living room. A nickel bag of pot was spread out on a Frisbee, seeds on the table, occasionally rolling onto the floor.

"What are you doing?"

"Nothing."

"I don't mean right now, I can see that for myself. What are you planning to do today?"

"Nothing."

"Well, I wish you would do something because I really need to work today at the typewriter after Lillian leaves and in order to do that I need some time in this apartment to myself. You know, I need to sit around for a while and listen to the radio and make coffee and smoke a cigarette and think and write a few pages and then play a record and write some more pages and I can't do that if you're sitting here all day long, Evan."

I tried to smile.

He looked distressed. Maybe I was too harsh.

"Look, why don't you read a book or something. I have a lot of interesting books. Here's one called *For Men Against Sexism*, you'll really like it."

"Don't you have *The Dharma Bums* by Jack Kerouac?"

"No, I do have Allen Ginsberg though."

"No, I don't think I want to read that."

"Evan, why ever not?"

"Well, he's—you know, he writes about those sailors and everything. I mean, I don't care about what a person does in private, but they shouldn't go imposing it on other people."

"He's gay, you mean."

"Yeah, I mean it's really weird here in New York, whenever I walk down the street these men are always looking at me and trying to touch me. It's really disgusting. They'd better watch out or one day I'm going to get really mad. That guy in the building. The one that wears women's clothes. He's really gross. The other day he . . . well." He looked at his Pro-Keds.

"Don't tell me he made a pass at you."

"Yeah."

"What did he do?"

"He showed me a poem and in it there was this guy who was a homosexual."

"And?"

"That's all—I mean I could just tell that he showed it to me because he was coming on to me, you know he was being so nice and everything. It makes me sick."

"That's why you like Kerouac, right? A good macho buddy-buddy, drinking wine and fucking waitresses."

"Yeah, that's America."

"It sure is."

I've known boys like this my whole life. They want to go on the road with Jack and Neal but they can't tie their own shoes.

When Lillian got back with the Sunday *Times* we went into my room and locked the door.

"You know Soph, if I were you, I'd be very concerned about having Evan around all the time. You never know what information he's picking up. I'd be real careful."

"Oh, he's just a pain in the ass but he's harmless. He's just a jerk, not a troublemaker. Believe me, I'm a very good judge of character. Now let's get to work." But just to be safe I stuffed towels under the door before flipping through the evidence.

"Let's see. Phone bills, rent receipts, bank statements, lots of good detective work here. Bills from Brooks Brothers, Lutece, Pleasure Chest . . ."

"Well, let's look at the phone bill. We can see if he made any weird or consistent long-distance calls. It's a good source for clues."

"Lillian, how do you know these things?"

"I read detective novels on my lunch hour. Three a week."

"The working girl's soap opera."

"Sophie, don't be so snotty. Some of them are really good. They're about all kinds of contemporary issues. There's even a gay detective. There's books about gentrification and capitalism and all that stuff that you like—only it's human, that's why I enjoy it."

We looked at the phone bills. It was a good idea. Seymour apparently called the same number in Elizabeth, New Jersey, every Tuesday at one o'clock in the afternoon. A definite clue. There was also one Westchester number that looked vaguely familiar, but so do all phone numbers.

"Okay Sherlock, what's next?"

"Well, according to King James—"

"Don't tell me, you read the bible on your coffee break."

"No, King James is one of my favorite mystery writers. He wrote about two hundred books. Anyway, his detectives are real professionals. They always know just what to do next. They're smooth and daring."

"Okay, I got the message." Sometimes I was happy that Lillian went home after three days.

"Sophie, why are you on this macho trip of having to be as tough as Spencer Tracy? You act so big with all these unreasonable expectations and then you can't even keep a weak schlep like Evan from walking all over you."

I was getting angry. "I don't want to talk about it."

"Well, I'm not surprised."

I know, all right, I'm bad. I just don't like to talk about things, especially relationships. Other things on the list of topics I don't like to talk about are my character flaws, the workers, psychoanalysis, Sartre, when you did your laundry and what you had for breakfast. Also, haircuts.

Seymour had some bank statements recording a series of deposits. Some were marked with red pen. FUCK YOU PETER POPE YOU ASSHOLE was scribbled in the corner of one. I made a mental note.

"So you think Seymour could have had something against Catholics?

"I don't know, Sophie, look at this. Seymour got a rejection letter from *Esquire* magazine. 'Dear Mr. Epstein, I'm sorry but we have decided that we are unable to offer you an advance to write an article on the White Plains Affair. If you do complete the manuscript be sure to send us a copy. We do want to say that your choice of title "A Wolfe in Wolf's Clothing" is splendid.'"

"That cocksucker."

"Now Sophie."

"Well, can you imagine ripping off my title like that? He must think no one reads *Feminist News*. Well have I got news for him, he happens to be stealing from the Alexander

Cockburn of the feminist press. When this is all over I'm going to sue him for everything he's worth: the apartment, his leather jacket . . ."

"Oh my God."

Lillian was staring at the contents of Seymour's small metal box.

"Well, what is it?"

Silently Lillian lifted out a small plastic bag. It took me a moment to realize that the fine white powder wasn't laundry detergent. Cocaine, my nose started to run.

Three beautiful ounces of cocaine. So many times in my short life, I've come home from a long day at a boring job, or a long day without a boring job, worrying about money, dreaming of the paper bag lying in the street revealing a treasure of cocaine. Walking home nights from my job at a nursing home, I would fantasize a black car screeching around the corner into the night, bullets flying out the windows, another black car gaining on them. They hit a bump and a small briefcase flies out of the trunk, only they unknowingly speed on through the streets of the dark city. Unsuspectingly I wander over to the suitcase, snap the combination lock and reveal bags and bags of cocaine. Sometimes this fantasy includes cash. Then I have to figure out what to do with it. Knowing that ninety percent of the population of New York City would kill you for that much coke makes me want to get rid of it fast. I settle for one million in cash, a fraction of the street worth and give a big party, turning on winos to ounces of the best pot. "Don't say I never did anything for you," I'd snarl, throwing a bag of sense at some mean criminal type.

"Earth to Sophie."

"Hmmmm?"

"Look Soph, I know it's tempting but I really think we shouldn't touch this now. You just don't know what might happen. I just think we should put it back in this box and wait a while until we're sure everything's okay."

"Or we can snort it now and then everything will be okay."

"Sophie, just in case."

So, unwillingly, I agreed. We shut the box with the lock from my window gates and Lillian took the key. Before we put it away I decided to take one last look and noticed a small coke spoon. It was a souvenir spoon, like the kind you'd buy at the Statue of Liberty. The china bowl was silver rimmed, featuring a hand-painted portrait of the Leaning Tower of Pisa. The handle was made of silver filigree, carefully woven into a tree with small copper figures of frolicking peasants. At the top sat a tiny silver bust of a bald man with his mouth hanging open. Enameled into the porcelain plaque was his name—Galileo.

CHAPTER TWELVE

It was late Monday morning when they found Seymour's body belly-up in the Hudson River. The police were shocked by the sight of a three-hundred pound man in a leather face mask, leather thong tied tight around his neck, and wrists handcuffed behind his back. His floating body was surrounded by Clorox bottles tied together with plastic from six-packs. The *New York Post* suspected a BRUTAL SEX CULT. The doorman, Mukul Garg, told the *Post* that Epstein often came home dressed like that. He remembered a young white man in a leather jacket enter with Seymour, stay fifteen minutes, and then run out. The police broke down a locked door in the apartment, uncovering stereos, Cuisinarts and other hot items. Seymour was a fence.

I think it would be fair to say that terror ran through my body like traffic on the FDR Drive, and jammed up all my intersections. For the first hour I was in the most severe panic of my middle-class life. First I packed all my books. Then I unpacked everything except my feminist books. Then I repacked everything except for my feminist poetry books, and then I realized that packing and unpacking wasn't going to get me anywhere.

My next response was a desire to call Eva. Eva was my first girlfriend. We were best friends in junior high school and fell in love during the spring of ninth grade. We never ran out of things to say. We sat next to each other in every class, spent the afternoons together drinking Tab and eating Fritos with dip. On weekends we went to movies. *Persona, Cries and Whispers, The Story of Adele H;* we saw ourselves in every lead character, as long as each spoke a different language. Then we would tearfully part at Grand Central as I headed back into Manhattan and she caught the number seven home to Elmhurst. At night, after our parents were asleep, we would hang out on the phone until we collapsed from exhaustion, and then meet the next morning for coffee and to sneak cigarettes. Always Marlboros.

It was the most passionate, lustful, loving, beautiful experience of my life and it was over before I was old enough to vote. The last time we made love was the night of the blackout in New York City. Two years later she got married. The wedding reminded me of a nose job. Eva, headed towards law school, glowing on the arm of Eddie Weinblatt, a recent MBA from Brandeis. The carnations were spray-painted blue and the band played "Windmills of Your Mind" as they walked down the aisle. At the reception I got morbidly drunk and began seeing all the guests as one large angry mob. When we were lovers we had to hide everything, but because he's a man, they get a party. After three whiskey sours I got sick and left before the consommé.

The last time we ran into each other, she was wearing a full-length fox coat. Once, about a year ago, I called her on a whim. Her maid answered and turned out to be an old friend of mine from when we waitressed together at the Brew and Burger.

"Mrs. Weinblatt" was "at the Hamptons."

But all said and done, Eva was the best friend I ever had

and whenever I needed a best friend, I needed her. There is a limit, however, to my self-deception. I knew she would not be amused to hear that I was involved in the murder of a leftie journalist with possible mob connections who I had stalked in a gay leather bar dressed as a man with a stuffed crotch. No, calling her just didn't seem to be the right thing to do.

At that moment the phone rang. I knew it had to be the police. I was trapped. There was no way out. They probably had the whole block covered with sharpshooters. At that very moment they might be handing my mother the bull-horn to implore me to surrender. "Sophie, Sophie, can you hear me you *schmendrik?*"

"They'll never take me alive, Ma."

"Sophie, how can you do this to your father and me? We're the laughingstock of the whole neighborhood. Don't give us any more *tsuris*. If you come out like a good girl, with no trouble, maybe if we change our names, no one will remember in ten or twenty years."

I decided I'd better answer the phone—otherwise they might burst in, guns blazing. "Hello."

"Hello, Sophie."

"Yeah."

"This is Vivian Beck. You remember me don't you? We had such a nice talk in SoHo the other day."

"Sure Vivian. How are you?"

"I'm fine. How are you?"

"I'm fine, just fine, sitting here, nothing's happening, everything's cool, peaceful, no problems, just a lazy typical afternoon."

"That's nice."

"So, what can I do for you Vivian?"

"Well, I really enjoyed that little talk we had the other day and I think I might have some more memories that could help you with your story. That is if you are still interested."

"Sure."

"So, do you want to get together sometime this week? I thought Thursday might be a good day. In the afternoon?"

"Yeah, that's fine. You teach at Hunter College, don't you?"

"That's right."

"So why don't I meet you under the Marine statue on Fifth Avenue at three?"

"Fine."

"See you then. Nice talking to you, Vivian."

Well, if the cops got me before Thursday, Vivian could read about it in the *New York Post*. I sat down on the couch. I knew I should review my life because it was about to be over. Maybe I'd be lucky and get thirty years. With good behavior I'd be out in twenty. Life begins at forty anyway. One thing was sure, I wasn't going to be able to concentrate with Evan in the house. He was playing the record player again. It was so loud the silverware was trembling in the kitchen. Someone should charge the boy with stereo abuse. For hours and hours I would first hear Bob Dylan, then Leonard Cohen, then Phil Ochs, then Neil Young, then Bob Dylan again. Lillian calls it angry young men music. It was the only kind he liked. I was beginning to wonder why I let Evan stay around. It was certainly far beyond the call of duty. But I had to admit that despite his disgusting habits of being, there was one perverse quality about Evan that made me sort of fond of him. We shared the same scope of self-perception. Either we were everything or we were nothing. There were no other possibilities. Anyway, by comparison to

Evan, my life felt successful.

"Don't you ever listen to anything else? Here, try this Betty Carter album."

"I don't like jazz."

"How can you say 'I don't like jazz'? What kind of comment is that?"

I taunted, ranted and raved, but little could jar his Midwest stupor. He had come to New York so full of himself and with unreasonable expectations. Now I knew what was happening. It was the same old syndrome, I'd seen it a million times before. New York is a great place to be if you're doing something and the wrong place to be if you're doing nothing. It swallows you whole and you disappear forever into an apartment or a job or a bar. Even if you have the courage and brains and luck to get out, you're never the same again, because you know all your life that you've failed in New York. Evan was lying sprawled at the bottom of the crevice.

"Look Evan, you just sit in this apartment and smoke nickel bags and listen to the same records over and over again. Why are you in New York? What's your purpose here? Okay, so you didn't make it in music. That's not everything. This is the most beautiful place in the world. Go for walks, look at people, explore, open yourself up, take guitar lessons."

"I already know how to play the guitar."

So he continued to sit there rolling another joint from another nickel bag. Sooner or later he had to run out of nickels; then, I guessed, he'd probably go home. In the meantime I needed some air to get my head straight. I put on my black sunglasses and started to walk down Second Avenue through the Lower East Side.

CHAPTER THIRTEEN

Tears welled up in my eyes as I looked at the familiar buildings. How beautiful they were. Soon I would be gone, underground. My people, will I ever see you again? The cold sweat of fear started to turn into bristles of excitement. I would miss the neighborhood, my friends, the people hanging out on the stoops drinking Colt .45, but I had no choice. If I was to carry on my work, this was the only solution. Better to be free and move with the wind than spend the rest of my life in prison. On the lam. My picture would replace Germaine's on the walls of post offices around the country. Young mothers would whisper to their daughters "There goes a hero." From safe house to safe house, people preparing for my arrival. "Sophie is coming," they would nod knowingly to each other.

The light changed. Wait a minute, asshole, wake up. This is ridiculous. I haven't done anything for anyone. I've just spent my life being a bourgeois feminist. No, no Lone Ranger for me. It would be solitary life. An anonymous life. Wandering from town to town riding the freights, working on an oil rig here, in a Holiday Inn there. For the rest of my life I would be a woman without a name, a lady without a country, a stranger in a strange land. First I'd hitch to Montreal, a wedding band on my left hand for protection. I'd say my husband is in the service. The truckers would tell me their army stories. Then, I'd hop a tanker for Europe where I would spend the rest of my life under an assumed name. I tried out aliases: Emma Goldman. No, too obvious . . . Emma Goldstein.

As a young girl I had walked these streets with my grandmother on the way to the Yiddish theatre to see "The Dybbuk" or "Yoshe Kalb." She'd clutch my hand as we rushed past the Fillmore East where barefoot kids in painted faces sat laughing at nothing. Afterwards we'd eat kasha varnishkas at Ratner's Dairy Restaurant where every table got a whole basket of onion and pumpernickel rolls for free. All those memories made me hungry. If I was going to have to go underground I should at least allow myself a little treat. I stopped at the B & H Dairy for a good knish. That was the only place left that didn't microwave. Tears ran down my cheeks dripping into a glass of cold schav with sour cream.

Stumbling home I saw an omen on the marquee of the St. Mark's Theatre. Maria Schneider? A Maria Schneider double feature. What bliss. I would do anything for that woman, anything. I would even sit through two hours of Marlon Brando and two hours of Jack Nicholson for her. Rumor has it on the lesbian grapevine that while she was filming *Last Tango In Paris,* her girlfriend got hysterical at the sex scenes and had a nervous breakdown. Maria, tried and true, moved into the psychiatric hospital to be near her lover, only leaving to go to the set. Well, supposedly it was in *People* magazine. All right, it may not be exactly true, but it makes a great story.

When the films were over I felt a whole lot clearer. Retracing my steps I found it hard to believe that I would get caught. The only people who really had a good look were Seymour and Mukul Garg. Mukul wasn't a problem. Only Lillian knew the real score, and Melonie thinks I used her toys for some illicit fun. The thing to do was be professional. If I ever wanted to get picked up by one of the big dailies, I would have to make it my business to get some more scoops. Make an underground name for myself. I had to put my petty fears aside, my ego in check and solve this mystery. Who killed Seymour Epstein? Where is Germaine Covington? And what about Laura Wolfe?

CHAPTER FOURTEEN

Tuesday morning I woke up to the sound of typing from across the alley. It had started about three weeks before. I guessed another writer had moved onto the block and I felt a warm camaraderie. Some mornings we'd be typing duets, our different rhythms coming together in a symphony of productivity.

Walking up with a glass of tea and a bialy, I dialed the Elizabeth, New Jersey, number. I rang seven times.

"Hello," I shouted.

"You got a phone booth here."

"Where?"

"On Elizabeth Avenue and Broad Street, next to Schulman's dress shop, across from the courthouse."

The familiar Westchester number was busy so I lit a Winston and resolved to take a bus to Elizabeth that afternoon for the one o'clock call. It might be interesting to see who was waiting to answer the phone. It would be a stakeout. I started trying on black T-shirts when the phone rang.

"Soph—where have you been? I've been trying to call you. Dad passed out on the street." It was my brother Lou. "It's not that serious, he'll be back home soon, but the family's still pretty upset. He was just walking to the dentist and fainted in front of the emergency room of University Hospital. They gave him a room on the twelfth floor for tests. Mom really wants you to come over. I think you should. She asked me to call you. I think she'll behave herself, Soph. I can't promise, but I think so."

Sigh. I knew it wasn't going to be easy. But, being my mother's daughter, familial duty weighs heavy on the conscience.

I stumbled into my clothes and down six flights tripping over the three winos who had recently taken up residence on my front stoop. They gurgled as I raced off to the subway.

I dreaded these family emergencies. I dreaded any contact with the family whatsoever, except for Lou of course. He's always been cool. But the parents had reached the point of no return long ago. I'd tried every possible strategy for cease-fire once it became clear that our mutual disapproval wasn't just a phase.

I'd tried fighting: "Just because I don't want to go to Israel does not mean that I am a 'self-hating Jew.'"

I'd tried arguing: "How can you say it's unnatural—can't you see that sexuality is a social construct?"

"Don't social construct me," my mother would say. "Don't give me this social construct," my father would say.

"You're psychopathic," my mother would yell. "You're like a drug addict. All you want is your next shot. You wear your problems like a banner on Fifth Avenue."

When my article "A Jewish Lesbian Speaks" appeared in a progressive magazine, my parents threatened to sell the business and move to New Hampshire. "At least no one will know us there," they said.

Then it came to me one day that I didn't love them. It happened when they hurt me again, and I wasn't surprised. In fact, I expected it. It's made life easier to have a way to measure these things.

Last year I did a late night talk show, midnight to 3 A.M., a call-in program. For three hours in between cosmic communicators, a woman who meowed, wrong numbers, inebriated fantasizers and Nazis, an older man with an Eastern European accent kept calling in.

"Kill all gays." Then he would hang up. He must have called twenty times.

A week later I attended the wedding of a Lubavitcher cousin, Rivke, in Crown Heights. Born the same year as me, she was set up in an arranged marriage to a *yeshiva buche* from Israel who she met the day before the wedding. He was a pasty, bitter and pale young man with thick glasses. He was one of those orthodox boys who study from the moment they're able to sit up in a chair. She had to shave her head for the wedding and was wearing the traditional wig of a married woman. The next day the two of them would go off to Israel. At the party following the service, men danced together as befits the passion of the Lubavitcher. The whirling, jumping and kicking went on for hours. Even my father danced on the table. Off in the corner I stood, the perennial observer in drag: my mother's dress and my sister's boots. At least here I could dance with the girls since mixed dancing is forbidden, due, in part, to the natural filthiness of women; but I knew that I still didn't exactly fit in. A large man with a large beard came to speak to me. A surprisingly muscular man for a scholar, he smiled wide and showed his yellow teeth.

"Sophela, I heard you on the radio the other night."
He smiled again.
I looked at him.
He looked at me.
That was the end of my search for my roots.

Now that the autumn weather was turning chilly, the heat had finally been turned off on the subway. Most of the windows were wedged open. Each passenger sat alone, together in the grey boringness. I took a deep breath as the train pulled into the 33rd Street station.

CHAPTER FIFTEEN

I felt a little chill coming on as I waited for the hospital elevator. It's not the Judaism that bothers me, it really is the family. The two are separate in my mind. Judaism and I made our peace last year when I was writing an article on women, orthodoxy and abortion. My photographer, Muffin, another Jewish lez, though a bit more assimilated, decided that we should do some fieldwork. So, one Saturday morning we dutifully prepared to meet with God.

In long sleeves, long skirts and dark stockings, with kerchiefs on our heads, we set off for the Eldridge Street synagogue. Built by Eastern European Jewish immigrants, it had once had a congregation of thousands. Now, its twenty paid members try to keep the roof from falling in on the Italian walls, walnut pews and hand-blown glass gaslights.

The old shammes told us to sit in the back, in the corner. We were the only women. Then they pulled the curtain. Not a light delicate lace curtain between the sexes, but a heavy, dirty, brown canvas curtain that cut us off from the men, the temple, the service and God. As the opening prayer started, we got comfortable. First we took off our hats, then our shoes. Realizing, as women before us must have realized, that the old men, praying to themselves, did not know or care what we were doing, we smiled at each other. I put my hand on Muffin's leg, pulling her skirt up high. We didn't know each other very well, but I sensed she'd be into it—this private communication with God. It was going to be a game. Muffin and Sophie on their first date. She stared ahead as if nothing was happening, but with a big smile on her face. Just like Andy Feldman in eighth grade, she stretched and yawned, ending up with her hand around my shoulders, inching down under my blouse, closer and closer to my left breast. An interesting moment, two grown-up lesbians sitting in shul trying to get to second base. In no time at all she had my shirt unbuttoned like a pro and was trying to unsnap my bra.

"Wait—let me do it," I whispered.

"Listen, I do this a lot, I know how."

Oh no, this would ruin everything. Everybody has something weird about them, some secret shame and mine is my bra. All right, so I wear those old-fashioned ones with underwire and three rows of hooks. That's how I'm built. My mother didn't consult the fashion mags when she made me. And it doesn't help matters when Lillian calls them "Your World War I underwear." I took it off myself. My breasts felt great in the cool air.

Muffin was agile and dark skinned. The kind of woman my grandmother probably made out with in the potato fields of Lithuania. With a very big smile she came and sat on my lap, facing me. Letting her shirt drop to the floor, she touched my breasts with her own and rubbed her soft, soft cheeks along my face. Her face and breasts felt like one skin. We rocked back and forth as she messily licked my face, starting with wet sloppy ones over my eyes. Then came small kisses, a combination of bites and long romantic ones that make you die a little bit inside. I lowered my face to the space between her breasts, hoping to soak in some more of that fruity waxy smell. I teased her, my specialty, placing my mouth dryly over her nipple, lightly biting it but keeping away my tongue, and then surprising her with the ever so slow long wet strokes and circles. I felt it harden between my lips as Muffin moved with me to the tune of the old men's prayers. As she reached down to stroke the hair between my thighs, my hand was down the back of her skirt. The monot-one chanting reverberated through the large and airy syna-gogue. The light streamed in from the crumbling stained glass windows highlighting the soft hair on Muffin's skin. Everything was cool, light and thrilling, like floating in water. As she pressed her body closer to mine, I felt her relax and I reached into her body, sliding over her asshole, vagina and slithery clitoris with first one finger, then two, then three.

"Shit."

"What's the matter?"

"Sophie, that's the last prayer. I remember from Sunday school in Hewlitt, the service is ending goddamnit, hurry up and get your clothes on."

We thanked the shammes for letting us have this golden opportunity.

"It was a religious experience," Muffin said.

"I certainly hope so." He smiled, inviting us to come again. Anytime.

Later, I felt really good, I had found my place in Judaism, behind the curtain making love with girls. Not per-fect, but no so bad either. As for Muffin, I sent in my story and she sent in her photos. She also sent me a small rain check, which I've still got in my desk.

CHAPTER SIXTEEN

I entered the hospital room with my mind on other things and forgot to prepare for the hostile faces of my mother and sister. Lou grinned from the corner.

"Hi Dad, how're you doing? I hear you haven't been feeling too well."

He didn't say a word.

"Hi Dad, how's it going?"

Mom took his hand. "Lenny, I know she's a *shanda* but at least you should say hello."

Nothing.

"Lenny, have some grapes. I bought them and washed them. They were $1.79, eat them, they're fresh."

My father sat staring, his eyes slightly glassy, with his right forefinger dangling precariously out of the corner of his mouth. It was that Sunday afternoon football game expression.

"So as I was saying," my mother continued. "Cousin Edith is getting married next month to a very nice boy, he's in computers, and Sophie, I want you should know that my beautiful wedding dress which I've saved for you all these years is going to be my wedding gift to her." She emphasized "her." "No use letting such a dress go to waste." Glare.

"But Momma," whined Amy, "What about my wedding? I could wear your dress at my wedding."

"Amy, don't tell me you're getting married too." I was always the last to know.

"Well, not right away but definitely before I'm twenty-four. I'm sure of that. How old are you now Sophie?"

She annoyed me. Always. Lou and I often wondered out loud how Amy could have lived and functioned for twenty years without ever having expressed an opinion or an idea.

"Yes dear, you'll have a lovely wedding with bridesmaids and fresh flowers."

"How many guests can I invite?" Amy smiled sweetly. I was getting sick.

"As many as you like. You've always been a good girl." Smile. "Not like your sister." Glare.

"Hey Ma, why can't I wear your dress when I get married?" Lou grinned from the corner. That boy knows how to pose.

She ignored his comment as I flashed a thank-you smile.

"Sophie, why don't you get some decent clothes instead of always dressing like a man?"

"Ma, do I really look like a man to you? Look at me." I stuck out my chest.

"Sophie, don't be rude." She turned back to Dad. "Myra's daughter just graduated summa cum laude from Radcliffe. She's going to marry a Harvard boy from a Jewish family in Colorado of all places. They're in oil. Have you ever heard of such a thing as Jews in oil? He's getting his doctorate in advanced particle physics, God knows what that is. Mrs. Long down the hall, her son just finished his degree at Columbia Law School and he graduated twenty-first in his class. Stevie Levy, you remember, his father was your science teacher, Sophie—well, he just finished a Fulbright to Rome where he is studying architectural history. What a lovely boy. I remember he rode his bicycle three blocks to bring you a Valentine's Day card. Don't you remember, he was so handsome."

"Oh," I said.

"Sophia, why can't you be more respectful?"

"Please, Ma, let's not start this now okay? Because I can't fight with you in a hospital room, so just hold it in for a few hours then you can call me up and abuse me over the phone."

"Don't you tell me what to do. Your problem is that you never accepted that you're a woman. Your father says it's all my fault because I took you to see Martin Luther King and that you hit your head a lot when you were little, the gay thing I mean. You never think about us, about how embarrassing it would be if this got back to the family in Israel. All you ever think about is your own life."

"Ma—"

"Besides, look at your poor father, he can't do anything for himself."

"Ma, he's always like this. Besides, he never does anything for himself, he can't even set the table."

"Well, he can set part of the table. He knows where the forks go."

The conversation was over.

CHAPTER SEVENTEEN

L ou and I sped out towards Elizabeth, New Jersey, in his 1961 Ford Falcon.

"I really appreciate you giving me this lift, brother. I have to get some local color for an article I'm doing on small New Jersey towns and their street corners."

"Sure thing."

Lou's really a good guy for a seventeen-year-old male in 1982 America. He doesn't like to go too deeply into things, mostly because he's so good-hearted; he can't stand to confront realities which are harsh. Most are. He also has an understanding of the war between the sexes which far surpasses that of most mortal men. Unfortunately he knows it, which makes him occasionally intolerable.

"Hey Lou, how's your new girlfriend?" I thought that would be a good typical older sister question.

"She's okay. How's yours?"

"She's okay too."

We drove past the Budweiser plant toward Elizabeth, another dying American city.

"She's okay Soph except for one thing. She sleeps with her brother."

"Oh."

"I mean, she likes me but she's in love with him."

We sat in silence for a while. I remembered the time I

did a speaking engagement in Staten Island about what it's like to be a lesbian and why people should support the gay rights bill. When I finished speaking and had survived the usual questions like "Do you do it with animals?" one woman stood up and said, "I've never had an orgasm. How do I talk to my children about sex?"

I thought for a moment and then replied in my feminist knight-in-shining-armor voice, "Tell them what you just told me. Tell them the truth about what you know and what you don't know. Speak from the reality of your experience. It'll be the most helpful information you can share with your children." The audience had exploded into wild applause.

"Lou, I just don't know what to say."

"I didn't think you would."

We were late. It drove me crazy. I can't stand to be one second late, not for a movie, a class, to meet a friend, nothing. It ruins my whole week. "Can't you drive any faster?"

"No Soph, are you going to pay the speeding ticket?"

I sat back in my seat and chewed on a Virginia Slim.

We turned off the highway onto Elizabeth Avenue. A hundred years ago, this town was one of the poor northern centers of the Ku Klux Klan. Later, Jews, escaping from the Lower East Side, came here to start small businesses. Now Black and Hispanic people inhabit this spot in the heart of the leukemia belt, downwind from the asbestos factories of Northern New Jersey. We drove past a dilapidated movie theatre playing *Five Fingers of Death* and *The Gore-Gore Girls,* up to the corner phone booth.

The courthouse clock said 1:05. Shit. We waited a few more minutes, but knowing what I already knew about the kind of company Seymour kept, they were never late. In those five minutes whoever it was probably came and went.

That is if they hadn't heard the news about Seymour's murder. That is if they hadn't *made* the news about Seymour's murder.

Dejected, I suggested to Lou that we find some food. We drove around for a while until it became clear that if there had ever been a deli in town, it wasn't there now. We pulled into a Pizza Hut and ordered. Sitting over mushroom pizza and Sprite, we shot the shit. I bummed a Kool from the cashier.

"Hey Soph, let's go play video games."

"I don't want to."

"You know Sophie, I've noticed something about you. You don't like change. You want to eat the same food and read the same books and play the same games you've always played. You never want to do anything modern like disco roller-skating or play video games."

"That's not true. I'm very up-to-date, I'm hip, I'm with what's happening, I have to be in my business. What kind of reporter do you think I would be if I didn't keep up to the most recent minute?"

We chose Ms. Pac-Man, a bone for each of us. First you put a quarter in and then the computer sings a little mechanized theme song. Suddenly Ms. Pac-Man appears on the electronic screen. She's in a maze. She has to gobble up as many little blue dots as she can before the monsters catch her. It's social realism about women and overeating. In about thirty seconds, the monsters had caught me three times and my turn was over.

"That's all you get for a quarter? What a rip-off."

Like a pro, my little brother smoothly manipulated Ms. Pac-Man in and out, dodging, weaving. It took all his concentration but she ate all the little blue dots.

"What happens now?"

"Watch."

It was intermission. We heard the theme song again and then the Ms. Pac-Man and a new figure appeared.

"Who's that?"

"That's Mister Pac-Man. They're going to get married."

Sure enough, the two little Pac-People merged and reproduced miniature Pac-ettes.

"I can't stand it, compulsory heterosexuality, it's all over the place."

I sat down and waited for Lou to finish. "Lou, you've got mozzarella on your ear."

"Kids really like these games Soph. Some kids in my school are addicted to it. They play video games twelve hours a day. They cut school and steal money just so they can play video games."

"What ever happened to basketball? Lou, if you don't start doing those normal teenage things you're going to be bald and fat before your time."

"Bald, do you think I'm balding?"

"No, silly, don't worry, it was just an idle threat."

"Besides Soph, I've got more important things to think about."

"Like what?"

"Like herpes."

I ordered another Sprite. Lou ordered another pizza. He's a growing boy.

In the ladies room I washed my hands and face and tried to get the tomato sauce off my shirt. I mulled over the evolution of this peculiar story. Things weren't exactly going great. I stared at myself in the mirror. Here I am, a twenty-four-year-old dyke. I took inventory: brown hair, brown eyes, full Jewish

86

lips, just like Ethel Rosenberg. Most of my girlhood friends are married or in professional school, or at least working nine to five and certainly not talking to me about it.

Times are hard. They always have been hard for most people and in my line of life they always will be for me too. Will I ever be able to earn a decent living, have nice clothes, keep my hair combed? Will I spend the rest of my life running around after women I'm not going to get and stories that no one's going to appreciate?

"I love your articles," one woman told me at a party, "but they're so long I never get past the fourth paragraph. Five paragraphs is enough to explain anything. Don't you think so?"

"Oh," I said.

I became increasingly aware of someone looking at me in the mirror. I caught her reflection in the eye.

"Hello Sophie."

Those brutal grey flashing eyes, those proletarian shoes, that Palestinian scarf. There was no doubt about it.

"Germaine." I could barely get it out.

"You think you're a piece of hot shit, don't you Sophie?"

"Germaine what are you doing here at Pizza Hut? Did you escape from the FBI? I thought you were a prisoner of the state."

"Shows what kind of detective you are. We followed you here from the phone booth. You drove around a while trying to shake us, didn't you? Don't try to shake me Sophie."

"I was just looking for a corned beef on rye. What do you mean *we* followed you? Who is *we?*"

"We watched you slink around in that stained black T-shirt like Sam Spade, making a fool out of yourself."

Times hadn't changed Germaine Covington. "Listen to

me Sophie. You're messing around in something bigger than you are. We know you killed Seymour Epstein and if you don't stay out of our business, we're not going to be the only ones who know it."

"Wait a minute . . ."

She waited. I didn't know what to say, the girl's timing was impeccable, and I was in serious trouble. Any jerk could've figured that out. I tried to be smart. "Wait a minute Germaine. How do I know it wasn't you? I know it wasn't me. How do you have all this information anyway?" I couldn't decide if I should try to play it cool or fall on my knees and beg for mercy. Something about her made you want to do that.

"Wait Germaine. I shouldn't ask that of you. I mean, you're a woman who's been underground for twelve years. While I was buying my first training bra, you were traveling in China and Cuba and North Vietnam—you've survived, you're strong."

She really was magnificent, even if she was a bitch. Neither could be denied. And those grey eyes really did flash, just like Seymour said in his *Voice* article. He must have talked to her after all.

"Oh don't be so naive Sophie, it's not as great as you think. Don't you read *Rolling Stone*? Years of being afraid, false identification, not being able to make new friends, in a sense making a commitment not to grow as a person, only as a political entity. Waiting, hoping, giving everything to build a movement and watching that movement crumble leaving people's lives as hard as they were before. Betraying all their faith in the possibility of change. Paying our bills on time, being afraid to cross a red light. Does that sound romantic to you?"

"No, I guess not."

I took another look. Her eyes were tired. Her hair had streaks of grey, but not too many.

"Germaine, please tell me what's going on. Did you escape from the FBI? Were you at that bank at all?"

"Think a minute Sophie. That doesn't really matter anymore, does it?"

"I don't get it."

"Even if you think otherwise, all the rest of America knows that Germaine Covington is dead. She died in jail of a drug overdose, self-administered, of course."

"So?"

"So, now I'm free, it's over. I can go where I want and live the way I want. Germaine is dead and I need your help to keep it that way. Sophie, forget about this story. Let me die in peace."

I looked at her, feeling something between us, wondering if she felt anything at all. That Germaine—she sure knew how to make you want to give her her way. It was almost a skill.

"You have my word Germaine. I won't betray you. Your story is safe with me." I felt like riding off into the sunset.

She dried her hands on a paper towel and stepped into a vacant stall.

"But, Germaine, just tell me one thing." I spoke through the closed door. "Who did kill Seymour Epstein? Just for my own curiosity of course. What happened at the bank, and by the way, where is Laura Wolfe?"

There was no answer. I looked under the door. No feet. I crawled in. The window was open. She was gone.

CHAPTER EIGHTEEN

I got home that afternoon looking as if I'd seen my own ghost in the mirror. The tree winos were still sitting on my stoop. While I fumbled for my keys, one of them lifted his head.

"Miss Horowitz?"

"Yes?"

"We're from the FBI." He wasn't gurgling.

That's how I ended up alone in my sixth-floor walk-up with three FBI agents dressed as smelly winos. Well, I wasn't exactly alone. Evan was there of course, but he just sat in the corner pulling hairs out of the middle of his head. The agents paced back and forth in my living room. It's about ten by twelve, so, with their New England prep school strides, they could easily take about two steps in any direction.

"Miss Horowitz. We have information, a signed affidavit from Frances Mary Marino that you have been fraternizing with known opponents of the democratic system."

So the animals had found my waitress.

"We know you are withholding information vital to the security and safety of your fellow Americans."

I tried to imagine him having sex with a twelve-year-old boy.

"Now Miss Horowitz. You can cooperate like a good citizen and tell us what you know."

A good citizen. It had a vaguely familiar ring. In Girl Scouts I'd earned a good citizen badge by serving as color guard, reciting the Pledge of Allegiance and learning how to properly fold and burn a flag that had touched ground. The latter skill did come in handy. We had to memorize the four freedoms. Freedom of speech, freedom of religion, freedom of the press . . .

"I'm a reporter and my notes are protected under freedom of the press."

"Miss Horowitz, I'm sorry to disappoint you but we are not playing any games here. So why don't you just keep that liberal crap to yourself."

"I am not a liberal."

"A bank was robbed. One of the women involved in this incident is currently a fugitive. We have reason to believe that you have information concerning her whereabouts."

"I think I need to call my lawyer."

They sat down and waited. Three FBI men squeezed together on my secondhand futon. Over their heads hung an "In Celebration of Amazons" poster announcing the Midwest Lesbian Arts and Music Festival.

I knew two lawyers. One was Barbara Hubbard, the nationally renowned feminist lawyer. She was beautiful, a dedicated woman with a head of grey, blue, black thick hair that looked like a stormy ocean. As the battles grew longer and harder, she started getting wearier. She would sit in meetings, trancelike with a dull, practiced smile on her face. A strong woman, whose commitment to losing causes had made her inaccessible as a human being. It made her exist, apart from and in a sense, above, all petty human conflict. The only other lawyer I knew was Eva. In eleventh grade when we were making out in the girls' bathroom, she promised me I could always count on her. "Winter, Spring, Summer or Fall, all you gotta do is call" she wrote in my high school yearbook.

In the background I heard Evan talking to the agents. "WOW, are you guys really in the FBI? How do you get into it? Do you have to take a test? I'm pretty smart, you know, I used to be a child prodigy." I resolved to get rid of him as soon as possible.

The phone rang twice, it was after six, she should be home making dinner for her little hubby.

"Eva, it's Sophie. Please don't hang up. There are three FBI men sitting here on my futon and I need a lawyer and you're the only one I know. I don't want you to think I've done anything wrong . . ."

"I know all about it. I'm working for the Westchester D.A. now, for Peter Pope. They're going to serve you with a grand jury subpoena as soon as you hang up this phone. I advise you to tell them everything. If you have nothing to hide then don't hide anything. Don't call me anymore. Sophie, grow up."

I stood making rhythmic yes sounds into the dial tone. It had a calming effect, the drone that follows the click that terminates an unpleasant conversation. I pondered the mysteries of life: My old girlfriend is a fink for the cops. I'm about to go to jail for information I don't have. Peter Pope, the name on Seymour's bank statements, is the Westchester D.A. Isn't life so full of surprises, it makes you want to vomit?

"My lawyer says I don't have to answer your questions."

They handed me the subpoena and left.

CHAPTER NINETEEN

Sometimes life makes you laugh. Sometimes life makes you cry. Sometimes life makes you sick to your stomach. This was one of those times.

I went to the bathroom. Evan had of course left piss on the floor and all over the toilet seat. Weren't fathers supposed to teach their sons these things? "Here little Evan-Wevan, first you lift up the seat and then you hold your little weenie so your pee-pee doesn't invade everybody else's life."

Evan blew his nose and left the tissues on the floor.

I walked into the living room. I sat on the chair. I screamed at the top of my lungs, "I'm sick and tired of you, you stupid, disgusting asshole, jerk fuckface, idiot. You yucky FBI lover, piss all over the floor, ketchup-sucking mongrel, you smell bad, and you're ugly and you stink. Get out of my house and never come back—do you hear me!"

Evan didn't know what to do. He held his head still, pointed in my direction, opened his mouth in a gape of horror and moved his eyes back and forth looking for some way out. Then he collapsed back in his chair and started to cry. Snot was dripping from his nose as his shrieks became more and more sorrowful. He wiped it off on the curtains. I took a drag off a Salem Light. I was considering switching to menthol.

Okay, so I was scared. It's not so terrible to be petrified

with fear. It's good for me to feel things that deeply. Why shouldn't I be scared to death? I had to get a grip on things. I needed to find a lawyer. I had to calm down. What would make me calm? Maybe I should think about what I was going to do that week. On Thursday I'd see Vivian. That should be nice. I had sort of a soft spot for her. But that was Thursday, this was Tuesday. What could I do that would take my mind off all this trouble? I could read a book. I looked at my books. *Inside the Third Reich*, that was a good book. I could take another look at Seymour's papers.

The bank statements were at the top of the pile. They were from the White Plains Bank detailing a series of small but regular deposits. None exceeded $500. Those pennies do add up eventually though. The balance seemed to hover around seventy-five thou. Enough to keep Seymour in leather, coke, boys and more. I couldn't keep my mind on the evidence. That blasted typing from across the way was getting on my nerves. I moved into the living room and started perusing the clippings on my walls. Yep, there it was in the newspaper of record:

> Peter Pope, Westchester District Attorney, personally presided over the arraignment of Miss Covington.

I bet he did. These might have been the documents stolen from the bank. Pretty slick. I poured myself a Spartan Dark and went over the sequence of events. But that typing, it was really bothering me. Making me nervous. So much was happening. I needed space to think.

Evan had finished crying and was now cooking some foul concoction in the kitchen. His ugly face was all red.

The smell was creeping into my brain. The typing from across the alley pounding away, the Bob Dylan music in the background, Evan in my kitchen, I just couldn't take it one minute longer. I ran to the window.

"Will you stop that fucking typing!"

It stopped. I lit a cigarette. The phone rang.

"Miss Horowitz?" It was a sweet old voice.

"Yes?"

"Hello Miss Horowitz. I'm afraid that I'm the typing culprit. I think perhaps, if you're not too busy, you might pop over and we could discuss this matter further, drink some tea, and have a little chat."

"Look, I'm sorry that I yelled at you, I'm sure you're very nice, but I've had a bad day and it's hard for me to concentrate."

"I know you've had a difficult afternoon," she replied sympathetically. "What a shame to have those three policemen waiting outside your building. You must be terribly distraught.

"How did you know they were policemen? How did you know they weren't winos?"

"My dear, I couldn't help but notice their ruddy complexions. Like a ski weekend in Vail. They had good figures, not at all undernourished like those poor fellows we've been seeing so much more of lately. Furthermore, Miss Horowitz . . ."

"Yes?"

"They always seem to be intoxicated, but they never drank anything besides coffee. Just sat there and gurgled like babies."

"I'll be right over Mrs. . . ."

"Noseworthy."

"I'll be right over."

CHAPTER TWENTY

"**D**o come in, Miss Horowitz. I've been interested in meeting you."

"Oh, do you read *Feminist News?*"

"No, no, heavens no."

She was, what else can I say, a little old lady. Not too old, but old nevertheless. Her hair was grey, her face was wrinkled, her dress went down below her knee. Her house was covered with books. Thousands of books. On the shelves, on the tables and chairs and floor. And none of these books looked familiar. They were all paperbacks—the kind that women read on the subway, with strange names like *Murder in the Men's Room*. Then there were more books, the kind that mechanics carry around in their back pockets or physics students read under the covers with titles like *Bulika, Chief of the Trayules*.

"Have we met before?"

"No dear. I've just observed some very nice people coming and going from your apartment. You seem to have some good kind friends who always look happy. All except for that poor wretched little bastard who's sleeping in your kitchen."

I looked out her window directly into my apartment. She was one flight higher, so I couldn't look back.

"Would you care for some tea?"

"Would you happen to have anything stronger? I've had a hard day."

"Old Grand Dad?"

It hit the spot. She was a nice lady after all, even if she was a bit snoopy. Probably had nothing better to do all day than read these trash novels. I noticed that one whole case was filled with books by King James, that writer Lillian liked so much.

"You like King James, don't you?"

"I am King James."

She smiled and I caught the twinkle of pleasure in her eye. "Sophie, I know you must be a little surprised, but don't underestimate me because I have grey hair. We needn't be macho to be powerful my dear. I've been writing science fiction, detective novels and fantasy pieces for over forty years. Seven hours a day, six days a week. Now I'm working on my five hundred and twenty-fifth novel. It should be quite a good one too. Now, Sophie, I know you have gotten into some kind of trouble and let me say for the record that although I don't enjoy politics very often, I do find the government rather unpleasant and the individuals that comprise it rather the same. So, I assume that if one of those horrid men is bothering you, you might be doing, as they say, something right."

So I told her the story. I needed someone to talk to about it anyway and she seemed to be the one. I told her the whole story from the radio announcement at the Key Food to Germaine's appearance at the Pizza Hut and all the sordid details in between. She sat quietly the whole time, rocking in her rocking chair and stroking the neck of her cat. I finished with Seymour's papers and sat back exhausted, taking the liberty of pouring some more Old Grand Dad.

"So, what do you think?"

She took off her spectacles and laid them on the coffee

table. "Sophie, I think you are a good and courageous young woman, but you are, unfortunately, an amateur. You have overlooked some very important evidence."

"Not inconceivable."

"Well, if this Seymour chap and this Germaine character, her poor, unfortunate stand-in and the District Attorney Mr. Pope are all in, shall we say, cahoots, we need to examine why. Why would Mr. Pope work with such an unseemly figure as Mr. Epstein? The answer lies, I believe, in the cache of stolen goods found in the apartment after the murder. If Seymour was what is commonly known as a fence, he had to get those goods from somewhere. Germaine wouldn't be the person for that, too risky for a woman in her position— but who better than a district attorney for access to stolen merchandise? Do you see?"

I saw.

"I assume Mr. Pope felt that his moment of reckoning was approaching, an investigation or the like, and he desperately needed to destroy any records of bank deposits that might connect him to Mr. Epstein. So, they developed a bank robbery, the investigation of which would conveniently be supervised by—"

"By the D.A. of course. This would be a great story. How do I pin it on him, Mrs. Noseworthy? Can you help me?"

"Ah—Sophie, this is one of those times when the *sagesse* of old age becomes a valuable item. You need to ask yourself some questions, Sophia. You need to ask yourself why."

"Why?"

"Why do you want to expose Mr. Pope? What will it bring to your own life? What insights will it give you? Do you really want to be the kind of writer who exposes politicians and covers boring crime and corruption?"

I looked at the floor.

"I thought not. Or would you rather transcend the interchangeable facts of daily existence and everyday events to capture and address the higher moral questions of human commitment, desire and ability? Do you see Sophia, your interest is in Laura Wolfe, because something in her story touches your own experience. This I can understand immediately. Looking for Laura Wolfe is a personal journey for you and I advise you to continue it. I would, however, be careful of that gentleman, the Asian physician who appears to be so helpful. No district attorney has the power to force a doctor to inject a patient with Thorazine against the doctor's medical judgment, at least not in a public hospital. It's just not done. I'm afraid Dr. Tsang has offered you some misleading information."

"Well, Mrs. Noseworthy, your ideas about Seymour and the D.A. are good ones, but I know Henry well. Maybe he's covering up some feelings that he didn't act responsibly, but I don't think he would consciously mislead me."

"Sophie, no one ever has the right answer to every situation. Even Henrietta Bell, my greatest detective, makes mistakes. Here's a copy of one of her adventures. I hope you enjoy it. I do wish you the best and urge you to be prudent in your judgments. As for me, I'm afraid I need now to return to my typewriter. I hope your new state of mind will make the typing more tolerable. I've only just moved here temporarily from my home in Nantucket. It's only for a few months while the renovations are done. My son lives here normally. He's a musician. He plays with a group of fine-spirited young people who call themselves Beverly Hell and the Five Towns. Have you ever heard of them? They're quite clever."

"Well, yes Mrs. Noseworthy, I saw them just a few weeks ago. They're very good."

"He's staying at his boyfriend's house until I can go home to New England. So, Sophie, we both must return to our work. I hope we can take tea again before I return to Cape Cod." She showed me to the door.

"Yes, yes, you've really been great. Thanks for everything. Bye."

I had been a long day. I crawled into bed with a copy of *Murder in the Missionary Position* and fell fast asleep.

CHAPTER TWENTY-ONE

We walked through the zoo and into the park. The trees were full and overgrown deep green everywhere. The cold air and thick brush hid the litter and created a pastoral scene as Vivian Beck and I strolled past the skating rink. Spray-painted on a tunnel in faded red letters was PNOM PENH'S GONNA FALL.

"Some archaeologist should rescue that relic." Vivian laughed.

"I have some vague memory of those anti-war marches," I interjected, trying to meet Vivian on her own turf. "My mother used to take us. I didn't really understand the chants, so I'd make up my own. Like 'Ho-Ho-Ho-Chi-Minh, the NFL is Gonna Win,' I never knew if that was for the North Vietnamese or the New York Giants."

Vivian was wearing fall colors. Soft browns and reds and olive green carefully arranged for effect. It had an effect.

"How old are you Sophie?"

"Twenty-four. How old are you?"

"Thirty-four."

"That means you were twenty-four in—uh—"

"1973."

She looked quiet. I didn't want to lose the moment. "So, we've both been young in difficult times. It must have been a disappointment for you after all that excitement and hope. It must have been hard to figure out where you were going next."

"Oh Sophie, you're so cute. I'm afraid you're romanticizing a bit though. You know, for some of my friends, nothing interesting has happened since 1972. It's all they've got to hold on to to prove that sometime in their lives they were vibrant. It's taken almost a decade for me to realize that nothing is going to turn the world over for me and I'm wasting my time if I sit around waiting. I have to make my own decisions now, I'm not going to be saved by social unrest, I don't know if you understand what I'm saying. Is your life exciting for you?"

"Well, when I'm on a story and have something neat to do it's great. I love running around sleazy parts of town, developing contacts and information sources, hanging out with all kinds of people, but it's usually for a story. Sometimes I think I'd stay home all day and cry if I wasn't working on a project."

I was worried she would think I was a punk in my sneakers and blue jeans. I'm not a kid anymore. Does she see me as a woman or a cute little boy or an androgyne or a friend? Vivian's eyes were as green as her sweater. Her lips looked soft. We were sitting in a small boathouse by the rowboat lake. Behind us was The Ramble. A lone boat quietly passed by.

"It's like sitting on the Connecticut River," Vivian said. "I haven't done that since I was a girl." She looked out over the water. She turned to face me.

I wanted to kiss her. We looked at each other. I wanted to kiss her soft so she would know what that's like and then kiss her hard so she wouldn't think that soft was the only option.

"Sophie, what do you think about this murder that everyone's talking about—Seymour Epstein?"

I didn't know what to say.

"I mean, I knew him from the old days, though we haven't talked in years, except over the deli counter at Zabar's. But I was so shocked at his death. You're a reporter. I thought you might have heard something."

"They think it's some kind of gay-pick-up-combination-murder. At least that's what the dailies are saying. Why, what do you think Vivian?"

I was thinking that I was a real jerk. Here I had deceived myself into believing that she liked me but really she only wanted to find out about Seymour.

"It could have been anyone. Seymour wasn't well liked in any circle. You can be terminally obnoxious for only so long without getting someone really angry."

"So, Vivian, you think it was a personal revenge thing?"

"Well, Sophie, don't quote me now, but it has occurred to me that . . . well, of course, I don't know anything more than what I've told you, but neither do you. It's getting chilly, I should be heading back to Westchester, it's so strange living in suburbia when I'm so used to the Upper West Side. You know, I totally forgot to bring you those pictures of Laura. They're still sitting on my kitchen table. We really should get together again some day and go over them. You know, I really enjoy these talks we've had. It's made me think about things I've successfully avoided confronting for ten years. I wish I could find Laura and talk to her about it. You haven't heard from her, have you? All right then."

She gave me a peck on the cheek and disappeared into the mist dividing the tall grey buildings from the park.

I sat by the lake for a moment. There was no doubt about

it, I had a serious crush on Vivian Beck. She just seemed so ripe for it. I couldn't restrain myself. It's such a special thrill, getting involved with straight women. My friends think I'm crazy because it's so dangerous, between their freak-outs and angry boyfriends, but I know that they're also grateful and that's very delicious. Even if they run screaming into the arms of their old man waiting in the car, you've become someone they can never forget. Besides, nothing beats the pure pleasure of watching them experience women in such an immense way for the first time. It's a thrill, almost a fetish. Some people are into little boys, others like leather. I happen to prefer straight women, it's my sexuality, and Vivian was going to be tough, but not impossible.

Now, it's not every straight woman in the world. Just the ones who seem never to have made heterosexuality their home, who want something more in their lives but can't imagine what. It's also the thing of taking something away from men, beating them out when they have everything on their side. Vivian's probably been thinking about Laura and what went wrong in their relationship. She's probably evaluating a lot of things. But I knew she liked me, I could just tell. She wouldn't have suggested getting together again if she didn't. Besides, she said that she liked being with me. I just had to play my cards right. I pulled up the collar on my black cloth jacket and started the long walk home.

CHAPTER TWENTY-TWO

"**S**ophie, you are out of your mind. It's the sad, sad truth. Why, why, why do you insist, against my advice, on wasting your time fooling around at all hours of the day and night with straight women, who have no intention of changing their ways? Hmmm?"

"Chris, I can't help it. I'm into it. I'm a fool for love."

Chris and I were having dinner at her place after a long collective meeting at *Feminist News*.

"Don't bullshit me gorgeous, we've been friends for a long time and I can remember a whole slew of hets of every size and color that you've chased around New York. How about that one who got married?"

"Well, that was an exception."

"How about the one who took you to California and abandoned you on Valencia Boulevard for a guy with a Porsche headed towards L.A.? What was that one, Sophie? By the way, who did you call collect from San Francisco in the middle of the night asking to be wired $200 with which to crawl home? Hmmmm?"

"Chris, I know you're Black but you remind me of my mother sometimes."

"It's a *schmatta*."

"You mean a *shanda*."

"Oh yeah, I forgot. Anyway Sophie Horowitz, I want to

make it clear now and forever that if you get fucked over by one more straight woman I am not helping you out. *Entiendes?*"

"Yeah, yeah."

"Don't look so hurt Sophie, I know you love me because I tell you what to do. Anyway, Lillian's a very special girl. She's sweet, you should hang on to her, she's a good woman and this Vivian sounds like trouble."

"You know Chris, sometimes you're so old-fashioned. If I get involved with Vivian it won't have any effect on Lillian and me. One has nothing to do with the other. Anyway, don't forget about Laura Wolfe, she's part of this too."

"That reminds me to tell you to keep away from that Laura Wolfe as well. Girl, don't you remember when she and her gang busted up the *Feminist News* community meeting last year chanting *struggle, struggle, struggle?* What's wrong with you Sophie? All you want is trouble. You're never happy with what you got."

"It's too boring."

"There you go sweetheart with your endearing convenient contradictions. After a full day of your one-thrill-after-another life you won't even taste my carefully prepared Haitian spices."

"I only like salt."

"Oh Goddess."

Chris had picked that up from the In Celebration of the Womb Moon conference that she covered in the spring. I started fumbling for a cigarette.

"Here Sophie, have a banana instead. You know I don't want you to die."

"Oh Chrissie, just one, be nice, you know I have to be in court tomorrow."

"You're right. Are you nervous?"

"Well, the clerk told me not to worry right away. This is just an appearance to set a court date. I don't know exactly what to expect though. I've never been in court before except as press."

"Well I'll tell you," Chris answered, digging into her dinner, "I have a story like that, it's not very anything, but I'll tell you anyway. It's not big Black revolutionary and it's not tough Black street kid."

"Chris, cut the crap, I know you're the average woman on the street. What are you eating anyway?"

"Chebri—goat, it's delicious."

"Well, perhaps slightly eccentric."

"Well Sophie, we all seem to have our ethnocentricities, don't we?"

"She took another bite and sat back in her familiar I've-got-a-story-position, fork suspended in midair, left hand wildly gesticulating, leaning farther and farther over the table, dramatically pausing for a drink of water. "I was in college. A snotty college. A white college. The board had decided to give a bullshit award to some famous person in order to boost the endowment, so they chose Robert McNamara, you know, the architect of the Vietnam war. They gave him an award for a 'lifetime contribution to international understanding.' It was too much for even the complacent students of the late seventies. '77 I think it was. So we formed a student protest committee to plan a demonstration. Most of the kids had never done anything remotely like that before and those who had were a little rusty. Being the only Black gay woman, I, of course, got immediately drafted onto every committee and speakers list. You know, 'We've got Chris so no more girls, Negroes or faggots.' Of course all the white boys gave big boring speeches about nothing and all this time, while they were talking, McNamara was getting his award across the street. So, when it was my turn, and honey, you know I was last, I said I thought we should stop the yakking and go tell Mr. M. what we think about him. Let him sweat a little, too. So we did, all one thousand of us. The police came of course and filled up one paddy wagon. I was in it. They charged us with mob action, disorderly conduct and resisting arrest. We ended up in Cook County jail—this is Chicago—which, take my word for it, ain't Old McDonald's farm. So we walk into the women's section. Eight white women and me and everyone in that prison was Black. They hooted and shouted 'What are you doing here? You don't belong here,' and when they saw me, bringing up the rear, they didn't know what to say. Well, that made me mad because I may have made the mistake of going to a snotty white college, but I am a proud Black woman and I was determined to find out what was happening. I talked to those women all that night and all the next day until the provost of the college came to get us out. None of them were criminals you know, they were mostly in there for prostitution or passing bad checks or something minor. Well, weeks later when we came to court, the room was filled with about eighty people, each waiting for their one and a half minutes of American justice. I saw one woman I recognized and went over to talk with her. Well, we hadn't even said out hellos when her fat white pimp comes over and starts hollering 'I don't want you fraternizin' with no colored trash' and she was a Black woman. So, anyway, later I went to visit her once. She lived in a housing project on the west side of Chicago called Cabrini Green. It was built as a series of high-rises and each apartment had a balcony overlooking the slums of Chicago. But, the crime rate was so high there that the city came and covered the buildings with wire mesh so no one could get in from the outside. Well, you know what? The place looked like a collection of giant hamster cages with poor Black people inside running on that wheel. So that's what it was like. Don't you worry Sophie, you know I love you, but they'll never put you in jail for more than overnight. You just don't have the right characteristics."

CHAPTER TWENTY-THREE

Chris finished eating and we started walking over to the Unitarian Church where some women were performing a "Night of Black Lesbian Voices."

"So what else is happening in your life Chrissie? You seem a little troubled."

"Well, do you really want to know?"

"Sure."

"Well, I'm seeing this boy, I don't know, he's very sweet with a feminine face, he hardly looks like a man at all, just like a little boy. I really don't know how this happened, we just started talking at a party and I thought, shit, I spend so much time in these important, transforming relationships, why can't I just do something that's fun? He's very feminist, he's real feminist, reads all the books. He's always saying things to me about how women are naturally superior, he's very sweet. But, unfortunately, he's boring. What do you think?"

"Chris, you're not going straight on me are you? I don't want to hear on the grapevine that you've started a group called Former Lesbians, or that you're married and moved to the suburbs."

"No, no, I'm a confirmed woman-loving, cunt-sucking lesbian, I'm just playing around."

"All right then, I hope you have a good time. How many times have you slept with him?"

"Once."

"So what are you worrying about?"

"Oh Sophie, you know how some women are, and I don't blame them really. They've fought so hard to be able to be out of the closet. It's scary to think that someone is buckling under the pressure, but this trick isn't about pressure." Her hands were shoved deep in her pockets as we walked along.

"Chrissie, I didn't say anything about that, why have you been getting a lot of shit lately?"

"I don't know. I know I felt a need that led me to this guy, I had decided to sleep with a man and I was attracted to him first, but there was more to that need than sexual desire."

"Well, don't worry yourself to death over it. You know, Chrissie, even I have fantasies about men sometimes."

"Even super-dyke? You're shitting me."

"That's the truth. Beautiful, vague fantasies about men who make love like women. But I know that even though I can think about it, if I ever got there again with a real man, I don't think I would really want to be there. I'm used to that skin you love to touch, I couldn't transfer to beards and bones."

The front steps were packed with women waiting to get into the church. When I went to white events I knew mostly everyone there. But after a few years of coming to Black women's things I still felt like a fly on the wall. All around me were women whose names and faces were familiar from book jackets. Sometimes I just felt pale and plain. Why would anyone here want to talk to a schmuck like me? It was easier to just sit quiet and not make any mistakes.

Walking home all high and excited, we headed towards

Veselka's Polish Home Cooking for some boiled beef with horseradish sauce and a chocolate egg cream.

"Chrissie, it's so weird to be here. This is where Laura Wolfe used to hang out. I'd come in here to read the paper and have coffee in the morning and she'd be sitting over in that corner arguing, or struggling with whomever. All the time, we used to glare at each other. Now she's gone and East Village life continues as if she'd never been here, as if she'd been just plucked out of the scenery."

"Don't get too nostalgic too quickly, Sophie, there are some of those Women Against Bad Things at the table behind you."

I turned around. They saw me, collectively. What could they possibly have against me now? I'd written that little piece on Laura for the paper and everyone knew I was working on a bigger one. I was certainly more sympathetic towards their fallen comrade than anybody else was. Those girls, they'd probably forgotten how to smile and thought that's what they were doing.

As a unit, they rose from their table and walked over to where we were sitting. One came forward and looked me in the eye.

"Sisters, we must struggle to move forward. Take our leaflet." She handed me five sheets of legal paper stapled together. Both sides of each sheet were crammed with single-spaced typing.

"Don't tell me, it's the new mobilization against egg creams."

"Sisters, this communiqué explains that we disassociate ourselves from Laura Wolfe because she is an individualist, opportunist, adventurist and doesn't understand the meaning of struggle."

"You're not supporting Laura Wolfe? I'm shocked. No I'm not. She's the best thing that ever happened to you little twerps."

I was surprised at how mad I was getting, but it was true. Even if Laura Wolfe is sort of a jerk, she's had a hard time. No one has ever had the courage to really love her. Besides, she's courageous, she did what she needed to do even though she didn't get any support for it. She's a good woman. Yes, I felt comfortable saying that. Laura Wolfe is my sister . . . so to speak.

"That's a pretty shitty way to treat your friends," Chrissie responded.

"It's not a question of friends. It's a political question. It's a question of comrades. Who are you anyway? I think you must be an agent."

"That's right, you little bitch, I'm an agent of the devil."

It had been a hard day all around. "Chris, I have to go home. I have to go to court tomorrow. I can't believe how many places I'm in in one day. I feel like five different people."

"Well, it's that New York state of mind."

"Yeah."

"Look Sophie, you don't have to get everything together at once. Just get through tomorrow, I'm sure you'll get a postponement. I'll be sending you love vibes."

"Thanks honey, good night."

"Good night."

CHAPTER TWENTY-FOUR

I spent Friday morning at the library reviewing old newspapers. Yep, Mrs. Noseworthy was right. Peter Pope had recently been under investigation concerning the disappearance of stolen property. It all made sense to me. Pope passed the goods on to Seymour who sold them through the black market and kicked back some profit to the D.A. via the White Plains bank. When the investigation got too hot, they set up this robbery to get the records and destroy them.

No wonder Laura Wolfe was hiding out. Poor kid, she probably knew too much for her own good. But how did she get into this mess in the first place? I was starting to grow fond of her. I remembered all the times she screamed at me and told me I was unprincipled. She'd send me three flyers every time her group had a meeting, and call me too. Once I did go. It lasted four hours. When I tried to leave after three, there were four of her girls at the door telling me I was unprincipled. The next day I saw her on the street.

"Hi Laura, how was the end of the meeting?"

"That's not the real question. The real question is why you weren't there."

Chris's way of dealing with them was that every time one of "those girls" would come up to her she'd ask, "Hey Laura, want to lend me $5?"

Still, it didn't seem so bad in retrospect. I guess I have been unprincipled in my time, and I did have to admire the way she hung in there when all her friends finked out. I remembered her slogan *Ho-Ho-Ho-Mo-Sexual, The Ruling Class Is Ineffectual.* I repeated it to myself as I entered the lawyer's office on 41st and Madison.

My lawyer's name was June Honeymoon; I found her through Lawyers for the Left. Like many of her comrades she was a divorce lawyer with a prosperous private practice on Central Park West. Her husband paraded himself as a liberal judge. Every three or four years she did a big splashy political case for free (*pro bono* she liked to say) thereby renewing her radical credentials. This was 1982 though and not many big splashy political cases were coming along so she'd agreed to take mine. Something about her manner told me we weren't going to get along. I think I started off with a bad attitude when I saw her office. It was arranged to be stylishly simple with Plexiglas furniture, area lighting and no books.

"Susan," she said, "I've reviewed your files and I think we can win this. Just trust me and you won't have to spend a minute in jail. What we need now is a theory of defense."

She frowned a moment, as if deep in thought. "I've got it. We'll argue that you didn't know it was illegal."

"Wait a minute."

"Now Susan, I know you believe in consensus and all that, but things are breaking fast, sometimes we just have to go with the current. Just believe me, I know what's best. My senior partner John Snort will argue the case. He carries a lot of weight with the judges."

"Sophie. My name is Sophie and I want one thing to be

clear from the beginning. I don't want a man arguing my case in court. Men are welcome to help out and I would be grateful if they do but I feel it's important for a feminist to be defended by a woman. That's why I chose your name out of the directory. I want a woman counsel." I liked the sound of that word *counsel*, like I knew what I was talking about.

"Look Susan, you are not considering the different factors in this very complex case. I am not implying that I am not qualified to represent you because I most certainly am. However, I also am capable of putting the best interests of my client before any petty personal desire for success as an attorney. My job is to get you off and only John Snort can do that. As far as your public image goes, well, I've never heard of you or that newspaper and I've lived in New York all my life. So, now, that's settled."

She was one of those short bitch types. One of the snotty kids in the school yard who would run around to the other kids in the in-group and say, "Sophie's hair is just dripping with grease." You just wanted to slap her.

"Besides," she smiled her snotty smile, "refusing to be represented by a man is sexist, it's the same as racist. It's a case of reverse discrimination and furthermore it's male-exclusionist."

Where did she get a word like that? I looked at the wall-to-wall carpeting, her tweed suit, leather briefcase, silver cigarette case and gold earrings.

"No," I said quietly.

"I must insist. I have already put in eight hours of work for you pro bono on this case. I didn't have to do it but I did. I think you had better consider that because you are sounding ungrateful and irrational."

She picked up the princess phone and started to dial. I

flipped through some copies of *Office Decorator.* She covered the receiver with her hand and hissed at me, "I have John Snort on the phone. I told him what your attitude is and he is very hurt. He's near tears. You call yourself a feminist but you don't mind brutally hurting the feelings of a very expensive lawyer who's trying to help you. He told me that he's never been so insulted in all his life. He also said that he refuses to represent anyone who claims they are being forced to be represented by him and if you don't say that you want him to represent you, he and I will walk off this case and you will walk into court twenty minutes from now with no lawyer."

She smiled.

"Now, before I forget, here is my bill for expenses incurred so far. Let's see. Three hundred for computer time, seventy for cab fare . . ."

We left together for court, still arguing in the cab. "Look Susan, I'm not a mean person, but if you do not listen to me and my expertise, you will lose. I don't mean to pressure you but I have to. It may sound unethical to you but it's ethical to me."

I wondered if ethical was anything like principled.

CHAPTER TWENTY-FIVE

When we got to Foley Square, the press was waiting but no John Snort. He was too hurt. June
went to prepare and I looked over the motley
crew. I recognized some of the guys from other cases I had
covered, which believe me, did not bring any great comfort.

"Hey Sophie, really got yourself fucked in the ass this
time ha-ha," called out the balding guy from ABC. Great.
Most of them are revolting. They get sent from one story to
another without any preparation or continuity and assume
that everyone's guilty or else they wouldn't have been
arrested.

"How come there's so much press?" I asked. "Did someone put this case in the UPI day book?"

"Naw," said the cameraman from CBS, cigar juice running down his second chin. "We're all here for the really
big news of the day. Someone in the Westchester D.A.'s
office was accused of moving stolen goods but the poor
schnook dropped dead before he could get to court. So
when we heard something was happening concerning that
commie lezzie case, we decided, what the hell, might as
well bring in something so the station don't go sending us
all over New York getting human interest location shots for
a story on the weather."

June and I climbed to the top of the stairs while the cameramen jockeyed for position. There was something about wearing a dress, the wind blowing through my short hair, my earrings glittering in the cold sun, that let me feel strong. This was, after all, my moment of glory. This was the switch from reporting news to making it. All over the country young girls would be looking up to me as an example of courage, independence and, well, principle. Just like I had looked up to Germaine Covington years before. Like hundreds of defendants before me, I read my statement in a cool, crisp inspiring voice.

"I am a journalist with no political or criminal involvement in this case. I am refusing to give testimony to the grand jury because I believe it violates my First Amendment rights to freedom of the press. Second, I oppose the very existence of the grand jury because I believe that its process . . ."

The cameraman turned off their lights and started walking away. Only the radio and print press remained.

". . . its process, in general, is a manipulation and an invasion into the lives of political people whose activities should be protected by the constitution."

It was a dignified statement, I knew that. It felt good to stand out with the buildings like razors against the blue autumn New York sky. We opened for questions.

"Why are you protecting criminals?" asked the *Daily News*.

"If you're not covering up for terrorists then why are you going to jail?" asked the *New York Post*.

I tried to explain how grand juries work. How they can subpoena anyone and ask them all kinds of questions unrelated to the case they are investigating. "They could ask me who lives in my building or who shops at Key Food. If I answer one question I have to answer all of them. Then, if you refuse to cooperate, they send you to jail for eighteen months without even charging you with a crime."

I was getting worried. This wasn't much fun at all. I mean, when the press conference was over they would go get a bacon, lettuce and tomato on white toast and I might be headed inside.

I hoped Evan remembered to water the plants. I hoped Chris was right, I could use a little of that white skin privilege. Was that a sick thing to think? I didn't know what I felt anymore.

We found John washing his face in the men's room. He filed some motions and argued some arguments and got the court date postponed one month. That evening I watched ABC News and saw reporters crowded around my father lying on our living room sofa, his finger still hanging out of his mouth.

"She's always been fascinated by terrorists," my mother said in her chatty, helpful way. After all, this was her big chance to be on TV.

"What about you Mr. Horowitz? Do you support your daughter's involvement with militants?"

My dear old dad took his finger out of his mouth and looked into the camera, right at me.

"They should go to Russia." he said.

CHAPTER TWENTY-SIX

Feeling in need of a little sisterhood, I walked over to the offices of *Feminist News*. Those women had been there for me through thick and thin, and I had been there for them. Three years it's been since we first started the newspaper in Chris's living room. Now we have a circulation of seven thousand and distribute another thousand free to women in prison. My column was called "On the Right and Left," which meant that I came under a lot of criticism from people, but my sisters always defended me. I remember once when I interviewed lesbian nuns and got bloody Tampax sent to me in the mail. Another time I criticized a prominent male leftist for sexually harassing his students and lots of his friends wouldn't talk to me for a year. Last spring was the worst of all—the spring of the sadomasochism controversy. I covered a conference on lesbian sadomasochism organized by a group called The Sexual Outlaws. It was held at midnight in a large basement packed with women in studded collars and leather shirts, some with crew cuts, all looking like desperados.

"How many women here do S/M" the MC asked.

About half raised their hands.

"This is a support meeting for sadomasochists. No one has permission to say anything negative about S/M. No one who doesn't do S/M has permission to speak at all."

They passed the microphone back and forth while women told their stories. One older woman, calmly dressed in sweatpants and a sweatshirt, took the floor.

"My name is Tina," she cooed. "I get off on creating a scene. Do you know what that is?"

No Tina, tell us.

"I create a fantasy involving you. You may not even know you're in it and once it starts you have no control over it." As she was telling the story, she started, ever so slowly, to unzip her sweatshirt and untie her sweatpants, until both dropped to the ground, revealing leather and chains draped across her torso and a silver dagger gleaming between her breasts. The outlaws oohed and aahed. I felt sort of nervous. Then, it hit me, so to speak, that she had just created an exhibitionist fantasy for herself and we were her unknowing and in my case, unwilling, partners. The women loved it. They cheered and clapped until their gaiety was broken by an angry voice from the back of the room.

"When you slept with Charisse in Northampton, you nearly killed her."

The murmurs of scandal rippled through the crowd.

Tina stood there proudly with her head held high, her iron- and leather-wrapped breasts thrust forward.

"Charisse never said stop."

I called my piece "A Sexual Outlaw Is Not Necessarily a Revolutionary." It was long but it made the point for women who couldn't get past the first paragraph. I got hate mail for months and an anonymous can of Crisco but my sisters stood by me. Even though they didn't agree with me, they were right there, dependable and supportive. Gosh I love them so much.

At the office my sisters were in deep despair. They

greeted my entrance with expressions of dark suspicion.

"Look who's here. Hey Bonnie, where's Clyde?"

After a few more minutes of succinct conversation the situation became clear.

"Look Sophie." Chris took me over by the window. "Paranoia is running high and wild among the feminists. Jackie thinks that Kathy is an agent and Gerri is checking Julia's references. We spent the morning accusing each other of being government infiltrators. Now we're breaking for lunch."

"What kind of community response have we gotten?"

"Well, as far as I can tell, no one is calling the office for fear that the phone is tapped. Advertisers are slipping notes under the door though, and then running away."

As we stood there a little slip of paper came floating in through the mail slot. We listened to the patter of army boots running down the hall. I picked it up.

> Dear *Feminist News,* please cancel all accounts for Feminist Exterminating Company and please burn all records that we ever did business with you. Please eat this message.

"Sophie, you know as well as I that without that revenue we'll never be able to put out another issue. Sophie . . . ?"

Chris was looking at the floor. "Sophie, if you don't resign, temporarily of course, you know, a leave of absence, we're all going on permanent vacation."

I looked out the window at the two agents sitting in an old Oldsmobile. I knew I had no choice.

CHAPTER TWENTY-SEVEN

A pariah to my friends, with $54 to my name, I was back pounding the pavement looking for work. I tried registering with temporary typing agencies but I didn't have the clothes to apply. My neighbor, Rick the Queen, claimed he could get me a gig in a restaurant downtown where some of his friends were enjoying stable employment. He came through for me, and by Monday evening I was walking to work at Yes Sir Mister President. My last waitressing job, the one at Brew and Burger, had ended when I tried organizing a Waitresses Collective with the slogan "Serving the Women Who Serve the World." The boss didn't care for it. Remembering Fran Marino and her animals, I walked into a dining room full of fat men in business suits.

The manager, Donnie, put me on the floor right away. "I'll just throw you in and see if you drown."

"Yes Sir Mister President?" I tried to smile but all I could do was raise my eyebrows. My first table ordered two Becks on tap.

As I poured the drinks, Donnie talked to me out of the corner of his mouth. "Serve your cherry with the beers, dear." So I put a cherry in each of the beers. What did I know? I figured they had to be regulars with weird tastes. I got a $20 tip. Something was not right. Experience had taught me that the only people who really leave good tips are other waitresses, or people who want something out of you that you don't want to give them. I stopped one of the other girls. Her nameplate said YES SIR MISTER PRESIDENT MY NAME IS JOANNE.

"Hey Joanne, those guys gave me a $20 tip."

"Honey, you'll have to wait until Shelley's through, you're next. You'll have to use the elevator."

"For what?"

"To suck them off, what do you think?"

For one minute I actually considered it. I considered sucking on the penises of fat Wall Street animals for $20 a shot. I've had friends who have done it. Linda, and old-fashioned bar dyke with a tattoo, put on a negligee and worked the reception desk for a whorehouse on East 27th Street. She had to say, "I have a lovely blonde for you. She likes sixty-nine, around the world and grecian urn. That's apartment 'P,' for pleasure." She made $150 a day. Then there was Judy, who was in my women's group some years ago. She worked as a masseuse to get through college. She said that you had to keep up with the porn mags to know what men were going to want. She said that if on Monday *Hustler* had some story about how the brand new kinky way to get off was to come in a woman's hair, then by Tuesday afternoon every man wanted to come in your hair. She said that she could read men like stop signs. She knew them so well, she could see one walking down the street and know everything about what humiliating, painful and boring things he liked to do. It would really be interesting to know men that well. I walked into the manager's office.

"Donnie, I'm sorry, I can't work here."

"That's all right honey. This isn't for everybody."

I walked out the door and into the night, later realizing I still had the $20 in my pocket. I wonder how long they waited in the elevator.

CHAPTER TWENTY-EIGHT

I was worried about money. Really worried. I didn't mind living on potatoes—in fact, I preferred living on potatoes. But the bills were piling up and resources were running out. On top of it I was getting depressed. I couldn't go anywhere, I couldn't do anything. I needed a way out. What would make a lot of money fast? Drugs didn't make sense with all this police trouble and besides, it was a field with a lot of competition. And then it fell calmly upon me like a beam of sunlight. Pornography. I could write pornography. It wasn't so bad. It wouldn't be too hard. I had a pornographic mind, at least that's what my mother says. I could write pornography for lesbians. Start a whole new market. This could be the beginning of something really big. I'd get famous and appear on the David Susskind show wearing a ski mask. The Lesbian Pornographer. It felt possible.

I went to my typewriter and began to get nervous. Usually I start hitting the keys before I even sit down, typing furiously like Little Richard at the piano. It was going to be harder than I thought, there were so many complications. First, it couldn't sound like regular dirty, sleazy porn. "He thrust his throbbing cock into her juicy cunt." That just wouldn't do it. Most nouns, verbs and adjectives were unusable. I couldn't bring myself to write words like "stroke," "wet," or "hungry." They're meaningless. Also, I certainly didn't want to make an unnecessary contribution to the world of things that men jerk off to. I wanted it to be meaningless to men and wonderful for women. But, that wouldn't be too hard, women can jerk off to the bible. I, for example, masturbate to *The New York Times*. The main thing was that I wanted it to be real. I wanted it to describe sex the way women really have it. The real thing is usually a combination of thrill and frustration, comfort and conflict. It's basically very delicious but surely more complicated than the gothics or paperbacks would have you believe.

I sat back with my feet up on the desk and took a hit off a cigarette. What was sex like with Lillian, or any woman? When does it start and stop? Sometimes it starts over dinner or before, when you're chopping and smelling and sautéing the food. It's funny with women, the illusions and fantasies don't come so much from TV or Mom or eighth-grade English. It's a special combination of what each woman brings to bed with her, her own courage or fear, her own private passions. I like the heavy physicality, touching and being touched in the same way, feeling the folds and wrinkles of her vulva, feeling mine being enjoyed in the same way. One woman called it "Writing graffiti on vaginal walls." It's a great urban metaphor. And there's also the thrill, every time, of knowing that everything in the world tried to stop this woman next to you in bed from being there, but she got through anyway, only because she wanted to and had decided to. All these feeling were what I wanted to synthesize into my pornography. I narrowed it down to one scene, to one seduction, to one moment of rising breasts with their red flush, to one minute of one tongue on my cunt, one minute of coming and kissing the mouth that

136

made you come from tongue to tongue. None of the words were right.

I tore the paper out of the machine and tried again. It all came easier this time. I typed for two hours straight until I had a nice short story, good enough for any stroke book, called "Cycle Suck," about two motorcycle men and their sailor boy. It should be good for $50.

Lillian and I talked on the phone the next morning.

"Don't you think it's a little unethical to write gay male pornography when you've never been a gay man?"

"Well, I've slept with one."

"Sophie, don't rationalize. If you're going to exploit gay men for money. that's okay, but you have to be honest about what you're doing."

I decided to sell it now and think about it later. Or maybe I could go back to restaurant work.

CHAPTER TWENTY-NINE

Two days later, after a series of humiliating inter-
views, I started to work at the Great American
Health Food Bar by City Hall. Secretaries with
painted faces and fingernails came in on their half-hour
lunch breaks to order glorified fast food like curried tofu on
pita bread with yogurt, brewer's yeast and a Coke. The staff
was composed of five lesbians, two Italian boys—one with
an Andy Capp tattoo and one with Jesus on the cross—and
a student at the Union Theological Seminary who was
about to be married. I couldn't help but feel bad. Every
time one of those secretaries spent her hard earned money
on alfalfa sprouts on toasted seven-grain bread, cottage
cheese with granola and a Coke, and the bill came to $7.50,
I felt bad. I felt so bad that I couldn't bring myself to
remember that she had four items instead of three. At the
end of the third day the boss came up to me.

"You don't like it here."

"Yes I do Bernie, I love it here, I really do."

"You don't smile at the customers."

"Bernie, I really try, I really do. Sometimes I can't actually smile but I do raise my eyebrows, see?"

At the age of twenty-four, with no degree and a reputation
to match, I was begging Bernie for a job that I didn't want.

Tears streaming down my face, I walked out into the

autumn air in my leafy green apron and carrottop hat, and walked home slowly through the Lower East Side. I really wanted to drown my sorrows in a fat kielbasa and mashed potatoes with sauerkraut and gravy, challah bread and a Tuborg dark, but I couldn't afford it. I really wanted to feel Lillian put her strong hands around my waist and roll me into bed or the tub. I really wanted to buy six different kinds of cheesecake and sit on all of them, squish ripe strawberries all over Lillian's body and squeeze a lime on her labia, slurping juice like oysters in their shell. But Lillian wouldn't be over for a few more hours and I needed something right away.

I walked into my apartment, surprising Evan. He was sitting in his usual place on the couch but this time he had a very guilty look on his face. Then I looked again. The coke! Evan was snorting lines from my cocaine. That was the last straw, that slimy pig. After all I'd done for him. Then I remembered I had better be cool. It had occurred to me, well, actually to Lillian, that it wasn't too hip to be doing all these illegal-type things with Evan hanging around. Who knows how much he'd already picked up? Now, if I lost my temper, he'd have enough information against me that for fun or profit—or even worse, good citizenship—he could upset this entire ship of fools.

"How's the coke, Evan?" I tried to sound friendly. It worked like a charm.

As soon as the drugs went up my nose I knew it was good quality. Two lines and I was really high. Soon I'd be wired and want to go running all over New York City talking to strangers on the street. I would separate myself from the city by leaning back and out of the picture, seeing it as one object, understanding its hugeness. But for now, it was important to just try and relax, enjoy the artificial clarity and see what came to mind.

Laura Wolfe came to mind. It was so weird, I'd thought about her a lot since that first cocktail with Vivian in SoHo. Poor kid. She'd come out at the wrong time and in the wrong place. No one would take a lesbian seriously then. There wasn't any support base for her. How frustrating it must have been to be so close to women like Vivian and have them be unwilling and unable to imagine being lovers with her. She had to watch them go through relationships with ego-tripping Left honchos, and they probably came crying to her for advice.

What am I talking about? Here I am with Vivian in the exact same situation. That woman is ridiculous, you'd think she would have realized by now that all the privileges she's supposed to get from men haven't given her any of the things she wants most. I mean, I had the benefit of lesbian culture, a certain cynicism developed collectively—it protects me. But Laura had to face aversion therapy, I can't blame her for becoming a fucking sectarian. She needs those politics as a way of surviving in the world. It's not my way, but it's okay. If no one else takes her seriously, she still has the guts to take herself seriously. All right, too seriously, but I mean, it could have been me. That's what it all boils down to. All these years I deceived myself into thinking that if I had lived then, I would have been as bright and beautiful as Germaine Covington, but I forgot one thing. I would have been one dead dyke, I would have been Laura Wolfe.

Is that why I'm so attracted to Vivian? Carrying on in Laura's footsteps. Or maybe she just turns me on. If she's lived thirty-four years and never been to bed with a woman she's got to be pretty scared, it's got to mean a lot to her.

From the way she talks about losing her friendship with Laura, it's clear she's got regrets. I guess there was a lot of love there. I'd sensed some deep sadness in Vivian. Some sense of loss, of disappointment, a layer of conflict. You could tell that she's a woman who has a private craziness. Who goes into her room alone and screams and cries and talks to herself and breaks things and doesn't clean them up and washes her face, puts on a dress and goes back out into the world for another round.

"This coke is good, real good." Evan sniffed.

I decided to do a few more lines. Lillian wouldn't really mind. How much more trouble could I get into? I decided not to answer that question. I took Neil Young off the stereo and put on Coltrane's *Ascension,* saw Evan wince.

He took the record off. "I can't listen to that stuff. How about *Bob Dylan's Greatest Hits Volume Two?*"

"No."

"*Volume One?*"

"No."

"Oh."

Wow, all I had to say to Evan was "No," like I was the boss or something and he'd listen. Why hadn't I ever thought of that before? God what a wimp.

"Let's compromise and play the radio," he suggested.

"Okay."

It was tuned to the public radio station.

"Welcome to the Feminist Men's hour. Brought to you by the Gentle Anti-Masculinist Men of Greater New York. Our slogan is 'It's okay.' Today we're going to be taking calls from other feminist men so that we can be the world's first on-the-air gentle men's support group. Here's a call now. Hello. You're on the air."

It all had to do with my mother.

It's okay.

I shut if off.

"Evan, let's do some more lines."

He laid them out with a razor blade. "Sophie, where did you get all this great coke? It hasn't even been stepped on once. It's the best I've ever tasted. I think it's pharmaceutical."

"Yeah it's really . . . what did you say it was?"

"Pharmaceutical."

"Pharmaceutical . . . pharmaceutical . . . where have I just heard . . . oh shit."

"What's the matter?"

Of course, Melonie Chaing. She had pharmaceutical coke and it tasted just like this. In fact, I'd bet my recipe box that it was this. How could I have been so stupid? I looked down at the coke spoon in my hand. Galileo's face was covered with white powder. Vivian Beck and her fucking Italian silverware. Germaine was right, I am a bad detective.

Well, they might have made a fool out of me once, but now I was going to turn the tables on them, those bums. Beck and Chaing were in cahoots somehow and the whole thing led to Seymour.

I ran into my room and looked at Seymour's phone bill. There it was goddamnit, that Westchester number was Vivian's. You can't trust those girls, I should have known that. I needed to call that Beck bitch right away. Wait a minute, what the fuck good would that do? I wanted to confront her fact-to-face. I had to be smart about this or I'd blow the whole show. There had to be a way.

CHAPTER THIRTY

L illian came over straight from the station.

"Sophie, there are three FBI agents hanging around outside in front of your building trying to look inconspicuous. Blonde boys from Utah wearing blue jeans, trying to fit in. The drug dealers are strutting around nervously thinking they're narcs."

"That's not all that's happening," I added glumly.

I told her everything that had been revealed in the last few hours while we cooked up some stuffed cabbage made with raisins and kosher wine, for that special sweetness. Soaking in the tub we laid out a plan. Lillian needed to create a diversion while I escaped and made my way to Vivian's.

Quietly, I smoked a Tarryton, chewing on the charcoal filter, watching Lillian sit in the bath. It was one of those moments when I could see her age. Her neck and hands were getting rougher, not smooth and pudgy like my own. She always acted like a kid, wearing crazy clothes and dyeing her hair all kinds of colors, bleaching her eyebrows and having a good time. But at some moments I could see her getting tired.

Lillian's smart. She's beautiful and courageous but willing to live a quiet minor life. Her friends, her cup of coffee, are enough for her. She doesn't have ambition. She doesn't mind working in the rape crisis center weekend after weekend and then getting up every day to work in the same office until five o'clock when she staggers home, tired. She doesn't mind adding a bit of jolliness and comfort to other people's adventures but she never wants to be the center of things.

"Lillian, are you sure you can handle it?" I regretted it the moment the words finished coming out of my coarse mouth.

"Sophie, don't you have any faith in me at all? Sometimes I think you really underestimate me. You act like I'm boring or something. Just because I'm not as glory hungry as you . . ."

"Lillian, relax."

"That's not fair. First you insult me and then when I get mad you try to smooth things over. It's not right. You have to let me get angry and not be so afraid of it. I'll show you what it's like to be bored—you're so worried about expending any of your valuable energy on mundane trivial topics like other people's feelings. How's this? I'm going to talk about that forbidden subject, what I did today. Today I did my laundry. I separated the whites and the colors . . ."

"Lillian, do you have to get hysterical? Is this necessary?"

"I used extra-strength bleach to get out those tough stains. Then I combed my hair. Then I bought a pack of gum. Juicy Fruit, I like it better than Doublemint." She was running out of steam.

We dressed silently. I knew I was supposed to feel bad but I didn't. Lillian is really a great person and she does take a lot of shit from me, but I'm just not interested in discussing our relationship. I let her talk—wait for her to finish and move on to the next topic. Talks like that can go on forever, like sports broadcasters, the same old stuff over and over again, you can't tell one game from another. In the

146

meantime the hours disappear and nothing interesting has happened.

She went down to the corner pay phone like we planned. The idea was for her to look guilty, act like she was paranoid, but didn't notice the agents. Then she was to call Information.

"May I have the number of the Armed Struggle Violent Revolutionary Council? Yes that's A-R-M-E-D as in bearing arms. Thank you."

It worked like a charm. The way she described it later, the agents all moved from the stoop to the corner booth, leaning conspicuously on the garbage can.

The drug dealers were losing patience. "You guys narcs or what?" they asked. "'Cause we don't need you guys just hanging out like you belong here, you are not fooling anyone, do you hear me? Why don't you just do something already instead of just hanging out, hanging out. Shit—it's annoying, man."

I hung out the bedroom window and dropped onto the fire escape. Climbing up the ladder I looked out onto the rooftops of the Lower East Side. It looked just the way it did when my grandparents came over in 1906, except for the housing projects of course. The twentieth century stood out in the background. All those massive glass boxes full of women typing and xeroxing and programming. Soon my neighborhood would be gone, leveled by greedy developers and turned into luxury duplex high-rises and condos. Young professionals, children of the white flight, were moving back into the city. The same city they spent their childhoods being afraid of. Hanging on to each other when they saw the *Nutcracker Suite* at a Christmas class trip. They were moving in with brutal rapidity. The drug dealers on the corner serve as the last stand between us and total homogeneity. I hoisted myself up onto the roof, stepped into the fire escape and made my way down into the neighbor's backyard, over the fence, and through the Polish sausage store to freedom.

CHAPTER THIRTY-ONE

In the train up to White Plains I thought more about the sequence of events. Melonie had offered to help me without me asking for anything. She connected me to Vivian Beck who had been real nice and helpful as well. Henry too, even though Mrs. Noseworthy thinks his story is screwy. But that day in the park, Vivian had acted like she barely knew Seymour. Yet her coke spoon and Melonie's coke were in his house and he'd called her on the telephone.

So I was being set up, that much was unfortunately clear. What could they possibly want from me, a nobody? Well, it was time to set them up. I had to go sweet-talk Vivian. If I really concentrated and used all my charm maybe I could find out what she knew. Anyway, I'd detected a certain hesitancy in her. Maybe she was having a change of heart? I called her from the station.

"Yes."

"Vivian?"

"Yes?"

"Vivian, this is Sophie Horowitz."

"Sophie, how nice to hear from you."

"It's nice to hear you too, Vivian. You know I really enjoyed the time we've spent together and I appreciate how open and helpful you've been in sharing your memories with me. Coincidentally, I happen to be up in White Plains for a story I'm doing on autumn leaves and I was wondering if I could stop by for a few minutes to see those photos you've told me about."

"Well . . ."

"It would save you the trouble of bringing them to me in the city. I know how busy you must be."

"Well, all right, if it's only for an hour."

"I'll be right there."

Great. Now how was I going to get over to her place? I had no money for a cab. I didn't even have enough money to take the train home. But, I was running on pure revenge and I knew it would get me through. I went up to a young blonde woman who got off the train with me. She was stepping into her car.

"Excuse me, I know this sounds strange, but I've come to visit a friend and I seem to have forgotten my wallet. You aren't going anywhere near Hartsdale Avenue are you? Could you just give me a lift?"

"Of course honey, get right in, I'm always glad to help out a stranger."

Uh-oh, a weirdo. I got in the light blue Pontiac and found out I was right. The dashboard was covered with little stickers saying *I believe in Him, Honk if You Believe in Jesus, Honk if You Believe in Elvis,* and *Jesus Was Once a Fetus.*

"My name is Sophie."

"I'm Kathleen."

"Pleased to meet you. I was just noticing your stickers here."

"Aren't they nice? I'm vice president of Westchester Right-to-Life."

This could be interesting . . . then again . . .

"I'm just coming back from a meeting in New York City," Kathleen said. "We're preparing for Saturday's activities. We stand outside of those horrible abortion clinics with photos of those poor dead, unborn babies. We do sidewalk counseling, trying to convince those desperate, miserable women not to kill their babies."

"What do you say to them?" I asked, sitting back in her blue velour bucket seat.

"Oh, we usually tell them that their baby is a God-given human being, that only God has the right to take away that life, that their baby might grow up to be a priest. Every day that we go there we save one or two babies."

I wanted to light a cigarette but I knew better.

"There are some weapons I always have to have with me. First, a 7' x 5' billboard of an aborted unborn child. It costs $22.95. I fold it up and carry it with me wherever I go. Then I have a twelve-week-old fetus in a jar. I had it on my desk for four days, but that poor precious unborn baby boy . . . now I keep him in my car."

I sniffed the air, checking for formaldehyde.

"Also the Lord gave me a free Xerox machine. I prayed and I got one."

"Have you ever been politically active before, Kathleen?"

"No, but nothing has ever been this horrible before. You know, abortion is far worse than what the Nazis did as far as I'm concerned. The unborn are more helpless. It was the fact that abortion was legal in Germany in the twenties that made Nazism acceptable. It's fascinating, the things one learns as a crusader in God's army."

"Yes, fascinating."

"Well, my dear, here's the address. Remember, there's the east way, the west way, the north way and the south way, but the one way is the Lord's way, Amen."

"Amen."

She drove away, abandoning me in Suburbia.

CHAPTER THIRTY-TWO

The street was dark and cold as the wind blew across empty yards. It had been a long time since I was last in the country. Well, it wasn't really the country but there were more trees than people so it wasn't a place where I belonged. It made me nervous, all those trees moving this way and that.

I rang the doorbell. Vivian answered. She looked really bad, like she'd been crying and smoking too much.

"Hello?"

She had been drinking too.

"Vivian, what's the matter, you look very upset." Her skin was pale and chalky, beads of cold sweat on her brow.

We walked into the living room and sat down. My eyes immediately caught an old Dutch hutch filled to the brim with souvenir spoons. There were examples from Disneyland to Disneyworld and all the area in between. The international collection was sitting on an oak bookcase.

"Vivian, sit down next to me and tell me what's wrong."

"It's stupid."

"No, it's not, you look really upset."

"I'm confronting all the self-deception I've burdened myself with for the last twenty years and I have to accept that it's my fault. No one did this to me. I did this to myself."

"It sounds like you're feeling out of control." Straight

women always feel out of control.

"Yes, I think that has a lot to do with it."

So far so good.

We talked for a while longer while Vivian poured cognac into souvenir snifters from the Knoxville World's Fair. "It's my boyfriend. I don't know what to do about him. There are some pretty wonderful things about him and then there are some pretty awful things about him. If only I could be beautiful, charming, witty and passionate all the time, he would be a lot more interesting."

"Vivian, that sounds a little off."

"Yeah it does."

I lit one of her cigarettes, Marlboro Lights, just like Lillian, but that's where the resemblance ended.

"Sometimes I think my life with men is such a pitiful stereotype. Sophie, why don't you like men?"

"Well, I wouldn't exactly put it that way. I like some men, my brother, the drag queen down the hall. But you know, I'm never close enough to any of them for them to be able to do anything to me, except those obnoxious types on the street. I guess I'm a little out of touch. One thing for sure is that I don't like the way they run the world, and I don't like the way their world intrudes into mine."

"I don't know Sophie, thinking about my relationships makes me feel like a cartoon character."

"What happened to your other husband, the one you married after Jerry got into Scientology?"

"Yeah, you know he sells video games now? I just found that out. Well, Daniel, that was his name. I met him in graduate school in Philly. He was one of those gentle men, you know, strong enough to be tender?"

"I've met the type."

She was feeling better now. I could tell. She just needed someone who would listen to her.

"Well, he read all these books on feminism, making love with him was different than with other men. He seemed to be really interested in how my body worked. With the others I always felt that they were fiddling with me, like tuning up a car. Yet, at the same time, I had this forboding sense that he wasn't getting much out of it except achievement, that being a good lover was more of a burden than a thrill. We married in '76 and I accepted a teaching/doctoral student package at Columbia in Italian Lang and Lit. We moved back to the city and started making friends with other old radicals who had found themselves wandering through the deserts of academia. I joined a Marxist-Feminist study group."

"Why Marxist-Feminist?"

"Well, you know, when I was in the New Left I never made a decision for myself. Either Jerry or Laura told me what to think. But on my own, actually with some other women in the same pitiful predicament, I started getting my politics together."

"So, what did you decide? Come on Vivian, I want to hear the word."

She took a deep breath. "Well, feminism is clearly ahistorical and insufficiently materialist but Marxism has an inadequate analysis of gender relations. I even wrote an article for a theoretical journal in which I stated that women's relationship to the mode of production is determined by her relationship to reproduction."

I scowled. "Vivian."

"Well, it can't be all feelings, there's got to be some science."

"Yeah, but it can't be all formula either, it's like Bach without sound, it's all math."

"Well, I lost interest soon anyway."

That Vivian—a bundle of contradictions. Sometimes I saw her as this feeling, open woman, other times as such a jerk. "So what about Daniel?"

"Daniel told me that he was gay and had contracted a case of venereal warts. I went without sex for two years. But I did finish my dissertation and published my book and spent more time alone in my apartment. I started an intricate and organized filing system for newspaper clippings and seriously developed my collection of souvenir spoons. Then I started teaching at Hunter. My life was getting stabilized. I went to the movies, I built my own life as one solid unit. Any relationship was an invasion, but I knew I needed relationships because I liked having other people who I could tell what I was doing. Then I got involved with the chairman of the department. I spent a lot of time in the lobby of his building pretending I was invisible whenever he would step out of the elevator accompanied by his wife, you know, when I was expecting to spend that time with him. Afterwards he would call me up and say how much he wanted to fuck me."

"What did you do?"

"I made friends with the doorman. One night we went out for a drink. Then we went to bed together. He wanted to move in. When my sister's husband got transferred to Idaho, they offered me a house to sit for a year while they tried it out. So here we are."

"You and your doorman."

"Sort of a post-modern romanticism, don't you think?"

The cognac was making me nervous. "Vivian, let's look at those pictures."

She brightened up and pulled an old album from the shelves. "This is me and Laura at a demonstration in Washington Square Park. Look, we're both wearing flowers in our hair. The woman over there turned out to be a police agent. The other woman in the back, she was killed by the National Guard."

"You two have certainly been through a lot together, haven't you?"

"We certainly have. Even when we're not together, sometimes I think that so much of what I've gone through alone has something to do with Laura. Sometimes when it feels like a dream, I try to figure it out. Then I realize it's too complicated to understand. That's how I know it's real life. You know, I've always been a little paranoid. Never really trusted that people who were nice to me really liked me, I always thought they were after something else. After a while I got used to feeling that way. I decided it was just part of the package of being a neurotic woman in her thirties. Then, two years ago I got my FBI file under the Freedom of Information Act. I found out that the last year Laura and I lived together we were followed every day by agents. Can you imagine that? No wonder we both had nervous break-downs. That kind of surveillance creeps in under your skin. That whole period was such an unnatural thing to live through. I don't know if any of us have really recovered. I don't know if we really want to."

"I didn't know you had a breakdown too. The same time as Laura?"

"Yes, right after I got married."

"It sounds like you and Laura have a rather intense connection."

"I guess you could say that. You could think that." She

poured herself some cognac. "You can think whatever you want to think, Sophie, about me being repressed or permanently in the closet. I think you have this thin but solid layer of contempt for me. Heterosexuality hasn't delivered on any of its promises to me, but I *have* been straight all this time and there has to be a reason. Either I'm pitifully repressed or I really am straight. You know Sophie, I've never even kissed a woman. Can you imagine? Oh I've come close, very close over the years, but at the last moment I could just never go through with it. I think I knew it would take all my courage for that first step, and that it would only be a first step. I once tried to make a list of how many steps there were to go through before you are actually lovers with a woman and I realized I didn't have enough stamina to make it through all of them."

The cigarettes were empty but I had to have one. I took out some rolling papers and started unwrapping the butts. "Well, what are the pros and cons for you?"

"Well, the pro would be that I'd like to be in a relationship with someone who was nice to me. That's a revealing fantasy isn't it? I guess I still hold some fairy-tale view of women together. It's so strange, you know, in the early seventies, one day, half the women's movement came out as lesbians. It was like we were all sitting around and the ice cream truck came and all of a sudden I looked around and everyone ran out for ice cream."

"Everyone but you."

"I didn't know where they had all gone. Oh lots of those women are straight again, but at least their sexuality gives them some sense of movement . . ."

"And the cons?"

"Well, I guess my major con would be that I would freak

out in the middle and really not want to be there, or worse, that I would like it so much I'd never go back and my whole world would be turned upside down."

"That's a con?"

"I mean, it's embarrassing, Sophie. I'm scared that I don't know how to make love to a woman. I wouldn't know how many fingers to use when or what rhythm, or how to tell if she really liked it. It's embarrassing for me. I'm used to being competent. I mean, I wrote my dissertation, didn't I?"

I smoked my precious cigarette. "Well, there's ways to be involved with a woman, Vivian, that takes all these fears into account. I mean, you could do it in stages. You know, set limits for your time together so that you know exactly what you'll be dealing with and then it would be up to you to decide when to move on to the next stage. So you could really enjoy a woman's breasts without being worried that you're going to get in deeper, over your head so to speak."

We both blushed. "That way you'd have some control and responsibility and wouldn't be doing anything you didn't want to do."

I could see her thinking it over. It did make good sense. I silently patted myself on the back. We were quiet. For one moment we looked each other full in the eyes. I saw what she really looked like. Sort of beautiful and hideous and vulnerable, her teenage acne scars showing through. I was glad she wasn't wearing any lipstick.

"So Sophie, what would the first step be?"

This was my moment. I had to play those cards.

"Well, we could lie down together and be close."

"That doesn't sound too good. I think I might start giggling." She was negotiating.

"Well, then we could just kiss, which would be really nice

because I'd really like to kiss you."

"Yeah, I'd like to kiss you too."

I thought I was going to die. It was so intense. We sat there for a moment. She turned her head to mine and then backed away.

"Vivian, would you like to kiss me?"

"Don't push me okay?" She was tense. "Just let me be. Just let me sit with it. Let me be the aggressor, I'd like that better. Just let me do it."

I waited and waited. Shit, I thought. I really blew it. Now I had to get out of the house with my integrity intact. Then she leaned over and we kissed just like two women. Cheek to cheek, bites and licks, lips melting into each other. It was wonderful.

"It's wonderful," she said.

When her arms were around my neck and her body was pressed closely to mine, I reached into my pocket and, with one hand on her waist, said, "Vivian, is this yours?" holding up the silver coke spoon.

CHAPTER THIRTY-THREE

We drove along in Vivian's Volkswagen bug. It was about two in the morning.

"Where are we going, Vivian?"

"I don't know. I'm just driving."

"Where can you go in Westchester when you need to talk in the middle of the night?"

"I don't know."

So I'd played my card and now Vivian was pretty shook up about it. I didn't feel much like a smart guy hero. I didn't know what she was going to do, but I had the sense she didn't know either. We'd been driving around the burbs for some time.

"I need some gas." We pulled into a service station on the fringe of a large shopping mall. "Could you hand me my wallet? It's in the glove compartment."

"Sure." I opened it to a picture of a rather mean, unpleasant looking man with a short haircut. I couldn't see that well in the gas station light, but he seemed to be wearing army fatigues. Something about him was uncomfortably familiar. "Who's that?"

"My old man. He's a mercenary. That picture's from when he was in the Green Berets."

"You're shitting me. Vivian, you're full of surprises aren't you?"

"Yeah, I make one mistake after another. I don't even know how I got in this relationship. Look Sophie, I know you think I'm some dirty double-crossing manipulating bitch, but I'm really not. I just don't have the energy to explain everything to you now. Who are you anyway? Where did you come from? I didn't know you from the moon and all of a sudden I owe you all these explanations. How do I know you're not a cop?"

"Don't give me that bullshit."

She signed her credit card slip and we drove on.

The lights were on at the mall. Cars were cruising in the parking lot. Kids were hanging out smoking pot and drinking bottles of Boone's Farm Strawberry Wine.

"Why all the action?"

"It's Christmas-shopping season. The town council decided to keep the place open twenty-four hours this year as an experiment. It creates jobs."

"Yeah, I bet."

She parked by the side of the Rite-Aid and turned on the radio.

"So, tell me more about your hulk. Is he still opening doors for adulterous university professors?"

"He's saving up his money. He wants to go to Angola." She looked stoned.

"Wait here, Sophie, I'll be right back."

I thought about saying something like, "okay but don't try any funny stuff," but decided against it. Vivian already had too much cops and robbers in her life. "Hey remember to get some cigarettes," I yelled out the window.

"What brand?"

"It doesn't matter."

I watched the kids dancing and drinking and having a

good time. Poor kids, growing up in the suburbs must be so goddamn boring. Either you spend your life in "extracurricular activities" or you're a greaser, wasting your brains on scuzzy rock and roll and bad drugs. Unless you're rich. Then you go to business school, grab a condo in the East Village, buy our Gussie's Pickles and open a wine bar.

"Here, I got you Lucky Strikes. Should put some hair on your chest."

"Very funny."

I couldn't tell if Vivian and I were fighting or what. I was waiting for information. She was waiting for morning. She took a bottle out of a Rite-Aid bag and swallowed three pills very quickly.

"Vivian, what's that?"

"It's for my nerves, they're prescription. I'm a little stressed-out right now and I don't want to get depressed or else I'll just crash, bottom out all over you and it won't be pleasant. I just want to get my head clear."

"Yeah, but three? Isn't that a little much? Vivian, I hope you're not considering suicide in Westchester as the final solution to this little problem we're having. Soon it'll all be over. You'll see. A few years from now, you'll be able to look back on this night and understand it. It'll be a fond memory."

"Sophie, never in my life has a single moment ever come when I've looked back at times like this with anything but questions. Disturbing, depressing questions."

She started the motor. We drove past Scarsdale High as the football team was just starting early morning warm up. The sun was rising over the goal post.

"Sophie, I'm going to be sick."

She pulled over and stopped the car. As soon as the

door swung open, a stream of vomit poured out of Vivian's mouth. I let her vomit it all out. I put my arms around her. She felt so thin and tired. I kissed her hair and whispered into her neck that everything would be all right. I wiped her face with my shirt and she buried her head into my breasts and cried until we both fell asleep.

CHAPTER THIRTY-FOUR

I heard Vivian sit up and start the motor but I didn't feel like opening my eyes. Kids were screaming in the school yard and the sun felt warm on my face. It was one of those mornings. Like when you've been driving all night just to get across Nebraska and when the sun comes up you find out you still have Iowa to go. No point in getting excited.

By the time I started stretching and looking around we were turning onto Hartsdale Avenue. There seemed to be an awful lot of cars parked on the street for a quiet suburb. A lot of cars, including police cars. When we pulled up in front of the house, a whole crowd had gathered in Vivian's yard. They were gawking and stepping all over the bushes. Policemen in uniforms and plainclothes were writing things in little notepads. We slowly got out of the car and walked up to the front door.

"This is my home. What is the trouble, officer?"

Then I saw her. I almost swallowed my tongue. Eva, the true love of my teenaged years, that bitch. But there she was in her tweed suit and leather pumps. The man standing next to her was tall and tan. She strode over briskly, not batting an eye. The sun god spoke first.

"Miss Beck?"

"Yes?"

"I'm Peter Pope, the district attorney for this area. Do you know this man?" He flashed a picture of Viv's doorman guerrilla.

"Yes."

"I'm afraid, Miss Beck, that he is under arrest for murder."

"Oh."

Vivian wasn't surprised. I couldn't tell if she knew all along or had just gotten habituated to massive disappointment and heartbreak.

"Eva, take down this lady's name while I consult with Miss Beck." He walked Vivian away into the house.

So, after years of wonder, anger and fantasy, Eva and I were finally alone together again. She in her nylons and me in my vomit-stained shirt.

"Name?"

"Lainie Kazan."

"Occupation?"

"I sing at the Rainbow Room. Eva, what are you doing?"

"Relation to suspect?"

"We carpool together."

"Sophie, I don't know what your problem is but you should not be here. You are under subpoena in a totally unrelated case. Now, if you're smart you will just get out of here and never talk to any of these people again. I'll give you one chance."

She looked me right in the eye. I remembered those baby blues with lightning streaks of yellow and green. "Just tell me," I said, "who did her old man rub out? Some political assassination? Was it a contract job? Did he use hand grenades or poison gas?"

She looked at me again. I remembered how pink her

lips were. I remembered that they were the same color as her nipples.

"He killed a fairy."

She walked away.

"Thanks, Eva," I said to myself. "Thanks for letting me off the hook."

I turned around to walk off into the crowd and stumbled right into Lillian and Mrs. Noseworthy. "Hi girls. Do you come here often?"

"Sophie." Lillian threw her arms around me, tears pouring down her cheeks. "How do you feel?"

"Like I'm coming down off an LSD trip. Lillian, Mrs. Noseworthy, what is going on here?"

"Sophie, get in my car and we'll tell you the whole story." Mrs. Noseworthy's grey hair looked beautiful against the yellow and red leaves. She pointed to a small foreign job.

"Mrs. Noseworthy, you drive a lavender BMW?"

"It makes me feel young."

"I bet."

We drove away from that sordid mess. I felt high from not eating but my imagination was dulled from overuse. I wanted to be there for Vivian but knew that I couldn't be. I just hoped she'd make it through so I could see her again. Something about seeing people at their worst usually makes me fond of them. Well, not all the time.

Lillian put her big arms around me and I settled back into her softness. "Okay Lil, give me the scoop."

CHAPTER THIRTY-FIVE

"You know Mrs. Noseworthy, my most consistent emotion during this case has been nausea. Do you think that's normal?"

"Well, Sophie, most detectives have little idiosyncrasies. Nero Wolfe never leaves his apartment, Spenser is a gourmet cook, King James hasn't slept with his wife in ten years and likes peppermint Life Savers. I'd say that nausea is a fine quality in a detective. Especially since making a business of snooping into other people's lives is a pretty disgusting way to pass your time."

My head was hurting.

"Are you really feeling bad Soph-a-loaf?" Lillian was unusually cheery.

"I'm starting to feel so bad I can't think of anything else to say."

"Sophie, if you can't think of anything to say, you must be dying." She chuckled. What was Lillian so titillated about?

"So, Lily, tell me the story already."

"Well, after you left I was pretty angry at you. I sat in that ugly apartment of yours with Evan and got upset. I was sitting by the window, crying, when the phone rang. It was the sweetest, most comforting voice—Mrs. Noseworthy. Did you know that she's King James? Why didn't you tell me? Well, she was so nice and invited me over for tea and we just talked about her books and your case. We went over all the facts."

Lillian smiled at Mrs. Noseworthy in the rearview mirror. "That's when we got to Mukul Garg."

"Mukul Garg?"

"Seymour's doorman. Remember him?"

A chill ran through my body. Something very unpleasant was about to fall right into my little lap.

"Well, just to find out some more about him, Mrs. Noseworthy and I went up to 350 Central Park West and spoke with the other employees in the building about him, and some of the tenants. One, this older man, a professor or some such, was most helpful. We found out that Mukul lived in White Plains and that, as a matter of fact, he lived in the very same house as—"

"Vivian Beck."

My head hit the roof.

"That's right, Sophie, Vivian Beck's boyfriend was the doorman. But you must know all this by now, seeing as you've been to the scene of the crime."

"Uh, sure Mrs. Noseworthy, I figured it all out after a while."

"What clues gave it away to you?"

"Uh, intuition, I'm a great judge of character."

"Well, dear, when we realized you were unsuspectingly walking into a potentially explosive situation, I made an anonymous phone call to the police, in my best Italian accent. I thought it would be appropriate for the occasion."

"Sophie, you should have been there, she was just great. She tipped them off that Seymour's murderer would be found at the Westchester address. She's been to Italy and everything."

The Saturday afternoon traffic was picking up the closer we got to the city. It'd been a long time since I'd done anything fun like go to a ball game. Maybe I needed to take a day off. Play some chess, look at my stamp collection. Take in a museum. Hey, that might be a nice idea.

"I guess Vivian's implicated in the murder."

"Well, I thought so too, at first." Mrs. Noseworthy always seemed so even-tempered and clear. Maybe it comes with age. Probably not. "But since then I've been convinced to the contrary. We got out to Vivian's house early this morning, right before the police did. It takes them such a long time to do anything. This man has to check with that man who has to get permission from the other man. It precludes any imaginative spontaneity. Except when it comes to violence, of course. At any rate, we sat in my car here in the early dawn having a rather pleasant chat."

"About the fauna of the Cape and how it compares to northern Michigan." I'd never seen Lillian so enthused.

"Yes it was quite pleasant. Then that Mr. Pope and his associate drove up with four or five police cars. All full of fat balding men carrying guns. They surrounded the house and called for Mukul to surrender. He came to the window and looked out at a sea of police officers pointing guns at him. He was in his pajamas. I guess his soldier's sense told him it was not the moment to die a hero and so he attached a little white handkerchief to his electric toothbrush and waved it out the window."

We drove down Ninth Avenue. The horns were honking, the peddlers were peddling, the bums were panhandling. What a relief.

"By this time a crowd had gathered. As soon as he came out of the house Mukul started to cry. You know he looks like a gorilla but he really seemed to be quite soft inside. He said he knew his wife was having an affair with Seymour and when he realized what kind of sex Seymour was into, he couldn't stand the thought of Vivian as Epstein's . . . well . . . dominatrix. No, I don't think that's the word he used."

"Slut . . . he said slut."

"Yes, thank you, Lillian."

"Oh God, the poor schnook," I said. "All along Vivian was selling coke to Seymour and her old man thought it was nookie-nookie and goes and kills the slob. Shit. God, what was Vivian doing with a guy like that? Everything else about her makes perfect sense. You could predict it. But this Marine doorman with an Ehrlichman haircut. I don't know."

"Oh Sophie . . . You shouldn't be so surprised really. It's part of the burden of heterosexuality. I'm sorry Mrs. Noseworthy . . ."

"That's all right Lillian, we're all entitled to our opinions."

"Thank you. So Soph, you know, they try and try to find a man who's different and all they get is false promises, deception and a passivity that passes for gentleness. They just can't stop. It's a compulsion. I guess Vivian just reached the point where she got involved with a man who made no pretenses about being different. He was honest about how much of an asshole he is and she was able to accurately assess exactly what she was and was not going to get out of it. Maybe it's not so disappointing that way."

We were walking up the six flights to my apartment. "Lily, I have a confession to make. I've been making a fool of myself over a straight woman."

"Not again."

"I'm afraid so."

"My poor baby. Let me run you a nice hot bath."

CHAPTER THIRTY-SIX

It was Monday afternoon. Melonie and I were having breakfast. Two shots of Jim Beam Sour Mash and a Molson wash. Melonie was coming off a gig looking fresh as a kumquat. She wore khaki parachute pants, a white shirt, a black leather jacket and a blue sparkle tie. She looked really sharp. I wore my pants and my shirt. I looked really tired.

"Okay Melonie. I want it straight from you this time. I hope I don't need to tell you how annoyed I am. Listen to me. I was almost implicated in a bizarre murder, came face-to-face with Public Enemy Number One, got subpoenaed by a grand jury and just missed running into a Da Nang alumnus while I was making out with his neurotic girlfriend. So now why don't you tell me the truth for a change. Hmmm?"

"Well, Sophie." She was cool as a cucumber in Montana in December. "I fronted that coke to Vivian when she told me what she had in mind. Helping Laura."

"Laura?" I ordered another round.

"Yeah. Vivian still sees herself as the only person in the world who really cares if Laura Wolfe lives or dies. She hasn't heard from her yet, but Vivian's counting on some message coming through sooner or later and she wanted to have a large sum of money waiting to help Laura get out of the country or whatever." Melonie took out a pack of Rothman Internationals. The kind with the gold band.

"Hey Melonie, you want to know what the fuck I figured out all by my little stupid self?"

She didn't even raise an eyebrow, I got the feeling she was adopting her psychologist persona: Go ahead you little nothing, yell and scream and tell me everything. I'll write it all down in my book. I won't tell you a thing. Go ahead, I dare you.

"Yes?"

"It was you who told Germaine Covington that I went to Seymour's that night. Am I right? It had to be you. You're the only one with enough information to figure it out."

"Well, I don't know you intimately, it's true, but I am a good enough diagnostician to know that if you, Sophie, were borrowing leather it could only be for a story. Since I was familiar with Seymour's proclivities and your discussion with Henry, it all fit together very nicely until Seymour was murdered. Then I had a lot of questions."

"So did I."

"But mine have been answered."

She had a point there. "So Melonie, you have been in touch with Germaine all these years."

"Someone had to stand by her. She's a revolutionary you know." Melonie's eyes blazed. I recognized that look. That cold, blank look. I didn't want to know any more. The more information she gave me, the more trouble I was in. I tried to start wrapping up this discussion.

"Well Mel, it's been great talking to you but I have some clothes in the dryer and I think I left my typewriter on."

"Listen Sophie, I'm older than you and there are some things you don't know about, so pay attention. I grew up in

Chinatown. I was the only one who spoke English so they used to bring me out at age six to translate when the man from the city came to inspect the family store. So I was smart and got sent to an all-white school for quote intellectually gifted girls. There were five of us from Chinatown and we used to bring our lunches from home in cleaned-out plastic containers and eat together every single day. We thought we could do anything, for a while. I wanted to study literature and write stories. But no, I was Chinese so I got tracked into all the science classes. They pushed me into honors biology and got me a scholarship to Barnard, another all-white school that wanted me to smile and study hard and spend the rest of my life in a laboratory. I managed to convince them to let me go into psychology. I spent every day working in the library so I could afford to keep working in the library. Then I met Henry."

She brushed her hair out of the beer. "He didn't know Chinese but he knew he was Chinese. He wore a patch on his jacket that said "Yellow Power." That was an attitude I'd never run into before. He took me around to meet his spoiled angry friends who were throwing away their chance at a good education. They all liked me, wanted me to be in their groups, at their parties. Do you know why Sophie?"

Of course I knew why.

"Because I was a Third World woman." She was shaking. "Only one person didn't treat me that way. Germaine Covington. She had more charisma than anyone I had ever seen off a movie screen. She didn't tell me my studies were bourgeois or that I shouldn't take a straight job in a straight clinic. She was smarter than that. She wanted me to know she had faith in me. She knew I had to come into changes on my own, and that I would. She believed I would find my own way. Then, when Germaine got into trouble, she came to me. She came to me and I agreed to help her. I didn't need to think about it. It was pure instinct. I was strong enough to know what was right, and it invigorated me, doing what was right, it gave me power. I'd work all day at Payne Whitney connecting names to ridiculous categories and watching psychology fuck people over. Then at night I'd be getting credit card numbers and false identification cards. I felt a buzzing throughout my body. There was a hidden electrical wire running under my skin, burning, and only I could feel it. That wire's name was Germaine Covington." She looked me right in the eye.

"So how does Germaine connect to Seymour?"

"I'd been selling drugs to Seymour for a long time. I began to realize he had some illegal money sources and that the asshole couldn't keep a secret. He always was an asshole. Germaine blackmailed him on the basis of the information until he agreed to set up this robbery. At the same time Pope started to come under investigation and he needed an easy out. The three of them set up the whole thing. Pope got the records, Seymour gets the story and Germaine gets killed off."

"But Germaine wasn't really killed."

"No, but someone was. I don't know anything about that side of it. Pope set everything up."

With a little help from Henry, I thought to myself, and immediately changed the subject. "So what about Laura Wolfe?"

"I don't know. No one has seen her. I hear your interest in her goes beyond professionalism. I hear you're a little in love with her."

"Come on Melonie." I coughed and walked over to the

jukebox. We were in an old Polish bar on Seventh Street and First. Most of the songs were polkas but they did have a few golden oldies. I played Janis's "Get It While You Can," and ordered another round.

"Don't try to bullshit me Sophie. You have excellent diversionary tactics."

"Look Melonie, if you think that psych stuff is bullshit then don't use it against me."

"It's bullshit but it's good for one thing. It gives the person who uses it power. And I'm interested in the gathering and maintenance of power. Henry says you have pictures of her all over your walls. He says you know every detail about her personal history. Forget about her Sophie. She doesn't even know you're alive."

Physically high and spiritually low, I stumbled home past the dealers, the bums, the Polish women getting their hair done, the Puerto Rican men listening to Tito Puente, the gentrifiers buying quiche. After an arduous climb up the stairs I collapsed in my apartment. I thought about giving up drinking. I'd taken it up for effect and now it was starting to have an effect. I had to get my head straight or at least clear. The fact that Henry, Melonie and Vivian were acting on their political convictions and personal relationships didn't take away that they lied to me, and that hurt. God those connections were strong. Vivian had barely spoken to Laura in ten years but was willing to risk everything for her. They'd become each other's art. It was interesting but I still felt embarrassed, like a little kid who just realized that she wasn't really invited to her parents' cocktail party. Or planning to meet a woman somewhere and having her show up with her boyfriend. Little subtle messages that tell you you're nothing. I started eating some cold potato kugel.

The story was almost over. Soon I'd have to sit down and write it. There's a certain relief when that moment comes. I'd lived with these people and this information and now that time was almost up. I could say goodbye to them.

Sometimes it's sad, but it's always scary. Maybe the magic won't come back, maybe another interesting event won't present itself. It makes me want to hold on for one more episode. I never know for sure if I'll again be able to find a story where no one else has seen one. That chance to sit in my apartment, typing and at the same time communicating with thousands of people without having to talk to anybody. Then, those golden moments of glory when a really good article appears and suddenly I have friends. Or the times when a poor excuse for journalism shows up under my byline and I don't hear from a soul for weeks. But good or bad, when each new issue hits the stands, everyone forgets forever about the ones that came before. It's a stark moment, that beat between stories, when I'm left alone with myself and the warm purring of my Smith-Corona.

Evan appeared with a backpack on his back.

"Evan, are you leaving my lovely home?"

"I'm going to Hawaii."

"Evan, how are you going to get to Hawaii? Swim?"

"I'm flying Pan Am. First Class. I made some money."

My coke. "What kind of money?"

"I've been watching you write at that typewriter. It didn't look hard. I'm pretty smart you know."

"So you've mentioned."

"So I wrote an article . . . for *Penthouse*. It's called "What Makes a Woman Good In Bed." I got $3000 for it. I'm going to Maui. I left some food in the refrigerator—ketchup and mustard. You can keep it."

I felt like I was sending my son off to Boy Scout camp. Maybe I could write an article for *Penthouse* called "What Makes a Woman Good In Bed," but maybe I needed to do a little more research.

CHAPTER THIRTY-SEVEN

It was a really good idea to take the day off. Originally I'd wanted to go to see the Yankees with Lou but he told me that the season was long over and besides, the Yankees had been out of contention for weeks before the Series. So, I ended up walking up Fifth Avenue, all bundled up in the beginning of winter attire, heading towards the Jewish Museum.

Before I learned that there were upper classes and lower classes I learned that there was uptown and downtown. The German Jews lived uptown and the Russian Jews lived downtown. Actually, by the time I was born this was no longer the case, but my grandmother forgot to mention that fact, so the Jewish Museum, overlooking Central Park, has always meant German Jews to me.

Most of their exhibits were usually about religious issues, artifacts ranging from pots to candlesticks or particular artists who happened to be Jewish. I like two topics: the Lower East Side and certain aspects of the Holocaust, not the guilt and suffering part, but all the intrigues, the history and the infamous cast of characters.

There's a whole generation of Jews like me who are obsessed with the Holocaust the way other teenagers like Mick Jagger. We see each other embarrassingly slink in to see the four-hour version of *The Sorrow and the Pity* for the third time. We go to every exhibit, film or show about fascism and have hardcover editions of *The Rise and Fall of the Third Reich* sitting on our bookshelves. Lillian says that watching documentaries about Nazis with me is like watching the Academy Awards or the Superbowl with anybody else. I'm always saying "See, see that's Martin Bormann, he stayed in Hitler's bunker to the end and then split, Nuremberg sentenced him to death *in absentia.* Look, look, that's Ernst Roehm, he was gay, he got the axe in the night of a thousand swords." I know all the guys and their vital statistics. One thing I've noticed is that most exhibits, books, films, etc., focus on either the horror of the victims, or the horror of the victimizers. But the thing that's always interested me is that short quiet period of time, after the war, when Jewish women in Brownsville and the Bronx were hanging up their wash one day and a letter came telling them that their sister, mother, neighbor, friend, village, country had been exterminated. What did they say when they learned this? Did they speak to each other about it? What vows did they make? What did they resign themselves to? These are the questions I bring to the Jewish Museum. I don't ever see the answers. But I keep on going. I keep waiting for the exhibit on Jewish lesbians, I've got plenty of time.

I passed by exhibits on the Jews of Istanbul in the eighteenth century and took a look at Contemporary Jewish Painters. My eyes raced through the paintings as if I were looking for a name in the phone book. There was nothing there that spoke to me. Wait. Over in the corner—now that was a familiar scene. A large, comfortable beat-up old armchair on a beat-up old rug. Next to it a magazine stand overflowed with copies of the *Forward, Commentary* and *Hadassah News.* Facing the chair sat a big old TV from the forties covered with a doily, plastic flowers and bar mitzvah photos. It was home. I sat down in the chair. Automatically, the lights dimmed, the TV turned on.

An old woman in glasses and an apron appeared on the set and looked right at me. "What are you doing wearing that *schmata*? You're a *shanda* for the goyim. You should only get a good job and earn a living so you shouldn't be a schnorrer."

The set turned off as the lights came back on. I looked at the nameplate. The piece was called "Grandma." Now that's what I call good art.

I wandered around a bit more. I was pretty much alone except for this nun. Nuns, they make me nervous. Chrissie says most of them are lesbians anyway, but I don't know. I just don't trust them. Someone told me they're all married to Christ. That seems sort of out to lunch, you've gotta admit.

I stepped into another gallery, the nun came in after me. I went up the stairs. She glided after me. This was really weird. Was I being cruised by a nun? Is that possible? There was only one way to tell. I headed for the ladies' room.

"I'm sorry, we're closing," interceded the guard.

"Oh yeah, sure, thanks." I stumbled out the front door. Well, if she wanted me that bad she could follow me into the park. It was six o'clock, there wouldn't be many people there.

When you tell someone you're from New York they usually ask two questions. "Do you ever go out?" and "Do you carry a gun?" The trick is that dusk in autumn is the best time to go into the park. The muggers haven't gotten used to the cold and you have one of those few opportunities to be alone, outside, in New York City. Besides, the greyness is eerie, like the moors in *Wuthering Heights*. It makes me feel like I'm in a fairy tale.

I looked over my shoulder, yep, there she was, Sister Mary Heroin or whatever her name was. Goddamnit, oops I didn't mean to say that. Maybe she wanted to ask me for a donation.

I walked a little farther. We passed the Alice in Wonderland statue by the sailboat pond. That's where the fifty-year-old Irish maids hang out together with their little rich kids. We passed the 68th Street entrance, that's where the twenty-year-old Black maids from the islands hang out with their little rich kids and with their Rasta boyfriends. I passed the children's zoo and walked under the tunnel just in time for the clock to strike 6:30. The zoo was completely deserted. I sat down on the bench opposite the empty seal pond and watched the little concrete figures dance around the clock singing "Silver Bells." You can't get heat in your apartment, the subway never comes on time, but come November 1 you know that goddamn clock is going to play "Silver Bells."

I lit a Kent Golden Light 100 and took turns switching smoking hands so my fingers wouldn't freeze and fall off. Yep, there she was again. She was a little nun, a young one. She sat down next to me.

"Hey Sis, what can I do for you?"

"My name is Laura Wolfe."

CHAPTER THIRTY-EIGHT

We sat in the bar at the Waldorf-Astoria. It was decorated according to a jungle theme. The mirrors had snakeskin trimming, the walls were covered in leopard skin. A blonde waitress in a safari shirt and tan hot pants came over to us.

"Would you care for a drink, Sister?"

"Oh no," she giggled piously, "I'll just have some orange juice please."

"I'll have a triple shot of rum, neat and a side of OJ."

"Here Sis." I poured half my drink into her glass. "You'll like this place, they serve macadamia nuts."

Laura Wolfe was calmer, softer, more serene than I remembered. Although, who knew what lurked under that exterior? She told me her story.

"I hadn't spoken to Germaine since she ducked out. She always treated me badly because I wasn't a big shot like her. But I didn't let her power-tripping get in the way. I put my personal feelings aside and supported her anyway, for ten years. It was the principled thing to do."

It occurred to me that I'd been spending a lot of time in bars lately. "Laura there's something I've been meaning to ask you for a long time. What is this principled-unprincipled thing? What does it all mean?"

She took a deep breath. "Principled is like honorable.

It's when you put your personal ego and petty jealousies aside and do what is the objectively right thing, no matter how hard it is. You may lose a lot personally, but the revolution wins in the end. That's the contradiction, the commitment of the white middle-class American revolutionary. You are actively agitating for your own demise."

That Laura Wolfe. She has these bizarre ideas and they somehow seem to make sense.

"Laura, I don't know what it is but something about your perspective, although it has many fine ideological points, seems hard for me. It seems a little dehumanized."

"Well, what's your program?"

"What?"

"What's your program for making a revolution?"

"Well, I don't really have one. You mean like a ten point how-to plan? No, I don't have one."

"Next question you need to ask yourself, Sophie, is what will society look like after the revolution?"

"Well, I don't know. I guess it depends on what people are into."

"No, that's how fascists come to power. We have to have a program that is both pre- and post-revolutionary in its vision. You, you call yourself a feminist. What does that mean?"

"Wait a minute Laura, I didn't go through all this shit to end up fighting about politics with you."

"Just answer my question."

"Well, I don't know really, it sort of means that people should be able to control their own lives and that we all have more options and open up our imaginations and try new ways of living and challenging . . ."

"See, you have no program." She took a contented sip.

That Laura Wolfe. All my fantasies of reforming her were hopeless. I wanted to tell her that first of all, right now, there is no revolution. Second, when there will be one, if it's a good one, which is a big if, it won't be because people threw their humanity out the window. I knew then what I had to do.

"Wait right here, I have to make a phone call. Chrissie is expecting to meet me at *Feminist News*. I don't want her to worry."

I smiled at the waitress and ordered another round on the way back to the table.

"So for ten years, not a peep," Laura continued. "Everyone else I knew had seen her or helped her in some way. Then, about three months ago I got a telephone call. She told me that she'd been watching me, that I was the real revolutionary, that I was in the Vanguard."

Oh, that word.

"You have to understand Sophie, all my life these women have been laughing at me behind my back and sometimes to my face. Like you and Chris. I know what you all think and say about me and it hurts, it hurts every single day, but I can't give in to that. It would be like trying to change myself to make friends with the popular girls. What's the point? So, when Germaine called and said that I was really radical, I believed her. When she invited me to join her new underground fighting cadre, I believed her. It was only when I got to the bank and realized what was going on that I understood I had been played for the fool. So here I am, thirty-four years old. My group disowned me, the police are looking for me. What's going to happen to my life?"

God, everyone I'd talked to lately was thirty-four years old. I made a mental note to get together with Lou as soon as possible. We could just listen to the Allman Brothers and not worry about things like this.

"What about your friends? What about Vivian?"

"Vivian? You know, I've been thinking about her a lot lately, after years of not thinking about her at all. Do you know her?"

"We've met."

"God, Vivian. It's been so long. We were really close, I was so in love with her. We used to sleep in the same bed together with our arms around each other but we never even kissed. Everyone around was coming out, but not Vivian. She was stuck in something and no matter how much love I gave her it wasn't enough. So you know what I mean?"

I had an idea.

"At first I thought it was just a question of being patient. I thought that there was real love and desire there and she knew it. But after a while I realized that she was holding me back. If Vivian couldn't face and validate her own feelings then she couldn't and that was it. It was sad but I had to leave her behind. I mean she couldn't stop herself from loving women, she just couldn't act on it."

"It must have been impossible for you in the student movement, Laura; it sounds so male and heterosexual. Yuck."

"Well, it was hard, I'm not going to claim otherwise but it made me strong too. I mean, I admit, I used to die a little every time my work was overlooked or when they wouldn't listen to me at meetings because I wasn't fucking anyone and I wasn't going to fuck anyone. But it was double-edged, you know, I really didn't want those men either, so I was glad that they didn't want me. When Vivian would come home crying after Jerry hurt her, I knew I would be able to put my arms around her and kiss her hair and whisper into her neck that everything would be all right. Then she would cry and we'd fall asleep like that. Those were our best moments together. But I was young then. Soon I learned that it isn't friendship that makes a revolution, it's comrades."

"When did you learn that?"

"Around '69 or '70."

"When you went to the hospital?"

She brushed her blonde hair back into her habit. "Oh, I get it, the investigative reporter does her homework."

"That's right." It didn't feel great.

Laura looked younger than Vivian. She was thin with bouncy ringlets and blue, blue eyes. Maybe it was because she dressed differently. I tried to remember how she used to look picketing all my events. No color coordination, no style, just clothes. Of course, she did look smashing in a nun's habit.

"Where did you get that getup anyway?"

"Ripped it off from this shelter where I was staying, Sisters of Perpetual Bondage or something like that."

Hey, she had a sense of humor after all. One thing I noticed looking at all those pictures of her on my wall every day was that Laura Wolfe dressed a little bit like me.

"So what was that about, the hospital I mean?"

"It's pretty much what you can imagine. They strapped me down and showed me pictures of women pretending to make love to each other. Not real women, not real love, more like those board school pornography shots, the kind that men like. Then they gave me electric shock. At first I wondered why my friends didn't come and rescue me but then I remembered the pain of the Vietnamese and knew the doctors couldn't break me. I could live like them."

"So you formed Women of the Roots."

"Right, which then split over the question of Cuba into Some Women of the Roots and Women's Committee for the Roots. There's been a lot of change since then in the formations' efforts to build a mass base. You can't convene a revolution you know, it has to be slowly, painfully and precisely built."

I looked at the zebra-skin clock. It was time to go. The check came.

"Hey Laura, guess how much orange juice costs at the Waldorf-Astoria?"

"I don't know."

"Five dollars, and it wasn't even freshly squeezed."

I signed the check. "That's room 48," I told the busy cashier, and off we walked into midtown Manhattan Monday night.

"Where do you want to go now?"

"I don't know Laura, let's just walk. Are you hungry? Maybe we can get something to eat."

We walked all the way down to the Saint Mark's Theatre. They were having a Faye Dunaway festival. *Chinatown* and *Mommie Dearest.*

As I expected, Vivian was standing under the pink marquee lights. When they saw each other the whole city lit up with the power of the hope in their faces.

I stood back a bit and let them talk and touch and look at each other. It was getting cold. God I love this neighborhood. Soon it would be overrun with sushi bars but right at the moment it seemed so much a part of me. There would always be something interesting happening here. If I was sad or lonely, all I had to do was walk outside and I could feel life wrap her arms around me and let me crawl into her.

Laura got into Vivian's Volkswagen leaving the two of us looking at each other across the sidewalk as punks and tourists and Ukranians hurried by between us.

"Vivian I . . ."

I didn't have the words to tell her what I felt. I was surprised by the sharp flash in my side, it was a precious and short moment. I wanted to hold on to it but I didn't know how.

"Sophie you used me and I used you. I know that. It doesn't matter what we think passed between us. Everything's too confused to figure out what part of it was real."

"No Vivian, please don't throw me away like that."

"Look, I'm sorry I have to tell you this but I do. Melonie and Henry are friends of Germaine's They've been protecting her for a long time and they're not going to stop now. Do you understand? There's only one person who really knows what happened at the bank and that's Laura. Look Sophie, what I'm trying to say is that you've been set-up okay? I know you have a big ego and this is going to be hard for you to take but we fed you information because we wanted you to lead us to Laura and you were naive enough to take the bait. You believed that all this was naturally falling into your lap. Only now I want Laura for different reasons than they do, than I did two months ago. If it makes you feel any better, I've changed and it's because of you, okay? Now I just want to get Laura out of here and see what kind of lives we can rebuild somewhere. I'm sorry Sophie."

She leaned forward to kiss me, changed her mind and ran into the car. They drove off down Second Avenue.

It was all over now. It was over. I fumbled for a cigarette. I was out. It was time to quit anyway. It was really time to quit.

191

CHAPTER THIRTY-NINE

I stayed up typing the White Plains story for the *Feminist News* deadline. I worked straight through until the phone rang at nine in the morning. It was June Honeymoon.

"Well Susan, I wanted to be the first to tell you that you were wrong and I was right."

"Congratulations June, you're the first."

"Yes, they dropped your grand jury subpoena. Turns out the Westchester D.A. was involved in the whole affair. Transporting stolen goods etc. He's been under investigation for weeks. His assistant broke the story. A woman, Weinblatt, or something like that, I thought that would make you happy. She wrote an expose about it for *New York* magazine and now she owns the movie rights. It's very exciting. Anyway, so his word is worth ca-ca if you know what I mean and the police and FBI are suspending the investigation until that whole mess is cleared up. I have a few expenses, I'll send a messenger over with the bill. Don't forget to tip him. Bye."

I was sorry that she called because it made me sit still for a minute. It made me think about Vivian and Laura and miss not having them in my life anymore. Women. The world is full of these brilliant, beautiful, delicious women and all I want to do is love them and be good to them. But they're all so damaged. I could spend my life trying to put them back together again. And how about that Eva, I never said she wasn't smart. Now that she's rich, maybe she'll get rid of that jerk. You never know, maybe we could get together again someday. She was nice to me at Vivian's, maybe she still likes me. Maybe I should give her a call. I looked at the clock. Oh shit. I had to get my copy over to the office before ten.

The collective took my copy to read over and discuss as I went across the street to Maude's for a glass of seltzer with lime and a plate of nachos. It was a good story, one of my best. Writing, it's like making love. First you dream about it and then one day it finally happens and it's nothing like you imagined. After a while it can be better than you ever thought or the absolute pits. Maybe I could really make it as a writer. The kind that goes on talk shows. I'd never have to really work, just write all the time and get invited to a lot of parties. I'd meet other writers and artists. Filmmakers would ask me to do their screenplays. A bestseller, a TV series, I could write the first lesbian situation comedy. It would be great. I came into the office smiling.

"We're not running it." Chris looked at her shoes.

"Chrissie, every time I see you lately you're looking at your shoes. Did you just get a new pair or what?"

"Look Sophie, don't come down hard on me just because I'm the only one in this place who had the guts to tell you to your face. We're not printing it. It's a glorification of women who are male-identified. They embrace a male-Left ideology and support violence as a strategy. You don't even criticize them. They're anti-feminist and besides the article is too long. We can't run it and that's all there is to say about it."

I threatened, I yelled and argued and bargained and cajoled. They were firm. I ran outside. It was the first snow of the year. It was falling. It was falling on me. Everyone in the street looked happy, remembering when they were kids, playing in the snow.

Sometimes I worry about what's going to happen to me. Sometimes I fantasize about the easy life, but really I don't expect it. I just want to enjoy things, have friends and keep my life interesting. If I stick to my instincts, the world will follow. I have to believe that. It was a cold day but I had two left gloves so I was warm. I lit a cigarette and walked off into the skyline.

GIRLS, VISIONS AND EVERYTHING

ACKNOWLEDGMENTS

I am very grateful to everyone who took the time to read this manuscript and to discuss it with me in detail, especially Beryl Satter, Julie Scher, Stephanie Doba and Teal Frasier. I am also thankful to Maxine Wolfe and Bettina Berch for their attention and recommendations, and to Peg Byron and Leslie Gervirtz for the champagne.

I also want to thank Sally Brunsman, Faith Conlon and Barbara Wilson for their intelligent and precise editorial work.

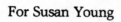For Susan Young

PART ONE

ONE

Lila Futuransky always knew she was an outlaw, but she could never figure out which one. She wanted to be free but couldn't decide what that meant. Yet, endlessly persevering, she continued to believe that she could construct any kind of life that she desired to live. And, because she both understood the phenomenon of process and felt that, at twenty-five, she was still young and had time, she continued to be a general dyke about town, alternately entertaining and antagonizing the people she bumped into, tripped over, walked with and the women that she slept with.

Lila felt pretty good about herself that night in May, on her way to meet Helen Hayes at ten. Her black hair stood up, all spikey and energized by a brand new haircut that was half queer, half punk. She had a Jack Kennedy jaw and a Katharine Hepburn dazzle and she wore her pants tight. Her tank top was silky and showed the shape of her breasts whenever she wanted them to be seen.

This date with Helen confirmed in Lila's mind that she had perfected that combination of softness and electricity that let her pick out the women she wanted to sleep with and then enabled her to do so. Waving to Ray, a friendly drug dealer working the corner of Saint Mark's and First, she walked into The Pyramid Club with complete confidence. This time, she was sure, everything would turn out right.

Despite Helen's reputation as female trouble, Lila had resolved to make love to her after three viewings of Helen's show *The Girls in Apartment Twelve A* at the local lesbian clubhouse known informally as The Kitsch-Inn. What had attracted her to Helen in the first place was her pop-television combination of neurosis and sick genius. As though lesbianism was just another category on *Hollywood Squares*. Helen's delivery was somewhere between Gloria Swanson and *Gilligan's Island*. There were always lines about being wet and breathless at the shopping mall. Plus, Helen was little and skinny and physically vulnerable and jerky-looking. Lila thought she was just so cute. Finally, after carefully planning her delivery to correspond to Helen's aesthetic sensibility, Lila walked right over to her and said,

"So Helen, when are we going to have an affair?"

"Anytime you want," Helen replied, batting her false eyelashes and wriggling up too close. "I've actually been considering you too, Lila, for a little cheap and meaningless sex."

Lila had guessed right on the button. Helen was not the sentimental type.

"But not too cheap," Lila said. She'd see what color Helen's nipples were, and how she liked to have them touched. They'd have fun together and feel good about each other later.

"I'm free tomorrow night," Helen said, "after the show at The Pyramid Club. I'll leave your name on the guest list."

And there it was, right on the guest list, just like Helen had said it would be. There was no reason to be nervous, the whole thing was sewn up. Now Lila could just sit back and enjoy it. The star of her own personal movie, Lila ordered a scotch and boldly put herself in the front row to look closely at Helen's little body and watch her deliver those lines with a perfected East Village deadpan. The audience was in-the-know enough to go for it and Helen had them right where she wanted them.

When the show was over, Lila casually held back, letting the crowd cluster around Helen with handshakes and kisses, who handled the attention with a skill derived from a precise combination of grace, diplomacy and fierce ambition. Lila figured she'd make her way over there when the place thinned out. Here's the scenario she had in her head:

"Great show, Helen."

"Now that you're here it's going to get even better."

"I liked watching you up there in that polyester dress."

"Oh Lila, you're so observant. So, why don't I change my clothes and then you can come home with me for a little brewsky and the other delights that await you. I've been thinking about that tongue of yours all day long."

Lila mulled over these lines, wondering if they were the right shade of camp to please Miss Hayes. She really wanted to please Miss Hayes. Where was Miss Hayes? Lila was searching by the video games when Helen whizzed by, surrounded by her entourage. Lila sinkingly followed.

"Helen," she hissed, "what's going on?"

"I'm in love," she said, over her shoulder.

"What?"

"I meant to call you, but we just had an all-afternoon honeymoon."

"You meant to call me?"

Helen looked up from under her pillbox hat.

"Just put it on hold Lila, there's still something there. Just put it on hold."

What an actress. She was so rude, it was practically art. So, now Lila had mud in her eye. She had serious mud in her eye.

TWO

When the dust cleared Lila was standing alone on the sidewalk almost giving in to tears. But, priding herself on her good nature and ability to rebound from any situation, she walked back, softly, into the Pyramid Club. Leaning on the bar for a moment to regain her composure, she glanced around the place, to make sure there were no witnesses. Then she saw Emily Harrison sitting quietly on a corner stool looking demure in a neato black lace hat of her own making.

"Hi Emily, I just got mud in my eye. You know what that means? I just got humiliated by a woman. Shit. Want to dance with me?"

It was Thelma Houston singing *Don't Leave Me This Way*. They boogied around a bit, sort of weirdly, until Lila tried to really dance, twirl her and everything. To her surprise, she ended up being twirled instead, since Emily's arms were much stronger than she anticipated. Still, they never did quite get in sync with each other.

"Hey Emily. You feel like talking? I kinda want to talk."

They walked outside, headed towards the Kitsch-Inn where Emily spent every spare moment working on shows. She'd been sleeping there too, on the make-up table, when nothing else was available. It was hot for May, everyone was out on the street. The sky was clear.

"So Lila, what do you want to talk about?" Emily's face was shining in the night light. Lila couldn't look her in the eye, and watched the city instead as they walked along on the sidewalk. Lila felt okay about Emily. She didn't know her very well. They'd only been together over a few joints. It was always a fun conversation which would end very politely as though nothing really important or intimate had gone on. Still, it had occurred to her that Emily had a chameleon's beauty. She was bland in a crowd but somehow mysteriously alluring one on one, if anybody bothered to look.

The first time Lila every noticed her was in a performance at The Kitsch-Inn. It was a lesbian version of *A Streetcar Named Desire* and Emily was Stella Kowalski. She'd looked exactly like Stella with thin arms in a sleeveless cotton dress, clearly defined neck bones, a few lines in her face. Like she really was pretty, but just a little tired.

"That Stanley," she'd said, and Lila had really believed she was Stella, picturing how her naked legs would wrap around Marlon Brando when he carried her off to make love.

"Stella's not strong," Emily said, sitting on the floor of the Inn, "but she has balance. I'm the same way. I work at a textile factory, always lifting things, working the machinery, and the guys can't figure out where the power comes from. They think it's cute. It turns them on."

Lila understood why. Emily was attractive in a soft way, the kind of pretty that deceived men into thinking they could easily have her because that's what that kind of pretty women are for.

"Lila, do you want to smoke some grass?"

She liked the way Emily said *grass*, an old-fashioned word. They sat and talked about performing and traveling. Then Lila needed cigarettes but was afraid, in a way, to go out, because that might mean the discussion was over. She took the risk anyway, all high and everything, and when she came back, Emily suggested they go to the apartment where she was house-sitting so she could feed the cats.

The walk was misty, quiet. So calm, it had to be a movie set. They were quiet together and Lila liked that. Then Emily babbled things, the kind of things you babble when you're high, and she wasn't embarrassed. Lila liked that too.

"Emily, look at that woman in the gelatti store. The one with her hair dyed black and bleached blonde on top. She's an Italian lesbian named Tina. You lived in Italy, right? You might want to meet her. She's real pretty. Some of my friends told me about her. They're going in for gelatti three times a day just to make conversation. Want to stop and say hi?"

"No thanks. You can if you want to. I'll wait outside."

Lila was embarrassed again. She had invited someone into her fantasy and they had refused.

"I'm sorry, I guess that sounds sort of coarse. I don't know what I'm talking about. I'm just high. Forget I ever said it."

But Emily saved the moment with a wide smile and Lila felt her body dip into the warm breeze filling the space between them. This was a friend.

In a tenement on East Fourth Street, on the fourth floor, the window overlooked a silent summer street. Some Black men murmuring, someone playing the drums, a lone bicycle. She was a pretty woman in a small apartment on a hot night.

Their talk was full of memories and associations, comfortable as old friends, but with the excitement of describing themselves to each other for the first time. Eudora Welty, The Allman Brothers, *Giovanni's Room*, Top Cat, reading Dostoyevsky in high school and finding out there were things to think about in life, like how much control you have and when to take it. They talked about woman things too. About rape, about abortion, about being straight.

"When I lived in Europe I went out with men a few times, but I decided to wait until I met lesbians."

This was a women who waits.

"I liked being straight," she said, "some of it. But, after three months or so I wouldn't want to have sex with them anymore. I would feel repulsed."

"I haven't touched a penis since 1979," Lila told her. "I do have this one friend though, Sal Paradise. He lives in my building. We hang out together. One night, about a year ago, we were up late in my apartment drinking and talking and I felt so close to him that I wanted to reach out and make love with him but he said no."

"And now...?"

"Now we get along fine. What the fuck. People want to sleep with each other at different times for different reasons. It's no secret. It doesn't have to poison everything."

First Emily sat across the floor from Lila and then she sat next to her. Lila brushed some ashes off Emily's leg without thinking. She liked her. She felt like her friend. She wouldn't have minded curling up with her and kissing, but not for romance. She just liked her.

They sat and smoked cigarettes like men do in Hollywood versions of tenement apartments and Lila wondered if Emily was considering kissing her too, or if she was just waiting. Everything felt good and calm. So, Lila, knowing the ways of the grapevine, decided to tell the sad tale of her plans for Helen Hayes, just so Emily wouldn't find out later from someone else. Lila really liked talking to Emily and wanted her to know the truth. She told all the gory details and was genuinely surprised when Emily started laughing out loud.

"You mean you've spent that much time thinking about Helen?"

"Well, it's not like it was the most pressing thing on my mind," answered Lila, a bit defensively. "I just noticed her. Listen, I have lots of crushes all over the place. I just sit back and look at them and think, some of this will come to be and the rest won't, so I'll just enjoy imagining it all for now.

Emily's response was to realize how late it was and how sleepy she was getting, since she had to be at the factory by seven the next morning. Lila put on her shiny shoes and linen jacket and Emily got back to the business of feeding the cats, as if Lila had just stopped by for the rent check, or to deliver a package.

"Come by the Inn and visit."

"I will," Lila said, "I will," and stepped out into the early morning.

THREE

L ila came home feeling all sexy and silky. She sat down at the typewriter and worked until the sun came up. She knew she'd be a wreck in the office, but she didn't care, she wanted to get down every detail of her adventure with Helen Hayes at The Pyramid Club. It was too good a story to lose. She washed her hair, changed her clothes and went down for cigarettes and the mail. There was another rejection letter. This time from a lesbian magazine in southern Pennsylvania. She'd sent them a story about going to the country and getting a crush on a sign-language interpreter for the deaf who she met while hitch-hiking on the back of a pick-up truck. Her intention had been to use their interaction as a metaphor for urban-rural relations. The editors obviously missed the point. Lila re-read their letter three times on the subway to work.

"We like your writing," they said. "You have a wonderful sense of humor. However, there are a few problems with your piece. First, on page one, you refer to *fat* farmers. Why did you have to say they were fat? More important, how do you think fat women will feel reading that word? We also felt this way about page two where you mentioned a *pock-marked local*. We don't want to spout jargon, but who has pock-marked skin? Not rich people. The other thing had to do with the *tiny pink nipples* on page five. If you would not walk up to a woman and say to her face *I think your nipples are a drag*, should you expect us to say it by publishing your story? Thank you for thinking of us and good luck in the future. Signed, The Collective."

As soon as Lila said good morning to her co-workers, sorted the mail and re-filled the xerox machine, she turned on the office's IBM Selectric and wrote back, in one draft.

"Dear Collective,

"I'm sorry that the farmer was fat and that I said so. If only I had said that he was tan instead, that the pock-marked boy was blond and the woman's breasts were like porcelain instead of egg whites with tiny pink nipples. If only I had seen something different than what I saw, or written something different than what I saw, then my work would have appeared in your magazine.

"Either you can let me tell people what I see, or you can decide that they should only know about ways of seeing that aren't anything like fat farmers. Sincerely Yours."

After she mailed the letter, which one always needs to do immediately with letters like that, Lila remembered one of her heroes, Lenny Bruce, and how his solution would have been to climb up on a large billboard somewhere in the state of Pennsylvania and write on it, in careful black letters, fifteen hundred times, *fat farmers*.

FOUR

Work was always there taking up time and rarely meant much short of the postage stolen off the postage meter and the xerox paper stolen for writing and the pens, white-out and xerox copies stolen for Lila's personal use. It was always there and then it was over, leaving her with some kind of need to do something worthwhile, or at least enjoyable, as soon as possible.

She sat in The Cafe Kabul on Saint Mark's Place waiting for someone she needed to see come by, and sure enough, Muriel Kay Starr came walking down the street. She needed to see Lila too, so they walked over to the Futuransky home, stopping off at Punk Chinese for some asparagus to go and saying hello to Tony, a drug dealer on the corner of Ninth and First. He'd probably figured out by this time that Lila and Muriel were lovers.

It took those two women a few years of misunderstanding and unfulfilled expectations to figure out the right way to do it, but eventually they did. Lila was Muriel's permanent affair. It would never be more than that, since everyone knew that Lila Futuransky was not the marrying kind and Muriel, while not ready for the altar, needed to have a primary girlfriend and needed to know where she was every day. Over the years

Muriel's love life had consisted of a series of main lovers, with Lila on the side plus assorted others every now and then. The girlfriends accepted the situation because they knew that Lila wasn't going to take Muriel away from them. From Lila's point of view there weren't many drawbacks except for a few lonely moments now and then when the main girls came first, but she and Muriel could always talk about anything and not worry. Like best teenaged buddies, they would plot together, discuss their problems and usually made love very well, though they didn't mention that fact very often. Once though, Lila did send her a note just to say that Muriel made her cunt feel like butter.

They lay down together on the bed, arms fitting as comfortably as an old, old couch, while Lila read Muriel the story of The Pyramid Club, a copy of which she had just mailed to Helen. Muriel told how she had finally gotten up enough courage to ask out the beautiful Italian woman, Tina, who worked in the gelatti store, even though Roberta, Muriel's main girlfriend of the moment, did not think she was ready to put up with another of Muriel's flings. Maybe Tina would take her off someplace too beautiful, like Brazil. She was ready for anything, as long as it was new.

That seemed to be the latest theme around town. Everyone was looking for something new. Not that the old thing wasn't working out, but just for the sake of change. It all had to do with the weather. First it was cold, freezing cold for months and very private with never enough heat. Then, one day, quite unexpectedly, spring came. People's minds were splitting open right there on the sidewalk, stretching, trying to take in all the images rushing by, trying to synthesize them into some kind of sense. It had to do with the sudden appearance of countless astounding colors combined with having your skin feel the air again. Everyone was out on the street with something to say, giving in to the desire to just emote for a while. But, before anyone had time to get ready, it was summer, and heavy and humid and dark with heat, promising nothing but the same for three months. At that point, each person who still had it within themselves to dream, dreamed. Each person who still believed that those dreams could come to be, started to plot about how they were going to get the hell out of there and get to something new before the heat set in.

This time, though, Lila was thinking she might just go with it, stay and sweat. They say New York dies in the summer, but everyone's still there. It must be the haze rising from the concrete that makes it go private again. But, what if she just stayed with it this time? Somewhere along the line she knew there'd be girls, visions and everything.

FIVE

Muriel called to tell all about her night with Tina. It sounded really nice over the phone to Lila, who was spread out on the floor looking at the big dark tree hanging over her window. It was that exciting warm, cool, fucking weather. She could mess around at home or go out looking for something. What was there to read anyhow? *The Trial? Portnoy's Complaint?* No, four times was enough. *On the Road?* Lila often asked herself why she tried to write lesbian fiction when she never read any. She had a lifetime of stories piled up in cardboard boxes over her desk. Someday they'd all come crashing down on her head. She could see the New York Post headline: BRUNETTE BURIED BY UNPUBLISHED MANUSCRIPTS.

A writer who never published anything had a hard time convincing other people that she was really working. Take Emily, for example. Anyone could walk into The Kitsch-Inn and there she would be, covered in paint, scraps of material all over the floor. Even if no one knew exactly what she was doing, they could be sure it was something. As for Lila, she thought of her ideas alone, wrote them down alone, took them to the post office alone and got back the rejection letters alone. The only evidence were those goddamn cardboard boxes. The other problem was that, lately, Lila had been writing faster than she had been living and sooner or later was bound to run out of material. Maybe she should read *On the Road* again. Only, from a different angle this time. The trick was to identify with Jack Kerouac instead of with the women he fucks along the way. She could easily get into his kind of head. Everyone else just sits around, but Jack *does* it! No grass grows under his feet.

But the night was too clear to waste, so, she stuffed Jack into her back pocket and jumped out onto the street, heading towards Sally Liberty's garden over on East Sixth. On her way she ran into Isabel Schwartz in her purple jacket and purple sneakers, just coming home from her waitressing shift. She was talking to herself very intently and wheeling her purple bicycle. There's an expression, *two Jews, three opinions,* and lesbians are exactly the same way. So, although Isabel Schwartz was also a drama dyke, she was coming from a completely different school of thought than the Kitsch-Inn crowd.

"Miss Schwartz, you look like you've got something interesting turning over in your brain."

"Miss Subways, yes, I've got an idea for a new show."

Isabel always called Lila "Miss Subways" because she said it was an appropriate name for a soon-to-be underground hero.

Isabel Schwartz worked forty hours a week slinging burgers and saving her quarters until she had enough to put on a show. Her plays were tales of average lesbians and the little things they knew and cared about. Then it was back to the burgers.

"It's going to be called *Job Revisited,* about God and the Devil and there is no good and evil, but they keep tempting me with promises of love and success. I haven't got it all figured out yet, but what I do know so far is that, in the first scene, the Devil will be a rabbi and God will be my mother. In the second scene, the Devil will be my mother and God will be the rabbi. Finally, in the last scene, they'll both be my mother."

"What is your mother going to say about all of this?"

"She loves it. I've done nine shows, each one about my mother, and she loves them all. Except the one before last where I killed her. She didn't like that one."

Once Isabel and Lila went to an off-Broadway theatre to see what shows were like when you paid twenty-five dollars for a ticket. The piece was by a playwright from Missouri, with actors from Chicago and an audience from New Jersey. All were pretending that they were dramatically interpreting the reality of New York street life. The actors strutted around, jiving like bad imitations of Eddie Murphy imitating a Black teenager imitating what he saw Eddie Murphy do on TV the night before. The lesbian characters kissed each other and hit each other. The gay male characters made jokes about the sizes of each other's penises. The Black characters ran around with afro-picks in their pockets and occasionally stopped combing their hair long enough to play three-card monte while saying "motha-fucka" a lot and grabbing their own crotches. All of this provided an appropriately colorful background for the white heterosexual characters to expose their deeply complex emotional lives.

"You know what gets me the most," Isabel said after they walked a few blocks home in silence. "Everyone runs around complaining that New Yorkers control the world. But it's not the people who really live here. It's the ones who came from somewhere else, you know, like Americans."

Lila nodded her head, paying close attention to the way Isabel had of figuring out what was really going on.

"Then, after they're here a while, they write these plays and books and songs about what it was like coming here from somewhere else. As if this was a city full of golden angels getting off the Greyhound bus with a suitcase full of dreams battling their way past the local slugs until they get to their righteously deserved pot of gold."

"Yeah Miss Schwartz, I know what you mean. Like Dustin Hoffman, or someone like him, who grows three days' worth of beard, grunts and thinks that means he's playing a real person. He hasn't been one for so long that he can't see the difference."

"That's called fake social realism," Isabel said, and a new category was born.

SIX

L ila turned down Sixth Street to Avenue B. Once she got past all those stupid art galleries, it was still a nice block. With the creepy, crawling invasion of gentrification into the neighborhood, it was becoming harder and harder to find a quiet street. Things were so bad that even Avenue A was unlivable. The Good Humor man had been replaced by tofutti-selling teenaged boys in teased Mohawks. Polish and Puerto Rican mom and pop soda fountains featuring Breyer's ice cream, vanilla or chocolate, bowed to the pressure of imported ices. Tanned Europeans in skimpy t-shirts sold one dollar and fifty cent scoops-du-jour. But, over by Avenue B there was still life on Sixth Street. Lila passed an old Irish bar with a pool table, a few bodegas and the combination Jesse Jackson for President campaign headquarters and thrift shop, until she got to the former vacant lot on the corner. For years it was full of garbage and served as a shooting gallery for junkies, but that night, in the dark, Lila could make out three silhouettes laughing and talking in the rubble. Sally Liberty, Lacy Burns and, surprise, Muriel too, looking pretty as usual. The real surprise though, was that once she climbed over all the bricks and things, Lila stumbled into a few little gardens, here and there, with mari-

221

golds and tomato plants. Just little patches where Sally, a short white woman from West Virginia and Lacy, a tall Black woman from Queens, had gone out with pick axes and lemonade, digging up little sections of the dead earth and bringing it back to life again. At night they hung out in their gardens with their kids and lovers and friends, spending the hours telling tall tales.

"Lila, have some wine." Lacy took out another paper cup.

"What's the occasion?"

"Sally's taking off for California on Monday in her big green school bus, so we're having a farewell party."

"Plus," Sally added, "Lacy is getting another book published."

Lacy had that look of embarrassment that meant there had been too much talk already about a real accomplishment and since she wanted to keep all her friends, she changed the subject as graciously as possible.

"Enough ladies, we are here to enjoy the garden. Lila, you come by for a visit next week and I'll tell you all about it."

Lacy leaned back, the shadow of a marigold hanging over her shoulder.

"You bet. Hi Muriel."

She was all curled up, glowing from the heat and a joint, looking up at the empty buildings to the south and the remodeled ones to the north.

"Sally, have you gotten the bus in shape for the Rainbow Gathering?"

"We're all set, except for the garden."

"Why? It looks wonderful to me."

"It looks great to me too," she answered. "That's the problem."

Sally was in her forties somewhere and thought like a Yippie, which meant giving away food for free, helping out retarded kids at the Special Olympics and going on The World Cannabis March. She had lines in her face from a little too much party. Lila found herself easily seduced by that kind of attitude, so she always stayed two steps away.

"You won't believe what's been going on around here. The other day, me and Lacy were putting down some dirt and this lady walked up in brand new blue jeans and told us that the City of New York is so proud of our garden that they have decided to adopt it into The Green Apple Program. She handed us a little plaque of a green apple and then told us she was our official organizer."

"But you don't need an organizer," Lila said, "you're already organized."

"That's the truth," Sally nodded. "Then, last Friday, this woman came back and announced that from now on all the gardens had to be square and ours is round. So, she demanded that we take it apart and make it square."

Muriel lay back quietly while the rest really got into shooting the shit and getting blown away by the stupidity of things.

"Look around you," Lacy said, "there's thousands of abandoned apartments and people with no homes and all the city cares about is our garden. They called a meeting and we went. We made a proposal that said we could keep our garden round. That lady just happened to be the one taking the minutes and first she wrote it down and then she crossed it out because she didn't like it. So, Sally starts screaming. . . "

"Yeah, I was so pissed off, I started screaming, YOU FAS-CISTS, ONLY FASCISTS MAKE PEOPLE HAVE SQUARE GARDENS. Then I told them, YOU CROSS ME OUT, I CROSS YOU OUT, and I tore up the minutes."

"But they kept saying THE PLAN, THE PLAN and. . . well, you know how I get around the bureaucratic unimagination," Lacy smiled, "I stood up, very properly and then screamed at the top of my lungs, FUCK THE PLAN, and tore that up too. We hope they'll stay away but with the city, you never know. We'll be out here a lot this summer, me and Arthur and Kwame, holding down the fort while Sally's on the coast."

Everyone got quiet then, like they all ran out of breath at the same moment and sat back, satisfied at having told a good story.

"I'll be here all summer too," Muriel said.
"I guess we all will be."
Then there was a quiet breeze.

SEVEN

ila's mind kept drifting back to Emily Harrison and the good feelings that had passed between them. A few times she considered going over to The Inn to pay a call. The only problem was avoiding Helen Hayes, who also hung out there. On the other hand, maybe she should get the humiliation over with and just show her face before she lost it. Maybe not. But, to be sure, she climbed the fence in front of a lot down the block and made her way over a whole alley's worth of garbage and rusty bed springs to peek in through the back window. Yep, the lights were still on. Something was happening, but she couldn't bring herself to knock on the window. Lila guessed she'd been a little bold before and had gone too far. Now she was feeling some timidity on the rebound and wanted to avoid looking like an asshole at all costs. So, she walked the streets for a little while longer.

Lila cruised First Avenue between Seventh Street and Tenth Street quite often in the course of her daily life and every time she ran into three men: Ray, Tony and Solomon. Each one had their own personal story but they were also part of the same old story of men hanging out, just hanging out.

Ray was her favorite. The other dealers called him the old

man because his beard was almost grey, but, at age fifty, he was in better shape than most of the young junkies who worked that strip, with his shiny black skin, his cool beret and tight t-shirts to show off his pretty muscles. Ray had been around, of course. He had organized for The Black Panthers at Wayne State and somehow ended up selling nickel bags in the East Village. He had a girlfriend for a while, a white woman named Asia. But after her kid was born she split and went back to North Dakota where she knew Ray would never follow.

One night Lila and Muriel were drunk and dancing and teasing the slam dancers who had just started coming around the neighborhood. They didn't have their own bar at that time so they hung out occasionally at The Park Inn where there was some Hard Core on the juke box and drafts were still seventy-five cents. A little after midnight Ray stepped in for a break, looking sharp as always and needing some company. Well, he liked Muriel right away, with those aquamarine eyes, and she was in a party mood.

"Ray," she smiled, genuinely happy to see him. "Ray, come see my new dance piece. It's a love story about two women, it's really romantic, you'll love it." With that, she threw her arms around his pretty neck.

"Uh... Muriel, Ray and I haven't exactly talked this through yet."

"Yeah," he said, looking around to make sure no one he knew was listening. "But I got eyes, Lila. You know I'm not what you'd call an unobservant guy. I see everything that happens in this neighborhood. Listen, I've been around this kind of thing before. It doesn't bother me. No problem. You know what I'm saying? No problem at all. I meet all kinds, all kinds. No problem."

She began to wonder if there might be a problem.

But the evening ended happily after some more beer and Perrier for Ray who, like a lot of dealers, never touched alcohol. Muriel gave him two free passes, though he showed up by himself. Ray sat quietly through the whole thing, even the part where Muriel made out with another woman on stage.

"You tell it how it is from your perspective," he said later under the flashing DON'T WALK sign, "and that's the only way that you can tell it."

So Ray was cool in Lila's book. That's why, one night, when he ran up to her and asked for twenty bucks, she said sure. In three years the guy had never done her wrong. She gave him the twenty bucks and the next thing she knew, the man disappeared. At first she was pissed off. Ray, why fuck up a friendship for twenty bucks? She checked out all his spots, Bryant Park, the west side of Washington Square, but no trace. Finally, after three weeks, she was riding her bike in Chelsea and a voice called out, "Lila, hey Lila." It was Ray.

"I've been laying low," he said. "You know I got into that cocaine and it started to kick my ass. It's costing me around two hundred and fifty dollars a day. I could have gone to the Virgin Islands. I could have gone to Hawaii. I've been chasing that cocaine like I never chased any woman. Finally I decided to get me some, you know, counseling. I got in touch with a center over here and I'm trying to stay away from those old places."

Good old Ray. She wished him luck, told him to postpone the loan until he got his shit together and rode off into the car exhaust of Eighth Avenue. About three days later, Lila got up to go to work and who did she see back on the corner but Ray, high as a kite, selling those nickel bags. From then on the pattern was set. He'd be standing around selling tiny bags of bad pot to cars with New Jersey plates or kids who hung around in front of the punk bars. As soon as he had enough cash to fill his freebase pipe, Ray would flag a cab, go off somewhere and be back about an hour later selling again. Lila worried about that man but there was nothing she could do. She could spend her life trying to save Ray, but it wouldn't work. She knew it would never work.

EIGHT

Then there was Tony, a young Puerto Rican guy from Tenth Street.

"Lend me five bucks," he said.

"No Tony, I'm not handing out any more money."

"Come on, just five. That way I can buy a bag and sell it for ten. With five bucks I can make a hundred."

"No man, I lent money to Ray and until I get it back I'm not lending out any more."

"That old man, he touches everyone. He only got twenty out of you because he knows that's all you're worth. If you had any kind of bucks at all he would have touched you for a hundred."

Tony slurped his Seven-Up.

"I'm getting sick of hanging out," he said. "I'm gonna take the civil service exam."

"What kind of civil service?"

"Correctional officer. I haven't got a record, or anything."

"Sounds great."

Tony was too skinny. He used to be good-looking but his eyes got too hollow. Besides, he developed a terrible twitch from looking out of one side of his face and talking out of the other.

"Hey Lila, you want to go out with me sometime? For dinner

or something? We can go eat, what's that called, lobster."

"I don't think so Tony."

"Why not?"

"I just don't think so."

"You got a boyfriend or something?"

"No."

"What's the matter, you don't like guys? You a lesbian or something?"

"Yeah, I'm a lesbian, but I'm friendly."

She didn't want this man to become a problem. You've got to stay on someone's good side if you're going to see them thirty-seven times a day. Anyway, Tony already knew that Lila was gay, he just forgot.

They'd met about two years before when Lila and her faggot friend Elliot decided they wanted to make an office space for lesbian and gay writers in the East Village where lesbian and gay writers had always flourished but never had an office. They contacted a housing organization called East Village Independent Livers and got introduced to Mark, a young, white nerdy guy who had just gotten out of college and wanted to become a "community activist."

"I'm Mark," he said. "I'm your organizer. I personally have nothing against homosexuals, but I don't think that the other people involved in this building project would want to work with you. They're all Third World."

"Why don't you let us talk to them?"

"No," said Mark, "I'm sure it wouldn't work. They're concerned with real survival issues."

At any rate, Elliot and Lila, using all the survival tricks they'd learned from years of queerness, wormed their way into the group and found out that it consisted of two Puerto Rican dykes who were lovers, a Black gay guy named Craig, a little guy named Fred, who was also Black, lived in the men's shelter and said he went "both ways," and Tony.

The building they were squatting in had been sitting abandoned for years. Each apartment had been lived in until the tenant died and in most cases, no one had ever come by to take away their stuff. So, each unit was packed with all the belongings of a person's entire life, from clothes to photographs to pots and pans. Only, it had all been tangled up and trashed by junkies and was covered with human shit and blood and used works. The hallways were full of garbage and broken down refrigerators. The grand finale, however, was the top floor. Some weird artist had lived there and filled one room from floor to ceiling with dirt and another room from floor to ceiling with hay. It took all of them and all of their friends about three hundred hours of physically hauling the stuff out before the place got cleaned up. They'd be there sweating while, every so often, Mark would stop by to say, "You're doing a great job, but we've got to keep on working."

"What do you mean we, white man," Fred would murmur under his breath.

On the last day everyone carried out about eight hundred filled plastic garbage bags while Mark spent the entire time fiddling with the lock on the front door. Finally one of the friends of friends went up to him and asked, with sweat pouring down her face, "What are you doing?"

"I'm the organizer here," he said.

The next day when everyone was ready to move in, they showed up at the building with all their stuff at ten in the morning and, coincidentally, the cops were there too, with a big strange lock on the door.

"What's going on?" Tony demanded.

They didn't get the full story until some weeks after, even though they could all see the landlord moving in hordes of rich bitch tenants into their nice, clean apartments. Tony filled Lila in on the details one slow afternoon on the corner, while chewing on a fried plantain chip.

"It was that turkey Mark," he said, looking around, as always, for customers and cops. "He was fighting with his girlfriend and bragging to her about screwing one of those girls from PR, just to make her jealous. You know it was bullshit to

230

make her jealous."

"Yeah," nodded Lila, knowingly.

"The girlfriend, who didn't have it all together upstairs since she was going with a jerk like that in the first place, wanted revenge, so she called the cops saying we was using needles in that building. They called the landlord and next thing you know, the people were back on the street."

He crumpled up the empty bag and tossed it under the car.

"Mark's still got that job, Fred's back in the shelter and you and me got nothing better to do than stand here and make conversation with each other. Haven't heard much about the girlfriend though."

Just then a patrol car turned the corner and Tony disappeared into Mercedita's bodega pretending he was buying a Seven-Up. Lila waited a few minutes till the cops pulled away, and was about to get going herself, when out of the corner of her eye she saw Ray flag down a cab.

NINE

Finally, there was Solomon. He was a different breed. Solomon was a hard working boozer in a dirty stetson who hung out on the stoop drinking vodka out of a paper bag. He was always willing to show a photo of his ex-wife in Haifa with their kids. Sometimes Solomon had a carton of Players cigarettes for five bucks. Usually, though, he was just working every day on the block, loading and unloading for a wholesale Italian grocer. The store's thirty-five years of business was about to end that summer when the lease expired and the rent would get jacked up so high only an art gallery could afford it.

After the changes in the neighborhood had started getting really dramatic, this new organization suddenly made itself known. The Concerned Neighbors for a Cleaner Block. Usually block associations were good, helping everyone get to know each other, planting trees, getting a new street light. But this one had a bad feeling about it. First they put up posters of a young white couple walking fearfully down a city street filled with menacing jungle animals, like baboons. The caption read "Clean Up Our Street." It hadn't taken Lila very long to realize that any group of people who wanted to "clean up" another group of people were usually bad news. With long-time tenants getting evicted left and right, all these people cared about was the drug dealers selling nickel bags. It bothered them. Of course, they all did drugs themselves, especially cocaine, but they did it in their apartments. The dealers were selling on the streets and that's what they didn't like. They couldn't claim it was bad for children, cause most of the children on that block had been evicted a long time before. Developers liked to tear out six apartments filled with kids and put in one luxury duplex for some kind of rich artist. Lila had seen the photos on TV. One day, she'd noted four of those posters within five feet of each other and almost bumped right into Solomon. He looked real bad, confused, like he had three hangovers at once.

"Lila, I have had bad times, bad times. I was working in front of the store last week. It's been hard work packing up thirty-five years of stuff. I was on my break when this little lady comes up to me asking if she can buy a nickel bag. I'm sitting on the olive oil and I said to her, *I don't sell no nickel bags. If that's what you want, ask him,* and I pointed to Tony. Do you know what?" He paused, leaning back on his hips, so that he towered over Lila, standing straight with an expression of pure disbelief in his eye. "Do you know what? She was a cop and she gone and arrested me then and there for accessory to a sale. I been in jail for three days now, no cigarettes or anything. Shit."

Lila called up the president of the Concerned Citizens and gave him a piece of her mind.

"You bleeding heart," he said, "You're living in the past. Do you want this street to be taken over by drugs?"

"I like drugs, I use drugs. Anyway, you can't go around arresting every Black person who walks down the block."

"Listen Lila Futuransky, I'm sick of your sixties-esque posturing. Just look out your window and you'll see that you're too late."

He was right. There were two policemen on *horseback* clip-clopping merrily along.

"Don't tell me you called in the Cossacks. Does this mean we're occupied?"

233

"Yup."

"Well, just think about this," she said. "When there are too many drug dealers, you call in the cops. But who are you going to call in when there are too many cops?"

Solomon had seen many hard days in his life and expected to see many more, so he soon settled back into his spot on the steps, drinking vodka out of a paper bag.

Ray, Tony and Solomon. Some of the men in Lila's life. She spoke to those guys more often than she spoke to her family, or any lover.

Speaking of which, she still had that Emily Harrison on the brain. Lila smiled at the thought of seeing her again. She firmly resolved to swallow some pride and check out The Inn one more time. But, it was too late. The door was all locked up. All the girls had gone to sleep. Still, Lila was buzzed and overflowing with street fever.

If she had been Jack Kerouac, she would have run right over to that apartment on Fourth Street where Emily was staying, climbed in through the fire escape and whisked her off on the F train to Brighton Beach, where, after hours of beer and all kinds of good talk and smoke, they would make love on the dirty sand when the sun came up. Or she would spend all night on the stoop, digging the Eastside night life, smoking cigarettes and tripping until the morning when Emily just might come down for a quart of milk and there she would be, disheveled and grinning. They would walk down to the water in the early morning cool, two women with bare shoulders, walking side by side, talking quietly as women have been known to do.

TEN

Bored again. Jack Kerouac had already gone through twenty-eight pages without having sex with anyone. He hadn't done anything substantial either, but he'd had a sensational time doing it. Lila was bouncing up and down the stairs, looking for fun on the Saturday afternoon of Memorial Day weekend. Every now and then she would stop in front of the mirror to say "Four more years of Ronald Reagan," realizing that that fact was a large part of how apocalyptic things felt lately. Then she'd go back on the street with Solomon, who had been trying to sell homemade leather belts to weekend tourists before the rain started. The afternoon got late and Lila took a few deep breaths to get her courage together before the start of whatever came next.

Then, just like the beginning of every night, the question got answered when someone familiar walked by, coincidentally at the very moment she needed to see him. There was Sal Paradise, looking pretty with his ponytail and clean-shaven face.

"Sal," and Lila was so happy to see him, and he was happy to see her too, because they both knew they could get down to brother-sister talk, have some beers and go anywhere.

"What happened to your beard?"

"I decided to come clean for Gene."

"Wishful thinking."

The rain broke as they ran into an old Polish bar on Seventh Street.

"I've been working ten hours a day on construction over at Thirty-Eighth and Eleventh. The boss is paying five hundred dollars a week in cash to create a completely electronic garage, installing luxury gadgets in limousines. The neighborhood is scuzzy as shit. I'm always seeing prostitutes and sometimes they're getting beaten up by their pimps. We're busy working on limos and don't do anything about it when we hear them yelling out for help. I just feel sick and don't say anything. I'm there for the money. One guy on the job has five thousand dollars hidden under his mattress. There are women who are so used up they have nothing left to sell. They go out into a lot with some pretty dirty men and do what they can for literally a couple of bucks. The others guys call out for me to come watch, but I just keep working on those limos. Yesterday I had this one that was so full of crap, we couldn't even install our gadget. It had a TV and a bar and a stereo and a telephone and those shaded windows. Someone is very ill to need all that."

The storm part ended and was followed by soft, warm drops, steady and harmless. They didn't care, and walked, all wet, over to Sally Liberty and Lacy's garden, but they weren't hanging out. Then Sal and Lila checked out a building on Thirteenth and A that was supposedly falling down. The whole street was blocked off with police cars and sawhorses. Puerto Rican families were sitting around on their stoops in the rain, drinking Miller beer, smoking Marlboros and watching the building, waiting for it to collapse. Lila and Sal smelled the sweet grass of Tompkins Square Park and sat in a pew at Saint Brigid's on Avenue B.

"Catholics always have the biggest churches," Lila whispered.

"That's because they have the best quality slaves to build them."

They started walking again, blending in with the muted colors, faded denim against the washed-out red of tenement buildings that had been really lived in.

"Sal, how's your sax going? I love coming home at night and hearing you play slower versions of Coltrane solos. Sometimes I just stand on the stairs and listen for a while. I haven't heard anything the last few weeks though."

"It's the job, it takes over everything. First I was coming home and writing poems about it. Now, I just can't, I'm so exhausted. Lila, I slept with a man again. That makes twice in ten years. I feel a little shy about it, but I do know I like sucking cock. I guess I can tell you that."

There were so many feelings going around at the same time. There was the global plane, where, frankly, things looked bad and no one wanted to face it. Like the neighborhood changing. Everyone knew it was going to happen and then that it was happening. Now it had finally happened. Just like the grotesque certainty of Ronald Reagan's re-election, no one could really accept how much more cruelty they'd have to see. But summer also brought new dimensions of feeling on the street, with different kinds of love and sex for each person. You saw someone and you wanted to touch them because you loved them, or because you didn't know them and they're pretty. Because they had a way of wearing an earring, or turning and smiling, or special long fingers. Your heart would just melt for that second and you'd want to kiss her breasts or suck his cock, the way Sal did. The air was murky and thick enough to hide anybody's shyness. Because, even when the shit is hitting the fan, people can still have good times.

Lila told Sal about Helen Hayes and about sending her the story of their evening with no response yet. About Emily Harrison too. About how Lila saw a woman and wanted to touch her, but it wasn't happening that way, so now, everything was unknown.

"But what the hell, Lila, go for it. She's already given you something special, even if she doesn't know about it."

Lila knew that he was right.

They swung back towards their building until she decided to go off in search of more girls, so Lila and Sal gave each other big hugs, boy and girl hugs. She remembered how some men have those muscle arms and you don't realize how much bigger they are until you get hugged.

"So Lila, when are we going to have an affair?"

Oh, yes, her words to Helen coming back to her like a gift. Just a little present to let her know she was not the only one searching out the company and the stimulation.

"One of these days."

She was ready again, refueled, and headed off to Lacy's apartment with a smile on her face. When there was no one home, she just left a note "Hi L, I will return," not knowing if it was true or not. Then back towards the Kitsch-Inn where she saw Emily sitting on the stoop quietly reading a book.

ELEVEN

Emily sat there with those same green eyes and thirty-something-year-old face, kind of like some actress somewhere. Lila leaped up onto the stoop next to her and started reciting from Jack.

"In their eyes I would be strange and ragged and like the prophet who walked across the land to bring the dark word and the only word I had was wow."

Then, in a swashbuckling mode, Lila invited her to the garden, which was the most romantic place she knew, but Emily didn't feel like entering strange territory, no matter how cool. So, they ended up on Sixth Street on another stoop, smoking joints and cigarettes and talking more about Emily's life. She talked about her constant travels all over the world, about her theatre work, about her jobs.

"I usually work in factories, sewing, printing, whatever's there. That way I can get materials for costumes and sets. Stage design? It's basically a matter of extending other people's ideas, making them look good. I want every detail to be perfect. Someone else decides what it's all about and then I decorate it, compensating for a weak script or a bad actress with a dazzling effect. When the audience walks in, I want them to take one look and gasp."

Lila paid attention. She was gathering information but didn't know how to put it all together. Instead she just watched the different expressions Emily's face was capable of. Sometimes she seemed like a dress-for-success executive whose bra was held together with staples. Then she became a silly girl sitting over a Tab in a coffee shop. Lila began to wonder, was she courting this woman, or were they just making friends?

They walked into a late night bookshop and stood quietly looking at a map of the world.

"I used to live here," Emily said, pointing to a spot on the page. "When I look at it I get so excited. I can hear the voices of my friends and remember the clove and dried flowers. Watch it shiver, reverberating off the paper."

Lila looked at the map, trying to decide where to go. It occurred to her that since the time of maps, people have been able to look upon other countries as empty pink and green shapes. Furthermore, Lila noted each country's maps projected different interpretations of size, boundary and centrality. Basically, though, Lila concluded, a map's first purpose was to state that the most important division in life was geographical.

They walked some more, not knowing exactly where until Emily suggested stopping for a beer. But, when they got to the bar, she expected Lila to pay, and then asked her if she played pool. Second thoughts began to present themselves. Maybe, Lila worried, this woman with a mysterious past was a pool shark. That would be interesting. To try to win the heart of a con-artist without losing your shirt. People who travel all the time are weird anyway, she thought. They spend most of their energy having introductory conversations and brief romances without going through anything with anybody. Their lives become focused on scoring a place to sleep and finding a job until the next train. Lila nursed her beer for hours but still couldn't get Emily to mention the name of any lover she'd ever had, even though they sat in that bar till way past midnight.

Emily decided to go home even though Lila could have

walked the streets with her all night. As the morning started to come their way, they passed by the locked up Inn and Lila saw, sticking out from under the door, the very letter she had sent to Helen Hayes with her story. Helen had never received it. Lila took that as an omen that she was on the right path and put the letter in her pocket. When the moment came to say good-bye, Emily started to run off, but Lila put her arms out for a hug and Emily kissed her instead and said it again.

"Stop by the Inn sometime."

As usual, Lila didn't know what she meant but felt freer somehow with that letter in her pocket.

It had only started on Monday, but already everything had come back full circle. There were still two days left to Memorial Day Weekend and time for another cycle to start and come to fruition. Or maybe everything would just sit there for a while and inspire Lila to move on to other adventures. That night, finally in bed, she lay with her shirt off, in her underwear and blue jeans, like Jack on his bunk, looking out on the shadows of the rooftops and doorways, watching the streetlight shine on her flat stomach. Lila listened to the trees tremble, getting ready for whatever came next.

PART TWO

TWELVE

"The arty types were all over America sucking its blood," said Jack Kerouac to Carlo Marx in Denver. From Lila's East Village vantage point, she could see that he was right. At least as pertained to the ART SCENE which was oozing its slime all over Second Avenue. The upscale New Yorkers who cabbed it down to the fancy spaces to see performers on tour from Europe, ate out afterwards in restaurants where Lila couldn't even get a job. It was an invading homogenous monster composed of a lot of boring people thinking they were leading wacky lives. Lila was beginning to regret her haircut.

Unfortunately the scene was getting older and more established and Lila had begun to watch its participants change fashions and pretensions as they passed her in the street year after year. From lots of overheard conversations and sterner expressions Lila deduced that as the person aged they'd often stop and take a look at how they'd been spending their art time. Occasionally that brought new insight and change. Usually it meant doing commercials or applying for grants. But for every dropout, there were three new recruits stepping off the commuter train.

Like Linda Kasbah, who had gone through a lot of changes.

She'd started out really wild, actually taking risks, not just dressing like she did. Linda worked nights as a go-go dancer in New Jersey for a while, endlessly whizzing by on the back of some guy's motorcycle. Then she got smart, and realized if she go-go'd in pretentious performance spaces and threw in some post-modern movements she could get somewhere, and did. In fact, she ended up with a tour of Europe with her show *Avant Garde A Go-Go* and dropped out of sight for a while, until the day Lila bumped into her in front of Leshko's Polish Restaurant. There was Linda, calm and restrained, standing next to a tall handsome man and pushing a baby carriage.

"This is John," she said, stepping into the frame of a one-celled nuclear family, "and this, is Jane."

Lila tried to be cool, chatting for a bit, inviting Linda over to try out a new idea she'd had, but Linda just nodded her head, and clutched Lila's arm with a ferocious urgency, startlingly tight and imploring.

"A new idea, yes, yes, it's a very different life, Lila, a very different life."

So that was one way out. One could also get thrown out, burned out, or even make it for a while, until the critics and funders who built you up decided it was time to tear you down. Some people never got anywhere but never gave up, clinging to their defeat until they died or got bored.

There was Muriel and her main girlfriend Roberta standing in front of Performance Space 122, wearing little white pinafores.

"What's going on?"

"It's about twenty-four hours," said Roberta looking kind of sleepy as usual. She was wearing her standard flowing robes, in their usual three shades of green, under her pinafore.

"What do you mean?"

"We're in a performance," Muriel sighed. "It's twenty-four hours long."

"What's it about?"

"Twenty-four hours."

246

"Oh."

"Here Lila," Roberta handed her a pinafore. "We need some more Alices, come on, let's go."

Inside the theatre some very worn out dancers were rolling around glossy-eyed in various states of dance marathon exhaustion. Lila, Muriel and Roberta ran over to a small crowd of women, all dressed in little white pinafores.

"Okay Alices," said the head Alice, "First we enter when he says *coming out of the woods*. Then we line up, then we break."

"What does *break* mean?" Lila asked Roberta.

"It means that after we're on stage and we line up, then you do whatever you want.

Lila decided to pay close attention to the stage activity for the next hour before she went on. The act of the moment was a woman in a thirties bathing suit reading boring postcards that her friends had sent her. Then some people pushed a bowling ball back and forth. After that, a woman who was a very important person to know and a man with a big grant danced with their mouths full of parsley. Finally, Lila could see a pattern emerging. First, you sort of moved around and then you said unrelated things in a deadpan. She could do that. She did that everyday. Suddenly, he said *coming out of the woods* and the Alices lined up and then they broke. Roberta and Lila slid down the middle of the floor and then Roberta said, to no one in particular, "I liked the parsley best."

"I counted. There are more artists than there are ideas to go around," Lila said, rather pleased with herself.

"I still liked the parsley."

This was really easy. Roberta starting jumping, so Lila took out a piece of paper, wrote down her phone number and handed it to a pretty woman in the audience. It was fun, but was it worth twenty-four hours?

THIRTEEN

Muriel and Lila needed a break. They went out in the rain to DiRobertis Italian Coffee Shop for a cup. Muriel was a dancer. She listened to Lila's stories and Lila went to see Muriel dance. Then they talked to each other about it. This was a gift they appreciated more than friendship. During those times they were not emotionally close. It was more about being colleagues. They took each other seriously and exchanged their most productive attention. This was not a dreamy time for come-on's and romantics. It was more like DiRobertis' warm silky coffee on a rainy day, which left them solidly awake with the smell of kitchens in their mouths. Whenever Lila thought about going home, she thought about the places where minds met like Muriel's and hers over coffee.

Talking with Muriel let her in to the head of a person whose concerns were completely different than her own. Dance wasn't Lila's way of seeing, but it was a way, and she was glad to know it was there. Muriel's issue was how to create the highest possible energy. She'd forget about wondering where the money was coming from and, instead, ask herself aesthetic questions about feeling a movement, looking to do this within the realm of some kind of emotion. Still, Lila knew that

Muriel's realm did not yet include anger or sadness. "Sensual and elastic," *The Village Voice* critic said, and she did look beautiful on stage. Even though Lila could see her resisting the effort to bring some feeling to all that grace. So, at that moment, there was no genius, but Lila loved her enough to maintain interest, sitting perpetually in Muriel's first row. This was the mood they were in over a coffee break from twenty-four hours.

"Muriel, I can't believe that you've been at this for an entire night and a half a day. Aren't you exhausted? I mean, I could see staying up if it was interesting or fun, but this. . . it's like LSD with no revelation."

Muriel lit a cigarette.

"Well, I did have a weird experience about eleven hours ago. I was performing a series of experimental dances, using haphazard movement without form. In the first piece I thought that Roberta and I were going into a slow contact, like a tango, and then we started dancing. But, she said *too slow*, so I moved out of the dance. Later, when I asked her why, she said I wasn't dancing *with* her, I was dancing *on* her, but I know that if my dance is refused during the improvisation, I just lose all my concentration."

Lila thought back on this conversation the next evening when she watched Muriel perform at The Dance Theatre Workshop and noticed Tina from the gelatti store, all alone, sitting quietly in the back row. Lila thought, *Wow, beauty and grace certainly take one very far*. She saw that Muriel had love whenever she wanted it and sex whenever she wanted it and someone to talk to in an intelligent way whenever she wanted, and that was too much for any one person. With so much diversion Lila would never be able to do the things that she loved best, like walk the streets for hours with nowhere to go except for where she ended up. She would never have the time to bump into a brand new person and give them her total attention. And with that understanding, she was happy to step out alone into the night's heat.

FOURTEEN

Lila's job was so fucking boring and disruptive and ever-present that she decided to try to write about it as a way of turning the mundane into the allegorical. It didn't seem to bother everyone the way it bothered her. Most people just accepted work. Some even enjoyed it because they had absolutely no idea of what else they could possibly do. Without white-out and collating and requisition forms there would be nothing to talk about over the dinner table during commercials. Lila was straining her imagination, looking for ways to turn these office items into symbols of time wasted and possibilities deferred. Unfortunately the greatest angle on all this had already been taken. It was an episode of *The Avengers* when these secretaries killed their bosses and they were the only ones who could run the company because no one else understood the filing system. The problem though, was that there were no more things like filing systems. Everything was getting computerized by the summer of '84, and it was happening so fast, a social critic could hardly keep up with it. Lila was having a hard time building a plot around a WANG word processor. This realization, in turn, stimulated a long rumination on the poor clerical of the future, trapped in her living room with a screaming baby, an unemployed husband and a radiating personal computer through which her invisible boss could monitor every key stroke.

In order to avoid spiritual meltdown, she gave Muriel a call on the company phone to see if she had any suggestions. Instead, Lila had to leave a message on the electronic secretary Muriel had just purchased, hot, on First Avenue for ten bucks.

"Hi Muriel. I know that you have a career to think of, but when I need to talk to you and I get an answering machine, well, it feels like riding on the commuter train, it's shockingly normal behavior."

Lila's metaphors always got a bit fuzzy when she was depressed.

About twenty minutes later Muriel called back, full of enthusiasm.

"I'm so excited," she said, "I bought my ticket for Madrid. Just me. Roberta is staying in New York. She's too tired to pack. I'm flying out on June 24th. . ."

"No," Lila said.

"Excuse me?"

"No, you're not. We have a show to do on the twenty-ninth. The Worst Performance Festival. Remember? Muriel?"

But she knew it was already too late. There was absolutely no point in going on about it. There were good things to Muriel and bad things to Muriel and this was one of the worst. She was completely undependable. Lila, on the other hand, if she promised one girl a cup of coffee and another offered her a weekend on a yacht, you know you would find her in the coffee shop, smiling through the grease. *Why should the rich and glamorous get everything?* she asked herself repeatedly in a combination of defiance and sincere wonder. Yet, there was no point in getting angry. The tension began to seep out of her body, trained, by experience, to transform anger into calm. *I'm deflating*, she though, *despite all my desire not to*. For one small and unusual moment, Lila felt sorry for herself.

She resolved to leave the office immediately and search out

some happiness, even though it was only four-thirty. Maybe Vicki the office manager wouldn't notice if she didn't try that one too often. Most importantly, Lila needed a shot of the city, so, after sneaking out the door, promising herself to be more careful in the future, she was right in it again. The buildings created a shining path that led directly to safety and adventure. Sometimes she would just put her head down and whiz right through, being part of the rush and the urgency. Sometimes she leaned back as far as she could until she was outside of it. Then she could enjoy how it was too enormous to explain and, at the same time, one solid thing. Nothing could ever be so beautiful as the city because it was a synthesis of people and objects and it felt every feeling and contained every possibility.

Soon she was ambling down Sixth Street where she found Sally Liberty putting up tie-dyed curtains on her big green school bus. Sally was getting ready to leave that very evening for The Rainbow Gathering. For one Jack Kerouac-second, Lila considered going along too, what the fuck. But then, as she sat on a garbage can, smoking a cigarette and trying to decide what to do, she remembered those other things like having no money, and the chance to enjoy the last days of the neighborhood. Lila knew that New York was closed; once she gave up an apartment she'd never find another one.

"No, goddammit Sally, I'm committed to here."

"Don't worry," Sally said, truly believing it. "There are many ways to fly."

That gave Lila a shot of hope again. She ran home as fast as she could, raced up the stairs and jumped in behind her typewriter like a race-car driver behind the wheel. First you turn it on, then you go. She pushed *on*, placed her hands on the keyboard, felt the electric buzz and started. Without any premeditation she found herself pounding out the story of Emily Harrison, about trying to figure her out and why Lila liked her so much. How Fourth Street radiated every time she passed it because she never forgot for a second that Emily was house-sitting there. It took her along in a flash and a daze until, suddenly, it was the end of the page and she had to wake up, put in another piece of paper and go again.

When Lila was a kid, people were always telling her that there was only one way to be and one way to think about things. It didn't take long for her to figure out that that just wasn't so. Writing had been subjected to the same fabrications. People who think everything through for themselves still write exactly the way their fourth grade teacher told them to.

"This is how to use time, this is how to use tense, this is what a sentence is."

But, if anyone had really analyzed it, the way Lila had, they would have seen right away that no one lives or feels or thinks in any consistent tense with subjects and predicates. People dangle their emotional participles all over the place. But, if you go ahead and show them something written just the way they experienced it, all of a sudden it's too scary or strange to comprehend.

The very first things Lila had ever written were for the local *Supermarket News*. That was great practice. There was a given event, say, the price of grapefruits. There was an audience. Her job was to describe the event through the lens of her own personality and writing style. There was no looking around for subject matter, only for description, a task she took very seriously. Did the prices *plummet*, or were they *slashed?* She would ask herself what the item really looked like. How the event really felt. She would shake herself, concentrating, grabbing finally and ecstatically at the one and only word that really said it. Now, though, with fiction, she wanted to write in any manner and about anything simply because she felt like it at that moment. She didn't care if the words were weird, indulgent, pretentious or honestly free. Sometimes Lila just let herself look at a lot of ordinary things in a magnificent way.

FIFTEEN

"**I**t sounds like you're just looking at a lot of things and saying WOW," Lacy said when Lila stopped by, "or OH
SHIT, or whatever you would say, Lila Futuransky. Nothing
wrong with that. What kind of music do you want to hear?"

"Nothing. Let's listen to the rain."

It had been pouring for three days and the rain was seeping
into everything.

Lacy was the only person Lila knew who had really achieved
what she had set out to do. Well, maybe that applied to Emily
too, only Lila still hadn't figured out what Emily wanted from
things, least of all, from her. Lacy had published a whole book
of poetry and was about to publish another. Lila wanted to ask
her advice about Emily and about writing but she wanted to
ask both at the same time.

"Lacy, what happens when you see something or someone,
but you see them in a dream and everything in your life
becomes a pursuit because you want to be close to beauty, to
bring it inside of you? But the thing is, you don't want to change
yourself. Can you follow a goal and not get lost?"

Lacy sat back and tucked her chin into her chest, which
meant she was thinking it all over very carefully.

The silence scared Lila, because it was too heavy for her to hear the answer that she wanted. So, she changed the subject.

"Where's Kwame?"

"Arthur took him to the movies. Every month or so Arthur decides that he wants his son to have exposure to some average American culture so he'll know what people are talking about if he ever crosses Fourteenth Street. That's the theory anyway. So he takes him off to the movies. Halfway through, of course, all the sexism and racism and gratuitous violence get to be too much. Arthur gets disgusted and they have to walk out. Poor Kwame's almost six and he doesn't know that movies are ever over. He thinks they're like the sky, cinematically endless."

Lacy was quiet for a moment, shifting in her seat, the way she always did right before getting to the point.

"I'll tell you the truth Lila, I'm honored to be able to publish and all that. I know few people ever get the chance. On the other hand, there's a lot of sickening components to this process. It often makes me want to spend the rest of my writing career developing handbooks for urban gardeners."

"That's not a bad idea," Lila noted, filing the concept away for later.

"First you spend many years staring at bookshelves thinking how incredible it would be to be up there with your greatest heroes, existing apart from yourself. Then you have ideas. Then, somehow, one day, you actually finish writing them down in a reasonable way you find pleasing. When I finished *Crossing The Border*, I thought *Thank God it's finally over. I actually did it*. But no, no, no and no again. You have to sell it, which can take longer than a lifetime. When it was placed I breathed a sigh of relief until the next phase revealed itself. Prepublication."

Lacy was gesticulating wildly, as though she was a young girl conducting a symphony alone in front of her mother's mirror.

"What's that?" Lila asked, finding out about yet another reality.

"That's a great euphemism for endless screaming over punctuation and *no, it is not okay to have a woman in a bikini on the cover, and no, I will not be marketed as the next Lorraine Hansberry*. They have to compare a Black woman to a Black woman, that's revealing enough, but then they compare a poet to a playwright. The guys in marketing probably looked through a book called *Great Negroes* and the only woman in it was Lorraine Hansberry.

"Anyway, years after you write the thing, it finally comes out and of course you don't like it or agree with hardly any of the things it says, but now you have to sell it, so you run around pretending that you do. The publisher, in the meantime, wants to know when you're going to have another one exactly like the first. Lila, I'm not even rich or famous. Imagine how gross it would be to have a big success. Every famous person who ever talked about the experience described how it ruined their life. But we don't listen to that, do we? No, no, no. We don't listen to that. Arthur, home already?"

"*Indiana Jones and the Temple of Doom*," Arthur muttered, his fishing hat soaked with rain. "Racist trash."

Kwame followed him into the kitchen, leaving a trail of water.

"See, what did I tell you," Lacy laughed, relaxing again.

"But Lacy, what about the revenge factor?" Lila asked, trying to absorb all this new and troublesome information.

"The what?"

"You know, where you saw the world one way and recorded it that way in defiance of all the people who tried to say it wasn't like that. When you got screwed in life and could punch them out on paper."

"Lila," Lacy said, looking tired for a minute. "I find that any character I try to hit on paper will hit me back ten times harder. And as far as making an impression on the living goes, it's my opinion that you only impress those people who already like you or don't know you and what does that mean? The ones who couldn't stand your ass before are going to like it even less after. Look at my mother."

"Rose?"

"Rose. Here I am, thirty-eight years old. A Black woman with two books of poetry. Something to brag to the neighbors about, right? Well, after the first one she was still bugging me that it wasn't too late to go to law school and make some money. But, I thought for sure with the second one. . ."

"No go?"

Lacy smiled again, though her eyes looked sad. She kept her wine glass full and wrapped her body in an old comforter. They were silent in that quiet damp apartment in the East Village in the rain. They could hear the sounds of Arthur and Kwame getting dinner.

"She said to me *Good thing there are exhibitionists out there to entertain the rest of us. I believe some things should be kept private.* You see, *some things* is momma's code word for S-E-X. But, still trying to win her over, I asked, *Momma, don't you like to read and go to the theatre and listen to music? Aren't you glad people took the risk to make those things?* And she answered, *Exhibitionists. They're all exhibitionists.* No, some people you will never win over no matter what you do."

Kwame walked in eating a banana.

"Mom, that movie hurt my head, it was too big."

"I know baby, I'm sorry."

Satisfied with this response, he wandered back into the kitchen.

"You know Lacy, for years I've been trying to figure out parents, since I've never been one, just had them. But now, I get it. They live their lives and then they want to live yours too. Gives me an idea for a story. Something about parents who only want one thing in the world and that's for their child to fail so that they can prove that they were right all along."

"Finally win the argument once and for all."

"That's right Lacy, that's it."

"Lacy," Arthur called. "Come here and tell me if the melon is ripe."

Lila went over to the stereo to put on some music. Oh-oh, it was a tape player. It had been so long since she had lived with a music machine of any kind that she only experienced the last decade of technological advances in high-fi equipment through contact with new models at other people's houses. She didn't even know which way the tape fit into the little plastic envelope that opened when she pressed *eject*. Then there were arrows pointing back and forth, then double arrows doing the same thing. Little meters lit up green next to a square of red plastic that flashed on and off. All this was in addition to knobs labeled with various vague concepts like *tuning* or *tone*. The tapes were the same way, either so new that Lila had never heard of them or so old that Lila had never heard of them. She turned on the radio.

"What are you thinking about these days Lila?" Lacy asked, offering some cantaloupe.

"It has to do with time and girls and Jack Kerouac. With living in a Jack Kerouac novel and one particular mystery girl but a cast of many regular ones too. Something happens in chapter one which gets into Jack's head and leads him through to chapter five where he understands it. In chapter seven, all is reconsidered again because of some revelation about to present itself. That's what it feels like anyway, but my changes are still in their early stages."

"I get it," Lacy said, bouncing back from her author-like somber air and into a round garden playfulness. "Then in chapter thirteen of *Lila Meets The Subterraneans* you ask some Vision of Cody to send you a letter and pretend to put it in chapter fifteen, but actually throw it away and only in chapter twenty does Dr. Sax call you personally to find out why it wasn't there, you Dharma Bum, you."

And Lila knew she understood.

SIXTEEN

"**S**ee Isabel, when Emily was a kid, her parents changed jobs every few years. As a result, by the time she was sixteen, she had an intimate knowledge of most major suburbs in America. When she grew up she kept moving, only across oceans too. By the time she came to New York and the windowless back room at The Kitsch-Inn, she had lived on four continents, working tedious jobs with her hands and eyes, sewing, cutting and dyeing. She made things in large factories and small shops. Emily knows a lot about the difference between cultures as well as the reality of solitude and hard physical labor. But she never learned the mundane responsibilities of consistent, dependable intimacy over time. It's like, her primary relationship is with her own ability to create. I think it's been that way since she was a little girl, making things alone in the various houses she passed through and the hotel rooms in between them. She spent her childhood cutting, gluing, putting together, drawing, planning and imagining because she was, at the same time, enormously gifted and in need of something to buffer her loneliness."

"Listen to me buddy," Isabel Schwartz said in response to Lila's story. "Girls like that, you have to watch out for those girls."

Lila was sitting at the counter of Burger Heaven, hunched over an iced tea, cooling off in the air conditioning and listening to Isabel toss advice over her shoulder as she glided back and forth between the tables and the grill.

"They're not like you or me," she continued on the rebound with a ketchup bottle. "You think you're making friends with them because they tell you to *stop by the Inn.* But it's just part of the trap." Her voice faded away as she delivered a mile-high cheeseburger to a smelly man in the corner. "Oh God," she muttered, swinging by the counter again, "he wants another order of raw onion. Why don't people just stay home?"

Finally things quieted down and Isabel could take a seat on the worn out squeaky stools and drink a coke.

"The next step, that's when they talk about sex. That's all they do, talk, talk, talk. You'll be having these all night sensual conversations and the next thing you know you're sleeping over in her bed. Just sleeping of course. I'm telling you, watch out for those girls."

"How do you know so much?" Lila demanded.

"Miss Subways, those girls, they think they're better. They're broke too but they think they have other options. You don't have a chance buddy, not a chance. I don't mean to rub it in your face but didn't you learn anything from the Helen Hayes fiasco?"

Maybe Isabel's right, Lila thought, stepping out again into a gust of hot air, *maybe she's wrong.* Walking through the putrid air of another stagnant early evening, Lila knew that she could never back down without finding out for sure. The problem was approach. This was the time for a new method. Maybe she should try relaxing and being normal. On that note of inspiration, Lila went right home, ironed her famous blue luau shirt, Tennex'd her hair and donned a pair of mirrored sunglasses. It worked. She felt as though she had a tan. Her fingertips tingling with hope and anticipation, Lila walked slowly over to the Inn, on the thin pretext of going to see the show.

As usual Emily was at the door greeting everyone and smiled

largely when Lila made her entrance.

"Hi darlin'," Emily said in her cute nervous way and Lila felt so happy just being around her, she almost forgot to take a seat so she could work on being relaxed. Lila sat in the back row to get a good view of the real show, the usual assortment of local lesbians who made up the audiences at places like this.

Whenever she was in a roomful of lesbians, Lila fluctuated between two points of view. First, she would have a sentimental rush of feeling, overwhelmed by the beauty and the courage of all these women who had gone through fire and ice just to find each other. Every meeting place, tradition or ritual was built with nothing but their own determination, which kept everything vaguely together. But, a split second later, Lila looked more distantly and the scene would be transformed into a room full of victims. This one had her child taken away, that one got locked up by her parents, that one's girlfriend got queerbashed in front of her and there wasn't a thing she could do about it. It made Lila wonder if they really weren't just a bunch of weirdos hallucinating all this fragile dignity. The fact was, that after almost fifteen years of hard core propaganda and heavy publicity, nobody, outside of lesbians, had bought the line that they were strong, determined survivors. To everyone else they were invisible or pitiful and most straight people were plain glad they weren't queer. Still, thought Lila, if only they could put over a *Black Is Beautiful* line of advertising.

Actually, Lila had often considered the question of marketing lesbian popularity. She looked at other groups of outcasts who had managed to make a name for themselves. The ultimate failures were Communists. In America, they were still at the bottom of the charts. After considering various historical examples, she concluded that the most successful model was that of the Beats. Guys like Jack, William Burroughs and Allen Ginsberg, some of them were smart and had some good ideas and wrote some lasting and inspiring work. Mostly, though, they weren't all the geniuses their reputations implied. The thing was, they had made a phenomenon of themselves. They made themselves into the fashion, each one quoting from the other, building an image based not so much on their work as on the idea that they led interesting lives. Lila firmly believed that was exactly what lesbians needed to do. Why not make heroes out of Isabel Schwartz and Helen Hayes, and make The Kitsch-Inn the new mecca? Let kids from all over America pack their bags, sneak out at night and flock to the East Village to hang out with the lesbians. Soon there'd be lines around the block for the Inn's midnight show bringing those hungry for stimulation flocking to catch the last word in Lesbiana. They'd have magazine covers, syndicated situation comedies, do the lecture circuit, maybe even walk down the street without being afraid. Who knows? In Amerika, anything is theoretically possible. The next time she saw Allen Ginsberg buying cannollis at Veniero's, she would be sure to ask him how he did it.

SEVENTEEN

When the show was over, Lila lingered a bit until Emily finally invited her to come along to a party. They went with Sheena, who had just come back from Krishnaland, and Kitty, two members of the inner sanctum of Kitsch. Everything started to feel good again, happy and young and full of energy. Four fearless dykes out on the Friday night streets of their own turf. Just to prove that it was theirs, Kitty and Sheena started staring down motorists with Jersey plates, giving out dimes to beggars and singing old R&B tunes in loud boisterous voices. Kitty was known around as the prettiest Kitsch girl and everyone's old friend. Lila hadn't seen her hanging out for a while though.

"Where have you been, doll? I haven't seen your face since the Halloween Ball."

"Central Park South."

"Central Park South? What did you do, get a rich girlfriend or something?"

"Yeah. She's got two apartments, a building in the Bronx, a restaurant in the West Village and a little numbers business on the side. You want to hear some gossip? We're breaking up. But not till the end of the summer."

Kitty on Central Park South? She used to walk around with literally one dollar in her pocket and stay at people's houses, sleeping anywhere.

"How's that going to be, back on the edge?"

"I can't wait. Do you know what you have to do to be rich? You have to spend all your time with rich people. You have to do drugs even if you don't feel like it because that's what rich people do. Did you know that?"

"I've heard about it."

"You work all the time and then you have lots of things. I like fun. I'm going back to having fun as soon as the summer's over. I think so anyway, I'm not really sure."

"Groovoid," said Sheena.

They ended up at a party of gentrified straight people. It was in a former tenement apartment that had been *rehabilitated* in the style of an early-modern furniture showcase. The package was complete with built-in bookshelves, track lighting and parquet floors. Whoever lived there had a strange collection of books. An entire shelf was filled with volumes on chess. The next one only contained books about poker.

"What does the guy do who lives here?"

"He writes software," Sheena said, "so that lonely people who have computers can play chess and poker with themselves."

Lila walked out on the patio, which used to be a back alley, and ended up sitting with Emily on the lounge furniture. Emily was eating marinated mushrooms from the buffet table, but Lila was already so full with pretty things and the clear sky coming back after so much rain, that she couldn't eat at all.

"I can say some words in Italian," Lila said, looking for some more common ground. *"Cara mia, mi amore, que bella notte."*

"That's nice."

"I also know *dolce mia* and *va funcullo.*"

"No, don't say that." Emily's face was overcome by distaste. "I hate when people say that."

Lila knew it was time to try and change the subject, but she didn't know to what, until out of the blue she realized they were talking about sex, just like Isabel had said they would.

"Emily, do you have any lovers in New York?"

"No, not really," she said, absent-mindedly twisting a short curl with her painted fingers. "There are some women who I'm attracted to physically but they all seem to be matched with someone else. Around the Inn anyway, there aren't very many who are pretty, well, pretty to me. But no, except for a few nights with women I've met at parties or. . . well. . . no."

Lila was swimming in the night. She felt so free that she just said it.

"What about me? Are you attracted to me?"

"Yes. . . well. . . no. . . well."

"A little?"

"I don't really know you, Lila."

Lila had that feeling inside like soft evening and soft skin and soft wind and quiet, muffled street noises. Then there was a silence between them, a growing silence.

"I'm sorry if that was a conversation stopper," Lila said. "I wrote a story about you, for you. I even have a copy at home with your name on it. Sometime you'll have to come over and I'll give it to you. Also, I know there's no shower or hot water at The Inn. When your apartment-sitting is up, if you need a place to wash, you can always use my place."

Then they relaxed and partied around a bit, deciding to ignore the gentrifiers and to hang out in a corner with a Colombian lesbian named Olivia and her variety joints.

"This one is California sensemillia. This one is Thai. This one is Jamaican. Now, which one would you like to sample?"

A few hours later, Emily and Lila and Sheena went over to Maureen's, a neighborhood tavern run by a gruff old Irish dyke. Fats Waller was in the background, leftover Christmas lights on the walls. Emily sat in the foreground, her retro haircut illuminated by the flashing reds and greens. All three of them spun on their bar stools, smiling at the old movie posters and ignoring the old customers. They could have been boys or girls in any forties movie.

Sheena went on for a while about her energy and dyeing her hair blue, but Lila was waiting to be left alone with Emily and she thought Emily was waiting too. Even though the thought of being left alone together so late at night made Lila nervous. Still, it was a pleasurable anxiety somehow. As though they were sharing the same thought without speaking, just sitting quietly at the bar.

The events unraveled in such a way that Lila ended up going back to Fourth Street with Emily via an invitation to "watch TV," though it was well past two o'clock in the morning. She was a little surprised when they got there and Emily actually turned on the set. But, trying to go with the flow, Lila sat down next to her and watched *Soul Train*. She even made some conversation about how surprisingly artificial the dancing was, and ditto for the famous *Soul Train* fashions. They sat next to each other for a long time as ads for Ultra Sheen flashed on the screen. Finally Lila asked,

"Do you feel like kissing?"

She asked it because she wanted to kiss Emily so badly and besides, that was what she thought she had been brought there to do.

"Let's just relax," Emily said, curling up. "I'm feeling sleepy. Maybe I'll feel like kissing later."

In the meantime, with Emily's head on her lap, watching *Soul Train*, Lila touched Emily's skin by the TV light and was filled with feeling at how soft and oily Emily's skin was, especially between the fold in her neck, and how warm her curly hair was under Lila's fingers. Even though she ended up sleeping in Emily's bed that night, like Isabel Schwartz had predicted, she still felt happy the next morning that she had finally, in some small way, touched this woman. It gave her so many nice things to think about the rest of the day. Lila knew once again that life was holy and every minute precious.

EIGHTEEN

"**H**ello Lila? This is Emily."
"Emily. I'm so glad you called me. I was sitting here thinking about you."

"Oh good. Would you like to go to the movies with me? *Annie Hall* is playing at The Saint Mark's."

"I really would like to but I can't. It's time for The Worst Performance Festival to meet on my roof."

According to Lila, artists were supposed to show that there were other ways of seeing. Putting on a show meant calling people together because you had something to tell them, and that something, thought Lila, should not be the same old thing. In the art world, however, this was not the case. At the same time though a depression culture was rising on the streets. There was better dancing in Washington Square Park by Black boys or Puerto Rican faggots than in any performance space. There was Doo-Wop under the Washington Arch and excellent fusion jazz every night for free on Astor Place.

Noticing these contradictions, some of the girls, like Isabel, Muriel and Lila, decided they'd seen enough stupid performances and wanted to do something about it. They invited Muriel's girlfriend Roberta to come along too because she was starting to bill herself as Roberta La Moll and that looked great on a flyer. That was how The Worst Performance Festival was born. They were having their first planning meeting on Lila's roof that Saturday afternoon.

"The concept is," said Lila, "that we want to look at both sides of what it means to be the worst. Some performers are bad because they're about nothing but the audience loves them because the audience is also about nothing. Other performances are bad because they're really about something but that makes the audience uncomfortable, so they don't like it. That is the dialectic of worst."

"We have to help them understand the aesthetic of the worst performance," Muriel added. "Then they can have some criteria for choosing the best contestant since, frankly, almost anything is interesting for three minutes."

"So, what are the essential components of a bad performance?" Roberta asked.

"Well," answered Isabel Schwartz, "it should be something absolutely no one could ever identify with."

"It should be physically annoying," Lila added.

"It should definitely be inaudible," Muriel said.

"But, you know how people are always doing these self-indulgent things like *Disconnected Movements With Irrelevant Objects* where they make you sit there while they do something like count." Isabel wanted the Festival to be as realistic as possible.

At just that moment, the roof was filled with the startling appearance of brilliant colors in a shocking paisley motif. It was Helen Hayes herself, her bleached blonde hair highlighted by a hot pink blouse and turquoise flowered pants. Helen Hayes was in on the show and worst of the worst was guaranteed. She joined the group sitting together on the roof, getting high and talking about the worst.

"Listen girls," Helen suggested, picking up the vibes immediately, "How about a finale like this? *The next performance will be the greatest moment in experimental history, after which the avant-garde will officially be over. Yes, it's true, everyone who has ever won a National Endowment for the Arts grant will now come on stage and shit.* What do you think?"

That Helen cracked everybody up, so people forgot about the meeting and started running all over the roof, looking out over the downtown part of the city. The tenement rooftops of the nineteenth-century Lower Eastside were clear in the foreground while the steel and glass towers of the twentieth-century stood out, separate, in the dusky background.

"Here Helen," Lila said, when no one else was watching. "Here's a letter I sent you, but it got forwarded to the Kitsch-Inn where I found it again, so I decided to give it to you in person."

Helen opened it right then and there and read about how Lila had thought she was cute and smart but a real bitch. She even laughed out loud at the "I meant to call you" line.

"I'm a real nerd," she said. "I'll be sure to show this to Nancy, my new girlfriend, so she'll know what I passed up."

Lila had been carrying around a message to Helen about warmth and embarassment and being a jerk and leading the kind of life that they both led. Helen understood about uncertainty and experiment and unreasonable expectations. They were trying to do good work, have good sex, make meaningful friends, and do all this with no impetus except their own ambition and desires. There was no support outside of that tiny community of downtown dykes who understood being compelled towards an unlikely goal.

The idea was to keep feelings in circulation but still stay friendly, and it had worked. Everything was fine again. Helen knew she was still in Lila's life, even in a small way. Lila had come through that risk feeling good about herself and the people around her. Lila was on the right path.

NINETEEN

All the girls left except Muriel, since she and Lila hadn't had any time alone for a while. They lay down on a blanket on the roof in the last of the Saturday sun of early June and watched the sky.

"I know you're mad at me for taking off and leaving the festival, Lila."

That was exactly what Lila did not want to talk about.

"But you have to let me make decisions about what is best for me."

"Muriel, while theoretically I may agree with what you say, you always make your decisions based on what is best for you. Sometimes there are other people involved too, you know."

"I just want you to understand that I have to do what is best for me and it is best for me to go to Madrid now while I have the money."

"Muriel, I'm not trying to talk you out of it, but I'm not going to give you approval for it either and that's exactly what you are trying to get out of me."

Lila lay on her back with her hands over her eyes. All this tension was not worth it. She was willing to drop the whole argument. Why did Muriel have to push it too far? Now, how was she going to get out of this so they could be in a good mood again?

Lila looked at Muriel. They didn't look each other in the eye during emotionally intimate moments like fights. They usually talked over the phone or while sitting next to each other in an audience, or side by side walking down a street.

"What are you feeling, Muriel?"

"I don't know." She played with the tar-papered roof. "I'm feeling sort of vulnerable."

And then she cried. First Lila thought it was a trick of some kind because, when it came down to it, she didn't really trust Muriel. But then she realized that she couldn't remember that happening before so, guardedly, she felt for her.

"This weird relationship we have is so important to me, Lila, and I know that at any minute you could get really angry at me and stay away for a long, long time."

How could Lila help but hold her because, somewhere, she also had a need to tell Muriel how important she was to her.

"Muriel, I think if we cared any more for each other than we do we would never get along. It's always when we get really involved that we lock horns."

That felt like the truth. Their eyes met in a silent understanding. Then Muriel leaned in to kiss her. When Lila smelled her smell, she moved towards her with the same force and their emotional and intellectual feelings faded away to be considered another day, replaced by the power of sexual unity. Although the disagreements and conflicts were certainly irresolvable, there was a place of sexual confidence that kept them coming back to each other time after time. Then they sat back out of their kiss and were themselves again with different egos and points of view.

"Why don't we just stay here on the roof?" Muriel said.

Lila started to smooth out the blanket when she saw two men on the next roof staring at them.

"We have to go inside. There are two men staring at us."

They went inside and covered the windows so the men

271

couldn't see into the apartment. Muriel took off her clothes and Lila took off her clothes. Without any seduction or conversation they put their arms around each other's waists, held each other's asses and pressed their naked bodies against each other. They put their cool hands on each other's hot thighs. Every move was deliberate and strong. Their confidence in each other was so deep that Lila always anticipated the pleasure before it came. Plus, Muriel had the most responsive sexuality of any person Lila had ever slept with. Lila learned from the beginning that it was by making love to someone else, feeling how sopping wet she was, feeling her quiver, feeling her nipples change, that made Muriel excited. She was so sensitive to a lover's body that the higher she took them, the higher she went herself. When Lila was almost coming, Muriel would say her name over and over again, in her own rhythm. It all felt like one person sharing, not only the orgasm, but the climb, the floating, the coming and the falling. When Muriel came, her clitoris suddenly relaxed and Lila's fingers went through, right to the bone. Then there was a whimper and then kisses, cunty, hairy kisses between two very close bodies. Then they were themselves again, immediately, as Muriel jumped up for a glass of water. When she came back, Lila was sitting on the edge of the mattress. Muriel sat beside her, with her arms around Lila, the smell of her cunt, sort of sour, waxy apricot rising around them.

"It's funny how quickly we make love."

"It's fun making love with you Lila, I know that whatever happens, it's going to feel great."

She sat on the floor and touched Lila's thighs. She parted Lila's pubic hair and teased her cunt. Lila lay back on the mattress and let Muriel bring her face between her legs, like the breeze itself, but it was a woman, not an element. Lila forgot about thinking and lived through her cunt, perceiving the world as only warm and sweet and deeply powerful.

Then, Muriel decided to wake her up and take her somewhere else, so her tongue got more circular and purposeful. Eventually, Lila knew and could anticipate that, as it came around her clit, Muriel's tongue was going to flick suddenly, in the same place. Each time she wanted that moment more and more until that flicker became the entire feeling. Lila was taken over by the beat of perfect pressure, more and more, and she was moving and talking, crying out. Muriel's face started to turn, putting her head more and more into Lila's vagina. Lila saw her jaw go up and down and heard her gasping for air, keeping the pressure, keeping her tongue round and round until Lila pushed into her face and came, and fell back down on the bed as Muriel's large body crawled over her with kisses.

By nine o'clock they were buying apricots on Second Avenue and kissing good-bye amidst the uptown intermission crowd at The Orpheum Theatre as each set off into her own Saturday night.

TWENTY

The heat finally came and with it the loss of desire to move very far or fast, as well as a certain loss of hope. Lila sat naked, writing, knowing that it was too hot for anyone to care about seeing her pounds of flesh. She had work to do and wasn't going to dissipate her time by going over to The Inn to hang out. Why go? She'd see Emily and they would be awkward with each other, then the special mood between them would be ruined. Better to just sit home. But her chest started to tighten, the typewriter keys got heavy, cigarettes made her throat sore. She was dying, dying in the heat.

Finally, seeing no other option, Lila wandered off to The Inn where everyone was hanging out in the back, drinking beer and chatting. It was someone's birthday and the theme was poolside. There were little wading pools, Hawaiian shirts and bathing suits. These girls always had cute little themes to the things they did, it was more fun that way. It was tackiness as an acquired and desired aesthetic instead of tackiness because that was the only way one knew how to be. A subtle but crucial difference.

Lila talked to Sheena for a while about Krishna, the house-painting business and good places to go bowling. Meanwhile, a film of Helen Hayes mud wrestling was being projected onto a brick wall. Lila noticed an extremely tall muscular woman in a Straight to Hell t-shirt leaning against the wall, one booted foot flat against the brick. Even more interesting was the green dragon tattoo that seemed to be winding its way down her left arm. Her blonde hair was long and shaggy and she had a black bandana tied around her pants leg. Then Lila noticed that this woman was staring right at her from across the wading pool. When she caught Lila's eye she came closer, then closer.

"I'm Nancy," she said, dangling her beer bottle from two fingers.

"Hi Nancy, I'm Lila."

"I know."

"Oh, well, why don't you pull up a chair?"

But she preferred to stand. Helen Hayes' new girlfriend was not at all what Lila had expected. She thought Helen would go for someone little and dizzy, forgetting for a moment that there is a reason why there are butches and femmes in this world. Nancy was on a serious mission to check out the competition and make sure that Helen's honor was in no way compromised.

"I read that story you gave Helen. Everything was fine except for the part where you said she was jerky-looking. I didn't like that."

"Oh, don't worry Nance, it was all in fun, you know. I was just joking around, nothing serious."

"Good, because it's real between Helen and me."

"That's wonderful, I'm very happy for you both."

Lila had the strange premonition that she was about to be challenged to a duel. But suddenly the tone changed as Nancy grabbed a chair, plopped herself down and started a very friendly conversation about, of all things, theatre.

"You know I have a very strong background in theatre and Helen, she's so modest, she needs my encouragement and guidance."

"Oh yes, Helen Hayes is modesty personified."

"I'm glad you understand." Nancy relaxed now, opening a

fresh can of beer while making a perfect shot with the old bottle into a garbage can on the other side of the party.

"Helen feels bad that she doesn't have the exposure and the experience that she needs, so this summer I'm giving her plays to read to expand her theatrical sense."

"I know, she's so shy and retiring."

"Yeah, well, it's the least I can do."

Lila watched as Nancy proceeded to open a third beer with one hand and crush the empty one with the other. *Boy*, she thought, *Helen certainly knows how to pick 'em wild and woolly.*

"So I gave her these reading assignments, some Chekhov, for the characterization, *Zoo Story* for the vernacular, *A Doll's House* for the structure, *Death of a Salesman* for the death."

"*Cat on a Hot Tin Roof* for the tin?" Lila suggested, trying to be helpful. "*Breakfast at Tiffany's* for the breakfast?"

"What?"

"Never mind." Lila decided she had better learn to control her instinct to turn every conversation into some kind of sick joke.

Over their heads, on the wall, Helen and her challenger were rolling and romping, caked in brown mud. Helen's shirt was falling off and her nipples were smeared in dirt.

"Well, Nancy, I'm really glad we had this opportunity to talk, so you can be one hundred percent sure that there are no hard feelings whatsoever. I'm sure you and Helen will be very happy."

"Ms. Subways, there you are."

Thank God, it was Isabel Schwartz to the rescue. Lila smiled good-bye to Nancy and walked over to Isabel to hear her new ideas, since she had that I-need-to-talk-to-you-right-away-because-I-have-a-new-idea expression.

"Ms. Sub-Gum Ways, I have got a great idea for the new show. It's based on your experience with Helen. I'll play you and I'll keep running into different kinds of girls who promise all sorts of undeliverable delights and in the end, I become the Messiah, or better yet, Michael Jackson. We'll ask Helen to play herself. She'll do it, don't you think? Anything for Art. Miss Subways? What's the matter? You look like you're going out of order."

"I think I'm making a series of local stops."

"Hi Lila." There was Emily who smiled as though she didn't know what else to do and so turned away abruptly with that smile still plastered on her face and then walked back into the bevy of bathing beauties frolicking by the beach umbrella.

"That girl is trouble, buddy, I'm telling you. Girls like that don't go for girls like us. We don't get girls like that."

"Miss Schwartz, why not? I mean, why not? Know what I mean?"

"You don't understand," Isabel explained carefully after securing a purple shoe lace, "First of all, she's a WASP, they don't feel emotions deeply like we do. Catholics might stab you in the back, but afterwards they're upset if you don't like them any more. Protestants don't care what you think when they're through with you. They're just used to having everything their way. Besides, she's slumming it right now. They think it's boho to hang out with all these dark people with idealistic goals, but sooner or later they get tired of buying their shoes at Fava and go into antiqueing, or something useless like that. They don't know about the kinds of things that we know about and what's more, they don't care about the kinds of things that we know about. But, I know you can't hear that now. Well, maybe you'll get some good material at least. Remember, when your heart is breaking, write it down. When a relationship is over, what do you have? You have nothing. But if you write it down, you have material. That's the best a girl can hope for in these troubled times."

"What about you Isabel, don't you ever get shot in the gut from Cupid's bow?"

"I'm not falling in love until 1990. I refuse to be romantic during the Reagan era. I'm waiting for a Democratic president."

Lila intuited that Isabel was right. She was going to let herself get totally obsessed and ultimately used as a doormat by some woman just because she had neat hair. But, for old times' sake, she had to let herself sink, once again, into the muck and mire of failed pursual. It reminded her that she was alive. So, Lila hung out and hung out and hung out and drank beers and talked to girls and waited.

Emily came up to her some hours later, smiled again and said, "I'm glad you came. So many people that I like are here tonight."

Another appropriately vague, but pleasant comment. Lila got disgusted with herself and then she got sad, pulled herself together, resigned, and put her arm around Emily's shoulder.

"Emily, I'm going home now." She kissed Emily's hair, relaxed and natural, and turned away. Lila could hear the violins on the soundtrack as she stepped outside onto the deserted street and was in the movies again, walking off into the sunrise. But, for some reason having to do with the various emotional patterns that intersect in that field called love, Emily had followed her out and leaned against the building.

There was something very beautiful to Lila about the sight of a sweating woman leaning against a building on a summer city night.

"Lila, would you like me to walk you home? I'm pretty tired, but I like being around you."

Then there was a real smile and a wriggle, the way that women tremble sometimes when they're happy and excited.

"Sure Emily, I like being with you too. I really do."

And Lila was so very deeply touched.

TWENTY-ONE

There are moments that stand out delightful and clear like a black and white photograph. The first forty times you look at it, the whole event comes to life, your life with that person, frozen, smiling in her youth on a late night street corner, and that moment becomes the whole experience until, long after you've separated and lost each other, you have only one thing left, that moment. Lila had gone over it again and again in her head.

"I'm not a cold person," Emily had said and hugged her, held her face between her hands and kissed it, held her again and clasped her hand. "I don't want you to think I'm a cold person."

When Emily had walked with her into the apartment that evening, Lila was so overcome with shyness that she had to put on her mirrored sunglasses for the first ten minutes or so, just to be able to speak. But then, they eased so gracefully into their wonderful talks, full of understanding, like a gift with all its erotic properties.

Talk in the living room, talk in the bedroom, talk up on the rooftop, watching the never-ending light patterns of the city change their shape and sequence. And all the while Lila was thinking *dolce*, wanting to touch this woman. Wishing for it on a star, on a white seagull illuminated in the moonlight, on a green caterpillar inching across the concrete.

When Emily decided to leave, they walked silently down Second Avenue until Lila felt foolish, like a shadow who knows that night is coming, and turned to go back. But, like a worried lover, like an older woman in a thirties movie touched under a streetlight by the innocence of another, thoughtful, anxious, emotional, Emily hugged her, kissed her face, put her hands on Lila's cheeks and hugged her again.

"I don't want you to think I'm a cold person," Emily said, holding her hand before turning away.

And all the way home Lila was thinking *dolce, dolce* and looked up to see Tina, tired and hot, writing in her journal in the empty gelatti store. And everything seemed possible again.

PART THREE

TWENTY-TWO

June eighth was the first major demonstration of the summer. Old friends and neighbors greeted each other on the subways and buses as they headed towards the United Nations to protest United States intervention in Central America. In the U.S. people are allowed to be political as long as they don't actually have an effect on anything. So, the purpose of these gatherings was for the like-minded to see each other, try to get thirty seconds on the evening news and remember that they were not as alone as they felt reading the paper in the morning. Throughout, there was an unspoken hope that sooner or later someone would figure out a more effective method for accomplishing their goals.

The crowd was a fairly large one considering the one hundred degree weather. It hovered somewhere near ten thousand. The participants were mostly white, mostly from local peace groups and small political organizations. This included a lot of older people. Some were lifetime members of the Communist Party or upstarts from Another Grandmother for Peace, or both. They were joined by a small contingent of veterans of the Abraham Lincoln Brigade, fighters against facism in the Spanish Civil War. They got a big cheer from the dehydrated crowd.

This particular demonstration had been organized by Artists Against War and so, instead of long, boring, speeches, the Plaza was set up as a collection of simultaneous performance spaces from which a cacophony of overlapping productions filled the air. A Black woman rapped to a white man's saxophone while a Saint Mark's Poetry Project poet yelled his esoteric observations. Two women did an interpretive dance in very hot costumes to the synthesizer of yet another experimental band. At exactly the same moment, The New York Marxist School Chorus sang *El Pueblo Unido*. It was definitely different from the usual demo, Lila observed, but not actually better, being so chaotic and finally, meaningless.

After a few hours of disorganized mass sweating, the crowd started to march up Madison Avenue towards Reagan's re-election campaign headquarters. Having been around a bit, Lila managed to bump into a few people she saw only at protest marches. A theoretical Marxist who used to live down the hall. He had married a corporate lawyer and the two of them had just gotten back from Nicaragua. An old acquaintance from a now defunct food co-op was finishing her dissertation and had also just come back from Nicaragua.

"What are you doing these days Lila?"

"Nothing."

It was too complicated to go into.

Then she was faced with the usual dilemma of having to decide which contingent to march with. In other words, which part of her complex identity would be the base from which to express her opposition to the latest outrage? Ideally she would have loved to find a sign proclaiming "Girls Against War." However, the only banner relating in any way to anyone female came from a small left party that always had signs proclaiming "Women for Somebody Else." There was also a "Lesbians and Gays for Jesse Jackson" placard, but that seemed a little too specific, although she would definitely have carried one saying "Jesse Jackson for Lesbians and Gays." She tried the New Jewish Agenda Brooklyn Chapter, but after half a block decided, in all good conscience, she couldn't march with a group from Brooklyn. As always, she finally ended up with an ad-hoc collection of vaguely associated dykes, all without places to march.

They tried out a few creative slogans, since slogan writing is second nature to urban lesbians.

"Cruise People, Not Missiles."

"More Dykes, No Nukes."

And the old favorite:

"Two-Four-Six-Eight, Smash the Family, Smash the State."

But the t-shirted men with megaphones kept drowning them out with "No Draft, No War, US Out of El Salvador."

A noble sentiment, thought Lila, *but a very mundane delivery*.

After she got home and washed off the sweat, Lila dressed up in a red and black fifties print dress, tacky large earrings and a matching red and black imitation alligator skin clutch bag. She was off again to hang around outside of a women's dance, since it was too expensive to actually go in. She stopped off, of course, to visit Emily and invited her to come hang outside too, when that night's show was over.

Taking the circuitous route, Lila ran into Ray in his red "Enjoy Cocaine" t-shirt, cut off right above the navel so he could put his hands on his stomach muscles whenever he felt like it.

"Lila, I've been thinking it over and I figured it all out."

"What have you got figured out?"

"It has to do with those immigrants," he said, shifting his gaze now and then. "Look around at those Koreans who own all the fruit stands. They'll hire a Black man to stand outside with a stick and hit someone who tries to steal fruit. The Arabs own the delis, the Indians own the newsstands and wouldn't give credit on a pack of rolling papers. The way I see it, we, the Americans, used to be the insiders, but now we are the outsiders. Now, have you been to Harlem lately?"

"No."

"Well it's filled with everything but Black people. White people in brownstones, Orientals with those fruit stands, and when

I walk down the street they look at me weirdly, like, 'Are you a *Negro?*' Hey brother, I got good sense here."

Ray ran off to a brown Chevy to sell a bag. He was back in a flash.

"I know from the sixties," he said, scratching his grey beard and smiling with his eyes, "'cause I was around then and you were too young, but in the sixties, most people didn't understand what was happening, and I'm not talking color now either. Most people just followed the trend and said what they were supposed to say, but only a few understood the whole analysis. Fifteen years ago we turned Tompkins Square Park into a people's park. All kinds of people were sleeping there, talking about changing things and the police came to break it up. Last night just as many people slept out in that park but it was because they had no other place to go, so the police don't give a damn."

Another car drove by looking for stuff.

"Sense," Ray said, running up to the car. "I got skunk and sense."

So Lila went over to the dance and hung out on the sidewalk for a few hours, waiting for Emily to come, knowing that she would. Finally she saw her, standing off to one side, sort of alone in the crowd. Times were so bad that the sidewalk was packed and hardly anybody had paid to go inside where there was a live DJ. Someone had brought a radio and a big box and someone else had brought tapes and all the poor lesbians were dancing and chatting and having a good old time. And Lila had a good time too until it got really late and she accompanied Emily back to where she was house-sitting on Fourth Street.

TWENTY-THREE

They sat shirtless in the heat, on the fire escape watching the costume shop across the way bustle with sewing and cutting. It was the one lit unit, frantic with activity.

"Lila, would you like to sleep here tonight?"

Lila was beginning to grow accustomed to the idea that she rarely understood exactly what Emily was trying to tell her.

"I'd be real happy if you did, but I'm feeling kind of sleepy."

"Sure, hey, why not."

So, once again, Lila crawled into this woman's bed. This time though, their breasts were shiny from moonlight on sweat. Lila lay there, listening to Emily fall asleep and felt like a really stupid asshole. What was Emily trying to pull anyway? Was she totally out of it or was she purposely trying to make a fool of her? What the fuck was Lila doing in this situation? She should just get dressed and get the hell home. She heard Emily start to snore and some different levels of thought entered her mind. She really didn't want to let all this effort go out the window. Maybe Emily just wasn't meant to be her lover. Maybe Emily was her Carlo Marx or Dean Moriarty. Maybe she was someone to go out on adventures with and talk things over with all night long. Maybe Lila was being given the precious gift of a partner, a chum for adventures. Suddenly she wanted to jump up and read a chapter from *On The Road*.

"Are you anxious, Lila?"

"Me? Anxious? Of course."

"Are you changing your mind? Do you want to go home now?"

"No, Emily, I . . . look, I thought you wanted to sleep with me. That's why I came home with you. Look Emily, tell me the truth. What are you trying to pull here anyway? I mean, I don't always understand all the time what you mean by what you do."

"Why do I have to initiate everything?" Emily asked, with impatience in her voice, as though it was all so obvious.

"Oh. So that's how it is."

Lila touched Emily's hair and her face and the soft folds of her neck. At that moment, Emily moved the same way any woman moves when her aching skins finally gets touched in just the right way.

"I'm sorry I don't have a lot of energy," Emily said, reaching for her, "I'm usually too sleepy to make love late at night. I'll have to come visit you sometime during the day. Oh, I love your breasts."

And then it all began. You look at a woman and know she is a lesbian but you don't always know why until you find out one day how much she loves to suck your breasts. With bursts of hidden energy and force, Emily sucked Lila's breasts and looked up at her red nipple between her own red lips and flicked her tongue back and forth in Lila's direction. She kissed Lila so hard on the mouth that Lila could feel Emily's skull through her lips. Emily gave her her breasts to kiss, going back to Lila's breasts, to her mouth, to her breasts, her mouth, all with determination until she'd used her fingers to fuck Lila, until the whole of Emily's body was in her fingers, sweating and moving. . .

"Lila, am I hurting you?"

"What? No! You feel wonderful to me."

Lila looked closely at Emily's cunt, all sleek and symmetrical, following each fold and crease with her tongue until Emily pulled her up.

"You don't want me to come yet darlin'."

She was lying on Lila, sliding against her on a layer of sweat, putting her delicate face between Lila's legs, and when Lila came, Emily pulled herself up along her body, hanging out on her chest.

"Do you feel good darling? I want you to feel good."

Then she said, "I'm sorry I don't have much energy. Good night."

What Lila really wanted was to kiss her neck a hundred times and tell her how sweet she was and how good she'd made her feel. She wanted to whisper to Emily about how exciting it was to be held in her arms, strong from carrying boxes in the factory, in her fishnets. But instead, Lila just lay back and watched Emily sleep. Lila lay there with an enormous grin on her face.

When Emily woke up at six the next morning to go to work, Lila watched her put cocoa butter on her hairless legs and vaseline around her eyes. She watched Emily walk off with her red plastic handbag and powder blue booties. What a wonderful thing to have to dream about all the hot day long, Lila thought on her way to the office. This is what she wanted from her life. Nine o'clock on a blistering morning, riding up a stifling elevator to a stifling job thinking about Emily's fingers inside her, feeling them still. That was it.

TWENTY-FOUR

"**L**ila, sometimes I just need to be quiet."

It was Friday night out on the stoop and Emily didn't feel like talking. So, they watched the street a while longer until Lila got involved in a detailed conversation with an Italian Buddhist. Then they started walking slowly over to Washington Square Park, where they sat on the littered grass until it was too disgusting. They moved to some benches until men harassed them away and ended up at the midnight show of *Blade Runner* at The Saint Mark's. They walked in late and Lila couldn't figure out what was going on. Since she didn't have a TV, she found it harder and harder to tolerate movies, or even just to follow them. Her eyes hurt from too many screen flashes and all the marijuana smoke in the theatre and she didn't understand why Emily was being so stiff.

Finally they left that scene and wandered a bit, ending up on Lila's roof, lying on a blanket between the tarpaper and the open sky. Emily stayed distant and cool.

"I think touching somebody's body, well, I take it seriously, it's so personal. Sometime I get afraid of being abandoned. I like being with you Lila, like I said, but I'm not sure which way every friendship should go."

Lila watched Emily consider whether she should be her lover or not. She watched her have a thought, decide to articulate it and then do so.

"You know I'm not sexually adventurous. I'd rather not have sex and wait for something important and good for me to happen. You seem to have a lot of girlfriends, or at least try to, like you're not worried about being thwarted. How do you handle sexual fantasies about so many different people at once?"

"I always need to have some image in my head. Sometimes I feel like a certain kind of sex, then I look around to see what's out there."

Listening to her own words made Lila consider that she might actually be crass, promiscuous, coarse and in every way stupid. It was just at that moment that Emily abruptly put her face to Lila's breasts and started to kiss them. She put her face into Lila's lap and caressed her bare, hairy legs. This time Lila knew that Emily's cunt lived in her breasts and she looked at them, smelled them, felt their textures dry and wet, pressed her nipples, flattened them with her tongue and forgot that a few minutes before she had felt like a complete jerk.

"I love breasts," Emily said and Lila felt so close to her that she saw a glow of flush and neon light vibrating around Emily's face, like she was enchanted or emanating power. Lila wanted to talk while they were touching, to drown Emily in mush, to tell her how beautiful it was to make love with her.

"Lila, are you falling asleep?"

"No, no sorry, I just got lost in feeling you."

"Because I want to have sex, so wake up." She laughed out loud.

"Okay," Lila said, grinning, "Let's have sex."

But first, they stopped to share a cigarette, naked on the rooftop. Sitting together, they both reached over and felt each other's wetness while Emily smoked. Lila sat behind her, easing her into her arms, holding Emily's head on her breasts.

While they watched the night lights of the city, the red, white and blue Empire State Building, Lila reached down into Emily's cunt.

"Have you every been touched like this before, while you were smoking a cigarette?" she asked.

"No. Why?"

"Because of the suspense," Lila said and stroked Emily's clitoris around and around while the ash burned. As the smoke went up in a straight line into the sky, Lila held Emily's breast, feeling each duct of her large red nipple. Emily smiled holding that glowing cigarette, moved and quietly came, curling up relaxed and natural.

Later, after different kinds of sex and feelings, Emily was so soft that Lila kept thinking as she watched her, *I want to be close to this woman*.

Morning on the roof began at five-thirty when the sun suddenly and brutally came pounding down over the still-tired refugees from hot crowded apartments, starting the day off grimy and stale. They woke up and Emily's affection was gone again. Lila could have taken a shower and sucked Emily's breasts all morning but Emily went off to do something, leaving Lila sitting there sweating on the roof, watching the city get ready for another sweltering day.

TWENTY-FIVE

Coney Island still looked the way it had always looked. There were crowds of poor people in tacky clothing, thousands of screaming children and an amusement park becoming more and more fantasy-provoking in its imposing decline. Only, when Emily and Lila walked the boardwalk that Sunday afternoon, the poor people were Caribbean and Greek and Russian and East Asian and Hispanic. They sold *cerveza fría* and cooked crabs, freshly caught off the pier from the filthy ocean water.

Lila had finally found a lover who could out-distance her. A lifetime of playing it cool had not prepared her for the on-again off-again affections of Emily Harrison. Lila didn't like couples and she didn't want to know what her girlfriends were doing all the time, but, when she was hanging around with someone, she liked for them to be emotionally present. That didn't seem unreasonable. She liked to touch and kiss and play and say how much she liked being with them and how wonderful it had been the night before when that someone made love to her with her mouth, asking first,

"Lila, do you mind if I eat you out?"

Emily, however, who had spent her life moving in and out of

intimacy, was, by habit or caution, on the reserved side. Lila, feeling stymied, stared out at the Atlantic Ocean, picturing herself turning to mush, a nerd, a namby-pamby, a pansy.

When they got off the F train back from the beach, Emily asked,

"Do you want to come over?"

"Yeah," Lila answered, not quite sure of what she was expected to say. "I mean, as long as you don't think we've been spending too much time together or anything."

"Listen Lila, if you're going to sleep with me, you have to be my friend," Emily responded, appearing taller than Lila had ever noticed before, "You have to come and go as you please. You have to be a little more butch and not keep asking me if I want to be with you or not."

Lila swallowed her pride and went over to Emily's, took a shower and fell asleep naked on the bed while Emily sat on the floor sewing one of her creations. Hours later, waking up from a sleep, deep only as an escape from embarrassment, Lila felt Emily come sit by her feet. By this time, Lila knew enough to understand that Emily was not going to lie down beside her, put her delicious arms around her and whisper all the ways that she was going to make love to her. So, Lila took off Emily's clothes and they licked each other's vaginas, more for the fact of doing it than for a sexual feeling. Lila took Emily in her arms, and made love to her in a close, old-fashioned way.

"Lila, I'm worried that I'm not giving you an orgasm."

Lila found both the content and timing of this statement slightly surprising but she had already noticed that she and Emily saw identical situations with completely different eyes.

"I've been celibate for so long Lila, I'm not used to making love. When I think about this, about being with you, I think it's a good thing. We have a good sexual relationship, but I don't feel at all sentimental about it. This is something fun we can do together, but it has to keep that cutting edge of hostility so that it doesn't get boring."

"Sure," Lila said, thinking that if she tried to understand

totally Emily's rapidly changing moods and perceptions, she wasn't going to make any progress at all. "Now, how do you feel about having your asshole touched?"

"What do you mean? Putting your fingers in it? No, that sounds painful."

"I was thinking more about licking and sucking."

"That sounds alright," Emily said, "but not anything in it. Since I was raped, I can't stand anything inside me at all."

There was sand all over the bed.

"Sometimes Lila, I can't stand for certain people to even touch my breasts. What about you? What do you like?"

"Oh, everything. I don't care. Whatever you want to do is fine with me."

At this Emily laughed and laughed, pushing down on Lila's cunt just to check her out clinically. Then she made love to Lila, who helped, telling her where to put her hands and when and how fast, like they were making love to Lila together.

"You know Emily, I don't expect you to be the greatest lover I ever had. Just do what you want. Sometimes I make love to you with my mouth for you, and sometimes it's for me. I just feel a need for that shot of saltiness on my tongue. I don't care if it's not always the precisely correct motion. I like it when you move around. It makes me wonder what you're going to do next and I get turned on by thinking that that's what you want to do."

Since, by that time, it was late Sunday night and Emily had to be up by six to go to the factory the next day and then had to sew costumes for the Inn's new show all the next evening, they walked to the corner of Saint Mark's Place.

"Good-bye," Emily kissed her. "Come see me."

She kissed Lila again, smiling. "Call me even if you just want to talk." They kissed, surrounded by the late weekend throng. "Really darlin', don't lose touch with me." They kissed, they kissed and parted.

"You should be ashamed of yourself," Lila heard a male voice sputter from the crowd as she ran towards her home.

TWENTY-SIX

The office was so hot, Lila's sweat was dripping into the new electronic typewriter and she was afraid she would electrocute herself. Fed up with the glare of fluorescent lights, Vicki, the office manager, suggested they go out on the PATH train to her mother's house, pick up the car and some plants and drive back to the city. Vicki and her five-year girlfriend Beverly had recently moved from Jersey to Harlem as a way of being in Manhattan and still being around Black people.

Lila and Vicki's friendship had gone down some rocky paths. Like when Vicki got political and Lila tried to get political. They would sit and rap and think about everything in a new way. Sometimes it felt to Lila that she was on the border of earth-shattering revelations. Other times she wondered if this wasn't just another in a life-long series of mind-fucks.

"Have you ever made love with a woman of color?" Vicki asked.

"Well, no."

"That's what I mean," Vicki had said, disgustedly lighting another cigarette. "You white women who claim to support our movement, but you won't let a woman of color into your bed."

Lila didn't quite know what to think. Maybe Vicki had a

point. Why hadn't she ever come on to a woman of color? Of course, no woman of color had ever come on to her either. But then again, so fucking what? That wouldn't prove anything. Men slept with women all the time and they still didn't understand them.

Then Vicki became a macrobiotic. "Macroneurotic" Lila called it. Lila could just sit for hours watching Vicki eat her concoctions out of little plastic containers during lunch. She always ate a lot and fast as if it was the most delicious thing she had ever tasted.

"What's that Vick?"

"Want some?"

"What is it?"

"Miso-tahini spread on rice cakes."

"Oh." Lila could never get used to the fact that those rice cakes were really food. They tasted like a mixture of styrofoam and nothing.

But Vicki got awfully healthy looking, she lost a lot of weight and stopped smoking and stopped drinking and stopped eating dairy, meat, sugar, wheat and eggs.

"Lila," she moaned one afternoon, "I'm bored. I want a corned beef sandwich," and another chapter was over.

Lately Vicki had been trying to figure how to get out of her relationship with Beverly, which meant that she and Lila could drop the discourse for a while and just hang out, talking about women.

"The other day, my brother came over," Vicki said, "and I told him Beverly and I weren't getting along. He asked me if I was worried that she was going to leave me and I said, *Shit no, I'm worried that she'll never leave me.* I asked her to move out and the next thing she did was put in shelves. She doesn't want to go."

"Poor you," Lila said, teasingly. "You've got what most people in the world spend their whole lives trying to find, a devoted lover who will stay with you always. Life's tough."

"That's easy for you to say, Lila Futuransky," answered

Vicki, smiling and playing with her dreds, "'cause you're not hooked. Wait till that Emily girl gets a grip on you, it'll all be over so fast, you won't know what hit you."

They walked outside to the store to get some Doritos and two Cokes, past all the well-kept lawns and new cars lining the affluent Black neighborhood.

"Everyday I see a woman who's, well you know, sexy, fine legs or such, and I'd rather sit alone in a room and think about them than be eaten out by Beverly in a black bodice and whip. Maybe she'll get a girlfriend, I keep hoping. I tell her to go out with other people and if I hear that someone has a crush on her I invite them over for dinner. Oh Jesus."

They got in Vicki's car and started the drive past Elizabeth and Newark back to the city. They sang along with the radio for a while, but they didn't know any of the same songs so then they started talking about their grandmothers. Vicki's had worked the land in Louisiana, Lila's worked the land in Lithuania. Both of their moms used to take them to the library to read books. Both of their moms freaked out when they got new ideas from the books they read. Both had inherited remnants of poverty that they were the first generation to avoid.

"You know, one thing I retain from my grandmother," Vicki said, "is her thing about aluminum foil. I can afford aluminum foil, but just like when she came up to live with us in Jersey, I still save every teeny-tiny scrap and stick it in my drawer."

"It's wild how that stuff stays with you," Lila agreed. "My one grandmother was a peasant in Russia, destitution level. But life is so strange, one day she was eating potatoes in the Motherland and fifty years later she was watching color TV in New Jersey. But even when she had some bucks, she still added rice to stretch her chopped meat. My other grandmother was from Austria where things were alright for Jews. Her family was doing okay and had pretty high expectations. After the First World War they lost it all, had to come here and she worked in a laundry in Brooklyn for the rest of her life. But you know, that woman always had cream in her coffee."

At that moment two Van Halen fans drove by in a dirty white Chevy. One leaned out the window in Lila and Vicki's direction and shouted,

"Suck my cock you Black bitch."

They sat in silence for a minute.

"You take one step into America and look what happens," Vicki said, and then hummed to herself. "At least that's one way of looking at it." She snapped on the radio again and they listened to the interference as they drove through the Holland Tunnel. But by the time the car came up at Canal Street the incident was filed away along with the others and they were chattering like normal again. Scores of Chinese boys were waving at the cars, selling firecrackers for the Fourth of July. They were hawking and smoking, trying to look tough, like Rocky, with rolled up t-shirt sleeves holding hard packs of Marlboros, puffing out their chests.

"Oh no," Vicki said, "I hate the Fourth of July. Between the bombs and the flags, it's too American for me. Even uptown it sounds like a war is going on. I'm going camping this year, to get away from that red, blue and *white*."

Vicki dropped Lila off on Third Avenue instead of taking her to her door because Lila just needed to take a look at everything again. She passed the Polish butcher and the Korean fruit stands and the Chinese take-out and the Arab deli and the Greek coffee shop and the East Asian newsstand and the Jewish bakery. She realized that she had been getting lost in the world of romance and hadn't been looking at things as closely as she usually did. She'd been preoccupied with love and missed out on enjoying the beauty of the Lower Eastside everyday. Plus, she hadn't been thinking about Jack or tripping the streets or imagining adventures. It was like waking up when you've slept all day and you know it's night, but you don't know which one.

Then she remembered to run upstairs and turn on the radio right away because Lacy was being interviewed at that very moment.

"I'd like to welcome our listening audience to another episode of *Write-On America*, a program funded by the National Endowment for the Arts. Today we are pleased to have as our guest, Miss Lacy Burns, a Black woman poet who many people believe, and I agree, is destined to be the next Lorraine Hansberry. Tell us Miss Burns, you have a young son, am I right?"

"Yes, Kwame, and he's listening right now. Can I say hello? Hello, Kwame."

"Charming. And, how do you, a single mother, find time to hold down a job, raise a son and write poetry?"

"I am not a single mother. I have a husband. His name is Arthur. He's a painter."

"Oh I see. I'm sorry, that's what's written on this paper. There must have been a mistake in the research department. Anyway, let us move on to the next question. I assume that you have been heavily influenced by Nikki Giovanni."

"No, not really."

"I ask you that because I would like for you to talk to our audience about how you view poetry as a tool for social change."

"I don't know really. I don't know how many people read poetry and those who do. . . well. . . I don't know how many of them will be motivated to social action from reading about my son or my garden."

"Oh I see. Well, Miss Burns, that's very interesting. May I call you Lacy?"

"Why not?"

"Lacy, I enjoyed your first book a great deal and I'm excited to hear that your new one will be out this fall. The aspect of your work that I find the most inspiring is the brilliant way in which you capture the vernacular. How long did it take you to develop a voice rich with the natural rhythms of the streets?"

"Actually, that's just the way me and my friends talk."

Lila turned off the radio and poured herself a glass of milk. Everyone she knew or encountered had their own particular reality but what they all shared was a common difficulty with keeping to it in the face of mounting adversity.

TWENTY-SEVEN

There was Solomon on the stoop deep in conversation with a tall Black man in a Malcolm X t-shirt. "By Any Means Necessary" was printed across his chest.

"Hey Solomon," Lila called out.

"Lila, Lila, I am glad to see you. This is my friend Jonathan. Tell her what you just told me Johnny. This is Lila. Tell her."

Solomon took out a Players and put on a serious expression.

"There were about ten fellows come by to look at your building today. You better watch out. That landlord of yours is trying to sell it. He's asking seven hundred thousand dollars."

"For this piece of shit? He only paid sixty thousand two years ago. The speculation going on around here is unreal. There's mice, roaches, a leaky roof, the windows don't fit the frame so the wind blows through, the floorboards are coming up in spots."

"You know it, you know it." Solomon shook his head.

"You had better watch out. The new landlord's gonna want to double your rent roll right away, just to start to cover costs. You know Mister Pilinero, the old Italian in apartment four?"

"Yeah?"

"The old guy got pneumonia and went into the hospital last

week. This morning his apartment was advertised for rent in the paper for twelve hundred dollars a month and the man ain't even dead yet."

"Twelve hundred dollars! I earn half of that in a month."

"Well, you'd better watch your ass Lila. They gonna be turning off the heat, robbing your apartment, refusing to make repairs."

"Twelve hundred dollars," she repeated, "I can't get over it. What kind of rich person would want to spend twelve hundred dollars a month to live here, with us?"

"There ain't gonna be no *us* by the time they move in. That's where the master plan comes in." Jonathan was pleased because now he had an opening where he could launch into his *master plan* theory.

"This is landlord city, Lila, landlord city." Solomon was rocking back and forth, drawing deeply and pensively on his cigarette.

Lila's landlord was a notorious scum. A Hassid from Brooklyn, he claimed that the tenants had formed an association because they were anti-Semitic.

"Your building is owned by a rich synagogue," Jonathan said. "There's five millionaire rabbis and they own practically the whole block."

"Hey Jonathan, let's not get carried away with Jewish conspiracy theories please, because I really want to like you. Let's just say it's one lone snake."

"Five rabbis, I tell you, and they're all millionaires, every last one. Yep, you'd better watch your ass."

"This is landlord city," Solomon said again, his stetson pulled low over his forehead. "One hundred and fifty percent landlord city."

As soon as Lila got upstairs the phone rang. It was Isabel Schwartz calling from a pay phone.

"Ms. Subways, what are you doing this very minute? We've got to go over to the 8BC Club right away to see Jeff Weiss and Dorothy Cantwell. Come on buddy, two people who are actually good artists. Let's go."

So, Lila jumped. First there was 8BC and then there was Jeff Weiss, two mutually exclusive commodities co-existing in the same category of East Village theatre. The club was a renovated farmhouse on one of the most decimated blocks in New York City, Eighth Street between Avenues B and C. In fact, it was essentially one of the only living structures on the entire street, smack in the middle of a lot of smack. But, once through the unmarked doors, it was packed with young punkettes, NYU students and bisexuals, all who had descended on the defenseless neighborhood.

As for Jeff Weiss, he was another story altogether. The man was known as "the world's greatest actor" and if there was such a person it probably was him, plus he had a mythology to prove it. He did shows. He didn't care about reviews. He didn't care about grants. He barely cared if he had an audience. When you got a chance to see him in action, there might be five other people in the theatre because of his refusal to advertise, but one of them might be Susan Sontag or Meredith Monk, someone who thinks they know what's good. Or so the rumors went. Only a few people really understood the mastery of this crazy, aging writer, director and actor. His inspiration was as carefully sculpted as his pectorals, the latter the result of years of supporting himself at construction or working out on a Nautilus, whichever image appealed to your imagination. Those stories made the myth and the myth made the man. Jeff Weiss won an Obie, the off Broadway version of an Oscar, but he gave it back, and then he won it again, and gave that one back too. He was asked to sit on the board of a powerful grant-giving organization, but he refused.

"I wouldn't take your money and I certainly won't give it away."

What's more, he was good. Isabel and Lila were in ecstasy. Plus, for the same admission price they got Dorothy Cantwell, the woman who could play any part that Jessica Lange or Sissy Spacek got. A world-class actress. Another underground hero, custom-made for the give-it-all approach of Jeff Weiss.

Isabel and Lila slapped down their five dollars, and put in seventy-five cents each to split a beer, waiting for the scene to begin. First, though, Jeff had to step out into the empty club, and vigorously shake hands with Lila, Isabel and the three other people there that night. His words were so sincere.

"It's great to see you, really great to see you."

But his expression looked right through them as though he was talking to a mirror. That's because he was in fantasy land and he would bring them there too, soon enough. But first the flashlights. Everyone got one, to provide the lighting and then he shouted "One, Two, Three, Go" and they went.

In the first scene of the show Jeff did a moment between two men having sex with each other at The Saint Mark's Bath. He played both parts to perfection. The second scene was called "Connie Visits His Sister In A Psychiatric Hospital Two Days Before Her Suicide On Christmas." There was no introduction. Jeff yelled out "One, Two, Three" again and suddenly he and Dorothy took everyone to that place with all its futility and starkness. For the next seven minutes, the audience was absorbed and transported until, "One, Two, Three," it was the next scene. This time Jeff's character visited his best friend Izzy, the lesbian, played by Dorothy, who was drunk and lonely because she hadn't had a woman all winter. In eleven short minutes, the audience believed and understood Izzy's hunger, and the tender and reserved friendship between the two. And so the show went on.

Lila and Isabel were sure that they had just seen a masterful moment of human creativity. The three other people in the place agreed.

Walking home through Tompkins Square Park in the mud, Isabel had something on her mind.

"Tell me Miss Subways, is it possible to do the work for what it is, ignore the Arts Mafia, the critics and the scene and the grants, and still retain your social sanity, without having to be an outcast too?"

"Somehow, I don't think so. I can't articulate why. I just have this sense that something about doing the work makes a person lose their mind. Normal people can't live without approval for so long. What I can't figure out is whether that's a benefit or a disadvantage."

"That reminds me," Isabel said, "I think I'm getting fired from Burger Heaven, so I'm on the look-out for a new waitressing job. Let me know if you hear of anything. I tried some of those new places in the neighborhood like The Art Cafe and The Zen Cafe you know, those up-scale quiche spas with their endives. They'll never hire me. All the waitresses are punky or New Wave or Old Wave, or whatever wave is coming in at high tide, if you catch my drift. In other words, you have to be in style to be in servitude and let's face it, I'm out. I think I could end up with an attitude like Jeff Weiss, but am I talented enough to justify it?"

They walked on a few more blocks, Lila remembering that look in Dorothy Cantwell's eyes. At any given moment during the performance, the audience could look into her eyes and know that she believed everything that she was saying. It was reassuring somehow, to see true sincerity once in your life, even if it was on stage. *I wonder if we really have visions,* Lila thought, *or just a lot of energy.*

She was too inspired to go home now, so leaving Isabel at the edge of the neighborhood, Lila crossed Fourteenth Street and walked up to Kitty's girlfriend's apartment on Central Park South, just to take a peek at how the other one percent lives. Kitty would be good for a discussion on this topic. The girl had gone from rags to riches and would probably be back in rags before Labor Day. She'd gone uptown for a woman and was on her way back for the theatre and the girls, girls who were usually broke.

The apartment looked out over the park. When Lila walked into Kitty's lobby, the doorman stopped her immediately. First he made a phone call. Then he handed her a little slip of paper and punched for the elevator, which contained yet another little man. He pushed the button and accompanied Lila to Kitty's floor. He waited, watching suspiciously as she walked down the hallway, which was decorated in a late-Marriott hotel motif. Kitty greeted her at the door of her pad.

The place wasn't very large, but it had everything. Her girlfriend had a computer and a xerox machine and a cable TV hook-up with HBO in color and a stereo, Beta-Max and central air-conditioning.

"What does your girlfriend do again?"

"She's in the Mob. She has legitimate holdings like stocks and interests and various businesses and real estate, and then she has back room gambling and high interest loans. All I own are my clothes."

They looked out the window. Hansom cabs were waiting for rich tourists to step out of The Plaza for a late evening buggy ride.

"There's some government guy who lives next door," Kitty said. "Whenever he has dinner parties, the secret service closes off the whole block. I think he runs the UN or something like that."

By her own definition Kitty was married. She married for love, but into money and attributed the looming divorce to the mysterious ways of the rich.

"It's a different kind of butch/femme than we know about downtown," she confided to Lila, "where people change their mind every week about which one they are. Up here the butches sit around the table and make business deals while the femmes sit next to them. Sometimes I feel like jumping up on the table and screaming I WANT. But, I don't know what it is I want."

They stared at a silent Willie Nelson on the HBO, his face turning lavender. At the same time Marvin Gaye's last record spun on the stereo. When people accumulate a lot of gadgets, Lila noted, they like to keep them all on at the same time, just to glance at once in a while.

"You know I come from a real small town upstate. Two of

my sisters have never even been to the city. My dad worked at the state prison and sent five kids to Catholic school on an annual salary of seventeen thousand dollars. No one is supposed to even think of leaving home unless it's to get married. My mother came down here once, on the bus, just to see this place. She sniffed around, touching everything, wouldn't sit down. She couldn't figure out if I was a high-class prostitute or had just made a good match."

Kitty was a little better dressed than Lila remembered. She had on make-up and a few more grey hairs.

"Maybe I should just come back home to the East Village and pick up where I left off. I could get a job hanging lights for twenty dollars a day and handing out circulars or something."

"Kitty, it's not as easy as you think. The neighborhood has changed. The apartment situation is wildly out of control."

"I don't need an apartment. All I've got are my clothes. There's always someplace to stay."

"I don't know," said Lila, looking at the marble bathroom and the Cuisinart. "No moving around like the old days. New York is closed. Pretty soon it's just going to be bag ladies and rich people stepping over them, plus a few old timers hiding out in their rent-controlled apartments hoping no one's gonna notice. For everybody else, the city is closed."

They were quiet for a minute, not knowing where to look, till they both sat down at the same time and started staring at Willie Nelson, moving his lips.

TWENTY-EIGHT

Gay Pride Week was ushered in one rainy Sunday afternoon outside a bagel restaurant on Christopher Street. Emily and Lila sat there eating when sounds of sweet voices, three part harmonies carrying light church tunes, floated in off the street. Outside a group of happy young people were clapping hands in the rain, singing. They linked dripping wet arms to sway in unison to the verses of *I Believe In Him, Praise The Lord* and the ever popular *Amen*. It was the gay Christians from the Metropolitan Community Church holding a gay fellowship meeting to celebrate Gay Holy Week on Sheridan Square, right in front of the spot where Emily and Lila were eating cinnamon raisin bagels with scallion cream cheese.

Lila was staring very intently at Emily's face. She'd been doing that more and more lately, just looking at her. Sometimes Lila could see it made Emily so shy she would literally sweat, fanning herself with a paper plate like a Southern belle, like Blanche Dubois recovering her composure. Lila found Emily exquisitely beautiful. Not with the kind of glamour that made men gasp when Marlene Dietrich entered the room, but a more demure, quiet attractiveness that you had to take your time to see. She reached out to brush Emily's hair away from her forehead, touching it to make sure she was really there and once again Lila's gaze came to rest on the thin, deliberate scar just above Emily's hairline. Yes, that certainly was a mystery.

"Emily, I know I asked you this a few times before but I don't remember if you answered me or not. Where did that scar come from?"

"I don't know. It happened when I was very little."

"Didn't you ever ask your mom?"

"I think I asked her once. She didn't remember either."

"Your own mother didn't remember how you got a four-inch slice across your scalp? I find that hard to believe. Maybe she did it."

"Could be."

"But Emily, aren't you even the least bit interested? This could hold the key to some long repressed childhood trauma, unleashing waves of insight."

"I already have enough traumas to think about. Let's discuss the movie."

They had just seen *A Streetcar Named Desire*. There was Vivien Leigh as Blanche, with her old-fashioned master acting style, and Marlon Brando being something exciting that wasn't exactly Stanley Kowalski. They watched this movie and both agreed that the message was too sad. It said that life is a trap and anyone who tries to create their own magic will be destroyed. That wasn't Lila and Emily's message. Or, take Stanley. A guy who gives something sweet in bed and brutalizes all the rest of the day is supposed to be romantic. That wasn't Lila and Emily's message either. They knew they couldn't create three characters like Blanche and Stella and Stan, but they knew something Tennessee Williams forgot. Even when life is sad, people still have a good time. That's what these women and all their friends were trying to say everyday, in their different ways.

Emily and Lila were both inspired by their growing communication with each other, which had to do karmicly, Lila was convinced, with Gay Pride Week, a special and rare joy surpassing any other holiday including birthdays. Each year's festivities had their own special character since gay people as a group change very quickly and things become dated, then nostalgic, then historic, in a matter of months.

As Helen Hayes had put it,

"Today's kitsch is tomorrow's collectible."

Lila's first step into mass pride was a festival in Washington Square Park sometime in the late seventies. It was a hard time for Lila, working nights at the Baskin Robbins on Seventh Avenue South, across the street from a Puerto Rican gay juice bar. The guys used to come in really stoned at three in the morning and order pineapple sundaes with peanut butter ice cream and extra marshmallow sauce. Lila was eating ice cream for three meals a day, trying to survive on $2.75 an hour. So, when Bette Midler, fresh from The Continental Baths, stepped out on that stage and sang *You've Gotta Have Friends*, Lila's gay heart just melted. *Wow, somebody wants to be our friend.* Then the drag queens came on stage for their moment in the daylight. Drag queens are the barometer of gay time, meaning different things in different sociological moments, but persisting, nevertheless. At some point, early in the gay movement, they meant freedom. Faggots knew how important it was for a man to be able to walk down the street wearing a dress and tried to articulate this to the rest of the world. By the end of the decade, however, it took on other meanings. The original movement dykes were in serious negotiations with the boys and didn't take kindly to cocksuckers getting laughs by pretending to be women. Especially when their "women" were siliconed versions of every straight man's fantasy feline. A few women, in the stylish butch look of the moment, jumped on the stage and took over the microphone, in the stylish butch move of the moment, and announced "No more. From now on, this is *Lesbian* and Gay Pride Day."

The next march that Lila attended went off smoothly enough as everyone walked, sang, cheered and smiled in the hot sun up Fifth Avenue. When they got to Central Park, however, there were women telling women to turn right for the women-only rally, and men telling men to turn left to see Patti Smith and Lou Reed. Lila turned left. Patti was great.

As in every other aspect of life, the eighties had brought the doldrums to gay pride. Things had gotten frighteningly mellow. Instead of starting off the march with Salsa-Soul Sisters Third World Women Incorporated, the onlookers were greeted by the Gay Community Marching Band, in their maroon uniforms, John Philip Sousa tunes and American flags. Instead of queens, there was the Greater Gotham Business Council. Old timers hung on though, waiting for the tide to turn back again so swish wouldn't be so embarrassing. Like Rollerina, for example, a real trooper. He was a six-foot-tall queen in a prom dress, sparkle glasses, roller skates and a magic wand, blessing every contingent.

Eating her bagel, staring at Emily, Lila was convinced somehow that the old feeling of joy would come back in 1984. There was a need around town for lots of love and silly tenderness. Ronald Reagan and the AIDS crisis had sobered up people to the fact that the long haul was far from over. Even though each person had their own personal concept of what needed to be hauled and where to.

Isabel Schwartz had the idea to change the name to Lesbian Shame Week with thousands of dykes crawling down Fifth Avenue. She was even proposing "Lesbian Shame Awards."

"It's a new concept in anti-trend t-shirts," she said.

"Anti-trend t-shirts" were Isabel's code words for things that were fashionable because they were horribly ugly or in extremely bad taste.

So, Lila sat finishing her bagel thinking about all these crazy images and how they came together into one real thing that actually made sense, which was their community, and realized the nuances were only identifiable from the inside out. Still, she was inspired and looked Emily right in the eye, smiling.

"You know," she said, after all those thoughts, "I think something sweet is in the air."

TWENTY-NINE

Lila Futuransky's key to relationships had always been knowing how to properly exert restraint. She was considering this question on the way home from having spent three great days with someone she was just beginning to love and feel close to. According to her theory, the natural response on the fourth day was to want to see them again, immediately. This impulse, she always resisted. Lila was a firm believer that it was important to hold out until the fifth day, just to make sure it wasn't filled with leftover expectations from the fourth one. The sixth day was just right for some pleasant contact like a note or brief lunch visit. Just to let them know that they were still on your mind. That way things stayed pleasant, unpredictable and most of all, without desperation. But, that Emily tricked Lila by calling her on the Monday after the Sunday and saying that she wanted to see her simply because she wanted to.

Lila sat down on the stoop of the La Mama Annex on Fourth Street across from where Emily was house-sitting. She had a packet of Drum tobacco and a jar of grapefruit juice to pass the time until Emily came home from work. She watched the evening promenade of lovers strolling together, comforting each other, holding hands without talking, or deep in talk. It was pleasant to sit under Emily's window on a warm night thinking about her.

That girl was such a femme, she always wore her purse on the same shoulder. Once, Lila took her left arm by mistake and Emily asked her to stand on the other side.

"That's a femme," Lila said. "Never move the purse, just move the girl."

Then Lila giggled, thinking that Emily would love hearing something like that said about herself, giving her a place in all the sexuality of this world. But instead, Emily pushed her face into a pout, like a silly girl hurt by a silly thing.

"Don't be angry at me baby," she said quietly. "I love you so much."

"I'm not angry at you Emily."

"I know Lila, it's just that I've had this fantasy for such a long time that one day I would have a girlfriend who loved me very deeply and one day we would be having a petty disagreement and I would say *Don't be angry with me baby, I love you so much.* And now it's come true. I'm so happy."

And her face became one huge smile. Lila saw that expression again when Emily came home that night and found Lila sitting on the steps waiting for her. They sat there together laughing, entertaining each other, watching a Puerto Rican storekeeper and his wife dance outside their bodega across the street. They talked and touched each other's faces. Lila kissed Emily's forehead and they leaned back against the building to soak in the beauty on the street.

"Emily, when you were a kid, what did you want to be when you grew up?"

"A theatre designer or a fashion designer."

"I'm very impressed, Emily. I wanted to be a stewardess."

When Lila thought about Emily as a child, she saw her on a lifetime path of visual problems, spatial concerns, angles, shapes and color matching. Her descriptions were rarely anecdotal or populated. She had almost no stories about people. Instead she talked about the way the light was in the morning, the sound of the sea, or how her own body smelled in one place as opposed to another. They climbed the dirty stairs past the "Junkies Keep Out" sign and sat on the fire escape with the radio playing in the background.

"It's pretty strange spending so much time at the Inn when I'm designing or making things. It's usually late at night and people who can't sleep or don't know what to do with themselves stop by just to talk. Sometimes I feel too busy and sometimes I'm terribly shy. You talk to people all the time too, Lila. How do you deal with it?"

"I just tell them my most intimate thoughts."

"And they never bother you again."

"Right."

They felt like making love, but Emily wanted to wash her body first.

"I need to be clean for my girlfriend."

Lila sat on the edge of the tub watching Emily in the shower. She scrubbed her nails, getting out all the ink and paint from work. She shaved under her arms and carefully cleaned her asshole and vagina. She powdered and perfumed herself while Lila thought to herself that scents last as long as memory.

"What's the matter, don't you want to bring all the muck and mire of your existence into my body?"

"Oh Lila, I didn't know you were such an earth mother."

They both laughed loudly at that one, as Emily dried herself off, and then, on impulse, she pulled Lila's shirt right off her shoulder.

"I needed to taste your nipples right away," she said. And then she sat back for a while as Lila tasted hers.

"You get so much pleasure from your breasts Emily, it's beautiful to me."

"That's why sometimes I can't stand to be touched there, by certain people I mean."

"It's too close."

"Yes, that's it."

314

Lila leaned over and knew, for that moment, they were that close. Lightly, sexily with care and tenderness, they made love with each other. Emily was becoming a better and more confident lover. She would come up from Lila's orgasms smiling because she knew exactly what she had given her. Emily would purr and stretch, showing off like a proud, sleek cat.

The next morning, they left the house at half past six. On the way to Emily's factory, in a moment of silence, Emily grabbed Lila's hand. The city was already starting to broil and the two women's faces were damp from sweat. Emily stopped walking, right in front of the construction site where new condominiums were going up on the corner. She turned to Lila and said,

"You can sleep with me whenever you want to. We'll try it. Come over whenever you feel like it."

And Lila was changed.

PART FOUR

THIRTY

Once again Lila cut out of work early. She knew that by virtue of her own misbehavior this period of employment would soon be terminated, but she didn't give a shit. By the age of eighteen she'd already been through thirty-three different jobs. Most of them had gotten boring by the second day.

"If you liked school, you'll love work," said a poster on her refrigerator. And one on her wall said, "Work: A prison of measured time." So, knowing it was a corrupt institution, she never felt guilty about sabotaging it in little ways. Like pouring powdered sugar into word processors, or misfiling information on people who owed money for things they shouldn't have to pay for in the first place, like rent. She even heard about a programmer who programmed a computer to pay out dividends to all the programmers, but that was too high-tech for Lila's personal taste.

She sat on a bench in Washington Square Park smoking a cigarette and enjoying the bright afternoon. Two men walked by. One was sort of Italian looking, beefy, in a polyester double-knit, a gold chain and a rhinestone stud in his ear. The other was a skinny, tired drug dealer.

"Just sit here a second man, I'll be right back," the dealer said as he ran off to negotiate with an equally skinny, tired guy sporting an AC/DC tattoo.

"You making a drug deal?" Lila asked because she felt like making conversation.

"Yep. Hey babe, lemme get one of your cigarettes."

"Sure."

They sat and talked about how nice the weather was and how much easier it was to buy a nickel bag in the East Village than the West Village, because of all the undercover narcs.

"You know," Lila said, "I don't mean to deal in ethnic stereotypes or anything, but you look kind of like a cop yourself. Like, you're too healthy or something. I don't know why I said that. Maybe it's the earring."

"Why don't you tell him that," the guy said, good-naturedly pointing to the dealer. "He'd probably drop dead."

"No, I'm sure he knows better than me."

There was too much going on at the same time in that park to process it all. Junkies were dying, kids were racing skateboards up and down artificial lumps, called hills, chess players wildly hit clocks in games where speed was everything. She started to think about whether or not she had a roach buried at the bottom of her pocket that maybe she could light and get just a little high with this friendly guy. He probably had great stories. But, by that time, the dealer had returned, having made all the arrangements and Mister Polyester split without even saying goodbye. Lila finished her cigarette, watched the chess players and was on her way out when she realized that the skinny dealer and the guy with the tattoo were being led away in handcuffs by two additional undercover cops who had been posing as gay men cruising.

Lila stared, open-mouthed, at the guy who had smoked her cigarette. Her skin turned so cold she forgot who she was.

"You were right," he said, grinning ear to earring, and walked off towards Bleeker Street, satisfied at having done his duty once again. Lila, on the other hand, had come too close to something completely unnecessary and so headed straight for the nearest bar for a shot of anything.

It was a lonely bar that afternoon. One of the few remaining places on Bleeker Street where a regular person could afford to get drunk. The only other customer was Roberta, Muriel's girl-friend, in her usual forest green robes, moping under the color TV.

Lila just walked over and sat down very quietly. There was a silence of pure understanding between the two women, bal-ancing on bar stools. Lila told the whole story from beginning to end. Roberta didn't even ask one question.

"Cops," Roberta agreed, when Lila was through, "they'll never learn how to dress."

It started to get late after a while and the dreamy staleness of an old bar in the afternoon drifted away. By the time Lila got home, she remembered that she had a date that evening with Muriel, who had decided that they just had to go out with a gang of ex-patriate bourgeois Italians. She was being dragged along with them to a performance by someone from *Roma*, all because Tina was running the light board and had promised all her friends free tickets. Lila had to admit it was kind of nice to sit in a dark theatre surrounded by beautiful olive-skinned peo-ple with large blue or black eyes, rolling their tongues. Those Italians lean all over you, Lila noted. They touch you when they talk.

"Tina's so romantic," Muriel giggled in Lila's ear. "We were lying on the grass in Washington Square Park this afternoon making out, and she started to say *I will take you to the sands of Italy. I will make a bed of sand and make love to you by the waves at night*. Too much, no?"

"So that's why Roberta was in a bar alone this afternoon at about three o'clock."

"Yeah, three o'clock. What about Roberta?"

"Never mind."

Lila wanted to be with her own kind and left early, joining Sheena and Emily who were making plans for the Kitsch-Inn's contingent in the Gay Pride March. The year before, the Inn girls had become notorious for having walked the sixty blocks in prom dresses singing *Come on baby let the good times roll* over and over again. This year they were considering a march of mermaids.

"We could tie our feet together and hop all the way." Sheena said enthusiastically. "Helen Hayes can be the emcee and announce *These are the survivors of The Bermuda Triangle* when we get to the reviewing stand and no politicians are in it."

Lila didn't say anything, since she was still a novice when it came to the kitsch state of mind.

"What happened to our giant globe that said 'KITSCH' on it?" Sheena asked, obviously having moved on to a new concept.

"The mice ate it," Emily reported.

"Well, we can always go back to the original idea of being bathing beauties with machine guns. Now that would be nice."

"How about a float?" Lila suggested, suddenly feeling inspired, "A giant closet?"

"A closet?" Sheena asked. "Doesn't that sound a little grim?"

"Well, Isabel has been talking up this idea of Lesbian Shame Week."

Since no one could decide, they went to the former Polish Country-Western bar turned punk bar on First Avenue. The new owners changed the name to *Beirut* and decorated it with barbed wire. They hadn't gotten around to the juke box though, so the girls played *Ode to Billy Joe*, the Temptations and Santana, dancing around until a punk behind the bar turned on the TV, blasting a ball game.

"Has anyone seen Kitty recently?" Lila asked.

"Yeah," Sheena reported. "I went to visit her at her girlfriend's mansion on Fire Island. It's really beautiful there with ocean and beaches and hundreds of disco queens running around. Some of them are very hard to talk to because they don't know how to discuss anything. Kitty is spending a lot of time as a dresser for a drag show called *Viva Cherry Grove* about the history of Fire Island. The first scene has gay cavemen.

Then a gay George Washington sings *Don't Cry For Me Argentina*. She's crazy in a really great way. Remember last year when she turned The Inn into a church and we spent hours mashing Wonderbread to make the host?"

"Well, at least she gets a summer on Fire Island, which is more than I can see for the three baked apples sitting here." Lila often felt it was her duty to insert a sense of reality to these conversations.

"You'll see, wait until the march." Sheena was excited now. "New York faggotry and dykeness will come out in all its grandeur. Fifth Avenue will be ours. . ."

THIRTY-ONE

"**I** like it when you watch me eating you out," Emily said. "I know it sounds strange, but I like that you're absolutely sure of who is making you feel that way. I guess I want the most intimacy possible, even though the whole process makes me painfully shy. Sometimes it's like an evenly matched arm wrestle with myself to be able to look you fully in the eyes while I'm licking your cunt."

Lila, on the other hand, was turned on as much by the process as the act and was also entertained, especially at the sight of Emily's earnest nose poking out over her pubic hair. Plus, every once in a while, Emily would have trouble keeping her tongue going for very long and would take a tiny rest by sticking it out and moving her head back and forth to prevent lock jaw.

"There, that's better," Emily said, her face glistening. "I didn't eat my baby for three days and I was getting awfully hungry."

Then they hung out in bed until the conversation got serious, with Emily talking quietly about her own life. She saw it as a series of new places, aloneness and private rituals. Like stealing. She would go off by herself in whatever town her parents happened to have chosen for the moment, towards the local Penney's or Kresky's or Woolworth's, where she would carefully heist material, art supplies and, when available, good cloth. It was always something with which to make something else. Emily had cut every school she ever attended to sit in the various art rooms until, after trying out college for a minute, she fled university art studios for the safety of a room anywhere, where she could make whatever she wanted to, in silence.

First it was stealing, then it was leaving. She left because, as a child, she had to leave and because, as an adult, it was natural. She left when things were bad or boring or she was searching for a catharsis.

"Once I was angry at something and just took off in a bad way. I stopped at a rooming house sort of place because that's where my ride had dropped me off. I think it was a fight with my boyfriend, or something equally stupid. There was a bar on the ground floor of the house and all the locals used to come there to bore each other. One night, this one guy started talking to me. Quite a few times over that next week, he would come by to the bar and we would talk. Nothing revelatory, just conversation. Then, one night, he wanted to go out for a walk to the Seven Eleven, so I went along with it. We bought some cigarettes and walked back to the bar. Right before I went upstairs he said he wanted to show me something. It was a picture of Jesus. One of those three-dimensional postcards. He gave it to me. I held it for a minute, not knowing quite what he wanted and then he told me to turn it over. It was dark by then. Leaves and twigs were blowing around. The only light came from the Hamm's sign in the bar window. On the other side, Jesus was naked, with an erection, and a little girl was on her knees licking it. He laughed and laughed. All I could think was *You just had to be an asshole, didn't you*. It was the next night that I got raped."

Sometimes Lila would hold Emily in her arms after hours in a hot factory or after sweet loving and coming, and watch her sleep. Emily would sleep leaning against the wall with her arms over her head and the slope of her breast leading into the slope of her stomach, shining in the streetlight. Sometimes Lila would be making love to her playfully and kiss her so wetly, she'd lick her face.

"Don't do that," Emily would say, recoiling. "I don't mean anything against you, but please don't lick my face. When I was raped the first time he spit on my face. It's just not romantic for me, I'm sorry."

It was through making love with Lila that Emily showed more and more of her scars.

"Since then I try not to leave when things are bad." Emily's voice was very even, her pronunciation deliberate.

"It's taken on so much significance for me. I never know exactly why I go anywhere. People ask me that all the time, so I've learned that they need to hear a reason. But anything definite that I tell them is usually a lie. How can I explain what it's like to feel a new kind of weather for the first time to someone who lived with their parents until they were thirty? When people ask me, I just don't know what to say."

By this time they were wide awake and sat, wrapped in blankets, eating some old rice from the refrigerator. They ate as differently as they thought. Lila was quick and noisy, Emily precise and measured.

From Lila's point of view, Emily had vowed to live differently and so she did. Lila hadn't vowed anything at all but had done the same. Yet, Lila could see that they each retained huge chunks of the lives that they had left behind. For herself, it was her arrogance, believing that she had to right to live her life exactly the way she wanted to, no matter how laid back she felt like acting. In Emily's manners she saw a legacy of well-bred generations, which Emily said she cared nothing for, and a learned grace that Lila adored. Emily claimed it bored her.

Even though Emily tried to deny it, Lila found that there were things about her own ways that seemed distasteful to Emily. Like when Lila would enter an apartment as though she lived there, and walked room to room, touching things, pulling books off the shelves. Or when her friends would yell and scream at each other and five minutes later be laughing together as if nothing had happened. There were other things too. Like the way Lila ate.

"Lila, I know this is going to sound really crazy and after I say it you can forget about it, but I just want you to know how I feel. You're always telling me to talk about things that are on my mind, instead of keeping them in, so I'm going to tell you this. Please don't chomp when you eat. It makes me feel sick. Don't be angry at me baby, I love you so much."

"Just call me Noam Chompsky," Lila replied, smiling, but from then on she carefully checked to make sure that her mouth was closed whenever she found herself eating in Emily's presence, and that task made her feel unusually tired.

THIRTY-TWO

Gay Day finally came. The sky was teasingly grey but everyone knew that it never rained on the Gay Pride March. Lila stepped off the RR train at Columbus Circle, and it all came back in a wave of color. Who needed the Rainbow Gathering? It was right there on the sidewalks of New York. Fifty thousand homosexuals flaunted it that day, each having gone through their own personal weird shit and wild struggles to be proud. Even though they waved brilliant banners of soft colors and balloons and danced in the streets to samba music, gays are a very, very tough people.

Lila started out in the back, walking double-paced down Fifth so she could take turns marching with each contingent. This was her annual opportunity to be the generic lesbian.

"It's okay to be gay," she said to a Greek man selling sodas to thirsty fairies for two bucks each, "that's the theme for today."

In her Nina Hagen t-shirt, she marched and sang, offered a "Happy Gay Day" to every queen and stopped to exchange kisses with anyone who yelled out "I love Nina Hagen."

Lila marched with the Gay Psychologists and the Gay Bankers, Gay High-Tech workers and Gay Catholics. She walked with Gay Harvard Alumni, and the Eulenspiegel Society who, along with their affiliate, Gay Male Sadomasochism Activists, led each other by leashes past Tiffany's. She stood strong with Mirth and Girth, gays who like fat men, Gay Zionists, Gay Anti-Zionists and Gay Non-Zionists. She skipped the Gay Cops. Lila got militant with Gay Youth, chanting, "'Two, Four, Six, Eight, How Do You Know Your Kids Are Straight?" She sat down with Gay Teachers to protest the Catholic War Veterans counter-demonstration at Saint Patrick's Cathedral. They were in uniform holding signs like "God Made Adam and Eve, Not Steve or Bruce." She cheered Grandmas for Gays and felt, yet again, overcome to the point of tears at the sight of Parents of Gays, with their handpainted signs, "We Love Our Gay Children." Lila boogied for blocks with a Latin percussion band surrounded by thousands of sweating faggots and dykes just dancing freely under the buildings of New York City. She sang *It's Raining Men* with the Gay Men's Chorus, screamed "US Out of Central America" with Black and White Men Together and chanted "Rainbow Power is on the Move" with the New Alliance Party. By the time she'd made it to the front of the march, where all the girls were, it was already Twentieth Street and time to relax with the smiling unaffiliated lezzies. One day a year they got cheered, just for being gay. These few hours of approval brought out the dignity and the beauty in each marching queer.

"Hey Helen." Lila ran up to Helen Hayes in all her bleached blonde self. "It's great to see you Helen. It's okay to be gay."

"Yeah, but only for today. Tomorrow back to the same old shit."

"Hi Lila."

"I don't believe we've met."

"Sure we have," said the attractive red-head in a purple lame evening gown. "I'm Nancy, remember? Helen's girlfriend."

"Oh my God, you've changed." Lila quickly recovered her composure. "Where's the green dragon tattoo and the axle grease?"

"Anything for a show," Nancy smiled, having proven one of

her many points.

They started walking together and Lila felt a little nervous somehow since she still had the feeling that, regardless of her change in hair color, Nancy liked to keep a close watch over things. The longer they walked, the closer Nancy got, until they were shoulder to shoulder as if some very serious and discreet conversation was about to take place. A little further on ahead Lila could see Emily in a pink bandana looking very gorgeous in her sleeveless denim jacket, on the back of which was written in matching pink letters, CONEY ISLAND BABY.

"I've heard about your latest romance," Nancy was saying, like it was some big secret. "On the grapevine. Emily told Helen that you two had been going out for a while and that she would take Helen's rejects anytime."

"That's nice."

"Tell me Lila, just between us. Does Emily know about you and Muriel?"

"Of course. But that's not a romance. That's just how Muriel and I are friends."

"Right, right," she said, nudging Lila rather sharply in the gut. "But, just between us, how do you handle two women at once, if you know what I mean?"

Emily and Helen looked so cute giggling and laughing together a few yards in front of them. Nancy wasn't bad, it was just that Lila had no idea of who Nancy was, and therefore couldn't imagine how to answer her questions. There were always those fuzzy areas to lesbian etiquette, like how intimate are you really with the girlfriend of someone you once tried to pick up?

"I'm only asking you this Lila, because Emily has been repressed for a long time about getting close to people and she deeply needs to be loved, but I don't want you to hurt her. Be sure not to hurt her."

"Okay, Nancy, since you brought it up, I promise not to hurt her. But really, I'm sure Emily can take care of herself. Besides, well, people always have oversimplified explanations for things."

"Well, have it your way," Nancy said, taken aback but keeping her stride. "Be responsible Lila, do you know what I mean by that? Always remember that the other person has feelings that you need to consider. That's all. I wasn't crazy about your tone of voice just now, but I'll let it pass."

Lila ran up to her Coney Island Baby and threw her arms around her. They were getting down to Christopher Street by this time, where the sidewalks were overflowing with screaming, cheering gay people of every color and degree of faggotry, waving and throwing kisses. Emily put her arms around Lila, holding her like she had never done before, hugging her waist like she was her one and only girlfriend on the streets of Gay Day USA. They ended up with the crowd by the Hudson River, leaning against a concrete divider on what was left of the Westside Highway, next to a platoon of cops with demo-duty and across the street from both the river and the Ramrod. They were transformed into two sixteen-year-old girls in cut-off t-shirts, making out by the highway on the edge of the city. Lila hung on to Emily's neck and kissed her face right there in front of all those cops, just the way girls in spandex french-kiss by the cigarette machine in every lesbian bar in America. Lila felt the power of that old street greaser attitude. This is my girlfriend and I have to honor and protect her. In return she will hold me openly in the street, sexy and daring. That was what Lila was thinking when the rain came and Emily took her home.

THIRTY-THREE

The next morning, like what was getting to be every morning, Lila got up with Emily at six, even though she herself didn't need to stagger into the office until ten. At first it was out of courtesy and then out of guilt at how hard Emily worked for her paycheck. But, after a while, it became a silent, groggy and pleasant habit. They would step into the shower together, each one yawning while the other stood under the meager faucet. Each one waited with a body full of soap, while the other rinsed off. Even after she was clean, Emily would stand absentmindedly in the shower waiting for Lila to finish. She just liked being next to her. After Emily put on her medium brown eyebrow pencil and Lila found her cigarettes, they would head off to breakfast. Coffee for Lila and coffee and an English muffin for Emily. It was the only thing in her life that she did systematically every morning, whenever possible.

"I'm not paying for this," Emily said that morning, "Because it's cold."

Even though Emily's zipper was held together by a safety pin, Lila thought she was seeing traces of her Republican blood.

"Oh, forget about it," Lila said.

Actually, Emily had no intention of carrying out her threat

because as soon as she said it, she didn't really care any more. Lila, however, had a different reaction.

"I've never been able to talk back to waitresses," she said. "I can't return things to stores. I have a problem when the culprit is your common man or woman on the street. I can cross police lines, but I can't send back a cold English muffin."

They politely paid their checks and Lila ate it anyway because it was simply too disgusting to waste food when so many people were starving on Ninth Street. Then Lila walked Emily to the RR and turned around towards home for a few more minutes of sleep before getting on the RR herself.

Whenever Lila put Emily on the train she would picture what Emily's day would be like at the factory. It was called the American Fabric Association, where Emily performed a variety of skilled physical labors forty to fifty hours a week for five dollars an hour. As a result of the long hours and low pay, the other workers were all Hispanic men with dubious green cards. Emily said that she probably could get a better paying job but she didn't really care that much. She wasn't sure of how to go about it and this one would do, she insisted, until she saved up enough money to take another trip.

At noon, the phone on Lila's desk rang. It was Emily.

"Oh Lila, my boss saw me at the march. He told me this morning. He said I looked pretty and happy. I feel so good, I'm ecstatic. I just wanted to tell you about it. I love you more than ever."

The office wasn't too busy so Lila let herself sit and replay in her mind a fantasy Emily had told her in her low smoky voice. It started with Emily cutting fabric. In her right hand she held a razor blade tightly and repeated long, straight strokes, like swimming, but over and over again. With each stroke she would get further and further into a dream of the day when she would take her love away to Hawaii, or Greece. Lila would like Hawaii, Emily said, out on the sand on Big Island. All you needed was some shelter for when it rained. The ground was so rich, the fruit just grew, everywhere. Emily would build a roof

for her baby and they'd lie on the sand and watch the water between the sand and the horizon. In all that blue Emily would
take Lila in her arms and make love to her on the white sand in
the open air, free, in the middle of the day and Lila would eat
her, watch the waves, suck the waves, stroke the sand and
Emily would look up at the sky, so exciting.

But Lila couldn't push Emily's other realities out of her mind.
At the same moment she could remember Emily's voice dragging out her stories after long days at work.

"*When are you going to go out with me?* Johnny asked me for
the tenth time."

"What did you say?" Lila had asked.

"I said *never.*" Emily imitated his whiny voice. "*When are you
going to give me your phone number?* NEVER. I like working with
Eduardo better than Johnny. Eduardo never asks me out. He
does ask a lot of other questions though. The other day he said
Emmie, look, my wife is selling Tupperware. And he handed me a
catalogue. I told him he had picked the wrong person. I don't
even own a plate. I don't even own a fork. *Not even a fork?* He
couldn't believe it." Emily was smiling by that time, as though
just having someone to tell this to made it better. "I told him
that I never cook. I don't know how. I eat all my meals in restaurants." She had looked Lila in the eye. "I'm sorry baby, I
promised myself that next time I'm going to tell him that my
girlfriend cooks for me, since it is true. That would be the only
dignified thing to do."

At four that afternoon Lila got another phone call at work.
Vicki gave her that "don't chatter so much on my time" expression. It was Emily again, but her voice was solemn and
heavy.

"It was all a joke," she said, almost crying. "Everyone was
saying to each other all day *I saw you at the march, maricon.* Only
I fell for it. I forgot to be careful one more time."

She sounded so upset, Lila decided to cut out early once
again, even though she knew it would probably be the last
straw. On the one hand she hated putting Vicki in this position,

since, as office manager, she would undoubtedly fire her. But, on the other hand, Lila didn't give a flying fuck if she got fired anyway. As long as she had keys in her pocket she would be okay. It was only when you had no keys that your life was definitely out of hand. Lila got on the subway. There was one car with all the windows closed and that was the one that all the New Yorkers on board flocked to, because closed windows usually meant air-conditioning. All the other cars were populated by nodded-out junkies and tourists.

Sitting on the subway, Lila was struck by a series of ideas about Emily, about why she was so drawn to her. As her sweat began to cool and her thighs began to unstick she remembered all the times in her life, especially when she was young, when she was just wandering around, walking all night or being in the wrong place or ending up in no place. She was just walking around when everyone else seemed to have a place to go. All these years she had felt that she was the only girl in the world doing that guy-like thing. When women have no place to go they get married or kill themselves. Only guys walked around all night. Now though, she knew that back then, somewhere Emily had been walking around too.

Lila was sitting in front of the factory waiting for Emily to come out. She flashed anxiously on work one more time and then shrugged it off. Work should never keep you from living. There were other job possibilities. She could be a messenger again. Life in front of Emily's factory was the typical inner city industrial chaos of various men pushing various racks and stacks of things up and down the block with one hand and touching the body of every passing female with the other. After fifteen minutes, Lila took refuge inside the building, and by five-thirty decided it was time to liberate Emily from her usual stint of overtime without pay. When she got upstairs, she was surprised to find her at the front desk.

"Emily, what are you doing in reception?"

"I guess the boss couldn't take me using all the machinery correctly all day long. It was too virile for him to handle so he

335

banished me to secretarial. I don't even know how to use this stuff. These machines have been blinking and beeping all day and I can't figure out which button is *hold*. It took me an hour to find the *on* button for the typewriter."

"Well, come on now, don't give him your free time on top of all of that."

"Okay, I'll be down in a minute."

Twenty minutes later she stepped out of the elevator. Her fifty cent earrings looked, somehow, quite divine, fashionable and extraordinary. A late-shift rack pusher patted her ass.

"When are you going to go out with me?"

"I told you I'm gay," she screamed with a sudden, sharp and all-encompassing anger.

Lila looked at her and realized that her anger was always present but only showed itself when Emily was touched by the wrong person or at the wrong time or in some other way found her dignity to be under assault again.

"I'm going home to be with my girlfriend, pigfucker."

But he just laughed.

"I look into the future," Emily said that night, tired and sore but not admitting it, "and I see nothing, nothing at all. I know I'll travel, but aside from that I have no ambition and no fear."

"What about for yourself though? For your personality? I mean, Emily, aren't there things about yourself that you want to see change or develop or at least an expectation or two?"

"I want to go through the day without thinking about myself," she answered blandly. "From one thing to another. I want to talk to this person, make this thing, eat this food. I don't need drama. I don't think it's groovy anymore."

Before she fell asleep, Emily made little noises, like groans. They were calmer, more guttural versions of her own sex sounds and then she would quiver. The quiver told Lila that Emily had fallen asleep. For the next few moments Lila looked out the window into the La Mama costume shop. At that moment she promised herself that she would never betray this woman. She wanted to be the person in Emily's life who let her believe in love. Lila listened to the cats scurry and felt Emily's sleep sounds. Those images were imbedded permanently into her imagination.

THIRTY-FOUR

"**H**ello Arthur? Is Lacy home? This is Lila Futuransky calling."

"Hi Lila. Well, she's here but she's sort of busy. There's this fancy lady sitting in our living room who is trying to convince Lacy that she needs an agent. Wait a minute, hold on, here she comes."

"Hi Lila."

"Hi Lacy, Arthur says you're being recruited to the ranks of those with representation."

"Yes, yes, yes. I don't want to talk too loud, she's in the bathroom. Well, first she told me that *the only difference between artists who make it and artists who don't is promotion*. Then, later she said *if they read you once they'll read you twice*. I know I need an agent to protect me from publishers but who do you call to protect you from agents? Oh-oh she's finished shitting, bye honey, here's Arthur."

"Hello Arthur?"

"Yeah?"

"I just wanted to know when Sally Liberty was coming back. I need to talk to someone who has just taken a big trip."

"There are too many people taking trips around here if you

ask me," he said in one of those *you know what I'm talking about* voices.

"Not egos, Arthur, geography. You know, like a journey or a voyage."

"Lila, when you get a chance, you stop by here and see my most recent painting. It's a concave sunset and a convex sunrise so that night and day cave into each other in black and white paint and cigarette packages, to show the passage of time. It'll take you on a trip alright. You hang on now. Bye."

Lila had been reading and re-reading *On The Road*, she was almost through. But the closer she got to those final pages, the more doubts creepy crawled into her mind. She shared Jack's vision of women as sexual treasures and mystical beings who come in and out of your life like Arthur's suns, but there were still questions that Jack never touched on. Like, what do you do once you get to know them? He never stayed around long enough for that. All of this was why she had been seriously considering taking a trip somewhere, just to remember that Lila would be Lila wherever she was standing and it didn't have to be on those four square blocks below Fourteenth Street surrounded by those same old girls. She needed to take a trip like Jack's. But, then again, maybe it would be different for a woman. Maybe it didn't require a road at all.

"Let's pretend we're jumping in that pick-up truck and going out on the highway," she said to Emily. But Emily wasn't interested in that.

"I don't need an adventure everyday," she said.

Still, it was sticking in Lila's mind to take a trip.

"Buddy, you can't leave," Isabel implored as they shared her shift meal of Shepherd's Pie at Burger Heaven. She hadn't been fired yet. The lunch rush crowd was gone except for some old afternoon drinkers watching the Yankee game at the bar.

"Miss Subways, I need you—what about The Worst Performance Festival? It's coming up real soon."

"I wouldn't be gone for too long. Isabel, in some way, you're the one who understands me best. I know this because when you talk I agree so often that I don't need you to listen to me, you know it all already. Isabel, here, I am giving you my copy of *On The Road*. It is my gift to you."

"Buddy, I need you to write a scene for me, a trial. I don't really know what I want exactly but something about me dying and going to heaven, which is Grossinger's Hotel in the Catskills. First, though, naturally I have to be judged. The question is—have I really kept my integrity, or did I not sell out because no one was willing to buy? Can you picture a sort of Henry Fonda-Kafka-Job thing? Know what I mean?"

Somehow through the wonders of interpersonal communication, Lila did know what she meant. In fact, she was suddenly inspired and insisted at that very moment that they run off into the heat of midtown, over to The Jewish Division of the Public Library on Forty-Second Street to look at a very special thing right away.

The Jewish Room, being on the first floor of the giant main library building, had easy access and so became a resting place for those homeless men and women who were the inmates of the open wards of the city. Usually this room was noisy, smelled bad and was inhabited by a combination of religious Jews reading ancient texts and bag-ladies tearing up copies of *The New York Post*. Both sat there, rocking back and forth and talking to themselves. In the summer, it was hot and the windows were wide open, letting in the roar of the center city hustle outside. Two men collected money for a Black Museum that existed only in their dreams. Drug dealers promised Thai sticks, when it was only Mexican Cocoa-Cola buds. The Unification Church Missionaries, known as Moonies, drew diagrams explaining life and God with red and blue magic markers on portable boards. A bad saxophone player repeated over and over the theme song from *The Odd Couple* and then the theme song from *The Pink Panther*. All this drifted into The Jewish Room.

"The guy's name was Peretz," Lila told Isabel, looking through a fat card catalogue. "See how many cards are in his section? There's even a street named after him, right near us on Houston and First. Only nobody's ever heard of the guy. Here's the story I was telling you about. It's called *Bonche Schweig.*"

They politely put in their request and waited for the cute librarian to fetch the book.

"You see Isabel, it's like this. All these guys were writing, and women too, writing in Yiddish and trying out different ideas, forms, like writers anywhere. They had enthusiastic readers, critics, schools taught their books. Then came the war and their subject matter, their readers and their language was practically destroyed. Imagine sitting in a kitchen on Mosholu Parkway realizing that your career and your art form disappeared because your readers had been killed."

"I never thought about it that way before," Isabel said. "It reminds me in a way of when I saw this exhibit of Russian painters from 1900-70. First they were doing what everybody else was doing, except in their own Russian way. There was impressionism, cubism, all that. You're walking along the exhibit and all of a sudden there's a painting of an orange tractor with Lenin standing on it. History changes and the artist goes out of business."

The librarian came over with their book and gave them both a big smile. Isabel read it then and there while Lila watched her react. It was about a guy named Bonche who never had a good moment in his whole life. People would shit all over him and he consistently took it. What was more important, from Peretz' point of view, was that no matter what happened, Bonche never said anything bad against God. When he died, he had to be judged in the heavenly court. The defense attorney proved that no matter how much he suffered, Bonche had never cursed God. The court decided that since he died without having done anything wrong, Bonche won the trial and could have anything he wanted in all imagination. That was his reward. God would give him whatever he asked for.

"What I want," said Bonche, "is, everyday, a hot roll with some fresh butter."

Then, said Peretz, the prosecutor broke out laughing. That was the end of the story.

"You get it Isabel?" Lila was hysterical with enthusiasm. "In the end, the prosecutor really won. Bonche was turned into such a schmuck from never tasting anger or desire or revenge that when his moment finally came, his spirit was too dead to be able to do anything about it."

"Isabel," Lila asked over an ice cream soda at Howard Johnson's. "What's the difference between being stagnant and being stable?"

"Stagnant is what someone else wants you to be, stable is what you need them to be."

"Isabel, when God tells you that you can have anything you want, what are you going to ask for?"

"I don't know." Isabel answered, scratching her head. "I wouldn't want to get any of the things that I want too suddenly, because then the fun and the search and the dreams would all be over. It's not the satisfaction I'm after. I like thinking about new ways of doing things and then making up shows about the trying. Do you think God could give me something like that?"

"You've already got that."

"Oh, yeah. Well, how about health insurance?"

THIRTY-FIVE

Twice in one week, Lila got mistaken for a prostitute. She was walking home on Chrystie Street in the middle of the afternoon through Chinatown's warehouse district and two trucks drove by.

"Going out? Going out?"

She decided it was an honest mistake. Why else would a woman be walking down the street wearing a shoulder bag?

The next day she was on the corner of Tenth Street and Third Avenue waiting to make a phone call when a guy drove up in a cab.

"Hey you. Get in," he yelled out the window.

"I'm not a prostitute," Lila said. "She's a prostitute," pointing to a woman standing next to the phone booth.

"Oh," he said, shifting his gaze. "Hey you. Get in."

Then Lila got mistaken for a racist. Sal Paradise took her out to hear Ron Carter and then they went to Maureen's bar to play her juke box. Maureen had a Gertrude Stein haircut and a figure to match. She also had a great collection of forty-fives like Dinah Washington, Peggy Lee, Frankie crooning *Witchcraft*, very atmosphere-y. Everything got ruined though, when this man at the bar decided it was time to impose himself on the

343

general mood with his fucking presumptions.

"I work in a shoe store waiting on filthy rich people. Like, you know basketball stars, Lionel Ritchie, Herb Alpert, the tops. Those ball pros are the worst, let me tell you. The way I figure it, they would be spending their lives shooting hoops in school yards and turning into muggers if they hadn't hit the big time. They just piss all over themselves watching a white guy tie their shoes."

People don't look closely enough. They see tits and assume they're for sale. They see white skin and think they're among friends.

"I don't see it that way," Sal said. "I don't want to take away from you that you're working hard and rich people are being rude to you because that's real and it hurts. But it's success that makes people snotty, not their blackness. Maybe you could think about it again."

So, of course, the guy had to fall all over himself to justify the unjustifiable with references to "ignorant people," meaning someone other than himself. Lila just faded out and thought about MTV.

That very night she got mistaken for straight.

"Hey doll," the same guy at the same bar called out to a woman sitting alone in the corner. "Want me to walk you home?"

"Why don't you walk me home?" Sal said, trying to divert the guy's attention.

"Oh of course darling, lispen to me suger." The bar sitter flapped his wrists expecting, of course, that swish-baiting was just fine with everyone. It was another example of a typical American asshole who wouldn't know an emotion if it walked up and punched him in the eye.

Lila and Sal split immediately, feeling sorry for Maureen, who had to serve the creep for the rest of the night. They went to the Polish Country-Western bar turned Beirut turned gay men's fuck bar called The Manhole. God, things changed quickly as of late. The place still had a good juke box. There was

Psychedelic Shack and *Tell Me What I Say*. Half way through getting drunk and singing their selections, chatting with the leather-clad clientele and having a great time, Lila realized that she and Sal were going to go home together and have sex with each other. Surprisingly the thought didn't bother her or Sal one bit. So that's exactly what they did. There was no fucking or anything like that, since even before her voyage into lesbos, Lila the het had never liked fucking, she didn't have the stomach for it. But they played with old-fashioned sweaty boy and girl stuff, easy and light with a lot of energy. It was all vaguely reminiscent and fun, but most importantly, Lila found out that her pal Sal knew how to make love to a woman and it made her respect him all the more.

THIRTY-SIX

Emily was hard at work at The Kitsch-Inn, and Lila was trying, in her klutzy way, to help. The Inn had a new policy of putting on a fully produced play every weekend. This meant that Mondays they came up with a new idea, Tuesdays they wrote the scripts. Wednesdays were for blocking and costumes and late night set construction. Thursday was reserved for full-dress and tech rehearsal, and Friday and Saturday were for performances. Sunday there was always a party.

Even though she thought the shows were creative and charming, Lila's personality was much more suited to Isabel Schwartz' personal philosophy of theatre. This approach emphasized mulling over, developing, rehearsing and publicizing and then performing enough times so the show could become itself. Whenever Isabel did her shows, she would spend weeks before rehearsing, and after that, handing out flyers in lesbian bars, asking each woman individually if she would please come. Her approach was based on the idea that most lesbians in lesbian bars are never asked to come to anything that is made expressly for them. Usually this approach had some effect, but fairly frequently Isabel would be outside at the last minute, in costume and make-up, standing on Saint Mark's Place asking dykie-looking women in restaurants to please come to her show, offering to hold the curtain until they finished eating. She even gave drug dealers free passes on very slow nights.

The Kitsch girls, on the other hand, were less concerned with who and how many came to the shows. The theatre was so small and the casts so large that there wasn't much room for the audience anyway. Besides, spontaneity was the name of the game, and they relished being known as the "girls who would do anything." Somewhere each one of them privately suspected that if they got too organized they might turn mean, and each one knew how mean mean girls could be. So they kept it light, non-competitive and without an ounce of desperation.

Lila loved watching Emily develop her weekly creations out of nothing. The night before costume day, they would walk the streets for an hour or so. Emily would look around and suddenly seize upon a piece of old cardboard or some dirty clothing or a thrown away board, all from garbage cans and vacant lots and carry it back to the Inn.

"If I didn't think theatre could be made from garbage, I wouldn't be doing theatre," she liked to say once in a while.

Her budget for that week's production was six dollars and fifty cents, raised by auctioning off a bowling shirt. They had been working most of the evening when Sheena walked in with aqua-marine hair and a shirt saying "SLUT" in sequins.

"Hi Sheena."

"Hi Slut."

"I beg your pardon?"

"It's my new attitudinal band, *The Macho Sluts*. I need some people to be in it with me, so I'm holding open auditions. Anyone who answers to the name SLUT, is in."

"Well forget it." Lila already had enough no-future projects, especially with the Worst Performance Festival coming up so soon.

"Sheena," Lila said, without looking up from trying to thread a needle, "what's it like outside? We've been in here for hours."

"Well," Sheena reflected, chomping on some organic potato

chips, "the streets are filled with Michael Jackson imitators."

"Hey Sheena, you want to help me?" Emily called out from under a pile of junk.

"Sure Slut."

"Here I'm doing the new set for the show this weekend. Cast of thirty, all in period costumes. We're turning the Inn into The Triangle Shirtwaist Factory and I need fifty cutouts of sewing machines."

"Groovoid. How long is the run?"

"Two nights, the usual."

"Groovoid."

"I don't mean to interfere, girls," Lila injected, looking for a band-aid for her overpricked finger, "but why do you do all this chaotic work for one weekend when, if you would prolong your runs a little, the shows could get better and more people could see them. I mean don't you have any ambition?"

"No," they said in unison as Sheena started cutting sewing machines out of an old box of Tide.

Just then Kitty appeared in the doorway, her eyes red and puffy, clutching a small carrying bag. Emily crawled out from under her props to embrace her friend.

"What happened? Come in, what's the matter, Kitty?"

They all retreated to The Inn's beat-up couch while Kitty cried and shook with sorrow. Emily sat on her lap, Lila handed tissues and Sheena offered her organic potato chips. They each tried in their own way to show their friend that she was home.

"I left her," she said, blowing her nose. "We had a fight coming back from Gristede's. I offered to carry her bags but she didn't want me to. I offered to make her a drink, but she didn't want it. I asked her if she wanted me to leave and she said she didn't know. Everytime I asked her something she rolled up tighter and tighter into a ball and crawled deeper into the bed. I felt she didn't want to be in the same co-op with me."

"Maybe you asked her too much stuff?" Sheena said shyly.

"But I want her to ask me," she wailed, "I want her to ask me to do every little thing for her, to show me that she needs me."

"You know Slut, one thing you gotta get together in your head is that each person can only go so far. If you pressure them to go farther still, they're going to hate you. Just take what you can get. Have some more potato chips."

They talked more and took turns walking around the block with Kitty and deciding where she was going to stay that night. This went on until a white BMW drove up to The Inn and Kitty's face lit up with the joyful confirmation of being loved. She waved good-bye to her friends and climbed into the front seat.

Sheena, Emily and Lila sat in silence for a moment, each reflecting, in her own peculiar frame of reference, on the weird situations people get themselves into in the name of love. Then, one by one, they resumed the task of cutting out sewing machines from old boxes of detergent and mounting them on old wire hangers.

"The whole thing makes me think," Sheena said, "that sometimes love means finding out more about yourself than you ever really wanted to know."

Emily was busy gluing and didn't pay attention, so only Lila agreed.

THIRTY-SEVEN

Friday morning Lila woke up with Emily at six o'clock and found a small gift box lying on her stomach.

"What's this?"

"A good luck present for the Worst Performance Festival tonight."

Lila opened the box. Inside was a black lace brassiere with an underwire and a little pink flower stitched in between the cups. Next to it sat black lace underpants with another stitched pink rose. She shut the box quickly, and opened it again, slowly, to look more closely.

"Are you embarrassed?" Emily asked.

No. It was intimate, so involved with Lila's secret life that she was thrilled to the teeth.

"The right size and everything."

Lila imagined Emily standing thoughtfully at the counter, fingering the bras, deciding which one she would buy.

"I know my baby's breasts."

"I know you do."

The house was packed that night for the Worst, which was the third act on a bill at AVANT-GARDE-ARAMA, a former Ukranian restaurant turned performance club. Fortunately for

Lila, Isabel and Company, the opening piece was a woman eating a grapefruit and the following was a man walking around in a circle with a paper bag over his head talking about how much he liked to pee before going on stage. All the girls were there, except for Muriel, who was sunning herself somewhere on the Costa del Sol.

The lights came up on Helen Hayes and Mike Miller, the administrative heavy of the ARAMA. They were sitting at a panel-like table with official looking nameplates. Suddenly Lila rushed out into the crowd in tight black pants and a tight black t-shirt that said "Soon To Be A Major Homosexual."

"Good evening ladies and friends. I will be your emcee for this evening and I am pleased to be with this special audience. Who else but you, people who pay five dollars to come see this kind of work, could be better qualified to pick the worst performer of 1984? But first, before we begin, I want to remind you that all of us here together tonight, well, we are a community, a community of enemies. And we have to stay close to each other so we can watch out and protect ourselves. To give you an idea for the criteria by which to judge the participants, we have an excerpt from last year's winner, Amy Cohen. I will now read to you from her prize-winning text, *Artificial Turtle*:

Inside out. Empty Box as silence.
Empty box as monument to. . . emptiness.

"Isn't that just awful?"

The audience, getting into the groove, booed wildly, then, pleased with themselves, applauded and cheered. Isabel had promised Lila that they would. She understood the simple fact that people like to be insulted in public because they think it means they're important.

"Tonight we are proud to introduce our panel of minor celebrity judges from competing cliques to vote down each other's friends. First, representing the girls, from the Kitsch-Inn, The Platinum Angel herself, Helen Hayes."

351

Helen was dressed to her divaish teeth.

"It's simply terrible to be here tonight."

"Thank you, tell us Helen, how was your show at Dance-a-teria last night?"

"Pretty bad, pretty bad. I think it would have been competitive in this festival."

"That's great Helen, isn't she swell ladies and gentlemen? Thanks doll. And now, representing the boys, the Avant-Garde's head cheerleader, Mike Miller. Hey Mike, I love your beard. Thank you and enjoy the show."

Lila and Isabel had agreed before hand that Mike would have no lines and no microphone. Those boys talked too much anyway. As he sat there looking stupid, Helen announced the first entry.

"Our opening act tonight will be East Village Performance Artist Isabel Schwartz with her piece, *My Brilliant Career*, improvisational ruminations on nothing."

Isabel entered in her pink baseball pants, yellow sneakers and black sunglasses.

"Look, I don't have anything to say to you and you don't have anything to say to me," she sighed, looked as bored as possible, like she was too big for Carnegie Hall. "I don't even like you. I thought about coming here with the slides of my lesbian honeymoon at Grossinger's, but we're only getting ten dollars for this performance, so why waste a good idea for ten dollars? Instead, I'll read to you from my reviews. *Isabel Schwartz is a Genius, Isabel Schwartz is a whiz on stage, Isabel Schwartz is witty and exuberant.* That's all you deserve. Good-bye."

"Well," said Helen, "That was pretty terrible. Very annoying at times. It's going to be tough to beat. *Dance Magazine* called our next performer, *an actor with the wit, personal style and glamour of a young Dustin Hoffman.* Will you please welcome Ratso Tootsie."

Roberta walked calmly onto the stage, scratching her head, dragging her robes and drinking a beer. She took a cassette tape out of her pocket and dropped it on the floor. Then she took out a box of slides and tossed them uncaringly in the air. Finally she unraveled a film all over the stage. She finished the beer, spit on the floor and left.

"Thank you Ratso," said Helen, with an impeccable display of dishonest politeness. "The slides were very experimental but I found the film slightly opaque. Our next performer Patty Dyke uses time and space to interpret the self, herself, in all its post-modern incarnations. Patty's influences include Artaud, Rimbaud, Van Gogh, The Go-Go's and Uncle Ho."

It was Isabel again. This time she was dressed in a pink and green bath towel. She was plugged into a walkman and danced to the music that no one else could hear. But when the chorus came on, she screamed out, "Beat it, just beat it," and hit herself on the head with a stick. Helen, looking properly upset, tried to ease her off the stage, but Isabel, being the prototype horrible performer, started making a scene.

"I've given you everything," she shouted, running up to a stunned and silent Mike and pulling his beard, "everything, and you just fucked me in the ass you dumb prick," and then she threw off the towel.

After intermission, when the audience had calmed down, the lights came up slowly on the final segment of the show, "The Lesbian Nuns and Their Dirty Habits: The Real True Story (With Carlos)." There were Lila, Isabel and Roberta dressed as nuns with incense and chanting and holy water and Bach organ music played in slow motion in the background. The three of them were mumbling "Domini, Domini" and spraying holy water on everyone. When they finished their procession, each one assumed a pose in a different shadow and put on their name plates. Lila was "Sister Roger," Roberta, "Sister Fresnel," and Isabel, "Sister Bruce Weber."

Helen announced "The Flying Nun" and Lila pouted, slapped her thigh and said, "Come on Carlos, we've got to think of a way to save the convent. I know, a bake sale!" To which Helen, chomping on a cigar replied, "But Seester." Lila held on to her habit and made a few Gidget type moves to get ready for take-off.

Reading from her index cards Helen announced sister number two, Julie Andrews.

Roberta plastered a big smile on her face and began to teach the audience to sing Do-Re-Mi, until, right in the middle of *Me, a name I call myself*, she yelled out "Stop, stop. This is a sham. When I was a kid I was in love with Julie Andrews. I had her picture on my mirror. I dressed like her, I had a Julie Andrews wallet. My mother took me to all her movies. One day I got the address of her fan club and I wrote her a long letter. Julie, I said, Julie I love you, I love you. And do you know what she did, that bitch? She sent me back an autographed picture. I cried for days, my mother tried to console me with a Julie Andrews coloring book. Then Halloween came, and she took me to Woolworth's tempting me with a Mary Poppins costume but I said no. You know why? Do you know why? Because I didn't want to be Julie Andrews. I wanted to have Julie Andrews."

"And now," announced the lovely Helen Hayes, "Sister number three, The Singing Nun." At which point Isabel whipped out an electric guitar and started singing "Dominique." The others joined in. Unfortunately, they hadn't rehearsed this part of the show and none of them knew the lyrics so they just kept singing "Dominique-ah, nique-ah, nique-ah" over and over again until The Flying Nun took off, the Singing Nun switched to Hound Dog and Julie Andrews started making out with a woman in the first row.

Finally Helen had the foresight to turn out the lights. So went the Worst Performance Festival. Oh, well, that's show biz.

THIRTY-EIGHT

I t was a lazy morning and Lila and Emily were lying around in bed, with no where in particular that either needed to go.

"Lila, I'm so happy to be with you that I can't believe it sometimes. Just being in your presence somehow calms so many of my sorrows. I like feeling sexy, that I'm attractive to you, but it doesn't make me want to sleep around or anything like that. I know you want me to stay open to other women, and I'm trying, but for now I'd rather just think of you as my baby. Sometimes I wish people weren't so obsessed with sex in such distorted ways. Then there would be more energy for looking at how beautiful the earth is."

"I know what you're saying," Lila whispered, kissing Emily's neck, "But for me there's something incredible about two people getting it together to touch each other. I've learned so much about myself by having sex with different people, or just from finding out how someone does it. The dangerous part is when you use sex to justify hurting someone. That's the problem."

Like anyone who suddenly finds themselves in the presence of a compatible imagination, Lila perceived and felt daily occurrences with an insight beyond her own capability. When she was confronted by a more complex place of understanding, she knew it was not her interpretation alone but that of she and Emily together. Lila did not know if Emily would find this pathetic or wonderful. At the same time Lila began to feel a combination of panic and delight at watching someone be transformed by her love for them. But she had a more tentative enthusiasm for her own changes. Emily wanted the bulk of Lila's attention, which meant behaving a way that Lila had never even dreamed of behaving. Lila was learning a new way to live, where someone else had something to say about the decisions that she made in her own life. In fact, she'd never even had another person know so much about where she was everyday. She was trying it out half through resolve and half through an unclear kind of intimidation. Combined with her real love for Emily was the threat that Lila really wasn't a good person, that she was capable of all the abandonment and exploitation that Emily had experienced from others, and Lila was determined to prove that Emily's fears would never be justified.

The flesh around Emily's nipples was soft and wrinkled. There was enough give for Lila to play absent-mindedly, folding Emily's nipples into her skin.

"I think I admire that about you Lila, a little bit anyway. You desire someone and you try to live it out. It's too intimate for me, touching another person's body. That's why I haven't had as much experience as you, it's sharing your fantasy with someone. I mean, I have a lot of fantasies about women, but not about having sex, more like imagining doing things with them, having them in my life."

As Lila started to lick the softness under Emily's breast, they both felt the comfort. It had been a long time since Lila had been running out on the street all night, alone, figuring things out, chasing girls and conversation, but she didn't miss it that much because something special and sweet had come into her life. Maybe it was a gift to remind her that it was right to believe in love.

"I know I've fallen in love with you, Lila. I've been celibate for a long time, you know, but today at work I was thinking about how much I like having you as my girlfriend."

"Oh, you like having a woman pay attention to you and take care of you and make love to you? How unusual."

"Lila, I need to ask you something kind of strange."

"Sure babe."

"When you answer the phone on a phone machine and it's ringing, the light flashes on, right?"

"Yeah."

"So, if you need to put it on hold, you press down the hold button and the light starts blinking. If you want to speak to that person, do you press the hold button again?"

"No. After you press hold it pops up blinking silently. When you want to talk you press the blinking one."

"Thanks darlin'."

"Sure. Now I have a question for you. Why do you scotch tape your bangs to your forehead every morning before you get dressed and then take off the tape before you got out? Not that I think it's weird or anything, I'm just curious."

"That way my bangs will lie flat like Audrey Hepburn in *Charade*."

"Oh well, in that case."

Lila thought Emily was the cutest thing. She was at times prehistoric and then, suddenly, more Dior than Dior. But, even with her sophisto fancies, she had been in the world of needle and thread for so long that she hadn't caught up with even the most basic technologies, aside from industrial machinery of course. Like an intercom, for example. Lila watched her struggle for ten minutes one morning in Lila's apartment, trying to figure out how to buzz in Sheena, who was coming back from a visit to her mother on Avenue X in south Brooklyn. Emily tried to talk through the listen button and not press the talk button and then she couldn't hear who it was because the listen button wasn't pressed. Sheena got in though, because the downstairs lock was broken.

"What a place," she said, scratching the newly shaved part of her partially shaved head. "Everyone who stays there is crazy. They don't know why they're there but they don't know the names of any other places, and everyone is divorced by the time they're nineteen. But I did do some serious thinking about my future. I'm going to give myself one more year to find people to be in the *Macho Sluts* and then another year to see if we make it. If nothing happens I'll be a fireman, uh, person."

At least something was settled. They invited Sheena to go out for a walk but she had to run off to meet her friend Jenny who was supposed to have some information about a women's circus brigade in Nicaragua.

Emily and Lila went out anyway, strolling hand in hand through Washington Square Park. Lila saw all the drug dealing going on and remembered that she hadn't seen Ray for a long time, hoping that he wasn't in trouble or something more serious than that.

"Lila, I was watching you talk to Sheena and everything she said seemed to make sense to you. I realized that everything everyone says seems to make sense to you, which made me think that you must be fairly bizarre. And I must be equally bizarre to not have noticed for so long. I feel like I've been walking around the world, flying around it, like some character in Rocky and Bullwinkle who has a rocket attached to his leg. But now, I've been feeling love from you and all of a sudden, I'm paying attention."

On the way back they stopped every now and then for small kisses, and then for some gelatti. Not from the place that had fired Tina. The boss claimed she'd had too many visitors and couldn't keep her mind on the gelatti. Instead they stopped in at one of the many competitors on the same block.

"Oh look, they have the flavor *fig*. That's the same word as *cunt* in Italian."

So, of course they ordered fig and sat on a car in front of Lila's building to eat it slowly because it was so, so sweet. Lila rubbed her fingers over the nape of Emily's neck, through her dyed hair and then, at the same moment, they both keyed into the conversation going on behind them.

"That's gay liberation. They think they can do whatever they want whenever they want it."

About five men were drinking beer across the street and talking very loudly, obviously intending to be heard.

"You want to try it. Come on and try it sister. I've got A BIG COCK. See *mamacita*, I'd love to fuck your cunt."

Lila didn't want to go upstairs, because she didn't want them to see where she lived. They started walking slowly away, but the men followed.

"Come on you cunt, I bet you've got a nice pussy, you suck each other's pussy's right? I'll show you a cock that you'll never forget. . . ."

For Lila, this was a completely normal though unnecessary part of daily life. As a result she had learned docility, to keep quiet and do a shuffle, to avoid having her ass kicked in. Emily, however, exploded in a combination of offended innocence and righteous anger.

"Fuck you faggot spic."

Lila immediately pulled her into the building, trembling and overcome by layers of different reactions.

"Emily, Emily, listen to me. I don't want to tell you not to fight because you're right to fight, but once you get queer-bashed, it comes back to you over and over again because no one's going to be on your side. I don't want to tell you not to be angry Emily but please, don't say *spic*."

"I don't mean that against Spanish people," she said, after a moment of silence. "Out there are two men who tortured me for no other reason than that they felt like it. I'm going to kill a man someday. I'm sure I'm going to kill a man."

They sat upstairs in the dark, making feeble attempts to talk. The sounds of the men, drunker and laughing, came in through the open window.

"If I wasn't a lesbian," Emily said, looking out from behind the curtain, "I would be insane today. You know my rapes have changed me. You know better than anybody else that there are things I can't do sexually because they make me sick. I know you want to put your fingers inside me, I know you want to lick my face, someday you're going to reject me for that. You're going to get bored, I know it."

"Emily, what are you talking about. I love making love with you, we have a very deep friendship. Let's just calm down here and sit a minute."

"Don't condescend to me." Emily was walking back and forth around the tiny apartment. Lila had no idea what to do so she started smoking cigarettes, one after the other.

"I'm not groovy like you Lila, like you and your friends. This woman, that woman, this woman, that woman and a man. When is Muriel coming back? You haven't mentioned her for a while. I think it's a little disgusting to tell one lover about sex you had with someone else."

"What are you talking about?"

"*Fica ussatte.*"

"What the hell does that mean?" Lila was freaking out. She had absolutely no idea of what to do. The room was filling with smoke. Emily was pacing harder and harder and Lila couldn't imagine a way out of the whole thing.

"What does it sound like?"

"I don't understand Italian. You know that."

"It means *used cunt.*"

Lila was so surprised at how quickly everything had gotten out of hand that the only emotion she felt in touch with was a desire for the entire episode to be over. Emily's mouth got very smooth and tight. They were still for a minute and it seemed to Lila that Emily was dancing around the room and her emotions were a burst of colors that had all run into each other until they were muddy and brown.

"I'm sorry Lila, do you want me to go away?"

"No. Emily, just because we're having a fight doesn't mean that you have to go away. Why don't you sit down next to me, okay?"

"I'm sorry Lila, you know I get so tired from working with those guys hassling me all day long. When I won't go out with them they start talking about pussy right in front of me, and how they're going to go out and get some. I think if they knew I ate pussy for breakfast they would be pretty humiliated."

Lila tried to laugh, hoping everything would be better now.

"I'm driving you away from me," Emily said after a pause. "I'm driving you away when you love me because I'm afraid that if you leave me I'll be raped again. I'm safe when I walk down the street with you. Even if we get scared sometimes. I've been totally alone in strange places for so long. I don't want to walk alone anymore."

"Emily, listen, who gets raped, it's all haphazard. It could have been me instead of you. I haven't been raped yet but it doesn't mean I won't be."

"Pig-fuckers," Emily blurted out. "I won't let anybody hurt my baby."

Lila walked in the streets like someone who had always walked in the streets and for whom it was natural and rich. She walked with the illusion that she was safe and that the illusion would somehow keep her that way.

Yet, that particular night as she went out for cigarettes, Lila walked uneasily, her mind wandering until it stopped of its own accord, on the simple fact that she was not safe. She could be physically hurt at any time and felt, for a fleeting moment that she would be. She sat on a trunk of a '74 Chevy and accepted that this world was not hers. Even on her own block. She sat on that Chevy watching a young man pick through a garbage can, a young woman sell her shoes, fancy uptown diners in a Szechuan restaurant and a German tourist taking pictures of it all. Lila was full of questions about the power of defiance and its limitations.

PART FIVE

THIRTY-NINE

"**W**e were a hit buddy," Isabel was telling her over and over again. "The Worst Performance Festival was a hit. Isn't that pathetic? Critics were there and they actually liked us insulting them and telling them they were full of shit. It worked even better than we wanted it to. After all the good shows we've done, I can't believe we're getting reviews for that."

They walked out of the xerox store with copies of the first five scenes of *Job Revisited*.

"I'm sorry Isabel, I'm just not with it today. No, you're right. It's utterly sickening and predictable."

"By the way Miss Subways, that Kerouac book you gave me, there's something weird about it, like it has a magic power. Even though I hated the main guy, by page three I wanted to be him. I used to see that book in my brother's room when I was little, but I never opened it. Look at this."

She pulled a crinkled piece of newspaper out from her purple pockets.

"It says here that he died in his forties watching the Galloping Gourmet on TV in his mother's house. He was living with his mother and drinking beer all day long. Funny huh, how the author has nothing to do with the book. But even knowing what kind of person wrote this doesn't make its effect on me any different. I guess the road is the only image of freedom that an American can understand."

Lila couldn't answer. She went for a walk in Tompkins Square Park. Everything was so much more difficult than she'd thought. Which was better, the sad truth or the fun deception?

She saw Linda Casbah sitting with baby Jane and went over to help rock the stroller. Linda had her own analysis of this topic of sex, art, travel and success.

"I want to do a serious show about gender changes," she said, seriously. "When I was an underground go-go star, everyone wanted to interview me. I was invited to rich people's parties. They even brought me on tour to Amsterdam where somehow the Dutchies became convinced I was a transsexual and kept referring to me as *he*. I'd never been so in before. When I got pregnant though, and decided to live with John, everyone dropped me suddenly, like pregnancy was impossibly passé. Linda Casbah the transsexual go-go dancer is a lot sexier than mommy."

Her child at eight months old had that brand new skin that turned red when you touched it. She talked on and on in a happy series of garbled baby sounds.

"Pretty soon I'm going to find out what she has to say for herself. Now she keeps blabbing, but soon it will be words and the world will know what kind of person she is."

Like all babies who change their moods in a constant and intense sequence, Jane would finish speaking, take a breath and burst into tears for reasons known, perhaps, only to herself. Linda automatically responded to wails by sticking a piece of banana in her mouth. Jane switched into a passionate rush of soft, sweet security and banana bliss.

"It's her heroin," Linda said. "It's incredible how important bananas are to her. For example she has only two teeth. Having teeth is a new experience and she's starting to think about what kind of teeth activity to look forward to. When I brush mine in

366

the morning it gets her so excited that she literally becomes ecstatic with pure glee. Sometimes, when she won't stop crying, even with a fix of banana, I just start brushing my teeth and she starts fantasizing again about that day when she too will have teeth to brush. Just like mommy."

"I guess you're not bored with mommyhood then."

"Well, I was thinking actually about going back to Holland for a while, 'cause they pay for everything there. The only problem is that the enormous freedom is met by equally enormous passivity. Every once in a while people stop getting high long enough to actually do something quite good, but, you know how Calvinists are, completely without passion unless they are struggling to eat."

The sun was shining brightly and Jane was so happy eating her banana that Lila began to see hope again in little things, and maybe even in big ones.

"You should check it out Lila. They'll love you there. Lila Futuransky, the girl with the passionately unpretentious aesthetic. But, can you handle a label like that? Can you be the last moral celebrity?"

"Well, check this out Linda, Isabel Schwartz just told me that we've been invited to Nebraska to do The Worst Performance Festival there. They want us to be the imported comic, brunette intellectuals. You know, the conscience of the world routine. We said absolutely not."

Jane was busy reaching for things that were farther away than she could stretch. She held things too close to her eyes to actually see more than the color. Then Linda stood her up, leaning on a piece of bench, and Jane rejoiced, wide-eyed at the new experience of standing up, until, after a series of revelations about this perspective, she came to realize that she was standing alone. There was trouble on Jane's face, serious trouble, then distress, and finally a look of profound sadness until mommy picked her up again.

"All my life I've fought against dependence of this kind," Linda said, giving over the last piece of banana. "But I need to

367

remember that this one is natural, not neurotic. Here Jane," she said, peeling another banana, "have some smack."

FORTY

The third of July found Lila madly back at the typewriter, sweat soaking through her Lily Tomlin t-shirt. The radio was only playing songs with the word *America* in the title. *We're An American Band, America, Living in the USA* and Bruce Springsteen screaming that he was *Born in the USA*, followed by the Statler Brothers singing *My Baby Is American Made*. Lila knew that rock and roll was out of fashion but she loved that fucked up music and promised herself to keep working until they played Bowie's *Young Americans*. She would have done it too, except that Roberta appeared suddenly, sweating and smoking in Lila's living room.

"I've been in this city for two years and now that Muriel's gone I realize I don't know anybody. So, Lila Futuransky, when I wanted to talk, I came to talk to you. I got a postcard from Muriel. She's gotten a job teaching on some hippie farm in the south of France. Her course is called *Improvisational Balance*. I don't know if she's ever coming home."

Lila had the sudden thought that Roberta was a shorter version of herself. If she was writing a play, Roberta would have the lead. If she left town, Roberta would get her apartment.

"It's the clothes. I've been getting constant hassles lately

369

because of my green threads. It's worse without Muriel around because, usually, guys are so busy bothering her, they never come near me. Last night I walked into my lobby, got out my key and the next thing I knew a man was standing next to me, touching me, talking to me, telling me how green turned him on and he wanted to fuck me. I found myself in the ludicrous position of having to struggle to fight him off, just because he had decided on impulse to give me grief. I was screaming at the top of my lungs and eventually somebody came along, but they just stood there and looked. *This is serious* I yelled, *This is serious*. But they kept watching until he got bored and walked away. Just like that. I'm going to kill a man someday."

"That's the second time I've heard that this week," Lila said, rolling Roberta an emergency joint and offering her a shower. She cooked her some noodles with olives and poured a nice cold beer.

"I'm gonna kill a man someday," Roberta said again.

Then they went on to discuss other things because there is always more to a person than what somebody else does to them. They bullshitted and sang doo-wop versions of *The Last Train to Clarksville*. When they were both high-spirited, Lila decided to show off her collection of lesbian trash paperbacks from the fifties and sixties. That was always good for forgetting about troubles.

"You see Roberta," she pointed out, "some are stamped *Adult Reading* and were only available in porn shops or sleazy stores. It was one of the only ways lesbians could read about themselves. First the author would use a man's name, unless really sleazy, then a man would use a woman's name. Sometimes they'd add MD after it for good measure. A lot of them were written like medical discussions of case studies."

"What do you mean?" Roberta asked, opening another beer.

"Like, it would say *I recall my first lesbian client Anna Q. She came into my office to confess to me about a sexual encounter with a nun who passionately tore off her clothes, sucked her tits, ate her through three orgasms, ravaged her neck and left her blissfully dreaming of more.* They describe all this in the most graphic detail of course."

Lila was getting into it so she opened another beer for herself, while Roberta had a second helping of noodles. Lila felt like her older but wiser self.

"Then the patient says how guilty she feels, which reminds the doctor of another case that takes about ten more pages of lurid description."

"Wow," said Roberta, who was obviously feeling better. "These books sound a whole lot sexier than those morality tales we've been fed lately. Let's put the dirt back into dyke drama."

Lila was smiling from ear to ear, pretending she was the underground sex goddess of Lesbiana. Roberta opened another beer.

FORTY-ONE

On the night before the Fourth, the kids and old men and families hung out in the parks and on the stoops and rooftops drinking Budweisers, listening to the radio and shooting off firecrackers all night long. At the center of it was Washington Square Park, hot, dark and full of glory in all its blazing American contradictions.

A Black gay comedian told racist anti-gay jokes to crowds of cheering tourists, and made a lot of money. Break dancers gossiped and squabbled, spending more time negotiating than dancing. A country-western band found they would draw an audience only when they sang Grateful Dead tunes. All this urban conversation was punctuated again and again by ash cans, bottle rockets, rapid fire Chinese fire cracker and sparklers for the little ones out with dad. This went on in between the Rastas selling, buying and playing soccer. Kids, newer than New Wave, with frisbees and guitars, sang John Cougar songs for people who didn't know who John Cougar was. Suburban white people looking for nickel bags stood next to suburban white people who had never heard of nickel bags. Straight couples on dates didn't notice Puerto Rican faggots in mid-drift tops having dramatic jealous scenes and fabulous reunions.

Of course the cops had to come disrupt this natural wonder because, whenever all kinds of people come together for nothing more than fun, the police just have to show themselves, traveling in packs of three, each with a stick and a gun. They just had to come and announce that there would be no more singing in the park that night.

On the way home Lila and Emily stopped for plums.

"I'll buy you a plum," Emily said, as each woman picked out her own. Their plums rested on the counter. Lila's was dark, round with a tone of soft, rich purple. Emily's was tighter, not as ripe, in a shiny reddish skin. When Lila bit into her plum, it split and the inside was warm and sweet as she sucked it out of its bitter shell. It was red, it was golden, it filled every corner of her mouth and oozed its sweetness between her teeth. Then, Emily put her arm around Lila's waist as they walked along.

"There's a sweet dish. One for you and one for me," announced a male voice, emanating loudly from a doorway.

"Lila, kiss me," Emily said. And Lila did kiss her, brazenly and terrified, but she couldn't refuse the power of Emily's embrace and will.

"Thank you darlin'," Emily smiled, triumphant, because she had avoided another defeat, overcoming the violence with pure daring love.

They kept walking through the neighborhood. No matter how dark the sky, it was always day from below, with the store and street lights shining off everyone's eyes. And it never stopped. That was something Lila knew for sure, since one night she had tried to spray paint the latest condo which had displaced six families. At 3:30 in the morning she and Sal Paradise had snuck out, with their spray cans under their shirts and waited all night for the street to empty for five minutes so they could do the job. They ended up sitting there until the sun came up and the club crowds turned into the after hours crowds which turned right into the subway-bound morning work crowds. There was never an empty moment.

"Do you think that gay people will ever be safe?" Emily asked.

That kind of question was so often on everyone's mind that after a while they never actually asked it, just assumed it was always there.

"I don't know. We've always been there. You know I read this great story by Isaac Bashevis Singer, you know, the Yiddish writer."

"No, I never heard of him," Emily said.

"Well, he won a Nobel prize, which is its own story, but anyway, he writes these great stories combining spirits and sex and Jewish ways of approaching things. He doesn't clean anything up for presentation, which, somehow, makes me believe it even more. So, in this story called *Two*, he tells about two boys who met in a yeshiva in Poland and how they fell in love. After studying together and praying together, they separated over a minor jealousy, each marrying an arranged bride as an act designed to hurt the other. After the marriages were in place, they realized their need to be together and escaped to a far away shtetl where they lived as man and wife. One wore women's clothes, lit the shabbas candles and presented himself to the community as a woman. The other carried on a husband's religious and social obligations, presenting himself as a happily married man and pious Jew. Together, praying in their home, they acknowledged to God that they were living in violation of his law but that they still loved him and honored him from the depth of their devotion. Eventually, the one who passed as a woman became well loved in the village as a kind and gentle person. He was eventually given the responsibility of operating the mikvah. There, he happily cut the women's nails and hair and listened to their stories of woe and joy. One night, after many years, a new woman came to the mikvah with a special, fascinating aura. He was so entranced that he reached out to touch her and fell into the water, striking his head and then he drowned.

"When the townspeople learned that he was really a man, they turned from individuals, brethren and neighbors into an angry mob. In a fury, they marched to his lover's house, dragged the terrified man into the street and murdered him. Both bodies were dumped in a hole outside of the town, outside of the cemetery."

"Lila," Emily said, as they continued walking. "Maybe I should stop holding your hand on the street. Maybe it would be safer. I mean, we seem to get hassled by some man almost everyday."

Lila looked around. "Absolutely not. We've got to be together in this. We can't let them come between us."

As she was speaking, Lila felt that sooner or later she and Emily, or she alone, or she and someone else, were going to be attacked on the street and she had to be ready to be hurt and not be surprised.

Lila held Emily's hand tighter, noticing how sleazy the street looked. There was Tony, nodding out in a doorway. His clothes were filthy. During the day, bullshitting around, Lila sometimes forgot that he was really a junkie and sooner or later he would die. There he was, sitting in the garbage and piss, oblivious. He was drooling all over his pants.

They turned the corner past some more buildings in the process of being renovated into condos. The old Orchidia, the world's only Ukranian-Italian restuarant, was all boarded up. The landlord had increased the rent five hundred percent and thrown the owner out on her ass after thirty-two years. There was a rumor that Chirping Chicken was getting ready to open a store on that very spot, or maybe a Steve's Ice Cream so that all the uptown people coming down in cabs would have a place to get over-priced chain ice cream.

Lila and Emily passed a new up-scale bar filled with made-up women and greying men and almost didn't notice the four white kids standing in a line blocking their way. When Lila sensed the barrier, she looked up, almost walking right into two skinheads and their girlfriends. Their leather jackets said *HARD CORE*.

They weren't Hell's Angels types, or even just local toughs. They were rich kids who got turned on by not giving a shit. Violence to them was a game, not a way of life. The largest, baldest skinhead was holding out a wooden board, like a weapon, holding it at his crotch and stroking it as if he was jerking off his four foot wooden prick.

"Just fuck me," he said drunkenly, "just fuck me."

The two women stood still. Neither Emily or Lila could think of what to do. They didn't know how to talk these kids out of hurting them for the hell of it. Lila and Emily held each other's hands as tightly as they could and waited, expecting the wood to come crashing down on them. Expecting a blur and then a horrible pain, the splintering of wood. They expected to see each other crushed and screaming, bloody in the middle of their own neighborhood, in front of each other.

"Leave those ladies alone," screamed a slurred and pained voice from across the street. Someone was coming towards them, walking right into the middle of all that tension.

It was Ray, bloated and sick looking, stubbles of grey growing out of his shaved head.

"Shut up nigger," said the wooden hard-on, but the moment had passed. Ray had diffused the violence by crossing the street. "Come on," the kid said to his friends, and they went looking for something else to do that night.

"They shouldn't talk like that to nobody," said Ray.

He was wearing a shirt from the men's shelter and Lila flashed on all the times, in rain and snow, that she had stopped to talk to Ray, busy selling on the corner and never invited him up, not even for Thanksgiving. Because she knew that ultimately junkies rip you off. They move in and then they rip you off. A junkie's mind revolves around getting enough money for junk, and Ray the junkie had saved her and she had no way of thanking him, because all that his life boiled down to was cocaine.

"Ray, you saved us, just by saying something. So many people won't even say something."

"I'm sick Lila. You know what I'm telling you. I'm all fucked up."

And then he looked her right in the eyes and they understood each other perfectly. He was going to ask her for money and he knew that she would turn him down, because in her mind that was not a favor and meant nothing.

"I'll be alright tomorrow," he said. "People are fucking blind. They look at each other and only see color or whatever your thing is. You girls be careful now."

And he was gone into the darkness.

"Is he going to be alright?" Emily asked, wondering the same thing about herself.

"Eventually he's going to die. But we have to watch him get a lot worse before that happens."

Right then, another figure stepped out of the shadow, from nowhere, from the background glare of the steetlights, from the pink neon bagel at The B&H Dairy. It was an old, stooped-over woman, in an old wig and cheap, gaudy earrings. She wore a robin's egg blue polyester dress and shoes that could have been sold for fifty bucks in an antique clothing store. She was garish in her make-up, but approached Lila and Emily as if she had always known them. She spoke in the thickest Southern accent, coming so close to their faces they could smell the cheap toilet water.

"Good evening ladies," she said, in slow measured tones, like a television parody of southern gentility. "Ayh only need a dollah to get home. Would you young ladies be so kahnd as to help me with a dollah? Ayh am eighty-five years old this year."

"It's Blanche," Emily said, reaching into her purse and then handing over the whole purse. The woman grabbed the money and walked away before anyone could change their mind, but after a safe distance, she turned and smiled again.

"Ayh thank you kindly."

"Do tell," Emily said, staring after the disappearing figure. "Blanche, Blanche Dubois. So, you made it to the East Village, Blanche. Take your dollah. Now you can go home to the BMT or Grand Central Station or wherever you live. The Tarantula Arms, was it? Go home to your park bench Blanche. Go home."

Lila and Emily walked quietly for a minute. Then Emily turned to Lila.

"As long as someone knows where you are and worries when you're not home, you can't get too lost. Otherwise we all end up displaced."

As they were making love that night Lila thought that the more she had sex with Emily the more turned on to her she became, building an erotic fascination with every aspect of Emily's body and sensibility. As Emily rubbed her velvet breasts against Lila's breasts, pressed her wet cunt right into Lila's wet cunt, pushed her fingers into Lila's asshole, holding her every way, inside and out, Lila discovered that Emily's nipples smelled of sweat cream, and her neck a mixture of cocoa butter and tea rose, that their bodies fit together perfectly, that Emily's caresses carried her beyond knowing where she was being touched. When Emily sat up against the wall to hold Lila and make love to her, as though her hand was Lila's hand, helping Emily to curl up into her softness, Lila felt her cunt rise up into Emily's fingers, leading her body over her head, clit first, losing all sense of boundary. When Emily made love to her, Lila screamed so loud that hearing that sound come from her own throat was as liberating as any orgasm. It was knowing that she had sought this woman out, night after night, because she wanted Emily's hands between her legs, because she wanted Emily's fingers inside her, because Lila loved Emily's wrinkles, her unspeakably beautiful breasts, her grey hairs, the thrilling shape of her thighs, because Lila wanted Emily's hands tracing her stretch marks. It was knowing she had sought her out and now Emily was in her.

FORTY-TWO

The next morning Lila climbed up on her roof and sat there in the hot sun, looking out over the city. She felt very quiet. Her city was the most beautiful woman she had ever known, and yet, it was changing so quickly. More quickly than Lila was changing or perhaps in different directions.

Lila Futuransky had become responsible for another person. That meant making compromises, giving up things. In return she supposed she'd be a better person. She wouldn't be lonely anymore or horny or friendless. She would be a loved and understood person in this world, which is no small thing, and she would have a great companion. Everyone has to grow up sometime. Sooner or later she'd be almost thirty. Most women her age had families, now she would have one too.

A tear formed in Lila's gut. *I don't know who I am right now*, she thought. *I want to go back to the old way.*

She heard the rooftop door creak open and turned to see Isabel Schwartz step out in her lavender cut-offs.

"Isabel, what are you doing here? Aren't you supposed to be at Burger Heaven?"

"I quit," she said, with an expression of pure happiness. "I spent all night reading *On The Road* and then I went out this morning and saw everyone in the city get ready for another day or get pushed into another day that they'll never be ready for and, do you know what I realized Lila? Do you know what hit me?"

Lila sat quietly, never moving, while Isabel danced around the roof, pointing to the skyscrapers and tenements, using the bridges as her blackboard.

"Lila, think about every kind of person that you can possibly imagine. Then, take the ones who have enough guts to get out of wherever they are because they're driven by a higher fantasy of what is possible, or because the people around them throw them out. Then these individuals come here to a giant cacophony of sound and light and activity and they find out that what they imagined doesn't exist at all. But, there is something even more frightening and holy which is the spectacle of all these people having this realization *together*. Lila, you can't stop walking the streets and trying to get under the city's skin because, if you settle in your own little hole, she'll change so fast that by the time you wake up, she won't be yours anymore. Do you see Lila? Do you see? Lila? Lila? What's wrong?"

Lila stared at her own feet, she was too ashamed to show her face.

"Someone is asking me to do something that will never be right. And I'm going to do it because I love Emily, even though I don't know what that means. And all along I'll know that it will be an endless series of proofs that will never be enough. And my only excuse is that everyone has to do this sometime in their life."

"Don't do it buddy," Isabel was prancing, she was singing like Sal's saxophone, touching the whole neighborhood.

But Lila was sobbing so hard, she was swimming through her tears.

AFTER DELORES

For Julia Scher
and in memory of Jean Genet

ACKNOWLEDGMENTS

I am thankful to everyone who took the time to read and discuss this manuscript in various stages of development. Especially helpful were Susan LaVallee, Shelly Wald, Kathy Danger, Beryl Satter, Julia Scher, Bettina Berch, Steve Berman, Robin Becker, Anne D'Adesky, Carole Maso, Charlie Schulman, Maxine Wolfe, Migdalia Cruz, Susan Seizer, Erica Van Horn, Wendy Patterson, Ana Maria Simo, and Abigail Child.

My editor, Carole DeSanti, made consistently smart and creative contributions to this project.

For their generous support in times of great need I am thankful to Andrea Kirsch, Laura Flanders, Charlie Schulman, Steve Berman, Laurie Linton, Bettina Berch, Peg, Leslie, and the New York Foundation for the Arts.

The first draft of *After Delores* was created at the Mac-Dowell Colony. I am grateful to the administration and to the artists I met there for the affirming experience they made possible for me.

After Delores was developed, in part, as a personal response to the play *Pickaxe*, written and directed by Ana Maria Simo.

I was good but became evil because
I expected too much of other human beings.
                    —DELMORE SCHWARTZ

1

I walked out in the snow trying to get away from Delores's ghost. It was sitting back in the apartment waiting for me.

Snow was powdering up the sidewalk, but I'd seen too many winters to be surprised by how beautiful they can be. The sky became sheets of clear plastic that moved alongside me through the streets, turning the city into a night of transparent corridors. I walked through it to a few more beers, different places, and ended up at a big, gay dress-up party in the basement of an old public school.

There, the winter night that had been walls turned into men and women dancing together and by themselves and not dancing. One more drink and the skin on my face went numb. Then, for the first time that day I could relax. That's when I saw Priscilla. Some girl was dressed up as Priscilla Presley in a long black wig and miniskirt wedding dress that said "I'm a slut but I'm really a virgin," just the way Elvis liked it. She was so hot in that dress I surprised myself, watching her sashay around the hall handing out autographed pictures of The King and swallowing Dexedrine. When I caught her watching me, she came in like a close-up and said in the sweetest Texarkana voice, "Honey, take me for a ride in your Chevrolet."

"You look good in that dress," I said.

She was smiling then but I knew she was deadly serious.

"How good?"

"Real good."

It was all happening so quickly I was almost surprised when Priscilla walked me into a chair and pushed her breasts in my face. I slid my hand down the slope of her ass to the mesa that was the top of her thigh, and then pulled on the rubber seat of her panty girdle, letting it snap back with a slap.

Once we were out on the dance floor it got even hotter. I'd never gotten so hot so fast for a girl I didn't know before. She wrapped me up in her pink tulle veil and I could hear the crinkling of polyester as our bodies rubbed together.

"You really do it for me, Priscilla."

She looked up from her orange lipstick and tons of black eyeliner, smelling cheap like "Charlie" or "Sen-Sen."

"Honey, you got strong arms. My daddy is a military man and I know power when I feel it."

The music stopped, letting everyone mingle again, but now and then she'd look my way and I knew for sure how hot it was going to be.

There were maybe a hundred people there that night, but all I saw was Priscilla; otherwise I sat in the chair preoccupied, like sleep or just waiting. In that chair I dreamed that all my teeth were falling out into my hands. I kept trying to stuff them back in until I woke up to Priscilla standing over me red and shaking. Her demeanor was gone. So was her accent.

"That bitch," she said.

"What's the matter?"

I thought she was talking about me.

"That bitch in the leather jacket. That woman fucked me and then she fucked me over and I'm going to give her hell for it right now."

She flicked her bracelets down her wrist in a way that let me know Pris was just an old-time femme. She was ready to walk right up to Ms. Leather Jacket and slap her face, provoking a huge scene. Priscilla's blood was boiling. She stamped her feet.

"Ooooooh, that bitch."

"Pris," I said, getting straight right away. "Before you let her have it, why don't you change out of your costume?"

"God damn that bitch, she can't get away with this."

"Pris, darlin'." I put my hands on her shoulders. "Get out of the costume. You'll feel better."

"You think so?"

"Yeah. She'll never take you seriously in a white mini wedding gown. Come on, I'll help you change."

As we slipped into the heatless back room and she took off her wig, I realized that I had better get a grip on my drinking so I wouldn't keep ending up in situations like this one. She stepped out of her dress and left it lying in a heap on the floor. She washed the makeup off her face and put on her real makeup, took off her orange heart-shaped earrings and put on a nice shirt and nice pants. Then she went to tell that girl where to get off.

There was such a general clamor complete with queer goings-on in that room that night that no one noticed at first when Pris began to yell. Once they caught on, though, everyone pulled back and hung out unabashedly watching them go at it for a while. Ms. Leather was squirming, straining like a big dog on a short leash, trying to get the hell out of there. Pris didn't give a shit about what anyone thought of her. She just kept lashing away, not letting up for a second. I could tell from her face it was all rat-a-tat-tat. Some of the dancing fags enjoyed it for the dish effect while most found the whole catfight rather messy and unfortunate. But I was happy. Something about it was exciting to me. If you waited for the right moment you could eventually get revenge. Before that night I'd never considered fighting back. I was still afraid of consequences. But I got off on Priscilla's wagging finger, her swaggering shoulders, her mouth moving so fast it flew off her face. She was doing a dance called getting even. It had been a long time since I'd gotten a thing for anyone besides Delores, but maybe Priscilla was a fairy godmother with a bad case of fifties nostalgia. That's when I started thinking that I might have a dress-up fetish. But what kind of girl would want to dress up for me? I could practically come just thinking about it. But she wasn't really Priscilla Presley and that was that.

By the time Ms. Leather Jacket had crawled home and the mess was all cleaned up, I was deep in a dream and stayed there until Pris tapped me on the shoulder and we ended up back in the snow.

"This is a worthless winter," I said. "It doesn't give you anything. Not quiet, not stopping traffic, not everything white. Nothing."

Pris didn't have proper winter boots, so her feet must have been sopping in those thin things with the spiked heels. Still she enjoyed the sky full of snow, her face shining in the streetlight.

"Delores walked out on me," I told her.

"Let me guess," she said with a Miss Thing tone in her voice. "She hurt you real bad and all you need is someone to take you home and make you feel better."

"I didn't say that."

"You didn't have to." She was clapping her hands, catching the snow. "I'm little and I'm cute and enough women have told me that's *all* they want that I now know that's *all* anybody wants."

"You want a beer?" I asked 'cause I wanted one myself.

"Buy me a slice," she said, leading me to a pizza parlor run by stoned Arabs with big grins. It was yellow plastic, too much light, with posters of Yemen and grease-stained wax paper everywhere. Under her leather gloves were five long and polished nails on her right hand and three long polished nails on her left. The index and middle were cut, not chewed, to the cuticle.

"Southpaw?"

"I'm a left-handed lover," she said thoughtfully, holding her hand up to the fluorescent light. "When they grow too long it's depressing since I don't like to go without. But, don't get me wrong, I do believe in love." She had a dreamy teen-aged smile on her face. "Want to know what I know?"

"Sure." My voice came out like rancid butter.

"Okay, here it is, Priscilla Presley's philosophy of lesbian love. First, mistresses are fine, but when it gets too serious there's only room for one at a time. Two, it's got to be as over in your head as it is on paper. Three, everybody needs time between affairs to remember who they are. See how easy life can be?"

"But Delores left me," I said.

"Yeah, but she's still got you by the balls."

She picked the cheese off her pizza with those cherry red nails, grease dripping all over the floor.

"You're old gay, aren't you, Pris? You believe in honor."

"I never let a man touch me," she said. "And plenty have tried. I take myself very seriously."

I went next door to get a beer and picked up one for her too. Priscilla was some kind of angel with an important message. I had a question to ask her. It was "is love always worth it?" But by the time I got back, she was gone. Only she'd left her little black purse sitting lonely there like me on a yellow bucket seat. Inside it was her address book and a gun.

2

The breakfast shift started at six-forty-five but I punched in at seven on a lucky day. It was still dark outside, no matter what time of year. The crew was always waiting in their early morning attitudes.

"You look like you've been screwing all night," said Rambo, leaning against the register in his military pants, ready to start all his bullshit for the week.

"Smile," said Dino every morning, deep-frying bacon for the fifty BLTs he'd make at lunch.

"Come pick out my numbers," said Joe the cook. He was in the kitchen adding sugar to everything because Herbie, the boss, was so cheap he didn't want Joe putting eggs in the meatloaf or using spices. Finally Joe just gave up on flavor and added sugar instead.

Herbie's customers were living proof that you are where you eat. The breakfast club wasn't too fascinating except for the couple having an affair. They snuck in a few minutes together before work every day, the guy coming in first, staring nervously at his coffee. Then the lady came. Her hair was done up like Loretta Lynn and she always ordered American cheese on a toasted english and a glass of water with a straw. They'd hold hands across the table and say things like

"Did you see Mel Tormé on 'Night Court' last night?" Then she'd get in on his side of the booth and I'd leave them alone until seven-thirty, when she went off to work at the phone company across the street.

Every day was the same day. It started with breakfast, which is always simple. Most people want "two over easy whiskey down" or else "scrambled two all the way." You always have to ask them what kind of toast. Then they leave you a quarter because they think breakfast doesn't merit the same tipping scale as other meals. I'd like to remind them that a token still costs a dollar no matter what time you get on the train.

Herbie's mother came in at eleven carrying shopping bags full of discount paper towels, or honey cake left over from her daughter-in-law's party. Herbie could sell it for a dollar a slice. Joe called her "Greased Lightning" because she moved slowly but still managed to steal waitresses' tips right off the tables. If you caught her in the act, she might give it back, but Momma was one of those bosses who hated to see the employees eat because she saw her money going into their mouths. She hated to pay them or see them get tips because somehow that money should have been hers. Her son was the same way, cheap. Herbie claimed that spring started March first. That's when he turned off the heat, which drove a lot of customers over to the Texas-style chili parlor next door.

The lunch rush was a blur where I went so fast I'd forget I was alive and would dream movement instead, swinging my hips back and forth around the tables. That was the most fun because of the challenge and speed and the whole crew teaming up together, feeling closer. So, it was always a letdown when the place emptied out at two o'clock, because that was it, money-wise, and the rest of the afternoon was going to be a sit-around bore.

By three o'clock the workers got to eat, which meant sneaking around whenever Momma or Herbie would turn the other way and popping something in your mouth. Technically we could have egg salad or french fries, but Joe would pretend he was slicing corned beef for a reuben and leave a whole bunch on the slicer for us to grab. Then Dino would forget to put away the fresh fruit salad so we could all have a nice dessert. Only Rambo wouldn't play along. He always threatened to turn us in but was too much of a coward. Rambo spent the entire day leaning against the register showing off his tattoos or talking about the latest issue of *Soldier of Fortune* magazine and how he wished he could have gone over to Lebanon or Grenada instead of being stuck back here in the reserves.

Work was so much the same every day and business was so slow that I had nothing to do but read newspapers and after that stare out the window. That's when I would think about sad things. I couldn't help it. So, I started drinking with Joe behind the grill. I guess I just needed to sleep for a couple of weeks but I had to go to work instead, so drinking was some kind of compromise between the two. I knew enough, though, to keep in control of things or else the customers looked at you funny, which makes you feel paranoid and pathetic.

In the old days, I would come home from the restaurant and Delores would be there.

"Hi, baby, I missed you so much," she'd say.

I'd put my nose into her neck and say, "Mmmm, you smell great."

"You don't," she'd laugh, that strange Delores way of mocking and loving at the same time. "You smell like eggs and grease." Then she'd kiss me on the face and slap my ass, being silly and mean and cute.

Even after I took a shower, I never smelled as good as she did. I had to settle for being a nicer person and what the hell does that mean?

3

Priscilla had the kind of gun you'd expect from Barbara Stanwyck. It was tiny, with a pearl handle, deadly, sleek and feminine. I knew that if I hung on to it I would kill someone. Probably myself.

Delores used to carry a picture of Barbara Stanwyck in her bankbook. On the back was a copy of her favorite Stanwyck quote. "My three goals are to eat, to survive and to have a good coat." But Delores could never remember if it was Barbara the person who said that or whether it was a line from a movie.

Delores was out for the basics but she also liked being around glitz. She only took the kind of work that let you be near fabulous people. I remember one spring I got a job dressing up as a tomato and handing out fliers for a vegetable stand. Not Delores. She got a job calling up presidents of major corporations and asking them how they felt about their Lear jets. Both gigs paid five an hour, but when I was leafleting downtown Brooklyn, she was phoning from an office on Fifth Avenue.

"You never know who you might meet in Midtown," she used to say. "In Brooklyn, you can be pretty sure."

Also she loved *People* magazine. We used to go out on Sunday evenings to walk around Astor Place, where all kinds of people were on the street selling their stuff. You could buy somebody's shoes off their feet if you wanted to, that's how down and out everybody seemed. Some people would have good spreads of old books or coffee pots and radios that had obviously been freshly ripped off. But some people just had an old shirt or a couple of magazines they found in the garbage. That's where we did our shopping. Delores would buy week-old *People*s and some fashion mags for fifty cents, when they cost five times that in the store. Then when we got home she'd cut out the most outlandish outfits and paste them up on the bathroom wall.

"Isn't that fabulous," she'd say. "Really fabulous."

Delores's new girl friend was named Miriam Silverblatt but she changed it to Mary Sunshine when she got a job as a staff photographer for *Vogue*. It looked better in the credits. They met when Delores had a job in the garment district putting electronic price tags on minks.

It took ten hours to tag six hundred coats and by the end of the day you'd throw those coats around like they were garbage. Sunshine came in to take pictures and caught Delores trying on a full-length in the back. Thinking she was a customer going shopping and not a worker being paid six dollars an hour, Sunshine asked her out for lunch and the rest is herstory. You always fall for someone thinking they're something they're not. Sometimes I think that fashion was made for Delores, because it's so dependent on illusion. The people involved tell useless lies professionally and make money, then buy contraptions and use them to have sex. Sunshine had a loft in TriBeCa, invested her money and developed a good-sized dildo collection. She wore tweed pants and expensive leather jackets. I know this because I have investigated her thoroughly.

Having Priscilla's pistol in my pocket opened up a whole new world of possibilities. It might be the opening I needed to get Delores to take my feelings seriously. And if she still wouldn't pay attention, I could get even more serious. If I wanted to, all I had to do was go down to TriBeCa one morning, early, when the few remaining truckers were loading up. Then, when Delores and Mary Sunshine stepped out of their industrial doorway, I could blow Sunshine's brains right out of her head. I'd splatter them all over Franklin Street. I'd have to kill myself too, of course, since the world doesn't understand moments when there are no alternatives but murder. People don't see your pain when you are the killer. So I'd blow away my insides and Delores would have to live with that for the rest of her life. I could never shoot Delores. I love her.

There was something so attractive in that picture that I decided it would probably be better to give Priscilla back her gun as soon as possible. I tucked in my shirt and walked over to the address written on the inside cover of her little black book. There was an endless supply of girls inscribed in those pages, each name written in code with one or two asterisks before the exchange, like ratings on a movie marquee. Her apartment building was across the street from The Blue and The Gold, where Delores and I used to play pool every Tuesday night. We'd stroll over there together and put our quarters down. Delores was a mean pool player from lots of years of hanging out with a wide variety of lowlife. I wasn't bad myself from a couple of years of hanging out with Delores.

I don't own a television or anything like that, so we'd watch TV there, Tuesdays. In the summer they had air-conditioning sometimes too. Delores never knew what to order so she'd usually take a beer until I made her try a white russian, then she usually took that. But she never understood about picking the right drink for the right weather. I like bourbon in winter, but summer's right for gin and tonic or white rum and Coke. The rum makes you relax but the Coke makes you wake up, so you get drunk and excited at the same time.

Delores moved out about a month before the night I got a gun. She had cut out on a Thursday and the next Tuesday I went over to The Blue and The Gold secretly hoping that she would show up too and we could get back together. I was sipping my drink and watching the television when Delores walked in all right, but with Sunshine right behind her. They pranced around like a movie mogul and his aging starlet. I know they did that just to spite me, to make sure I got the message that Delores didn't care. Sunshine could have taken her anywhere in New York City and charged it on her American Express card. The Blue and The Gold only takes cash.

After I spotted them I sat still for a while trying to decide what to do. I could do nothing or I could start screaming in everybody's face. That's something I've considered seriously ever since I was a kid: jumping up and screaming in the most inappropriate places. But when I opened my mouth, the words came out in a thin, whiny string of spit.

"Delores!"

She didn't say anything but she did look at me.

"Delores."

"This is a public place," Delores said. "You can't control who comes in here. You're a control freak."

She was doing that fanatic bit where she opens her eyes real wide and pretends that means she's right.

"Look, Delores, if you had busted up somebody's family would you impose yourself on their party?"

"What party?" Delores asked. "Who's having a party? I don't know what you're talking about."

She started picking her teeth.

"Look, Delores, put yourself in my shoes. Don't you think you would feel bad if you were me?"

"No," she said. "I wouldn't care."

So I tried to man-to-man it with Sunshine.

"Look, Sunshine, you took away my girl friend five days ago. Can't you go somewhere else but my bar on my bar night?"

She didn't even turn her head to talk. She just let moldy growls drop out of her mouth.

"You can't tell me what to do," she said.

That's when I first got the idea to break her face. She broke my home, I had to break her face. She didn't need my bar the way I did. Sunshine had her own TV and her own video equipment. They could make videos of themselves fucking and watch it together on the VCR.

So I'd stayed away from that dive almost the whole of the new year until the night a gun brought me back to Priscilla Presley. I checked out the place across the street and when Pris didn't answer the buzzer I decided to stop in for a short one. It was worth waiting for Pris to come home so I could get rid of the gun and The Blue and The Gold is as good a place as any to wait. It's one of those bars where everybody is waiting on the same stools every night on the stumble home from work at five to bed at eleven. Besides, I'd never been there on a Wednesday before and there were whole new worlds of television shows to explore.

I was on my second one, staring at the still-blinking leftover Christmas lights, when a female voice came to me from the other end of the bar. It started as a tickle in my ear and then, for a second, I thought someone had the sense to record a quiet rap song, but when she got so close

I could see her reflection in my ice, I realized that a real person was talking to me. A blonde.

"Hey," she said, pulling up a barstool. "You want to buy a phone machine for ten dollars?"

4

We drank for a while until the girl asked if I wanted to see the machine. I was tired and needed to talk, so I just decided to tell her the truth.

"I can't. I have to give Priscilla Presley back her gun."

"Do you have to do it right now?"

"I guess it can wait. I'll show it to you if you want to see it, but we have to go into the bathroom."

"No thanks, I've seen guns before. You look kind of sad."

"I am sad."

Somebody played Patsy Cline on the jukebox and that made me even sadder, but in a pleasurable melancholy way, not a painful Delores-type way.

"Look," she said in adolescent earnest as I watched her recite from memory. "You have the possibility to make your life beautiful, but possibility is not forever and it's not immediate. Know what I mean?"

"Who told you that?"

"Charlotte. That's my girl friend. So, you want to see the machine or not?"

I paid the check, rang Pris's buzzer one more time but still no answer.

"She's probably live at Caesar's Palace," I muttered.

"What?"

"Never mind. Let's go see the machine."

First, though, the girl had to call her friend who was getting an abortion the next day to see if she needed her to go along or not. It was the last cold night in March and the wind was blowing dark and ugly. She used the pay phone on the corner as I huddled in the doorway with a cigarette and tried to push away the tiredness.

"You got your period," she shrieked. "That's great."

The girl seemed only five or six years younger than me but she was from a whole different generation. She wore those black tights and black felt miniskirt and over-sized shirt that everybody wore. Her hair was cut short on one side and long on the other with blonde added to the tips. My head was still in the sixties. The only thing that happened in the last two decades that made any sense to me at all was Patti Smith. When Patti Smith came along, even I got hip, but then she went away.

"How did she schedule an abortion without a pregnancy test?" I asked, following her little leather cap and one dangling earring.

"I don't know but she got her period. Isn't that great?"

She started walking east and then more east until it was too east. *There I go again,* I thought, *being old-fashioned.* The idea that Avenue D is off limits was a thing of the past. Now white people can go anywhere.

"Where are we going?"

"Charlotte's place. I have the key."

"How did you know it was okay to come out to me so quickly?" I asked.

"Easy. Charlotte taught me the trick. She says that if

you're talking to a woman and she looks you in the eye and really sees you and listens to what you have to say, then you know she's gay. It works every time."

"Charlotte sounds like a pretty unusual person," I said.

"Yeah," the girl answered, not noticing the cold men in thin jackets, staring silently as we passed by. "Only she's married . . . to a woman, you know, named Beatriz. I stay at her place sometimes when they've got gigs out of town. Charlotte's an actress. I'm gonna be one too. Beatriz is a director. They're different."

Our conversation was the only sound on the street and her part of it was much too loud.

"It's funny having Charlotte's key. It's like an older person."

"How old is she?"

"Thirty-eight. My father's forty. Why do older people always have keys?"

"Because older people have apartments. They're not moving around staying different places. They know where they live."

"Let's get some beer," she said, heading for the yellow light of a bodega presiding over the steely emptiness of Avenue C. I watched the Spanish men watching her. She was so young. She had no wrinkles on her face and wore a childish blue eyeliner passing for sophistication.

"Let's get a quart bottle of Bud and a small bottle of Guinness and mix it. It's not too bad."

I handed her two dollars over the stacks of stale Puerto Rican sweets and shivered. Even the apartment was cold.

"We make love here in the afternoons while Beatriz is away. Charlotte says she likes the smell of young flesh. She says it smells like white chocolate. Old flesh smells like the soap you use in the morning until it's really old and then it starts to rot. My grandmother used to smell that way but I loved her so it smelled good. One time Charlotte and I came up here and an old man passed us on the stairs. '*I can't stand that smell,*' Charlotte said. '*It's weak and worse than garbage.*' But I was happy because it reminded me of my grandmother. When you love someone they always smell good. Want to hear a record?"

She was smoking Camels without filters and playing albums by groups I had never heard of.

"Listen to this version of 'Fever.' It's Euro-trash. you know, French New Wave? Instead of the word *fever*, she says *tumor*. 'Tumor all through the night.'"

We sat and listened. My Punkette sprawled out on the floor. Me, freezing in the only chair.

"That was great," she said, pouring more beer. "Let's hear it again."

Her hands were short and white with badly painted black nails.

"I'm so in love with Charlotte," she said.

"How do you know?" I asked.

"Well, she's strong and she's a good lover. You think I'm young but I know the difference. Plus she has good information about life. Like, you know what she told me? She told me to tell all my secrets but one. That way you invest in the world and save a little something for yourself."

She grabbed on to one of the longer strands of her hair and started splitting the split ends.

"I know that she and Beatriz love each other and I'm trying hard to see it from Beatriz's point of view, so that someday we can all be friends. But for now I don't mind seeing her afternoons, I guess. I have to work mostly nights anyway, just a couple of lunches. I go-go dance in New Jersey. I told you that, right? On New Year's Eve I was so coked up after work and wanted to spend the night with her so badly that I wandered into The Cubby Hole at four-thirty in the morning and they still made me pay."

She had drunk all the beer by that time and smoked all her cigarettes. I gave her some of mine.

407

"Thanks. There was this yuppie girl there talking to me and I was so desperate I would have gone home with her but she didn't ask. Charlotte encouraged me to take that job, dancing. It's not too bad. Want to see my costume?"

She went into the next room to change and I started smoking. It was so cold. I had on a sweater and two blankets and was still chattering.

"Okay," she shouted from behind the door. "Now sing some tacky disco song."

"Bad girl," I sang. "Talking 'bout a bad, bad girl."

Then she came go-going in in her little red sparkle G-string and black high heels. Her breasts were so small that she could have been a little girl showing off her first bikini. She bit her lip, trying to look sexy, but she just looked young. I segued into the next song.

"Ring my bell, bell, bell, ring my bell, my bell, ring-a-ling-a-ling."

"Sometimes they hold up twenties," she said, still dancing. "But when I boogie over to take them, they give me singles instead. 'Sorry, honey.'"

Then I saw her eyes. They were smart. They were too smart for me.

"Charlotte says there's a palm at the end of the mind and it's on fire. What does that mean?"

And I thought, *This kid can get anything she wants, anything.*

She saw me staring at her eyes and got scared all of a sudden, like she was caught reaching into her daddy's wallet.

"I've never done that for someone I respected before."

Those breasts, I thought. *How could anyone make love to those breasts? There's nothing there, nothing at all.*

"Do you think Charlotte will leave her? What do you think?"

"You really believe in love, don't you?" I said.

She looked up at me from her spot on the floor, totally open.

"I don't know what you want from me," I said. "I'm the last person in New York City you should be asking about relationships."

"Do you think she'll leave her?"

Then I realized she saw something special in me. She trusted me. And I was transformed suddenly from a soup-stained waitress to an old professor. We were sitting, not in a Lower East Side firetrap but before a blazing hearth in a wood-lined brownstone. Charlotte was my colleague and Punkette, her hysterical mistake.

"Look, sometimes you have to cheat on your wife and sometimes you have to go back to her."

I looked into her eyes again. They were really listening.

"Maybe you'll get what you want," I said. "But you have to be patient."

And suddenly I wanted her so badly. I wanted to throw off the blankets and be vulnerable again, to roll on the rug with a little punkette in a red G-string and I wanted to show her a really good time. Nostalgia.

5

P unkette had mentioned a
bar called Urgie's in East Newark where she was working
nights and some go-go lunches. I telephoned ahead the
next day just to be sure and the bartender said a girl fitting
that description was working that afternoon under the
name Brigitte. I called in sick to Herbie, which wasn't a lie,
and decided to go see Punkette dance. The phone machine actually worked so maybe we could be friends.

When the guy started screaming on the subway to
Penn Station, I felt for Priscilla's gun in the pocket of my
spring coat. When the second guy started screaming in the
Amtrak waiting room, I felt it again. The terminal reeked
of urine-soaked clothing and roasting frankfurters. It was
repulsive. Danger lurked everywhere.

It wasn't until I got on the train to New Jersey that I
found Delores's old lipstick in my jacket pocket, which

brought back the fact that she still had my keys. Maybe that was a good sign.

Across the street from the Newark station was a run-down diner where I stepped in to check myself out in the mirror. Sometimes you just need to know what's going on with your face, to find out for sure what is showing. It was the same old me. I took out Delores's lipstick and put it on real thick until I had a mouth like a movie star—so caked and shiny that no one looks you in the eye. I slipped the gun into my right hand and posed, Wyatt Earp style, in the ladies' room. I wanted to see exactly what Delores would see if I stepped in front of her one afternoon clutching that little piece of metal. Except for the mouth I looked exactly like myself, but happier somehow. And it was all because the machine in my hand could make her shut up and listen for once. Boy would she be surprised.

It was raining in New Jersey that day, everything typically dismal. The sky was so full of industrial shit and car exhaust, it was all the same color, the color of sweat. New Jersey is a very sweaty state. The only reason girls truck out there to dance anyway is because they don't have to go topless like they do in the city and for the ones trying hard to maintain some distinct sense of limit, it's worth the commute.

Urgie's was a regular place, filled with regular guys from the bottling factory and some construction workers wearing baseball caps. It had fake wood paneling and pink and green disco lights like any tacky family business. Nothing about it was glamorous or half scary. Some of the customers were black, most were white and three had suits on. They drank beer and ate salami and provolone sandwiches. Everything smelled of yellow mustard. Punkette was right, it's not as bad as they make it out to be.

The stage was also on the tacky side and consisted of a hard plastic sheet laid over the pool table in the center of a circular bar. That way the guys could eat and watch at the

411

same time. After all, they only had an hour. Some girl in a white bikini was dancing around like it was nothing. She had nice legs and smiled a lot, but just a little smile. Every once in a while she'd untie the top of her bra and flash her nipples. Mostly the guys were busy talking and chewing but sometimes they'd look up. Sometimes they'd reach over and give her a dollar, which she'd tuck immediately into her panties. I calculated that if every guy in the place gave her one dollar, it would be exactly the same money as waitressing lunch.

I thought about what it would be like if I started hanging out with Punkette on a regular basis, or eventually got a girl friend who was a dancer or a stripper. You'd have to stay up late at night keeping an eye out for her and spend a lot of money on cabs. You'd have to bullshit with asshole men all the time and worry about being paid right. That dancer had a smooth belly, but it was flat, not like Delores.

I remember sitting in the bathroom in the morning when she'd come in to brush her teeth. She'd bend over the sink and I'd watch her ass hanging out of her baggy underpants. I loved it so much I would kiss it. Then, when I took a shower, Delores would come in too. She'd get clean first, but continued to hang out with me in the water so we could both dry off together. What gets me the most of anything is that I really thought Delores was my friend. I thought she'd love me even when she got mad. That's what hurts the most, being violated when you trust someone. Everything gets poisoned.

"Two IDs."

"Excuse me?"

"You gotta be over twenty-one."

The bartender had a tattoo of Andy Capp on his forearm.

"I'm way over twenty-one. Look at these wrinkles on my forehead. No twenty-one-year-old has wrinkles like that. Ask me the jingle of any game show that was on the air in 1960."

"Two IDs."

I dumped the contents of my pockets out onto the bar.

"Well, I don't have a driver's license and I don't have any credit cards. I don't have cards of any kind."

"Then you have to leave."

I stuffed it all back in my coat, leaving a crumpled five lying faceup next to the coasters.

"Maybe you can help me. I'm looking for a little girl who works here on and off—blond tips, red G-string. It's my sister."

He picked up the five and pulled me a draft.

"She ain't here. It's two bucks for the beer."

I put down another five. Didn't get any change. He belched in my face and went off to pour drinks around the bar. I drank down the beer and checked out the dancer. She was probably a psych major from Barnard. Then the bartender came back.

"Hey bartender, you know the one I'm talking about? A punk girl, goes by the name Brigitte?"

"You want another round? Got to keep drinking if you want to sit at the bar."

So I had one more and tipped him three dollars. He started to soften up a bit. This is America after all.

"Let's see . . . Brigitte? Is she the one with the Spic boyfriend?"

"I don't think so. She's more the independent type, clear eyes, kind of naïve, but sharp as a fresh razor blade, real hopeful, someone you'd want to be around."

"Flat-chested?"

"Yeah, that's her."

He wiped spit off his fat mustache with a mustard-stained bar cloth, leaving a nauseating streak of yellow across his already ugly face.

413

"She's got a Spic boyfriend. He comes in here all the time."

"No, that's not her."

I drank some more beer and tried to decide whether or not to tip the dancer. I didn't want to make her feel uncomfortable in front of all those men, but I did like the way she danced. Plus her cash flow seemed a bit slow. At a particularly dull moment, when I caught a flash of "boy is this boring" pass across her face, I stretched out over the bar, reached toward the dance floor/pool table and held out a dollar. Everything kind of stopped. One by one the guys weren't talking anymore and started paying attention until all you could hear on top of the disco music was the sound of them chewing salami and her feet shuffling against the plastic. But that little darling, bless her heart, gave me a big one-dollar smile, took the cash and stuffed it into her panties like I was a regular anybody. Well, I guess a dollar is a dollar, even if it's queer.

It took about thirty seconds for everthing to get back to normal and soon the growl of men's voices took over again. That's when it occurred to me that Punkette, being nobody's fool, probably got a better gig in a higher-paying place. She didn't need that dump. If I looked around long enough I knew I'd run into her again and we could be friends. If she and Charlotte and Beatriz could work out a three-way thing, maybe Delores and me and Asshole could do it too. I was feeling light and ready for one more beer when the bartender came over my way smelling like a rotting Blimpie.

"I'm not running no dating service for you, sweetheart. You're drunk. Now get the hell out of here before I call a cop."

I cursed myself all the way back to the station, getting drenched in the slimy drizzle. That asshole, pushing me around. Everybody's always pushing me around or walking out, or not showing up or somehow not coming through. And I'm the worthless piece of trash that's hurting like hell because of it.

It was just then that I jammed my hand into my jacket pocket and smashed my knuckles on a cold piece of metal. Then I remembered that I had a gun in my possession. I could use it any time I chose. I clutched it first and then tapped it slightly, running my forefinger along its chamber. I knew I didn't have to worry anymore, because the next time somebody went too far, I had the power to go farther. I had a gun. Now everyone had to pay attention. Nothing bothered me for the rest of the afternoon, as I stepped over the broken concrete, the New Jersey dirt turning to mud. It was the new me. I had Priscilla's gun in my pocket and if I'd wanted to, I could have turned around and shot the eyes right out of that fucking bartender's nasty head. But why use up a good thing? There would be better opportunities later on, and more deserving victims. Besides, this gun was a trump I could only play once.

6

When the news came the following Wednesday it came the hard way, during lunch in section two. At first things were fairly normal. The place was empty until the noon rush brought the operators and the one o'clock brought the lawyers.

None of the phone people actually earned enough to eat out every day, but it was too depressing to eat a sandwich at the same desk you sat at watching your life go down the drain. So, they scrimped and ordered a lot of little things, like a cup of soup with extra crackers and a small salad with dressing on the side and tea with extra lemon and water, no ice, which was three trips for me. I often got the feeling that the waitress was the only person in their lives that they ever got to push around, so they took full advantage of the opportunity. Joe always says that working people should help each other out, but the sad truth is that most people never think about who they serve. They just

416

accept it. But every waitress knows that a lot of side orders is a lot of work.

The lawyers were different. They lived defeats and victories every day, so there was always something to get over or celebrate. That meant a cheeseburger deluxe, which is one trip and a dollar tip, guaranteed. They'd wolf down the burger and a fattening dessert and then run off somewhere, so you could get two tables of lawyers for the same hour that one of the operators took.

By the time things slowed down on the floor, the guys behind the counter would go crazy with boredom. Joe had been drinking rum for an hour and had already picked out his horses. Rambo and Dino were usually deep in conversation.

"I know you suck dick."

"I do not suck dick. I eat pussy."

"Do you suck ass too, or do you only suck dick?"

"You suck dick, I don't suck dick."

I took a look at Dino's *Daily News*. U.S. ships were firing on the Gulf of Sidra. Reagan said, "I am a Contra" and, on page seventeen, next to a Macy's ad, was an old photograph of Punkette. She was standing over a cake, smiling. She was a brunette and her hair was long with little bangs. She wore a gold cross around her neck and too much eye makeup even then. The caption said her name was Marianne Walker, photographed at her fifteenth birthday party. She had come to New York City from Allentown, Pennsylvania, on the Greyhound bus and she was dead. The article said she'd worked as a call girl and a stripper up until the night that someone squeezed her neck until it broke. Then they dumped her in the East River behind the projects on Avenue D.

I looked at the picture and I just lost it. I lost it so bad I couldn't even walk out of the store. I kept on picking up tables and placing orders. When you hear something too awful like that, your whole body gets frightened. It jumps.

I looked around at the customers pouring ketchup on

their french fries and drinking Cokes. Urgie's customers in East Newark were just as tame. They weren't dangerous. They were normal. Punkette wasn't a hooker. The paper got it wrong 'cause it's all the same to them. No one was going to take the time to find out what really happened. People watch real life the way they watch TV, sitting in an armchair drinking a beer and talking during the commercials. They love brutality, it's so entertaining. They hate victims. Victims make them feel weak. But I cared about Punkette and someone else out there did too. Maybe it was the girl on the telephone who didn't need an abortion after all. Or Charlotte, who was almost forty and filled with passion and wise thoughts. I was sure, at that moment, we were all three sad.

After that I wanted a drink, so the second work was over I headed for the bar. But I couldn't step in the door of The Blue and The Gold. It stank. I found myself walking east again until the dirty bodega shined like a star from the corner of Avenue C just like it did that night with Punkette. I bought a beer and sat on a milk crate in the back drinking it in the store while the Puerto Rican woman on the register watched TV. I don't exactly understand Spanish, but you get used to hearing it and I could tell what was going on because the emotions were so huge. Men and women in fabulous costumes were fretting, threatening, falling passionately in and out of love. The characters yelled and screamed and cried and danced around. They felt everything very deeply. American TV actors just stare at each other and move their mouths. Sitting there watching those people on channel forty-seven let it all out, I learned something very personal. I learned that sometimes a person's real feelings are so painful they have to pretend just to get by. That's what I'd been doing. When you get hurt and can't trust people, they stop being real. Of all the people I'd been running into lately, Punkette was the most real because, in the middle of a lot of sordid business, she still had faith in love. I could picture her dancing away at Urgie's thinking about Charlotte, glowing. She probably even found something to relate to in that ugly bartender, because she certainly found something to relate to in me. When Delores was home I loved her every day, even when I was sick of her. Then she changed too fast and I was so used to loving her that I let her get away with it. There was a moment, in the bodega, when I loved Punkette instead, but it was too late for that.

In the back of the store they had three shelves filled with devotional candles covered with drawings of the saints. I bought one for Saint Barbara and lit it right there. The woman didn't blink. People probably made novenas on the spot every day, next to the cans of Goya beans. On the back of the candle was written

¡O Dios! Aparta de mi lado esos malvados.
O God! Keep the wicked away from me.

I had to laugh at myself, going to all the trouble of praying and then only asking for less of something. I didn't want more of anything, not money or love or sex. I was praying to Saint Barbara to take the pain away. When the Punkette died, something changed in me. That's when I decided to have a talk with Charlotte.

7

The next morning I tried Priscilla's one more time. Even though I realized that she was probably crazy as a loon, I had to admire her because she had the courage to live out her fantasy. She wanted to be Priscilla Presley instead of whoever she really was, some word processor named Ann Brown from Cincinnati or the like. So, she didn't let other people's opinions stand in the way of her pleasure. Pris was as brave as a drag queen, and just as tough. Even though no one was home, I went back happy Pris was in my life. Then I got ready to meet Charlotte.

I wasn't sure whether it was gift wrap or disguise but I knew to decorate myself for Punkette's lover. I powdered and primped, and put on long hanging earrings with silver filigree. It was almost a party mood, light and dancing, grooving all over the apartment. I was hopeful, like riding the open highway on a motorcycle with your hair streaming out behind you in the hottest heat of summer.

For the last month there hadn't been any clothes in my life, just five days of the same pants, with or without a waitress apron. But that afternoon in early spring, I searched for something pretty to put on my body. Tucked back in a corner of the closet was one of Delores's shirts, overlooked in her last-minute packing. Maybe she'd left it for me as a warning, maybe as an excuse to come back in case she needed one. She probably didn't want it anymore. The material was silky and billowing, the color, a rich teal. In her shirt I looked, all of a sudden, touchable and breezy.

Charlotte's block was different in the daylight. I recognized that particular brand of dingy that's not at all the same as poor. There was a special kind of neglect that felt like sabotage, and a lack of self-love evident everywhere. No mothers yelled to their kids from tenement windows. No music floated down from the lips of thin musicians in crowded apartments. No teen-agers cut on the radio to dance and flirt in lots and hallways under the nostalgic eyes of old people in their ancient folding chairs. No. Too many junkies had taken over too much territory. When the sidewalk belongs to junkies it lies cracked and bland. When there are people, but no signs of life, the buildings that carry them sag with the loss of expectation.

The lock had been torn off the front door of her building, a sure sign of rooftop shooting galleries. The stairs were covered with burn scars from men and women nodding out, cigarettes hanging from their mouths, then dropping to the floor with spit. I hadn't seen any of it with Punkette. The night was too cold and I was too drunk. Two skinny teen-agers in oversized jackets passed me on the stairs discussing crack hits, three for ten. A woman in tight pants, holding a large-sized bottle of Pepsi, let herself into an apartment, leaving behind the stench of menthol cigarettes.

I knocked at Charlotte's door and waited, then knocked again. The only sign of life came from the neighbor two doors down, who was busily installing a conspicuous contraption onto his front door.

"Excuse me, do you know Charlotte?" I asked.

"Hold this, will you?" he said, talking me over to his side of the hall, where I pressed two pieces of metal against the door.

"Putting in a new lock," he added, grimier than this job suggested. "They came in through the window the first time so I had to put in bars. Then they walked in through the front door. Try that again, cocksucker. See, all you have to do is tamper with the door and there's a little shock in store for you."

He waved me away without looking in my direction, flicked a switch inside the apartment and I jumped back as a sudden sharp vibration buzzed through the door, followed by an equally sudden silence.

I knocked at Charlotte's door with a little more urgency, ready to get away from that guy. Her peephole was blocked up with a matchbook cover, taped from the other side. When I looked through it I could make out the words *You too can get a high school equivalency* . . .

"She's probably at the theater," he said in a wasted drawl. This time he turned and faced me, so I had to look at him more closely and saw a wild mustache and bushy old-fashioned sideburns, like an antique image from a sixties album cover. He wore a torn, stained leather fringed cowboy jacket, the kind that hadn't been around for a long time until yuppie stores started carrying them in purple suede for girls. He had these shit kickers that were too heavy for the weather and too redneck for the territory. They were boots that could really kick ass and weren't good for much else besides attitude. This guy wasn't a left-over hippie. He was more Hell's Angels without the colors.

"Which theater?"

"Where they work. A few blocks up the avenue, next to Cuchifritos. Want a lift? I'm taking my cab out in a minute."

I've trained myself to avoid all potentially unpleasant situations with men even though I walk into them constantly with women. Once I realized women could be pretty nasty I actually considered boys for about five minutes until I remembered that they bored me very quickly, and if someone you love is going to bring tragedy into your life, you should at least be interested in them. So my "No thanks, I'll walk" was part routine behavior and part deliberate avoidance.

The theater was a boarded-up storefront on the ground floor of a tenement. It was quite large and long for what it was and had very low ceilings. You could tell it had once been an old-time bakery because the oven marks were still visible, scarring the worn-out brick walls. I came in quietly through the front door, which opened into the back of the audience area. There were soft lights up on the playing space, where two women seemed to be involved in a rehearsal. The one onstage was very tall, especially against the low ceilings. Her skin was the palest white and she was draped in soft black clothing that made her comfortable and classical, like the beautiful woman in a wine commercial stepping out of her lover's bed in the morning wearing his coziest sweater. It made you want to watch her. Another woman was sitting with her back toward me. All I saw were her curls of brown hair. She was watching too and taking notes as the actress recited her lines.

"I used to baby-sit for this family over by where the main road is before they put in the highway. I was baby-sitting for their son and afterwards, Allen, that was the father, he would drive me home. Sometimes, though, we stopped off at Nick's for cheeseburgers and played the jukebox. I liked being out with a grown-up man. It made me feel sexy. Anyway, one night, instead of driving me home, I just sat around in the living room and talked with him and his wife Jackie. And then they talked me into bed with them. So, that's how it went. After baby-sitting I would go to bed with them. Only I would never let Allen put it in. The thing that used to kill me was when I would make love with Jackie and he would screw her right in front of me. I hated it. I would sulk the whole way home in the car. I started going over there in the day when I knew he would be off working. Jackie was usually reading or in the garden. We'd chat, but nothing happened. Finally one afternoon she said to me, 'You know, I think you're a lesbian. You're a lesbian. You'd better not come round here anymore.' They moved soon after that."

It was only when she finished that I remembered it wasn't real. I felt like a spy in a private conversation, and when the conversation was over, I had a stake in it. When the actress dropped her hands and stood quietly on stage, I missed the character that she had become, and felt sad to watch her disappear. So, I let myself stay hidden there in the shadows, waiting to be thrilled again.

"That was shit," said the curly-haired woman.

"Fuck you, that was great," said the actress.

"What are you supposed to be thinking about when you tell this nostalgic little story?"

"You know," the actress said. "I'm thinking about being a girl again. I'm thinking about the different ways that women have said no to me ever since I was a girl, leading up to my lover who just threw me out."

"Well, if the events of the night before, the brutality, are not present in the telling, then this monologue has the sentimentality and saccharine sweetness of a greeting card."

"Don't be a cunt. Do you want me to do it again?"

This provoked the curly-haired woman, who jumped up onto the playing area and yelled, "How did she throw you out?"

I could tell that she yelled that way to get back in control. She wanted the actress to be responding to her, not the other way around. But the actress didn't say a word. She was significantly taller than the director and just looked down at her with a deep tenderness that was so insulting because it was obviously put on. That's when the director reached out with both hands and gave the tall woman a shove.

"Beatriz, don't push me."

"Let me remind you of what just happened, ten short hours before," Beatriz said with a distinctly abusive tone, punctuated by a series of shoves and jabs at the actress's long body. "'Get out,'" she continued, playing it all her way. "'Get out, I don't love you anymore.' That's what she said to you, isn't it? 'Get out. I have been trying for the last six months to get your stinking carcass out of my goddamn life. Now, get out.'"

The actress put her hands out to defend herself but she never hit back, either because she was afraid she'd hurt the little woman with the big will, or because she was afraid she'd lose. Beatriz kept telling her to get out.

"'You're so ugly, no one will ever love you.' That's what she said last night, isn't it?"

That's when the actress started to break down, crying within herself at first, like she was trying to hold back, but the tears came anyway and they were followed by absolutely convincing shaking and heaving shoulders. She sank down to the floor and looked up at Beatriz.

"Please let me stay. Please let me stay."

She said it over and over again, faster and faster.

"Please let me stay. Please let me stay. Five more minutes. Let me stay five more minutes."

425

"Okay," Beatriz said, dropping her arms, absolutely normal again immediately. "That's better. Now, do the scene again."

The actress took her original position and began. As soon as she started, the character that had been talking when I first walked in returned, magically, where a minute earlier she was nowhere to be found.

"'You know, I think you're a lesbian. You're a lesbian. You'd better not come round here anymore.'"

Then, without a beat, she jumped out of her character and out of her light, saying

"I'm so fake. I'm so goddamn fake," and punched the air with both fists. The second fist was the moment that she saw me, so she turned my way and spoke again.

"Can I help you?"

This woman had just transformed three ways in one moment. First she had been in character, then she broke it completely, becoming a temperamental actress stomping across the stage. Then she saw me and stopped on a dime. She turned courteous and charming and looked straight into me.

"Can I help you?" she repeated.

That was the first time I saw her eyes.

"Are you here about the job?"

"Yes, that's it."

I didn't know what she was talking about but it was the flash in her eyes that made me want to say yes.

"Great, I'll be right with you."

She wiped her face with a towel and drank seltzer out of the bottle. Beatriz didn't even turn around. She was busy writing. The actress came closer and extended her right hand. It was huge and carved with veins.

"My name is Charlotte. How strong are your secretarial skills?"

"Fair."

I thought she was playing a game, until she looked my

way again. Her face was different one more time. She was relaxed and familiar, like my lover, my closest comrade, my dream girl. Then she watched how I reacted. I was getting ready to tell her all about Punkette, that she was my friend and I wanted to find her killer, but before I could figure out how to say it, Charlotte handed me a pencil and the backside of an old flier.

"I'd like you to take some dictation. There's no dictation involved in this job but I just want to see how it goes. Where are you working now?"

"Herbie's Coffee Shop. Downtown. Three days a week."

She seemed to like me even though I gave her no reason to. Maybe it was Delores's shirt. I'd never worked clerical before. I always figured that if you went in for typing you'd end up a typist, and I didn't want to end up that way.

"I'll give you some sentences and you take them down."

"Okay."

"Number one. 'My last lover's name was . . .' fill in the blank."

I wrote "Delores."

She looked over my shoulder, smelling sweaty like a man.

"Where is Delores now?"

"She left me for Nelson Rockefeller."

"I see." She was prim and businesslike. "Number two. 'We will all go to heaven for this.'"

I giggled.

"Number three. 'When I laugh like that I feel . . .'"

"Nervous."

She took the paper and looked it over very carefully. I wanted to bring up about Punkette but I just couldn't. I couldn't disappoint Charlotte. I didn't want her to think

427

that I had lied about the job. I could get in touch later and explain everything.

"Thank you very much."

She held out that hand again.

"If you don't get the job I hope you will come back and visit."

And then she smiled the sweetest smile.

8

I don't like to admit it but women are the worst tippers. They put their heads together to divide up the bill and actually figure out exactly fifteen percent without taking into consideration how much they made you run around. Men don't talk about it. Each one peels a dollar off his billfold and quietly leaves it by the side of his plate.

It was a tough day at Herbie's because Momma was ragging on all of us. Joe and I were drinking rum, trying to stay out of her way. Some cooks make you feel tired, others are plain annoying, but Joe charmed me somehow into being more feline. With gold chains shining on his brown skin and a toothpick hanging from his lips, every favor he asked was a service, and his smile, approval. The way he'd say "got it, babe" when I called in my order, no matter how busy he was, always reminded me that he was my pal.

"Rum is good," he said in his Caribbean accent, "but it

can betray you. When you get the shakes, you've gone too far. Don't go that far, you're still a lovely girl. You're a sweetheart."

Then he looked both ways and poured some more into my coffee cup.

"But," he sighed. "What can you do? The world is so full of pain."

Then he'd scratch his big stomach and laugh.

"I'm going home to Brooklyn and smoke some cocaine and turn on the television. Oh I'm getting fat from all the sugar in the soup."

When Joe left I hung out with Dino, who was on the grill until closing. He was telling his war stories again because there was nothing at all happening on the floor.

"I was all over the Pacific during the war," he said. "They sent me to islands I didn't even know the names of 'til I was on 'em. Then we got two weeks of R and R in Hawaii. That was nice. Hotel, everything."

"Did they have segregated regiments then, Dino?"

"Yep. And drill sergeants of both colors. All of them ugly as homemade soap. Oh-oh, check out Rambo. Thinks he's so sly, that jerk."

Rambo was busy being the big man and giving away food for free to a cute Puerto Rican clerk from the hardware store. She was playing coy and hard to get. But, Rambo had picked the wrong moment to get off the register, because the place was too empty and Momma was keeping her eye on everything. That's when I realized that for all his tough-assed talk, Rambo didn't even know how to steal and get away with it. He was putting on his whole show right out in the open, wildly flagrant without choosing to be.

"That turkey is so overt," Dino said.

Rambo ran rampant all over the kitchen. He whipped up a plate of the rarest roast beef while Dino sat there chuckling and covering his eyes. The slices were so red and bloody that Momma could spot them from a block away.

"Thief," she shrieked with a shrillness that made the orange wallpaper tremble.

"What's the matter, bitch?" he said under his breath.

"Do you have a ticket for that? Where is the ticket? Thief, you steal the food out of my mouth."

"Fuck you, twat," he was screaming all of a sudden. He was screaming louder than she was. "Fuck you and your dead meat."

"Get out of here," she yelled. She yelled but she didn't move, like she had been firing people from that chair for forty years. Taking someone's job away involved such a natural sequence of events for Momma that it didn't require any energy anymore. Rambo picked up the roast beef and smashed it against the wall, which broke the greasy mirror. Up until that point it had been pretty interesting, but I didn't like it at all when the mirror cracked. A curse by Rambo would be hard to shake.

"I'm gonna kill you, you bitch. Watch your ass. I'm gonna kill you."

But he didn't kill her. He just walked right out the front door. The clerk from the hardware store kept sipping her 7-Up as though she didn't care about anything one bit. Me and Dino stood there without making a move. I did not want to touch that meat, lying in the crud on the restaurant floor, but I knew it would be me.

"Come on," Dino said. "I'll help you."

He started picking up the pieces of plate and beef and putting them in the garbage. Momma walked over, real slowly, watching us like we had been the ones who broke it.

"Dino," Momma said. "Those garbage bags cost thirty-five cents each. Don't use so many. Smash the garbage down with your feet. Don't be lazy. Be strong."

"I'm not lazy," Dino said calmly.

"And you," she said, pointing to me. "Find a doctor with a good practice and everything will be under control."

"That woman loves money," Dino said after she waddled away.

431

"She called you lazy."

"Don't pay her no mind. She loves money too much."

He picked out a penny from the garbage.

"I'll give this to Momma. Then she'll be happy." And he smiled at me. "Don't let it get to you, there are beautiful things in life."

But for some reason, I just started crying and crying.

"You got to get a grip on that drinking," Dino said.

9

Herbie's Coffee Shop was in the same neighborhood as Sunshine's loft. That's how I knew so much about her. She used to come in for breakfast with various models she'd picked up on shoots. They had to eat at Herbie's because all those Yup-Mex, blue-margarita places don't open until lunch. Sunshine was one of those customers who never thought their waitress was real, never recognized her, never learned her name. She'd leave the coffee sitting there while she made witty conversation and then call me over to complain that it was cold. Some afternoons I could see her and Delores whiz by on Sunshine's motorcycle. They were so cool I could throw up. TriBeCa was exactly where they belonged. There were a lot of offensive people living in TriBeCa, which was, in general, an offensive neighborhood. And in relation to those kinds of people, I was their servant.

There were still a couple of artists living around that

area, but only the rich ones. There was one in particular who was very famous. His picture was once in *People* magazine. He used to come in and talk about money for five to six hours at a time. He was always surrounded by people who said yes to everything he said, and he talked so loudly you could hear him in any corner of the restaurant. One day he was talking loudly again, as usual, and saying his ideas.

"I've just returned from my Eastern European tour where I developed great insights into the difference between communism and capitalism."

Just then Charlotte walked into the restaurant and took the table right behind the artist.

"Under capitalism, a family living in Harlem will never see Paris. Under communism, a family living in Budapest will never see Paris. But, the family in Harlem *might* one day see Paris. And that is the difference."

I was embarrassed that Charlotte should see me wait on someone so stupid, but when I went over to her, she leaned across the table like a co-conspirator.

"You want to know the difference between communism and capitalism?" she asked.

"Sure."

"Under capitalism people with new ideas serve people with old ones. Under communism it's exactly the same, only under communism you don't get tips."

And then I realized that Charlotte had come to see me.

"Did I get the job?" I asked, not knowing whether to laugh or not.

"I have to admit that there is no job. Forgive me?" She kissed my hand.

"Sure."

"I do these things," she said, "because I like provocation. Otherwise I'm bored and nasty all day long. Besides, I didn't want to talk about Marianne in front of Beatriz. You understand that, don't you?"

"Yeah, but, how . . ."

"Marianne told me all about you. She said you were very kind. You paid for her drinks. You shared your cigarettes. You gave her advice and you didn't try to get her into bed. I thought you'd show up eventually. After all, Marianne was a very attractive young woman, wasn't she?"

"Yes, she was."

"But we'll talk more about this later. What time do you get off work?"

She sat there for the next forty minutes making friends with Dino and Joe by imitating all the customers. Charlotte was amazing because she could be anybody at any time. She could be whoever you wanted her to be and still have total control of the situation. She was an entertainer all the way.

When work was over we walked to the park.

"How could you possibly get bored, Charlotte, playing characters all day long?"

"Acting is great," she said. "I love being hateful especially. It's so satisfying. It's terrible in life but on stage it's the best. That way everyone watches you more closely and then they want to soothe your sorrows and make you a better person."

As she talked I could see how smooth she was. She knew which facial expression to use to communicate every situation. Her face was capable of such refined emotions that she managed to convey what she was thinking and acknowledge what I was thinking and still be polite. But there were always surprises. Like I'd be right in the middle of explaining about Delores when, "Oh God!"

"What is it?"

"I saw a baby slobbering all over himself. It was great."

She was a kid, ready to grab and respond to anything immediately. She didn't let her life walk all over her.

It was just warm enough in the park to try out a bench. I could feel Charlotte breathing next to me. She smelled like a horse. It was so exciting. Charlotte really felt

435

things, just like those guys on Spanish TV, and it made me a little freer, being near her. My whole body was tingling, my muscles were breathing. No wonder Punkette loved her. Since Delores I haven't known how to relate to people sometimes because I can't tell how much they really feel. If they pay attention to me I don't know if they're doing it on purpose or if it's a trick. But, with Charlotte's voice on my neck, I realized how much I had missed closeness. I think I got too turned on, though, and kept interrupting maniacally, for no reason but to be in conversation with Charlotte. To see her teeth.

"Charlotte, when you were little, what did you want to be when you grew up?"

"Growing up has always been an elusive question in my life."

"What does *elusive* mean?"

"Fuzzy, changing shape."

Actually I think I did know what *elusive* meant, but I was so excited that I forgot.

"Let's see," she kept going, "I used to play games all the time. I had six brothers. One died. Three of them are priests. The other—"

"What kind of games? Oh . . . sorry."

I wanted to shut up, I really wanted to shut up.

"That's okay. Princes and dragons and buccaneers. We would—"

"Princes? Do you want to get a beer? I'm sorry . . . I am listening. I'm hearing every word you say."

I was. I was listening too hard. So, she got silent. Almost sullen. I had no idea at all of what to do until a derelict walked by laughing to himself.

"I don't like homosexuals," he said.

And I loved him for that because he could see the same thing in me that he saw in Charlotte. It put us on the same boat. I wanted her to put her arm around me but instead she flattened back her black hair and took off her earrings.

436

"Better get rid of these and back to my tough self."

Right there before me on a park bench, she transformed from the soft woman on stage, laughing and open, to an Irish butch with a set jaw and big hands, who comes home at night with tight shoulders, needing loving from her woman. I think that was the first time that any of Charlotte's personas struck me as real. She was a woman who wore suit jackets and men's pants. She'd stick her hands in her pockets and clam up when she really had something to say.

She was so close and within reach that I could no longer abide by the rule of touching and not touching. I put my hand up flat against her lapel, in the lightest way, and then pulled back, reaching for a cigarette and offering her one.

"No thanks, I don't smoke anymore."

That's what stayed in my mind all night, tossing and turning on the couch. Charlotte doesn't smoke. How could I ever be close with a woman who doesn't smoke? No bitter taste of tobacco on her tongue when I suck it. No late-night waves of smoke hanging on our shoulders. No red tip smoldering in the dark. No passing the butt from lip to lip. She would never love my smell the way a nicotine addict craved me. That's when I wondered if Charlotte was only my diversion, and I was nothing to her. But that thought was too bleak to possibly accept.

10

I'd kind of dropped the idea of giving Priscilla's gun back right away. There's really nothing that strange about having a gun. Most people in New York City seem to have one. It's normal. You're just expected to be cool about it and keep it hidden in a sloppy way. Then everyone knows you have one but nobody ever mentions it, like genitals or money. The truth was that after playing around with the gun so much, and practicing the idea of using it, I was getting used to the thought of shooting somebody.

Murder doesn't have to be a lonely tragedy. Especially in self-defense. I mean, I could kill Delores any day of the week and it would be in self-defense because she was hurting me around the clock. But that type of reasoning doesn't play in the public eye. You can only kill to protect a woman other than yourself if you want to get away with it. That's the trick, I think, that guys often use. They start out wanting to punch anyone in the mouth and then look around for the nearest rude drunk harassing some girl. That way they get their rocks off and can be a hero at the same time.

Let's say one night me and Charlotte would be on the trail of Punkette's killer. All the clues lead to an abandoned shooting gallery between a video store and a *botánica*. It's after midnight and we're picking through the garbage and human shit and used works by candlelight until some big dude steps, suddenly, out from the shadows. He whips out his knife and delivers a speech about why he killed Punkette including all the practical details. He tops it all off with a sinister laugh and lunges for Charlotte's throat. That's when I'd pull out my revolver and let him have it right in the gut. We'd leave his corpse for the rats and run out, euphoric, onto the street. Charlotte would love me forever for that. She'd throw her arms around me and cry real tears. I'm sure everything would feel better then.

If Charlotte and I were going to find Punkette's killer, we had to get started soon. I hadn't heard from her since that day in the park and it scared me to think she might be slipping out of my life. I couldn't let that happen. I put on Delores's shirt again. There are those of us in this world who understand nothing about clothes, about what looks good and why. When one garment succeeds, it becomes a permanent part of the repertoire, a habitual sure thing. Delores's shirt had worked for Delores and, so far, it had worked for me. Now there were other, more pressing, matters.

It was almost comfortable walking over to the theater. Charlotte's neighborhood and I were getting used to each other, or maybe I was becoming part of it. Some streets in New York City are fab and their people are fabulous too. Some streets are preoccupied and keep to themselves. Some are broken and tired. Some accept things the way they are. Charlotte's streets compose their own universe with their own personal sense of order and not too many questions or possibilities. They're not romantic or inviting but that's why they suck you in. Especially if you're the kind of person who doesn't feel like looking at the future right now.

The front door wasn't locked so I stepped into the theater's cool darkness. Beatriz was there again, alone in the front row. I knew I shouldn't disturb her, because she was busy thinking about something dramatic. And, I probably shouldn't involve her in the Punkette thing, because her feelings must be very mixed. But I was curious about what kind of woman would shove Charlotte around in order to get her to do what she wanted her to and then have it work. Beatriz seemed to be staring at the empty stage. Every once in a while she would make a little sound, a snort of recognition, and then, a note.

"Excuse me."

She looked up, interrupted but smiling graciously. A person with very good upbringing. Diplomatic. Not a common person.

"You are Marianne's friend, aren't you?"

That scared me right down to my fillings.

I thought Charlotte didn't want her to know about Marianne. Or was it that Charlotte specifically did not want Beatriz to talk to *me* about Marianne? Did I know something special or had Charlotte changed her mind? I wanted to get out of there but she beat me to it by saying, "Come in and sit down. I've been waiting for you."

She was miles ahead of me and flaunted it with style. She knew more than she should have known but was polite enough to tell me so. Beatriz didn't let suspense hang in the air like the melodrama of a waterfront movie, foghorns and mist. There were no raised eyebrows or padded shoulders and vampire nails. No, she said it like she was really thinking about something else, but in the meantime this little detail needed to be dealt with, simply that she knew more than I had told her and that was that.

"Beatriz Piazzola, like the musician."

She tapped the chair next to her with a pencil. Then we were both staring at the empty stage.

"I warned Marianne not to let strangers into a home, hers or anybody else's. But what can you do when children want everything to be so beautiful?"

She was Latin, but not from PR and not from Santo Domingo, with a soft accent and bad skin. Her English was shaped by a slightly British inflection, like someone who had studied in a grammar school with patient nuns, writing practice phrases in a small notebook, and presenting perfect papers. English had been part of her life for a long time.

"I'm working on a play right now, adapting a novel by the British writer Mary Renault. Do you know her?"

"No."

She smiled kindly as though my ignorance was nothing to be concerned about.

"It's the story of two women who live together on a houseboat on the Thames in the nineteen forties. They have lived this way for ten years, sleeping every night in the same bed and sharing, every day, their habits and imaginations. But they have never been lovers."

"Never?"

"No. Well, one night years before, but that is best not spoken about. They have, you see, a lesbian relationship but they do not know it. Enter, the American."

She held up one finger emphatically and laughed.

"Americans can provide the dramatic catalyst simply by entering. Because, for a foreigner, there is no difference between you and Hollywood. And, in fact, this particular American works in Hollywood. She eats lunch in the same canteen as Bette Davis. She is a walking movie and she is a lesbian. What's more, she actively pursues one of the Englishwomen and chases her into bed."

Beatriz was covered with ornamentation. She wore clashing scarves that flashed color when she moved and an extensive collection of detailed earrings, bracelets and

clips, a leather thong and a wooden comb. It was all somehow just right and comforting because, if I didn't want to
look at her eyes for too long at a time, there were perfectly
legitimate reasons to look at the rest of her. If you watched
Charlotte too closely she'd eat you up, but Beatriz was
designed to be looked at.

"This affair, of course, provokes a great crisis in the
friendship. You see, it forces them to confront the lie in
their relationship and their complicity in that lie, a lie that
has consumed ten years of their lives. Do you know what it
is to have to relegate ten years to a lie?"

The more involved the story became, the less expression Beatriz showed in her face. And I could see she
was capable of great anger.

"I feel that way about my whole life," I said.

"Good. Then you know exactly what I am talking
about."

"I've never heard of a book like that," I said. "I didn't
know it could exist."

"It doesn't." She was laughing again, the kind of laugh
you could pick out in a dark and crowded movie theater.
"What I have just told you is my dream of this book. On the
actual pages there is no American. There is only a dreary
man. And the secret, I'm afraid, is only in the enlightened
reader's imagination."

"Too bad, it would have been terrific."

"It will be terrific. We don't have to stop where the
writer does. That is only the first step." She sighed then.
"People help each other lie all the time. Then they call it
friendship, but it's not, is it?"

I searched her face for the right answer but she gave
me nothing.

"Little Marianne had no respect for what she didn't
understand, and I lie to Charlotte that this is an acceptable
invasion into my life, but it is not. I have given up many
things to be able to love this woman, but I will not give up

being treated with respect. I will not compete for attention with a schoolgirl."

"Do you think she was killed by someone she knew or did Marianne just walk down the wrong street at the wrong moment?"

"Honestly, I haven't let myself think about it. I accept murder in general without question because the causes of such events are far greater than the individuals who carry them out. But I will tell you two things. First, people do not dump bodies of strangers in the river. They don't care enough. Strangers' bodies are left lying in doorways or in backs of lots. They are collected, half rotten, by the police and carried away in plastic bags. Then a report is filed under the title 'Unidentified Hispanic Male 20–25, Assailant Unknown.' And that is the end of it."

"What is the second thing?"

"The second thing," she said, jumping up from her chair, "is that we're going to build a houseboat in here and a gangplank. The lights will be so beautiful. White and hot at noon, the way the sun falls directly on your head and dulls the water. Then in the evening it will be midnight blue, cool and cold, the breeze coming in off the sea."

She looked right at me again, her eyes very full.

"I am not a monster. I am just a woman in all her complexities. We must be able to accommodate a wide variety of simultaneous feelings within the confines of our feminine bodies."

I watched her skin, primarily, and the way her wrists moved. She had the manner of inner grace and intelligent beauty that women only begin to realize in their late thirties. Everything is texture and wise emotions. It was in her voice, her gestures, in every habit. A certain familiarity with obstacles. She glanced, not fleetingly from side to side, but up and down, to herself and then back to me. Her eyes were deep and tired with wrinkles from the sides like picture frames. Beatriz's veins stood away from her neck

443

and those thin wrists, so beautiful—there I could see every sorrow and useful labor. I got excited for the first time in a long time, realizing that this was in my future as well. Not just knowing her, but myself, becoming that beautiful. It had been too long since I had such hopeful imaginings.

"In this play, Charlotte is the abandoned friend, a woman who lies to herself. When you walked in I was planning a scene in which every line is a lie."

"Is that the play you were rehearsing when I met you the first time?"

"Oh no. That was a silly exercise. Charlotte doesn't play naïve things. She must always be very frightening."

"She sure scares me," I said. "I wouldn't want to get on her bad side. She looks like she could smash a chair over your head, just like that. Like she could destroy you if it happened to occur to her or she had nothing else to do."

"No, no, no," Beatriz said, a bit too aggressively. "Anybody can destroy another person. Only, most people won't admit it. A good actress admits these things for us. That's why we love them so much."

Beatriz had the voice of a reformed smoker, bluesy with a cough in her laugh. She was skinny from too much energy.

"Charlotte and I have been together for a long, long time. We have adapted to each other's failings. Charlotte has affairs and as long as she pays attention to me, I tolerate it. I do that because I love her and want to be together with her. What is more important to me than the category or theoretical concept of the relationship is that I love Charlotte the woman."

"Triangles are a big mess," I said.

"No," she answered curtly, as though I was misinformed. "Everything *can* work, but all the responsibility is on the new lover. A romance is always more exciting than a marriage, and a new lover has moments of more power than the old one because you are not so familiar with their bag of tricks. Unfortunately Marianne did not have the grace to adapt to the limitations of her role. The best newcomer is one with a great deal of respect. They have to respect me and they have to be considerate of me. Then we can all be generous and each one satisfied on some level."

She took a large bottle of seltzer out of a paper bag and poured it into two well-worn cups. Without the sweet shot of liquor that I was used to, it tasted sickly, like gas.

"My old girl friend, Delores, she wouldn't be generous like that to me."

"Well, then you're lucky to be rid of her. Don't worry, she'll do the same thing to her new woman when her number comes up. Then you can rejoice. People never change their modus operandi."

That made me angry. It started in my upper arms, they began to ache. I got jumpy like I wanted to smash everything and scream at myself in the mirror.

"She just didn't love you. It's obvious."

I wanted her to shut up.

"You sound like you don't even care that Marianne is dead. You don't even care that someone squeezed her neck until it broke. Think about how scared she must have been. Don't you give a shit?"

"She was my rival. I have the right to be cold. Charlotte likes those young women, I can't stand them. I don't like them aesthetically. I don't like their skin. It's too easy to be gay today in New York City. I come from those times when sexual excitement could only be in hidden places. Sweet women had to put themselves in constant danger to make love to me. All my erotic life is concerned with intrigue and secrets. You can't understand that these days, not at all. Lesbians will never be that sexy again."

I wondered if her hands were too small to have fit around Punkette's neck. And then I asked a larger question. What makes a person suddenly able to commit murder? It's easier to hate than to kill, that's for sure. But I bet the combination brings the greatest satisfaction. When

445

you kill the woman who took love out of your life, it can be an act of honor. But if you kill a woman because you saw her go-go dance in East Newark and wanted to feel her neck snap, then you too deserve to die. I marveled at how easily I accepted this difference.

11

There is a limit to what you can do for yourself. When the mess you're in is too scary and overwhelming to possibly unravel, you have the choice to call in outside help. The best candidates are smart, compassionate and creative. That narrows it down quite a bit. They have to have some free time, and finally they have to care about you a little. When I considered all the necessary qualifications, there was only one option: Coco Flores.

If everybody's got a best friend, I guess she's mine. She's always been a good talker but she learned to listen since she started working as a beautician. We met when she was managing an all-girl punk band called Useless Phlegm. Their name accurately described both their music and their personalities. When Coco suggested changing it to Warm Spit, they fired her. Then she enrolled in beauty school and got a job working a hair salon in the strip of new stores along the waterfront where the fuck bars used to be. Coco liked to hang out outside. She knew all the street people and they knew her. She knew the first name of every person begging for money between the park and the F train.

"When someone asks you for money you have to give it to them," she always said. "How can you say no? Dollars are best."

Of course, a beautician can't hand out dollars like business cards, so she developed a priority list which was topped off by two black dykes who regularly asked for cash. One worked the corner of Fourth and Second and the other stood under the scaffolding on Saint Mark's Place where construction workers had taken out a movie theater and were putting in a David's Cookies. They were definitely lesbians, Coco pointed out, and you have to take care of your own people first, so she saw them as her personal responsibility. There are more and more women in general panhandling on the street but women asking for money usually plead. They cry or they tell you what good reason they need the money for, like getting home to New Jersey. Not these women. They lean against buildings and talk to you real honeylike.

"Baby, can you give me a couple of dollars?"

Coco could get along with just about anybody and was, therefore, obviously unique. Somewhere in the background she was Puerto Rican on both sides, but they'd come over in the thirties so now she was more New Yorker than anything. Coco had never been a salsa queen but she did dabble in Latin punk and was always dyeing her hair a mulitude of colors. But Coco's most special feature was that she could talk poetry. She could turn it on and talk beautiful words that didn't exactly belong together but worked out all right in the end. Sometimes listening to Coco's stories was like swimming. You forgot where you were until it was over and then your arms felt freer. She'd read all the time, steal words for her spiral notebooks and then throw them into one-person conversations that others could only watch.

"Hey Coco, isn't it a beautiful day?"

"I know," she said, flipping her chartreuse frost over her shoulder. "It's the gold-feathered bird."

"What is?"

"The bird's fire-fangled feathers dangle down."

We were heading toward the Hudson River, trying to get across the highway, dodging in and out of speeding vehicles, so I didn't quite catch what she said.

"The bird's fire-fangled feathers dangle down," she yelled over the traffic. "It means believe in the imagination, but it doesn't mean politically like you *should*. The words just do it by example."

"Where did you learn that, Coco?"

"My three o'clock appointment took a course at the New School. Next year she'll take two. She told me about it waiting for her perm to take."

In a minute we were on the dock, sunny and warm. I had a beer. Coco had an iced tea.

"Tell me a story, Coco. Tell me one of your great stories about some girl."

"Sure."

Coco flipped her hair back again and looked out over the water. It was almost pretty the way the sun brought out the blue and hid the garbage and dead fish.

"We were both up in the country at the estate of a rich faggot whose boyfriend went to beauty school with me. She was married and older but we flirted the whole week-end in front of everyone, although her husband, thank God, was absent. Finally, with big smiles, we decided to meet at midnight but forgot to say where. So I waited in bed lounging, making myself fuckable, wet and sparkly. And, at the same moment, she was waiting for me, picking the perfect lighting and music, putting clean sheets on the bed. It got later and later, both of us waiting, wondering if the other would ever show. Finally, I decided I would not be disappointed and assumed my responsibilities as suitor by walking over to the guest house where she was staying."

At just this point in the story Coco took out a nail file and started doing her nails.

"I have a date later," she explained, grinning to herself.

"So anyway, the woods were dark that night, barely one star. Still I found the dirt paths easily and walked them without a light, since my excitement was fluorescent. I was bouncing along, feeling the night when, right then, ahead on the same road, in another direction, a single spot shined my way.

" 'Who's there?' she called out, knowing full well it was me coming to make love to her.

" 'It's me,' I said. 'It's Coco Flores.'

"Well, let me tell you, it was fun. Everything was happening just the way it should."

"What did she say?" I had to know.

"She laughed and said, 'Oh great,' and 'You're hot, you're really hot.' She said that to me because I was on her neck and scratching her fingers with my teeth outside in the woods. She held my hand in her leather glove. We were shy walking together in the night, but happy between kisses. During them we weren't shy at all. So, I put my hand on her ass like it was mine. 'You are forward,' she said."

"Did you do it right there in the woods?" I asked Coco and then felt bad for the crassness of the question.

"No, we made it back to my floor, and I, being taller, younger and the lesbian, unbuttoned her shirt until one forty-year-old breast showed with a nipple as dark as the eyes of Latin women. Do you know what was the most surprising? That she was so caring and willing to desire me. I was really touched, in that sexual way that leaves waves of sweet nausea that always end in the cunt."

Coco slurped her iced tea. She was really talking now.

450

"We enjoyed everything and kissed each other's mouths more than expected. 'Your breasts are great,' she said to me. 'Do all your girls tell you that?' When I went to her asshole it was a cave inside a rock formation. When her fingers went inside me they flew."

Coco got very quiet then, like she was feeling something dreamy and romantic, like all she wanted to think about was those fingers.

"You know," she said, "when you love women the way I do, when your life has been built around the pursuit of women's love, there are a hundred moments bathed in shadows cast from a fire or candle or the strange yellow light of an old kitchen. She was so tender with me.

" 'So,' I asked, 'when was the last time you made love with a woman?' And she said, 'Eleven years ago.'

"At that moment," Coco said, "I saw her pain right away. It jumped out at me. I touched her face and asked, 'She hurt you, didn't she?'

" 'Yes,' this woman said, so real. 'The woman I loved hurt me. She left me for a man. She was incredibly selfish. I wasn't heaven either but she was incredibly selfish.'

"I touched her face like she was my baby, because she was so brave to have made love with me that night. I knew the humiliation she had been carrying longer than a decade. I'd seen it many times before, across tables in bars, whispered in dark rooms and in the mirror."

Coco got sad for a moment and fixed her hair.

"So, she looked up at me beautiful and naked and said, 'Women are so much easier to love than men,' and I wondered what would become of all this because I was so very deeply touched."

Then Coco was finished. She took a little bow my way and started chewing on her ice cubes.

"Coco," I said. "That was a great story. What happened next?"

"Her husband came up the following day," she said,

sucking the lemon. "And that was that. Oh she called me a few times in the city, but she wanted to run around street corners where no one would see us, holding hands and kissing. I couldn't get involved in a trip like that. I want to have sex in my life."

12

Coco's stories helped me think through things. They were like therapy or hypnosis probably are. But as soon as I got home and was alone again, it was back into the real self. I couldn't get away from the spirit of Delores that haunted my apartment and clawed its way back into my mind. Every time I sat in that place the demon took hold. The only thing that led me away from my pain was to think about Charlotte. Then I could forget who I was.

I finally decided that the thing to do was to ask Charlotte if she honestly thought that Beatriz could have had anything to do with Punkette's death. If she was guilty, I wonder how long it took her to plan the murder. What was the final blow that made her decide "Yes, I will take this step now"? If I killed Sunshine, I wonder what would happen next? I'd probably just sit in the apartment waiting for the police to come. There'd be no need to run away.

Where would I go? Why? They'd come and take me to one of the women's prisons and I'd have to wear green smocks, trade cigarettes and learn how to play cards all day long with the other girls. When they bring you into court, is the press really waiting in a sea of flashbulbs, or does nobody notice, so you end up spending fifteen years in Bedford Hills taking Thorazine? Or, do you ever get away with it? Did Beatriz?

"You get used to the handcuffs," this customer told me.

She had been in Bedford for passing bad checks.

"'Cause handcuffs means you're going somewhere and somewhere is better than there. It's like a dog jumping around happy when he sees the leash."

I met her when she ordered an orange soda at Herbie's and sat there for an hour sipping it.

"All the girls don't feel the same about it. That's just my way of looking at things."

She had tattoos on her arm made from a blue pen and a pin.

"It gets pretty boring so you look for little things to do."

They were straggly and uneven. One tattoo said "Danger" inside a heart. That was her lover's name, she said. Danger got out first but they never did try to meet on the outside. She told me that women who were there for murder, some of them, told her that right after you kill someone who really deserved it, you feel great. But right away you have to pay for setting things so right.

The couch was getting pretty dirty from me sacking out there every night, but I could not bring myself to walk into the bedroom because as soon as I stepped into the doorway, all of Delores's lies came back to me.

"I love you so much," she said. "You're my family."

Sometimes it got so bad that all I could do was lie there on the couch and watch the sky. If I had money I would have gone to a decent psychiatric hospital, but instead I was just another pathetic person on the Lower East Side. Charlotte and Beatriz were really my only happy thought. I hoped Beatriz didn't do it. Some people's passions are so unique that reality doesn't have the right to invade. That's how I felt about her and Charlotte in general—that they couldn't be measured by regular standards. They were exceptional. They'd staked out a means of survival on their own terms, working together to take care of things. I'd rather think of them that way, then there was something for me to learn that was positive, instead of growing into another dimension of anger.

There were bars on my windows and outside them there were trees. I could hear radios from the street and at night, the moon peeked out from behind the projects. Sometimes I got so angry I thought my teeth would break. The only other thing I could think of to do was go find Charlotte. So, I washed out Delores's shirt and put it on again. It hadn't totally dried and was starting to look a little tired.

Being out on the street felt better for a minute because everything was interesting there and I saw different levels of pain and possibility in a combination that was somehow palatable, or at least diverting. It's only when you're open that the harshest thoughts pop right in. Delores and I, we had our honeymoon and then we had our crisis. That's when everything stops dead and you find out what the other person really thinks. It was that mundane. But all along I thought that if we could have stayed together through our little war, it would have been an opportunity to love each other in the most honest way. When you get informed, that's when the real loving starts. Now I'd have to explain myself to someone all over again. And, truthfully, there's so much confusion that the explanation seems to be an impossible task.

When I knocked on Charlotte's door, it was Beatriz who answered.

"Is Charlotte around?"

Beatriz stood there relaxed, wearing her little black stretch pants and red everything else.

"No, she's at her place."

I wasn't in the mood for any more surprises.

"Oh, I thought this was Charlotte's place."

"No."

"Oh."

"Do you want to come in?"

I stood in the dark hallway for one second too long.

"You mean this is *your* place?"

"That's right. Charlotte has a place uptown. Are you hungry? I'm just about to make some eggs. Is something wrong?"

"Nothing. I lost my breath coming up the stairs. Sure. Do you . . . uh mind if I look around?"

Everything was just the way I remembered it. There was one chair in the living room. The one I shivered on while Punkette danced. The tumor record was still on the stereo.

"Where did you get this album?" I asked, holding up the jacket cover. It was a black-and-white photo of a French clone trying to look like a forties American movie imitating a thirties French movie.

"That's Daniel, my son. He thinks he's white these days and spends his money on these atrocities. Have you ever listened to this music?"

"Once."

"So you know it's terrible. I said to him, 'Daniel, this is bad music. It is worse than what you hear on the elevators in department stores.' But all he can say is, 'It's wry, Ma. It's pretending to be stupid. You'll get it someday, leave me alone.' "

Beatriz had a huge personality in that tiny body, and the difference between the two was quite clear. One was sharp and dangerous, the other, simply adorable. Like you could cuddle her until she got completely bored and bit your head off.

"The Gambino family opened a punk club down the block and he's been wasting his mind hanging around there with the moneyed youth. He is sixteen now and totally beyond my influence. Last year he thought he was Puerto Rican. Even *refugees* from Argentina think they are better than all other Latins. Especially Puerto Ricans. Did you know that?"

"No, I didn't. Is that how you feel?"

"Not here in New York City, the great equalizer, where we all become Spics. Besides, I've never been a nationalist. Argentines are like Americans, master barbarians."

Beatriz started cooking up onions and scrambling eggs. She kept talking with her back turned, so I could choose between looking at her body or looking around the apartment and she wouldn't know the difference. I kept my hands in my pockets and tried to see everything, looking for remnants of Punkette. I was so uncomfortable and tense, I felt out of control and needed to do something that made an impact. Just so I could be sure I wouldn't disappear. I walked around a bit in the tiny kitchen looking for something to hold on to when, on a whim, I stopped by the front door and quietly snatched the matchbook cover off the peephole. Then I had a secret too.

"My son is ugly to me these days."

The onions were sizzling on the broken stove.

"The more manly he becomes, the more I find him so . . . unattractive. His face is too long. His skin is bad, like mine. He has no grace. The girls his age are so much more alive and brilliant. That's when I was the smartest, age sixteen. I knew everything I know now, but I didn't believe myself."

She could tell me anything. It didn't matter to her at all. I glanced, sideways, at the exposed peephole; it was huge. Beatriz was sort of humming and then she started laughing to herself. I was feeling nervous, sweating. She'd

457

surely notice the hole in the door, then what would I say? She started to set the table, still laughing. What was she laughing about when everything was so serious? She looked up, suddenly, and caught me panicking. Then the door slammed.

I turned around expecting Charlotte's black eyes, demanding to know what had happened to the peephole. But instead, it was an overgrown teen-aged boy.

"Daniel, why do you slam the door?" Beatriz said, knowing he was already in the next room.

Her son was homely and brash, filled with an authentic street cool of his own invention. His Nikes were laced, not tied, his cap was on backward. He had suspenders and wore his belt invitingly unbuckled. His style was too new and homemade to appear in any magazine. In two years it would all be mass-produced for white kids to wear, but for the moment Daniel was a happening young man. He was chill. He was fresh.

"Daniel, did you get the lock I asked you for?"

"I forgot."

"Well, don't forget again."

"All right Ma, all right."

He was filled with an energy that could as easily become brutality as anything, and had inherited his mother's masculine nature, a woman's masculinity that is too delicately defined to transfer well to sons. He smelled of the future and that future was frightening to me because I couldn't imagine ever being ready for it. There was too much in the present that I didn't understand. He kept going in and out of the bedroom looking me in the eye once in a while. I noticed his huge feet as he was out the door again, back to the things that were really important: matters of power and honor.

Beatriz was quiet for three heartbeats and then resumed her faint humming. I looked for something to say.

"How do you like living on this block?"

"Too many junkies. They're even stoned when they

rip you off. We got broken into but they left the stereo and took a cheap answering machine. Too stoned to steal properly. Can you imagine? Then, after a bit of time, they die. Probably only got ten dollars for it. Junkies sell everything for ten dollars."

Beatriz pointed to a dusty square on the side table where something had once been, something that was now sitting comfortably but underused in my living room. So Punkette needed small change and she needed it right away—or just wanted it, that might be more like her.

We sat down together at the table. Beatriz poured water from a clay pitcher and offered me good bread. She tore her piece in half and put it by the side of her plate.

"This neighborhood is a prison between C and D, Coke and Dope. You stay young in prison, did you know that?"

"No."

"In my country I remember a famous criminal who had been sentenced when he was twenty and when he came out he was sixty. People gasped on the street when they saw his photograph in the newspaper because he stayed young while they'd all become old."

Then she grabbed my wrist and pulled up my sleeve. Her grip was like iron. Even though she was half my size she was completely determined and in control.

"No, Beatriz, I don't have any track marks."

"Good. I hate junkies. They're liars."

"Well," I said, still feeling her fingerprints on my wrist. "Crack's the thing these days anyway. No needles, no marks, no AIDS."

She went to the mirror and started combing her hair, changing her earrings, changing her scarf. Her hands and feet were very tiny and her slippers, refined.

"Don't think that I'm afraid of death. It is the waste of time that disgusts me. In Argentina I killed a woman, but it was a political assassination. I can say this freely, knowing it means nothing tangible to you."

I was eating eggs with a woman who said she had killed another woman, at least one, because she had to. Claiming it was almost as good as doing it, choosing to be known as a murderer. I wanted to be repulsed, but discovered, instead, a twisted admiration. Beatriz stretched her mouth tight, waiting for lipstick.

"Now a woman is dead who would have been murdered eventually and I have survived into this life."

I looked back at the open peephole.

"You in America don't have this decision but everyone else in the world must choose between making love and making history. You Americans impact on the world simply by eating breakfast, with so many people working so hard so you can have it exactly the way you like it. For the rest of us, we have to fight to affect anything, or else just live our private lives of hope and sorrow. If I want power in the world, then the world must take priority, not personal habits like love. At precisely the moment when I become convinced of which direction is most necessary to me, the other presents itself. Now, theater, that can be made for love or history."

"And now you're making it for love?"

She smiled a tired smile. It showed the beginnings of a wrinkled face that would become increasingly exquisite with old age.

"I make theater with Charlotte. Sometimes in the early morning she is smiling, plotting in her sleep, being wild in her dreams. I brush back her hair and say, 'Bad, sleeping beauty, bad.' Because she is the mischievous imp in every fairy tale, and with a woman like that, all you can do is pretend. Those are the moments when I can see so clearly what we can make together. And you? What kind of family do you come from? What does your father do?"

"He's a narc in the Dominican Republic for the CIA."

"Oh, the intellectual type."

And we both cracked up laughing.

We were drinking coffee by that time and I could see

460

right through the peephole into the hallway. It completely altered the apartment. It was staring at me, like Beatriz was staring at me. I needed another question, quickly, so she wouldn't look at me so hard.

"How did you and Charlotte meet?"

She was really solemn for the first time that afternoon, as though all this talk about murder and politics was throwaway chitchat but Charlotte was a serious matter. Beatriz's eyes were like the nipples on Coco's lover. Dark and sharp as swords.

"On stage, of course. I'm not usually attracted to actors. In fact, they are my least favorite people in the theater. I could never say words I don't believe, not for money, or approval, certainly not for the principle of being convincing on any terms. Watch out when an actor tells you 'I mean what I say.' That's the biggest lie of all. With Charlotte, the first thing I saw was her way of holding a script over her mouth so that only her eyes showed, laughing."

She illustrated her story with a napkin at the kitchen table.

"Even though it was hidden, you could imagine the mouth and how wicked it was."

Beatriz poured more coffee into my cup and I realized that I was beginning to slide. Maybe there was a bottle somewhere. If I kept drinking coffee, eventually it would kick in. I hoped that would be soon.

"In theater there are many moments inside of one moment, so without the precision of emotion, the play is nothing. It is slop. Charlotte and I were working together for the first time and we were developing a nuance that had to make itself understood in a matter of seconds. I tell you, she had me crying. She was taking tears off her own face with her fingers and slowly painting them on mine until they dripped down my cheek and onto my tongue. I know she's selfish, but she can fool the magician. She fell in

461

love with me first, though, and I'll tell you why. It's because I'm not beautiful."

Yes you are, I thought.

"Beautiful women never take beautiful women for lovers. They like elusive faces and quirky impressions. It's because they want to be loved for themselves, but they also demand adoration. And they don't ever want competition. Especially from the same bed. But, she unleashes me. Our first night together we had talked all evening, strolling on the summer streets, with sirens and water pouring out of hydrants. Two elderly women were yelling in Spanish, their fat arms sticking out of cheap housedresses. When the time came to make love, I was sitting on my bed saying 'Come here,' and Charlotte walked towards me in a moment filled with wanting and compliance. She took those steps across a dark room. She didn't look at me, but there was volition and desire and her body coming closer with no affectation. It was a raw honesty that showed me then how much the rest of my life was lies."

13

I went straight from Beatriz's house to The Blue and The Gold and started drinking in a little booth behind the jukebox. When you begin to think about drinking and staying away from it, every dark street sends out a personalized path of light leading directly to a bar. It offers something to do, a place to watch the clock, and when you're drunk enough to sleep, you can go home. But, if you stay out of bars, there's nowhere to go but home, and then no place to go from there.

The news was on TV but they were bombing Libya and I couldn't handle that. Then the channel got changed to the ball game, which doesn't interest me at all. I had to find something to think about in a stein of flat beer and a bag of Dipsy Doodles. When that's your evening activity the beer goes down real fast and then there's nothing to do but buy another one. I was thinking about smashing Delores's face with a hammer, when I looked up and there she was. She was sitting at the bar, legs crossed, drinking a white russian. She had dyed her hair bright orange and was bouncing her foot up and down in Sunshine's clothes, expensive and too big for her. There was a white headband wrapped around her forehead that made Delores's skin pale and her wrinkles deeper. She didn't look hip. She looked silly like Grandma Bozo.

I wanted to run out of there, but where to? Or run right up to her and scream in her ear, or flash Priscilla's gun, which was home in my drawer. I wanted to spit on her and break her neck and beg her to come back to me.

Delores was so close I could hear her swallow. The sound of gurgling in her throat made me nauseous. If I listened to the rain the way I listened to Delores's spit, I would have drowned right there in the bar. She was the woman with whom I had been living and loving, and at the same time a monstrous orange thing.

The day she left I sat in the apartment, so sad. I didn't know how to be that sad. She was yelling at me and I just sat there.

"I'm leaving you for a woman who is going to marry me. You had your chance and now you just can't take it."

"I can't help it that I can't take it," I said.

What did I love about Delores? It wasn't something concrete that she would do or say, it was how I'd feel when I saw her. She was always so happy when I came home and she liked being next to me walking down the street. She'd slip her arm into mine and say, "Oh, I'm so cozy." It was a sense of well-being above anything else. The problems started when she talked about "forever." My idea was that we stay together for as long as it worked and then something else would happen. You never know which way a relationship will go, so you have to be creative. I couldn't say "forever" unless I knew for sure it was true. But, I believed that Delores was my friend, so whatever changes we went through, we'd go through them together. I had a picture in my head where we'd talk it all over stage by stage and try this or that, always being considerate and in touch. I wouldn't picture it any other way. But, as soon as Sunshine came along Delores split. Sunshine said "forever," so she wasn't interested in me anymore. It's not like we had stopped getting along or stopped having sex—everything was intact except the future. Man, was I surprised. I was so used to Delores being my friend and she changed so fast that I let her hurt me too deeply because I didn't know enough to treat her like a stranger yet.

"Delores, can't you just be nice and talk to me for one minute so we can figure something out?"

"You had your chance," she said.

See, from my point of view, Delores didn't play fair. When you dump your lover you should show a little consideration to the woman you've been whispering to in the dark for so many nights up until that one. Not Delores. She took what she needed and then cut out. She was not sentimental. She was seasoned. Sometimes I thought Delores didn't know how to take care of herself, so she needed to find other people who would do it for her. If they didn't do it well enough, she'd get rid of them. After all, Delores was no spring chicken and you get tired of hustling. People like that run into a lot of lowlife and sometimes they become lowlife themselves. Her lover before me broke her nose. The one before that took her money. Both guys. Some nights I'd listen to Delores tell me about the brutality in her life and secretly I felt frightened, but I didn't know of what. Then one day I wasn't hearing about it, I was living it. It wasn't just Delores's stories anymore. It became our life together.·

I remember one night we were walking home late along the avenue, both in suit jackets with girly decorations. We were both pretty. I looked up at her and I said,

"You know, I think you're my best friend, Delores." And she scrunched up her face in a kind of pure happiness you rarely get to bring out in another person.

"No one's ever said that to me before," she said. "That's what I've always wanted, a chum."

I remember watching her against the eerie glare of headlights knowing that I was the person Delores cared about the most. Now I'm the one she most wants to break. I guess that means I know her inside out. That's why I can't let go. Something organic keeps her right there, next to me. Whenever I move, she follows me because Delores left everything unresolved and that was a dirty trick.

Once, about two weeks after she left, I saw her across a subway platform in a crowd of people and she looked pretty, but seeing her alone and so close in that bar she looked terrible. I've watched that face say so many different kinds of things. I'm afraid when I see her now because each expression is familiar and would evoke memories that, good or bad, I wouldn't want to be thinking about if we were to meet. I'd rather just be present. That Delores. I don't know what was missing, generosity or need, but that last day, boy, she was on a campaign of slash and burn. She was screaming at me, jumping around in a carnival of hate, trying to destroy everything, and I just turned off. I knew inside that there was no way to react that would have changed anything.

So, when she came over and stood at my table at The Blue and The Gold, I knew I would be thrown into chaos.

"That's my shirt," she said.

"Hi, Delores."

"That's my shirt and I want it back."

She was holding her white russian with its little swizzle stick. I didn't get up but I could clearly see her expression. It was blank.

"Hey Delores, where's your yuppie girl friend?"

"She's not a yuppie, she's a lesbian."

"Okay, a preppie with a twist."

If I looked straight ahead my face would have been between her breasts. She was wearing her black bra. I could tell.

"If you don't give me that shirt right now, I'm going to tear it off you."

I was thinking how, if she tore it, she wouldn't be able to wear it, but instead I said, "Look, Delores, why don't you call me later and we'll talk about it. Let's talk about it later."

One of the underlying reasons I said "let's talk about it later" was that Delores had never called me since the day she left, not to give me her new phone number, not to pay the phone bill, nothing.

I got up to go to the bathroom and she kind of grabbed at the shirt, but let go before it ripped. When I got back she was still standing there.

"If you don't give it to me right now I'm going to make such a scene that they'll never let you back in this place."

Then I got scared. It wasn't losing the bar so much, it was the reality of the situation, of how Delores was angry that I was alive and she intended to obliterate me.

She yelled so loud, everything in that place stopped except the video games' repeating jingle.

"Give it to me now or I'm going to make a scene."

What could I do? I looked down at my table at The Blue and The Gold and slowly undid all the buttons. I handed her the wilted green shirt and sat there in my bra. You would think she'd at least leave at that point, but she took it back to her seat and sipped her drink. It was a while before Sal, the bartender, came over and told me to put on my jacket. That's when my head split open. It wasn't a headache. It was my skull. It cracked from the inside and nothing was keeping my brains together. I couldn't even cry. I couldn't do nothing.

14

All that night I lay awake in a dream of my own invention starring Delores as the phantom devil because no mortal being could have such impeccable timing. I dreamed I was wearing a white corset and it started to fill with blood. No matter how much I tensed my muscles, I couldn't keep it from seeping out. Finally the thing was soaked through and dripping red onto the carpet. I was in a fancy house with thick rugs and overstuffed sofas on wooden legs. I saw Delores coming and tried to hide the corset under the chair but no matter how much I shoved it back with my feet, it kept poking out from behind the upholstery.

My insides were sweating as the sun woke me up. Rivulets of salty liquid ran and dripped under my skin.

"You'll be sorry," I told her to myself, twitching like a rough cut in an experimental movie. "I should just kill you right now."

Where the fuck was she? I called her old job but the receptionist said she quit. Then I took Sunshine's number out of the phone book but got that fucking answering machine. I'm sure Delores was sitting there watching the color TV and screening her calls, that bitch.

"Bitch," I yelled, after the beep.

It was one of those days—cold on the outside but too hot under any jacket. I walked along the avenues realizing that all this time and after many incidents Delores continued to ignore the state of my emotional life. The time had come to put a stop to this, to let her know how I really felt. On a whim, really, I bought a postcard of the Statue of Liberty and scrawled angrily on the back

I hate you Delores. I walk down the street dreaming of smashing your face with a hammer, but when your face was right in front of me, I had no hammer. What have you done that someone who once loved and cared for you could be made to feel this way?

and I mailed it.

By the end of that week my living room was filled with thirty novena candles. They were all on their fourth day of a seven-day flame. That way, when I would lie on the couch, there was a warm glow, sometimes feeling like a funeral, with me stretched out, open casket.

The walls were ghost dances from the inside and from the street, gyrating disco-heaven. If I crashed on the couch with fire all around me, it was more peaceful. I had something to look at instead of nothing and something moving beside me instead of no one. I was lying in state when the phone rang.

"Delores?"

"No. This is Charlotte."

I didn't make a sound.

"Beatriz and I just had a big fight about Marianne and

469

I need someone to be with who cared about her. Do you mind if I come over?"

I looked around the apartment. It was a mausoleum. What's worse, Charlotte's answering machine was sitting on the floor right next to Priscilla's gun. I'd decided that morning that the two went together quite well.

"I'll meet you on the street," I said.

Since I slept in my clothes every night I didn't need to get dressed. I just paced back and forth across the room, thrilled to the teeth. I wanted to see Charlotte in my house. The possibility of her being there made living somehow easier. I wanted to watch her crossing her legs on my couch, thumbing through my belongings with her big hands, tough and bony like the Wild West under a big sky. I wanted to see her engrossed, thinking something over and coming to an important conclusion. So, I threw a bunch of towels over the machine and put the gun in the refrigerator just in case.

I was waiting so hard that I almost forgot to breathe, and so, got transported into a series of distant thoughts. By the time the buzzer sounded I was in a dream in which I had become something frilly and lilting, like a Southern belle waiting for her gentleman caller. I descended the staircase of my imagination feeling like Scarlett O'Hara at Tara, but probably looking more like Norma Desmond. Or maybe I was one of those blond creatures, a debutante at the cotillion drinking brandy alexanders, unconsciously garish in green eyeshadow. The drink left a frothy brown mustache that set off my wardrobe of various unnatural colors like beige or powder blue.

"Charlotte!"

She was sullen under the streetlight, her white skin luminescent in the night. My hero.

"When was the last time you changed your clothes?" she said. "You look terrible."

I watched myself grimy and wrinkled. Oh no, there were restaurant grease stains everywhere, baggy pants and

470

the worst, light green socks with a pink shirt. How could I be wearing light green socks at a moment like this when Charlotte was just about to fall in love with me?

"Come on, let's walk."

She started off with a quick pace, leaping over the broken sidewalk with those huge legs. She was talking, but I couldn't hear the words. I was in my private movie and Charlotte was the star. In this scene, she slumped into her gait, in a hurried dissatisfaction, like the Irishman she was in cap and stooped shoulders, glum over his dinner. The grouse, though, was all appearance, for she was easily content. She could happily watch television every night and drink her beer quietly in a corner while the other men played darts. Underneath the coal dust, she was really a champion, a resistance fighter, a king.

"We've been at it all week. It's about secrets. I can't tell her about Marianne because she wouldn't understand. If she knew I'd had another lover, it would hurt her and yet, it's on my mind all the time, of course. So you must never say a word to her about any of it."

She passed her thumb back and forth across her mouth exactly like Jean-Paul Belmondo in *Breathless.*

"You see, Beatriz knows intuitively that something is awry. But she can't put her finger on exactly what. I mean, realizing that your lover had a sixteen-year-old mistress who has just been murdered is not necessarily the first conclusion one jumps to when there's mysterious discord at home. She doesn't know anything for sure, and I want to keep it that way."

She grabbed my wrist and turned it until my whole arm turned with it.

"Do you understand?"

"Charlotte, what are you talking about?"

I loved the feeling of pain that was taking over my arm. But, as soon as she saw the pleasure in my face, she let go, and was sweet again.

"Beatriz is Latin. They have a sense of pride that is different than yours or mine."

She was lying. But she was lying so well, it drew you in. She had that expression on her face that some people use when they want you to know that they realize what's coming out of their mouths is rubbish, but they need you to play along so you do. Then it becomes your lie too.

"She would leave me in a second if she knew that I had been cheating on her. So, if you ever have more than a cursory conversation with my lover, I hope you will be discreet about what you know."

There was some information I had that Charlotte didn't want me to disclose. But I didn't know what it was. One thing was clear, though; I had proximity to one of Charlotte's secrets and that's why she needed to keep me in her life. The longer I held on to it, the closer we would be.

"Do you understand?"

"Yes, Charlotte, I understand perfectly."

A long time ago I learned that being alive meant playing by certain rules. Everyone knows that the specific choice of rules is an arbitrary one, but we agree on them to give ourselves something to focus on. One of the rules is that certain basic things—feelings, other people and responsibilities—are real. When they slip away, the walls cave in and there's nothing left but anger at what you gave up along the way just to play along. Charlotte was the last thing I knew of that I wanted to believe in, because she had power, enough power to love and be loved and still be in control. So, I loved her too, and let her have her way, even though I did know that she was lying.

"What did you like best about Punkette? I mean Marianne?"

"Don't deceive yourself. I did that out of pure vanity."

"But Charlotte, there must have been something about her individually that made you choose her. I know she was sexy and cute in a real touching way, without much passion. Was that it?"

Charlotte laughed, impatient at having to explain what was already so completely obvious.

"What did I see in her? The lack of pain. You can taste that on someone's skin. I like hope under my fingernails. You can smell it all day long like the insides of grapefruit rind. It's fresh and you think it can last forever."

I jammed my hands into my pockets. "But it's not forever," I said.

"Obviously, but who looks at a young woman and thinks of murder? I don't. Even if she was a junkie. A young junkie."

I only had to consider that thought for one moment. "No, I don't believe that. Punkette wasn't shooting junk."

If there was one thing I knew about, it was junkies. They're all over the place and you get used to them. They scratch their arms. They have nervous tics. They leave the water running and the fire burning. There's something very stupid in the way they glance around all the time. No, Punkette's eyes had no junk in them.

"Believe me, I was fooled too," Charlotte said. "But she started stealing things from my house and selling them. She took the television, the phone machine . . ."

Right then Charlotte did the strangest thing. She grabbed my head with both hands, like she was going to kiss my forehead, but instead, she slid her palm over my eyes and held them real tight. Her hand took up half my face. Then she talked to me in a high, faggy voice.

"Can you see?"

"Of course not, Charlotte, you're covering my eyes."

It was quiet for a minute as I waited without struggling, until she started laughing and laughing and dropped her long arms, letting one swing a full arc.

"That's what my brothers used to do to me all the time . . ." she said, normal again and seemingly happy, still swinging that arm.

There was something so brutal in her smile. She was a

473

very dangerous woman. She could really hurt me. And I realized that I wanted her fingers inside me right then. They were long and rough. If I was honest, I would have put my arms around that thick neck of hers and climbed right on top of her fingers.

15

I followed Charlotte into the theater. We were the only shadows passing under the streetlights. The whole block seemed deserted and black.

She stumbled past the chairs and threw a few switches on the lighting board. Then the stage had two eyes, one rose, the other, pale blue. She pulled me by the hand until we each sat in our own spotlight.

"Wait a minute," Charlotte said, bringing up a soft backlight so I wasn't alone anymore. There was enough light for each of us and between us too. I looked up into the heart of the stage light and started crying real tears. Then I knew that was how they did it.

"Are you okay?" Charlotte said.

"Okay," I said.

"Great."

She clapped her hands and jumped up. That was the

first time I saw how tight her ass was. She looked like a pressed flower lying in a book.

"Quick, this is our scene together, coming up. Sit at an angle so it looks natural to the audience. Okay: places, lights."

The lights were as cool as they could be, like the docks at night in a black-and-white movie. Charlotte was in character now looking dangerous and interested. I was respectfully quiet, waiting for her to happen.

"What do you learn from examining me the way you do?"

She asked that question with a slightly British accent, as though we were guests at a turn-of-the-century garden party where the emotional dramas of the upper classes were carried out in the calmest and most naturally inquisitive manner. I could see Charlotte, parasol in hand, strolling the rolling green estate in a white afternoon frock and large hat.

"I like looking at you, Charlotte," I said. "Because you're beautiful and you change all the time. I like watching the changes, they make me happy."

I said that in my usual voice and usual New York accent. It was almost magic, like I was talking to a picture show and still being myself. I could be my own character.

She waited for a minute, tightening her jaw and stooping over slightly so her chin dropped and her face got longer. It stretched as her eyes died a little bit.

"Jesus," she said, slowly bending over into an immigrant woman in Brooklyn somewhere in the days before the Big War. "Jesus, I've been beautiful my whole life," she said, wringing out the clothes and hanging them on the line between her fire escape and the O'Briens' across the alley. "I'm sick of it. People tell me I'm beautiful when they want something from me or they have nothing else to say." She brushed a wilted strand of hair off her sweaty face. "Beautiful." She was mocking now. "Beautiful as a spring flower."

476

"Not a flower, Charlotte," I said. "You're beautiful like a building with red brick and cornerstones. It took hundreds of men to build you and now you're solid and contain everything."

"Stop," she said. Then she screamed it. "Stop."

She screamed "stop" the way you yell at someone when they're just about to hurt you, so that when they do, your scream is embedded in their memory.

"Stop staring at me all the time, it's boring as hell."

For one minute I thought she might be serious and I felt so bad I wanted to say "shit" but instead I said, "Charlotte."

"You want to look at me?" she said. "All right, all right, God damn it, I'll let you look. Look!" And she sat down next to me and waited.

I could smell her. She was almost rotten. I could hear her breathing and watch her chest puff up and down. I saw dirt in her ears. I saw a neck like a mountain and hands that were dangerous. They were murder weapons. Charlotte could kill me easily. It wouldn't take a thing.

"Let me see your legs," I said, and she lifted up her skirt. They were chimneys.

"Finished?"

"Yes," I said. "I'm finished."

So she became Charlotte again and turned up the house lights.

"There's that strange moment in rehearsal," she said, "where a good actor tries something new and it looks silly. Then, all her moments seem suddenly transparent as though she's just a fake, not an artist. I love when that happens to me because then I have to start all over again."

Fuck you, Charlotte, I thought. *This is no goddamn rehearsal. This is true.* But I didn't tell her the truth. I hid it in a statement designed to contain both undying loyalty and bratty insolence.

"Beatriz knows all about you and Marianne. I didn't tell her."

"What did Marianne say about me?"

She watched me very carefully.

"Marianne told me that she loved you, and she really wanted things to work out. She felt lonely when she couldn't be with you. She told me some things that you like to say."

"Like what?"

"She told me that you said there was a palm at the end of the mind and it's on fire."

"Yes," she said quietly. "It's burning. And there's a bird. Its fire-fangled feathers dangle down."

"What?"

"Its fire-fangled feathers dangle down."

"Do you know Coco Flores?"

"Who?"

"She said that same thing to me just the other day."

"It's a famous poem by Wallace Stevens. A lot of people know it. What else did Marianne tell you?"

"She didn't tell me anything else. Charlotte, I don't think I know what you think I know. I just don't think so."

She was sitting on her knees with her hands folded in her lap, looking like a middle-aged nun. She had knees like the man in the moon. When she knelt before me they were as large as my face. I could lick them for an hour and still not cross all the mountains. Here's how I would make love with Charlotte. I would dress her up in feathers and have her hold me by the ass, carrying me around the room. I'd squeeze her waist tight with my legs and bury my face into the stone of her neck.

"Beatriz does know about Marianne," Charlotte said. "I just don't want her to know that Marianne was on junk. That's something Beatriz is not capable of understanding. Okay?"

"Okay."

I knew Marianne was not on junk.

"Can I trust you?" Charlotte asked, turning her head so fast her hair flew. "No, I don't think so."

"I'm sorry, Charlotte," I said, deeply ashamed. "Do you want me to go away?"

As soon as I said it I remembered that that's exactly what Delores used to say whenever we'd have a little spat. She'd say, "Do you want me to go away?"

And I'd say, "No, Delores. I love you. We're just having a fight. It's no big thing."

I'd say that because I wanted to be able to persevere with people, to have faith in them. But I was so, so stupid. Thank you, Delores, for showing me how stupid I've been.

"Yes, I want you to go away," Charlotte said, laughing, as if she could have, just as easily, asked me to stay.

16

All the way home people were asking for money. Some were young, sane and homeless. Some were boozers, stumbling in speech and movement with swollen lips and gray faces. Some were psychotic and poisoned. I believed every word they said. Each one wanted money from me. When I gave I was blessed and when I refused, they cursed me. I stopped giving then, just to see how many curses I could accommodate in one city block.

I didn't want to go home but I didn't know how to find anyone to talk to, so, at least at home I could talk to myself. Sometimes on the street, waiting for the light, I'd try to talk to somebody but nobody wanted to except some sleazy guys. I got as far as my front steps when someone called out, expressly for me. I turned around and saw Charlotte, running to catch up. My eyes opened so wide and happy that the night came inside.

Oh God, she knows my name.

I was breathless and my skin began to burn with joy. She followed me upstairs and didn't mention all the fire around my couch, where we both sat, right on top of the sleeping bag and rolled-up towel.

"You know," she said, "it's wonderful to have a crush on someone but it can get frustrating when you can't do anything about it. When it's impossible."

That shamed me into looking down at the floor, and then was embarrassed for that, so looked at the wall instead.

"Do they always know about it?" I mumbled.

"They know," she said. "They know when you're sitting across a table and you want to kiss their neck. They can always tell."

"Well, if that's the way it goes," I said, "then no one's ever had a crush on me because I've never felt a woman kissing my neck across a table if she hasn't already done it in real life."

Then Charlotte looked at me and I looked at her. She let me look for much too long. She let me look at her huge legs with their beautiful bruises. Then she let me look at the skyscraper that was her neck. And I was so thankful she had taken the time to let me admire her like that.

"In my drawer are two nightgowns," I said. But I wasn't being sexy. I was being overwhelmed and looking down too much. "One is silky, light green. One is pink and frilly. They're both for summer. I pretend that different women come to sleep in my bed and we wear these nightgowns, talking like high school girls and looking at the moon outside the window. After we giggle and snuggle down cozy under the quilt, they run their hands along my bare skin and we sleep so soundly, with our arms around each other, that no dream can disturb us."

"Do it to me," she said.

"What? What do you mean?"

She looked like a maniac. She was strange.

481

"Charlotte? What are you doing? Are you acting?"

"I'm going to do it to you," she said.

I got so angry, I got furious. Charlotte knew I couldn't have sex with her, I was too crazy. Besides, she had a girl friend. I would never take love away from another person. What would be the difference between me and Sunshine if I did that? I could have punched Charlotte, I hated her so much.

"No," I hissed. My teeth were clenched so tight, my face was somebody else's face.

She slapped me. I was crying. I wanted to kill her. Where was my gun? Charlotte didn't kiss me. She pulled down my pants. She pressed her whole body so I couldn't move and jammed her hand inside me. I was pinned by a rock that was Charlotte. I didn't fight her. I wanted her. Tears and snot were everywhere and her breath was dripping wet all over my chest. Her fingers were huge and pried open the muscle. My body was the only thing left to me and now she was breaking that too.

I heard myself whimpering in a way that makes people despise you. Charlotte pushed and pushed until eventually she pushed me into a feverish clarity. I could see everything. I was burning. I could see that there was so much more pain than I had ever imagined and I didn't have to look for it. Those closest to me would bring it with them.

Charlotte was sweating all over me. When she stood the couch was wet and sticky and smelled foul. I couldn't sit up. I could feel her scratches, the impression of her grip inside me.

"Charlotte," I said. "You're just what I deserve."

But she was already bored.

17

Ever since the Rambo incident Dino had been acting sort of hostile toward me. He smiled like he hated me. He was always saying how good I looked and how I should marry him. Instead of saying "Smile" every morning he'd started saying "You sure look healthy, momma."

"Let's get married," he'd say about three times a day.

"I don't want to get married, Dino."

"Oh come on, Mrs. Monroe."

He called me "Mrs. Monroe" because his name was Dino Monroe.

"I need a good wife."

"Good luck," I'd say three times a day. "Because a good wife is hard to find."

Charlotte had left bruises on the insides of my thighs and she'd scratched my cunt so that it stung every time I pissed. It was hard to walk around that restaurant all day because the welts would rub and then start to bleed.

"What's that between your legs?" Dino finally said.

I had to stop serving the blue plate specials and tell him straight to his face.

"Dino, be polite, man, because I want to like you. Be my friend, okay?"

Then he shut up for a minute but came right back to the marriage rap.

Momma was still doing her routine. But, since she was too cheap to replace Rambo, she'd started working the register herself. Only, she was practically blind, so she'd ask each customer how much the check was and how big a bill they were paying with. When it came time to go to the bank, she'd roll up the deposit in a paper bag and stick it in her girdle before waddling off. That's when we'd eat the corned beef.

One day, who comes into the place but Rambo himself. He was weirder than usual, he was unsettlingly calm. He had the collar of his jacket turned up and the visor of his baseball cap pulled down and he smoked Lucky Strikes very quietly, staring at the ashtray. None of the crew said anything to him. I had to talk to him, though, because I was his waitress.

So I said, "Coffee?"

And he nodded.

Herbie's is one of those places that rich people think are quaint and the poorest people are always welcomed. Anyone who can scrape together one dollar and sixty cents for the breakfast special will be served. It's not the kind of place that anyone gets thrown out of. Even if they can't pay the check, we just let them leave. That's what dive coffee shops are for. So, no one thought to throw Rambo out. He just drank and smoked and thought things over.

"Look at that poor boy. He can't get a job," Joe said whispering in the kitchen. I nodded. Most of the crew couldn't get a good job anywhere else. That's why they

484

were all working at Herbie's. Take Joe, for example. Joe is a great chef and a good guy, but he's from Saint Kitts and he doesn't know how to read, so we have to pretend that he can. I put up all my checks with the orders clearly written, hanging on the line, and Joe stares at them all day long, checking back and forth every once in a while. But all the time I'm whispering, "Chopped sirloin, mashed and string. Burger well, L and T."

Joe wouldn't last a minute in a fancier place. They'd get someone who knows how to read. He was right about Rambo. The guy probably couldn't find anything else and had to come in to ask for his job back. Joe bet me a joint. He'd get it too.

After a whole hour Rambo got up and kind of shuffled to the bathroom. The back of his pants were dirty and stained. I could tell he'd been sleeping out on the street, really falling apart and punishing himself.

Rambo would have to hate himself and give up everything he believed in to crawl back to Herbie's and beg Momma for a job. She looked at him conspicuously over her glasses.

"You look like a bum," she said, too loud. "I can't take you back looking like a bum."

That did it. I would have done the same thing in his place at the same moment. I mean, I don't like Rambo, but to turn someone down before they ask, when they're just thinking about asking, takes away their dignity to make the decision to ask by themselves. It was unnecessarily gross. When Rambo blew his cool, he did the weirdest thing. He stared at Momma and then he turned around and jumped behind the counter. He leaped, like they do in basic training, and grabbed a big prep knife. He stood there, in battle, pausing for a moment to remember where he was and then plunged the knife into Dino's arm. There was blood everywhere. The customers started screaming and Rambo started running and Joe rushed over to Dino while

Momma called the police. In the middle of all this, I stood in the corner of the restaurant and thought, *Why Dino?*

Then I realized. It's just too damn hard sometimes to give up on somebody. Momma was his boss, telling him what to do for three years. All that time Rambo had been phony polite to her every day. He couldn't let go of that. Somewhere inside he thought he still needed her. That's why Rambo took it out on one of us. On Dino. On someone just like him.

Then I went over to Dino. His apron was covered with blood and he was looking old and shaking but he didn't say anything. Not even a moan or cry. He just tried to keep it all together by thinking about other things. The ambulance came and the cops came and when everything was cleaned up and settled down, Joe and me were the only ones left in the store. Eventually new customers started coming in again, looking for menus, not knowing about anything that had gone on before. So Joe and I looked each other in the eye, he heaved a sigh and we started working again—me taking orders and him cooking them up.

18

Spring can be the best time in the city because it's so emotional, but some years it only lasts a day. This year it rained cool and gray for two weeks, which gave everyone enough time to think something over. But as soon as the sun came out it got hot and that was the end of that.

I woke up that morning right in the middle of spring and it was too early. The sun had already come up but no one was taking advantage of it yet. Although some kind of breeze stuck its hand in through the window every now and then, it was obviously just a matter of time before the heat became unbearable.

There was nothing in the refrigerator except a beer and the gun, freezing away on the top shelf. I brought them both back to the couch and stretched out, naked, my skin so soft. All I could let myself understand on that beautiful morning, balancing a gun on my belly, its nose nestling in my pubic hair, was a profound sadness.

Everything was in confusion. A young woman was dead with no explanation, unless Beatriz killed her to defend her honor. But, was honor reason enough to kill a sixteen-year-old? If the answer was yes, it was certainly reason enough to kill a photographer from *Vogue*. Charlotte and Beatriz held a secret for me, but I couldn't tell if their answer lay in love or violence. Whenever one was apparent the other stirred in the shadows. I could not integrate those two feelings into my life the way they fit together so perfectly in theirs. Charlotte and Beatriz maintain their passion and brutality with each other but I have to face all my anger alone. Before the first hour of this new day had gone I was already angry again, punching my fists into imaginary faces and hearing the echo of old lies. Then I finished my beer.

By late morning I was agitated and sweating and decided to go outside. On the street, people were moving very slowly. Some of them had been drinking already too, usually tall, warm beers in brown paper bags. They drank Colt or Bud, a dollar eighty-five a quart. I could afford rum. I was working.

It's men, for the most part, who drink outside in the morning in the park. They sit placidly on benches with shirts hanging from their belts, nipples brown like roasted coffee beans, listening to a Spanish radio station. I wanted to listen too, but they started talking to me and I couldn't hear what they were saying. I just stared because they moved slowly like branches, like movie screens as the projector breaks down. It was like the last moment of a dream when the telephone rings and you desperately want to keep sleeping because you know there's nothing at all for you out there.

This bag lady that I know was looking in the garbage for deposit bottles. She had white hair and a thousand wrinkles. Her face was like crushed velvet, like you could peel it off her and she'd be young again underneath. It's too awful to be so old and sleeping in the shelter.

"Let me tell you something," she said. "Let me tell you something."

"All right, ma," I said. "What is it?"

"It's awful," she said. "It's awful when you ain't got no place to go and they put you in the street. To get a place you gotta have a thousand dollars. How can I get that?"

She wore an old winter coat. She wore everything.

"I don't know, ma," I said, giving her two dollars, but she didn't move on right away.

"It's awful," she said, starting to cry from realizing for the thousandth time that day how awful it really was.

"I know, ma."

I was crying too. It was so hot. But the whole time it was like she was on a television set and I wasn't crying for her because there are people just like her everywhere you look. I was crying for me because I didn't know how to live in this world. I had no idea.

"Let me come stay with you," she said. "In your house."

"No," I said. I looked her in the eye and said no. I didn't even think of a reason why.

"Okay," she said. We weren't crying anymore. Now it was back to business. "Okay," she said holding on to the dollars I gave her. She went on to the next garbage can and I had another hit of Bacardi.

19

When I woke up from my nap someone had snatched the rum bottle and I had a sunburn on one-half of my face. I was grimy from head to toe plus Coco Flores was standing right over me taking notes in her little spiral notebook.

"You make a great metaphor," she said.

"Huh?"

"You look like a fucking wino. Get up. Come on."

She didn't lift me from under my arms, or even offer a hand-up. She just stood there and told me what to do.

"Listen," Coco said. "Do you know that I like you?"

"Yeah, yeah."

It was embarrassing and I was still sleepy.

"Do you know why?" she asked, pointing me toward the water fountain.

"Why?"

I was really thirsty and then we washed up. I say "we"

because Coco was standing there making sure I washed my neck and also my ankles, which somehow hadn't been washed in a long time.

"Because you see the world in a really individually twisted manner and so do I. If we don't stick together one of us is going to get put away, and I don't think I'm first on that list. Do you understand? So, don't lie around in the park like that. Any crazy could come along and smash a bottle over your head or spit on you."

Her hair was streaked magenta, lavender and some other color.

"Amethyst Smoke," she said, fingering it playfully. "We just got it in the shop. Cute, huh? How many Puerto Ricans can you name with hair that's colors like Amethyst Smoke? Huh? That's really living."

"Yeah."

I felt like crying.

"Listen," Coco said. "It doesn't matter who Delores was, why you loved her then and why you hate her now. Delores is a hallucination so the facts are irrelevant. What's important is how hurt you are. You're so hurt that regardless of who or what she is, Delores has control. In other words, you lost, okay? That's the reality of the situation. Look, I'll tell you the truth. I never liked Delores anyway. She wouldn't even ask me how I was doing, you know? She's not a friendly girl. There, does that help you feel better?"

"What do *you* do to keep it together, Coco?"

"I'm busy right now experiencing life."

"What's the difference between living it and experiencing it?"

"Now I'm seeing it with the narrative eye, you jerk. Take a look around. It's all there."

I started checking out the park with Coco, and it gave me so many memories of all kinds of people. There were winners and losers and gays and straights and me and

Delores. There were too many dogs, though, and the whole place smelled of piss.

"Hey look."

Coco pointed through the busted-up playground, next to the art gallery over by the condos where Cher was supposedly moving in soon. Two white women had been stopped by two white cops in one police car.

"Busted," Coco said. "Come on."

I followed her closer and closer until we were practically on top of the whole procedure. The cops were going through one of the women's pocketbook, taking out her personal things and laying them on the hood of the car.

"Let's get closer," Coco said. "If they know that someone is watching, the cops won't try any brutality. They hate it when someone watches them do a bust. They lose their cool."

The woman being searched was definitely a junkie and couldn't keep a straight face. When he found a little piece of aluminum foil, she started jabbering away with half-baked explanations, as if talking as fast as you could would keep him from opening it. She was freaked out, scared, like she'd been inside ten times before and could not stand the idea of going in again.

Me and Coco were staring at the cop's fingers as he slowly unfolded the foil. He looked up once, looked right at us like he was nervous as hell. That's how close we were. He unfolded the first fold and he unfolded the second and then the third and then it was open. But there was no dope inside. No white powder, nothing. He couldn't believe it. He turned it over and over in his hand but there was nothing there. Then the woman remembered something. She started laughing and laughing. She remembered that she had gotten straight an hour ago and put the foil wrapper back in her purse. It was inside her, so he couldn't get his piggy paws on it or her. She was laughing really loud too. Then me and Coco were laughing and laughing. We all laughed until the cops drove away.

"Come on," Coco said. "It's time for the Hard Core matinee."

And still smiling, I followed her to the club.

20

Some guy with an Iron Maiden tattoo vomited in our direction as Coco led me past all the new condominiums and few remaining flophouses left on the Bowery. We passed the shelter for homeless men, the lobster place with singing waitresses, putrid Phebe's and walked through the grimy doorway of CBGB's, the punk palace. The people inside were loud and overwhelmingly ugly. Each one had processed their hair into such an advanced state of artificiality that they deprived everyone close to them of touching it soft or smelling it sweet. It was teased up, Stiffed into spikes, shaved, extended and always dyed, in a procedure utterly boring and out of date. Didn't they know that Sid Vicious was the stuff of Hollywood movies and they too would soon be petrified in their hard-core state if they didn't get hip to a new thing real soon?

Everywhere there were kids and the kids were making deals, or imitating what they saw as the rough-and-tumble world of deal making. Deals for bands, for gigs, for dope and sex. Deals that were nothing but big talk and small return. Deals because there was nothing else to talk about and the music was usually too loud to discuss anything substantial.

Also too many boys. Dirty boys trying to look mean, in training not to give a shit. Lots of boys in black boots, not a single one was pretty. The girls who hung on to them disappeared, but the girls who came in with each other were cute, chubby fourteen-year-olds with fake IDs, one shock of dyed black hair hanging over one eye. They were young enough to still be giggling from behind one cupped hand. Just like I used to do.

"See that girl?" said the sceevy boy standing next to his greasy friend. "She's an awesome fuck."

Then the band blasted on again.

CBGB's walls were covered with remnants of torn-off posters. Thousands of little corners still Scotch-taped to the wall, and then some larger scraps advertising the Nihilistics, False Prophets and the Spineless Yesmen. The air-conditioning worked.

Napalm was the band that afternoon. They all had the same haircut, shaved frontal lobes with backside shags that made them look like moles coming up through Astroturf. Their other common denominator was big, dirty fingernails that no woman should ever let near her body. Three of them had old underwear sticking out of the backs of their pants, which had been bought at a fancy Saint Mark's Place boutique years earlier when they were still NYU students. Now, though, the asses sagged, the colors faded and their entire wardrobes were stained from Stromboli's pizza and puking. Phone numbers scribbled on torn Marlboro packs, learning how to smoke and drink, not enough love, just rock-and-roll bands with no personality, filled that room that afternoon. Two rums for me and then an oblivion of noise.

Coco and I stumbled out of there both drunk, since Coco was susceptible to influence and my influence was a bad one.

"Hey Coke, do you mind if I call you Coke?"

"Only if you let me call you asshole."

"Listen, Coco, there's Daniel, Beatriz's son."

"Who?"

"My friend's son Daniel."

He was leaning against a car looking as cool as a sweating teen-ager can look at four in the afternoon, deep in conversation with some white guy with dyed black hair.

"That's no Daniel," Coco said, leaning on my arm a little bit. It was one thing to be drunk in the air-conditioning, but out there in the sun it really took its toll.

"That's Juan Colon. Last year he was Juan Colon at any rate. This year he changed his name to Johnny. He's from PR."

"That's no Juan Colon, I'm telling you." I really wanted a cigarette and started feeling up all my pockets and casing the crowd for a good person to grub from. "His name is Daniel Piazzola. He's from Argentina."

"No, man." Coco was looking for cigarettes too and pulled out two crumpled Virginia Slims from the bottom of her bag. "I know him. He's from PR."

Now we had to find matches.

"Excuse me, do you have a light?" I asked some gross shithead.

"Coco, talk to him in Spanish and listen to his accent. Then you'll know where he's from."

"What? Are you crazy? I don't speak Spanish. One, two, three cocksucker. That's all I know. Let's go to your house and smoke some herb."

But I had to talk to him. Johnny Colon, what a liar. Well, he came by it honestly, that's for sure. Charlotte and

Beatriz created a legacy of lies and deception combined with certain elements of beauty that couldn't easily be discounted. But the closer I got to this gawky boy leaning against a car, the more clearly I could see the packages of neatly folded aluminum foil, wrapped up in a rubber band. I saw how gracefully he hid them in the palm of one hand, making change with the other and always watching out.

"Daniel?"

"What do you want, C or D?"

"Remember me? I listened to your 'tumor' record. I've been in your house."

"Yeah? What for?"

It was really hot now, the car-hood metal was sizzling but I sat on it anyway because the pain kept me awake and kept my eyes glued to Daniel's.

"I knew Marianne too," I said, suddenly remembering the words of Urgie's sick bartender. "Her Spic boyfriend." "She said you used to watch out for her once in a while, even going to New Jersey some late nights."

I was very still while he made small movements with great agility and grace, the kind that can be used for baseball or sex or waitressing or selling drugs on the hot cement.

"I liked her, you know, but she was a baby. She couldn't keep her opinions to herself and got mixed up in everybody's business."

"Someone told me she was a junkie," I said. "But I didn't think so."

"Who said that? Bullshit. Bullshit. Marianne never used except on holidays. But that's like everybody. Even the president does that."

"So what did she need big money for, then?"

"She liked to eat in restaurants. She liked to buy new shoes at Manic Panic and get her hair done at Hair Space. She always bought the most expensive shampoo. She got

497

messed up in too many deep things because she was a kid and never figured out who to say no to. Okay? Now, leave me the hell alone."

I had to act quickly because my time was running out on Daniel's meter. He started to shrug his shoulders a little too much, like he really was tough and tough guys don't have time for too many questions.

"Charlotte said she was a junkie. It was Charlotte told me that. I figured she should know."

Suddenly everything changed. Daniel stopped talking out of the corner of his mouth. He stopped making change swiftly with his right hand. He stopped acting like a man when he was only a boy.

"That's bullshit, man. You can't believe a word that bitch says. Let me tell you something. If anyone's a dope fiend around here, it's Charlotte. When this whole thing happened, the first thing I thought of was that Charlotte got Marianne more high than she could handle and ended up dumping her in the water because she was too stoned to think of what else to do. That Charlotte is a real cunt. Don't believe anything she tells you. Okay, okay, you happy now?"

He jumped off the car with a jerk, as though I had upset him so thoroughly he couldn't stand to be in a place where I had just been. He started walking, troubled and slow, around the parking meter, easing back into doing business. Every now and then he twitched, eventually loping over to a third car, where he hitched his little ass up on the hood again and made change.

Of course it was Charlotte. How could I have been so blind? But never would Charlotte be part of something so sloppy and accidental as Daniel's scenario. I remembered those giant hands that would fit so perfectly around Punkette's neck. Those hands were the size of taxicabs. First they would stroke Punkette's hair, one hand covering her entire skull. Then they would caress her little breasts and slide between her legs, sloshing around in her wetness. And, in that quiet, out-of-breath moment, right after she came, Punkette would look up, flushed and grateful, to see Charlotte's hands, with the same ease, crawl up her neck and break it without any effort at all. Without a thought.

21

What's the matter, you don't eat anymore?" Coco asked as I cracked open a fifth of Bacardi that I kept stored back in the apartment. "This place is a mess," she said.

I hadn't said a word all the way back from CBGB's. I wasn't thinking about anything either, except how to get drunk as quickly as possible. I really was too tired to think about Charlotte killing anyone. I didn't have the energy to strategize or negotiate or imagine. I was just beat.

"Still no stereo?"

"There's a radio."

She plopped herself down on the couch, putting her dirty feet all over my dirty sleeping bag.

"Any more books?"

"No, Coco, I still have one book. It's over there behind the candles. Buy me another one if it bothers you so much."

She stepped over a new wave of burning novenas.

"Think you have a future in mortuary science?"

"Don't be a drag, Coco. Look at the book."

She dug out the battered copy of Patti Smith's poems which I'd kept over since she was hot, and now that there are people who have never heard of her, that book is becoming harder to find. But thank God it is still available if you really need it.

"Show me the good ones," Coco said, throwing the book in my lap. "Show me the really great ones."

That was easy. The book just fell open to them.

"It's all about Judith. A woman Patti loved called Judith."

"But she's not gay," Coco said, completely relaxed. "She's married with a baby and living in Michigan."

"So what, she still loved Judith. Listen."

And carefully, I read aloud, knowing it would fill Coco with inspiration and happiness.

When all else failed:bird, magician, desert mirage, the prospect of gold and riches beyond the cloak and sleeve of marco polo, I attached all to a woman.

"More," Coco said.

Blushing monument:pink sphinx, sizzling squirrel. fallen pharaoh. the exhaustion of the mind which attempts to penetrate the mystery of her.

"More," Coco said.

> I love her like the jews love the land.
> I love her like judas loved jesus.

"Yes," Coco said. "Yes, how beautiful. How wonderful. What joy in words. It's making my mind work overtime. It's setting my heart on fire."

"I know," I said. "I love Patti Smith."

We both sat there for a minute. Then I said, "Coco, tell me a story about a woman, a happy story."

"Okay," she said, flipping through the long-ago back

pages of her notebook, looking at her messages and talking them together into a story right then and there. A story that never happened but would always sound true.

"The story is called 'This and That,'" Coco said.

And I repeated, "'This and That.'"

"And it's also about Judith. The same Judith that Patti loved, but years later. She came to my house. It was three o'clock. I left the door open and was cutting strawberries over the sink, listening to her climb the stairs.

"'Hello, gorgeous,' I said before she stepped in.

"'How do you know I'm gorgeous today? You haven't even seen me yet.'

"That sentence started out in the hall and continued through the threshold of the apartment as she took off her sunglasses and laid them on the counter with a bouquet of orange tiger lilies. All for me.

"'I love how they jiggle,' she would say later, fingering them, 'like breasts.'

"But at that moment she was still nervous, having come from the bed of her other lover.

"'I just knew,' I said, kissing her, being very quiet because inside I was thrilled. I was so happy that she had come to me.

"After some tabletop talk over tea and a joint I could embrace her from behind, naturally, because I love her so easily.

"'Relax, darlin', you can relax.'

"And for that moment, I felt her love me. For the rest of the day, though, I was never sure.

"We talked about this and that. It was interesting, but what's more important, I was watching her. Then she said, 'Let's go' and stripped to the waist like a sumo wrestler. We kissed, almost dancing, naked, feeling each other and the sun. It was so sunny and bright. Then we went to bed doing this and that.

"'When I was making love with you,' she said, 'I was thinking about Sappho and how her fragments are just

502

what it's like. Everything wet for a moment and then something different like a rising passion and then something else.'

"She was lying in my favorite position on her back with both hands under her head, like a guy, really. It's the masculine things about her that I'm most attracted to: her gravel voice, her wiry arms, her thick black wristwatch. When she lies on her back like that and talks I could say a prayer on her chest.

"Also, she's always thinking. Sometimes too much, but that's where I come in because sometimes I can be girly and help her relax. I can make her laugh. I know how to make her feel better. This is the Judith who is the woman who loves me in the afternoon."

"That's a nice story," I said. "But I'm really worried, Coco, because I think that Charlotte killed the Punkette and I don't know what to do about it."

"What are you talking about?" Coco said.

"Daniel said that Charlotte is a dope fiend."

"Well, at least she's not a junkie."

"Why do you find everything so fucking acceptable? You know, Coco, some things are just too outrageous to let them go by."

"Like what?" She had on that insolent attitude where she could focus in and out of sincerity. I think she learned it from Useless Phlegm.

"Like fucking Delores," I said, really loud. "Like when fucking Delores said she loved me but she was really looking for a place to live. Do you think that's something I should take lying down?"

"Do you have a choice?"

"Fuck you, Coco Flores."

"Well, fuck you. Did you ever even ask her why she does what she does so you can drop it already?"

I saw that Coco couldn't decide whether or not to give in and let me say what I needed to say.

"Yeah, I asked her. I asked her why she said she was my friend and then didn't act like one."

"So what was her answer?"

Coco looked around for something to do and ended up lighting a cigarette and flicking the ashes on the floor.

"She said, 'I changed my mind.'"

As soon as I said that, I remembered the whole scene, like it was playing again on the video screen that sat somewhere between my mind and the back of my eyes. I remembered the day Delores said 'I changed my mind.' She was sitting in the living room shaving her legs with a plastic bowl and disposable razor. I sat opposite her wishing she would cut herself. She was wearing green, sequined hot pants and those legs were so white. I wished she would slit them open so I could watch the blood run all over everything like spilled paint. Her face was blank. It was the ugliest thing I had ever seen.

She left the bowl lying there, where Coco was now smoking. It was filled with little hairs. Then she put on some perfume and went over to her new girl friend's house. I was stuck here with my nostrils full of Chanel. It hung in the air all around me and I had to sit and stare at that tiny bottle on the dresser, waiting for the scent to settle in my gut. I wanted to smash it.

"I don't understand you," Coco said. "You think normal people are running around killing each other and then you blame everything on Delores. You're just drunk."

Right then I got so angry I wanted to punch everyone. I was one of those people who talks to themselves and punches the air.

"Delores was a cunt," I said. "Sex with her made me sick. She always did the same thing. Whenever she wanted it, she'd pull her shirt up and bounce around, shoving her tits in my face."

"I don't care about you and Delores," Coco said, putting out the cigarette with her heel like we were on some street corner. "I used to but it got to be too much. You're sick. You need counseling. Here, let's talk about something else. Look at this fluorescent paint I bought. Hot pink."

I picked up the little jar.

"Let's paint my house," I said and smashed the jar against the wall so there was pink glass all over the place. "Let's slam-paint my house."

"You're too weird. It's not eccentric anymore. I'm going home."

"I'm going to cut Sunshine's face open with a can opener."

"Look," Coco said. "Your feelings are too large for the moment, okay?"

"Why?"

"Because everything in life is temporary so you have to live only for the moment and this is not the moment for which you should be living like this."

"No."

"What do you mean, 'no'?" Coco said, exasperated. "Yes! If you would believe in and be satisfied by what I just said, you would be a much happier person."

"No," I said. "It's just too much. I'll never give in like that. My anger is justified, therefore I need to maintain it until I get justice."

"Then keep on crying," Coco said, as if it was nothing.

I picked a little jar of green paint out of Coco's purse and threw that against the other wall so there was green glass too.

"Look," Coco said. "The first time was weird enough but the second time was sick because by then you knew what was going to happen but you did it anyway. That paint cost me eight bucks."

I didn't feel like saying anything right then. Not "fuck you" or "shut up," so I just sat there and Coco sat there too. Then she started braiding her hair. Then she left.

When the door slammed shut I pulled out my gun from under the couch and held it, first in the palm of my hand, then gripped it cowboy style. It smelled like stale licorice or polished wood and it tasted like Delores. I decided that day that I would carry it with me at all times, until it took me directly to her. Then I would make Delores suffer. It was the only way that I could be happy.

22

All day at Herbie's I wore the gun wrapped in a clean side towel, in the middle pocket of my apron. It felt great, hitting against my pubic bone.

Things were slow that day, so by three o'clock Dino and I were taking a break on the back stoop smoking his Kools, which he always pulled upside down from the bottom of the pack. We were talking about what kind of day it was and what those kinds of days reminded us of.

For Dino it was about remembering being in San Francisco when he was young, "a few years back."

"It's the weather," he said, "that makes them all feel like that. It's like you're on vacation every day and can take a bus in either direction. I had a friend, Max, who worked at the Do-City Barbeque. Eat Your Ass Off was their slogan. Old men be sweeping sidewalks anytime they got around to it because it's bright morning all day long.

There's nowhere else I've ever been where you can take it so easy and still be in the middle of everything, except down south, but that's another story altogether."

I looked up, leisurely smoking, when I saw Delores coming down the street. Her eyes were glazed over all fanatic like and she moved as quickly as the Wicked Witch of the West, pedaling that bicycle through Kansas. In her left fist she clutched my Statue of Liberty postcard.

I jumped up as fast as I could but she still caught me square in the chest.

"Don't think I care about your fucking postcard," she said, shoving me again with a strength I remembered immediately. I stood there with no expression and let her shove me all around the back lot of Herbie's Coffee Shop. The gun was banging back and forth, cracking me in the bone.

"Don't think I care," she said. "But everyone else is going to care a lot. I have some friends now, you know."

Well, the truth is, I never felt better. I felt successful. Delores looked so ugly that I didn't even have to shoot her. For the first time ever she knew exactly how I felt. I had touched her. Delores finally got the message.

I watched her stalk away and picked up the beat-up old postcard she had discarded on the sidewalk.

"Shit, Dino, I mailed this months ago. God, the mail is slow. Man, it has really gotten out of hand."

Cocky as all hell, I delicately dropped it into the mailbox that was standing, conveniently, right next to the streetlight.

Dino was blinking, dragging on his cigarette, looking calm and very handsome.

"Funny," he said. "Funny how sometimes you're just sitting down having a smoke and all of a sudden you're in a movie. Right up there on the silver screen. And then, you're out of it again."

I was smiling away, feeling that warm spot on my chest where Delores had put her hand.

23

The next day I made a big mistake. I started looking at old photographs of me and Delores. There was this one that really got to me. It was taken one weekend the previous August. We'd gotten shriveled and passive from surviving the city all summer, and, when a customer at Herbie's recommended Ocean Grove, New Jersey, as not too expensive and not too far, we decided to stretch the budget and check it out.

About a half-hour after we got there it became evident that the whole town was run by Christians and everything was closed by nine usually and all day Sunday. Delores started calling it "Ocean Grave." The hotel that we were staying in was more like someone's home that got too large so they rented out a few rooms. In the foyer were born-again Archie comics and a board game called Bible Trivia. I remember that Delores and I pushed our beds together over by the window so we could see and hear the ocean. When we made love we had to be quiet because we were scared of getting caught. But the next morning we took a little stroll down the beach and found out that one town over was Asbury Park, home of Bruce Springsteen and the famous boardwalk. We jumped in and out of that scene, playing ski ball, eating fried clams at Howard Johnson's, going to a rock-and-roll revival concert of the Marvelettes singing "Please Mr. Postman" for the seventeen thousandth time, and then we looked at the water. On the way back to bed, Delores and I crowded into an old-fashioned photo booth and took a strip of four shots. The first three were black-and-white with Delores sitting on my lap. But, at the last minute, she grabbed my face between her hands and kissed it so deeply in front of the camera that my face got drawn into her face. When the pictures came out of the little slot she snatched the strip right away, tore off the three posed ones and threw them in the garbage, handing me the kiss.

"Here," she said, being nobody's fool. "I want you to have this one."

That's why I still have it and it hurts too much. Looking at it again made me realize what a pansy I have been, what a Caspar Milquetoast, letting her walk all over me. I conveniently turn to putty as Delores bops into my life for one second to cause total disarray and then she walks out of it again whenever she pleases.

That was it. There was no more beating around the bush. No more pretending. The time had come for me to take that step and get Delores. I walked around the apartment with my gun for a while. It felt good. What was more important, it felt natural. I wasn't going to shoot Delores and throw my whole life away. I was just going to scare her. Then she'd have to be polite for a minute or two. All I wanted was to say a few things to that bitch without having to hear her snappy comebacks. First, though, I had to get her into my house.

"Hi, Delores? This is me. I just wanted to tell you that

I'm very sorry for any inconveniences that I may have caused you. I've thought it all over very carefully and I've decided that you are right and I am wrong."

I was talking to Sunshine's answering machine.

"Delores, if I had known that you were going to smash me because I wouldn't get married then I would have married you. Being married to you could not have been worse than this."

I was trembling just a tiny bit.

"Well, anyway, Delores, I would really like to make things up to you in person. I would really appreciate it if you would stop by here soon and I could tell you how wrong I've been."

I poured myself a short one.

"Eight o'clock," I said.

Then I hung up.

The plan was in motion. The first step was to finish my drink. Maybe then I should reassess the plan. Maybe I should take the gun and shoot my face off as soon as Delores walked through that door. Then I had another drink and looked out the window.

"Everyone's a liar."

I was talking to myself out loud by this time and gritting my teeth. "Take Charlotte, she's as big a liar as Delores."

I hated her.

"'My house, her house.' Charlotte almost had me fooled into thinking that she cared about me, that we shared a secret, almost like best friends. But, the real reason she didn't want me talking to Beatriz was that Charlotte thought Punkette had told me something about Charlotte liking to get seriously high every now and again. In the meantime there's that Beatriz looking for tracks on *my* arm when *her* lover and *her* son were probably high in front of her every single day."

I was getting ready to walk right over to Charlotte's

place and give her a piece of my mind when I heard someone knocking on the front door.

"Delores?"

"No."

I opened it to find three women standing there. They looked exactly alike, even though one was rail-thin and the other two were not. Looking alike was what was unusual about them. Separately they would have looked very usual. Their hair was dyed the same color, black. And it was all the same style, ugly. They looked, at the same time, like a bad hallucination and very familiar. But I couldn't tell if that was because I was drunk. I couldn't tell which was more familiar, having hallucinations or them. Maybe they really did look like everybody else.

"We're from the Rape Crisis Center."

"What?"

"We're from the Rape Crisis Center."

"Are you collecting clothing for a thrift sale?"

"You have commited violence against women."

"What is this?"

I was not in the mood for this at all.

"You have threatened the life of Delores," they said in unison. "We have evidence." One of them pawed a greasy, crumbled Statue of Liberty postcard.

"But I just mailed that yesterday."

"With the New York City postal service, you never can tell. Anyway, you threatened to smash her face with a hammer."

"I didn't say I would smash her face with a hammer, I said I wanted to. It's not the same thing. Anyway, that's not the issue. The issue is who the fuck are you and get the hell out of here."

"Delores is a victim," the greasiest one said. "She is your victim. You are a rapist. You have metaphorically raped her."

"Why are you doing this?" I asked, almost crying.

512

"For justice," the skinny one said. "To get justice for Delores."

"Who's going to get justice for me? Where were you when I asked Sunshine to stay away from my bar on my night and she said 'You can't tell me what to do'? Is that right? Where were you when I asked Delores why she said she loved me when she only wanted a place to live and she said 'I changed my mind'? Where were you when Delores took my shirt off in The Blue and The Gold? Where were you when she was pushing me around Herbie's back lot?"

"We don't care about that," the middle one said. Her face was pasty-white and bloated like she ate cortisone for breakfast.

"Why not?"

"Because your name is mud in this town," they all said in unison.

They each had their street names painted on their identical leather jackets. Their names were Dubble, Trubble and Boil. Then I remembered where I had seen them before. They weren't from any Rape Crisis Center. They were Useless Phlegm. They were that horrible rock band that Coco used to manage.

"You're not from the Rape Crisis Center," I said. "Your names aren't Dubble, Trubble and Boil. Your names are Debbie, Amy and Lynn. You have the three most boring names in America. You're not social workers. Social workers drive Le Cars and carry appointment books. They really want to care. You don't do anything for anybody. You must really need bucks to walk around giving rape crisis counselors a bad name."

"Your name is mud," they said.

"What's the matter?" I said, walking past them and down the stairs. "No more gigs at the blood bank? Can't find any more health clubs that will pay you to hand out circulars? Couldn't find enough deposit bottles? Is that why you let yourselves be hired out as Sunshine's paid goons?"

"Why?" asked Boil. "Can you make a better offer?"

"I hope you got cash first," I said. "Or is she lending you her video equipment so you can make a music video of your band?"

"Video?" the one who wasn't skinny said. "All she promised us were free glossies."

"You are just bullies and cunts," I said. "Bullies and cunts."

"Your name is mud," they said. "All over town."

"Shut up," I said, slamming the front door behind me and running off down the street.

"Mud," they yelled after me. "Mud, mud, mud."

I ran all the way to Charlotte's house, but when I got up the stairs to the door, staring me in the face was that peephole. It was cavernous. I could have crawled into it. I didn't need to knock. The peephole would let me in. My palms left sweaty handprints when I pressed up against the door to look inside. The light was out in the hallway, so I stood, like a thief in the night, like a traitor committing espionage. I looked in and they were naked. Charlotte sitting strong and beautiful on a kitchen chair with her arms around Beatriz's tiny waist. They were sweating and so terrific. Their bodies glistened in the yellowed old kitchen.

Beatriz was curved and slithering, snakelike, looking down at the seated Charlotte with the greatest tenderness. Charlotte holding her so closely, her jaw relaxed, actually looking content. I could smell them from the hall. I felt great love for them. I became their accomplice. I would never betray them. Charlotte killed a lover with her hands and hid that behind a high while Beatriz covered it all up with lies so they could make love together in a tenement kitchen in the afternoon. Their lies enabled them to keep a passionate relationship. I was one of them now. I was so evil. I was in love with them.

I raced down the stairs onto the street, running, running again as fast as I could. My lungs were aching but I kept running, the gun bumping against my hip. My legs were sore and slapped against the pavement, but I kept running until sweat poured down my face and sliced my skin. I ran to Priscilla's house and she let me in.

24

I waited in the living room while Priscilla got comfortable. She brought out a bottle of good vodka and a nineteen forties ice bucket with long-stemmed art deco glasses, pink. Everything was something. Nothing was regular. It couldn't be just a chair. It had to be tacky or exquisite or a great find. There were too many details, like coasters from various world's fairs and ice tongs from here and there an an overload of truck-stop ashtrays. But, bless her heart, that little dollface stepped out of the bedroom all dressed up just for me, in her gown and panty girdle and even that black fall. She put on rhumba records and we danced around laughing and drinking from the bottle in between sloppy, drunken kisses. Then Elvis sang, "Wise men say, even fools fall in love."

That's when I murmured "Don't be cruel," and fell on my knees at Priscilla's feet, burying my face in her polyester. I rubbed my whole body in it. Polyester was my everything. I chewed on her girdle and she tightened the grip of tulle around my neck.

"I'm a terrible lover," I said, tonguing her thigh. "I'm the worst. You can still get out of it."

"I know you stink," she said, scratching eight long nails and two short ones under my shirt and down my back. "As long as I know the truth, let's just do it."

She put her hand on my thigh.

"Cool," she said.

She put her hand on my cunt.

"Feel how hot," she said. "You're burning up."

Pris tore off her Playtex and rocked back and forth over my face. So, I ate her the best I could, which was like riding a bucking bronco, because she was not shy when it came to getting what she wanted. And there is little in life that is more terrific than being put in that compromising a situation by a woman who outdoes her own fantasy. But then, surprise, surprise, Priscilla got all soft and dewy-eyed. That's when it hit me.

"Priscilla, you're the kind to fall in love immediately, aren't you?"

"It's true. I've never been able to kiss through walls or any kind of protection. That's why I need to carry a gun."

We lay back on the floor, quiet and out of breath. She raised herself up on one elbow and brushed my hair off my forehead.

"Honey," she purred. "What made you know I would let you in like that and give you exactly what you were looking for if you just presented yourself at my front door?"

"Well, Priscilla," I said, noticing her face under the makeup. "You're dangerous. You're dangerous and I'm crazy. We smelled each other out in a rathole so I thought it might work. By the way, while we're on the subject. I'd like to ask you a favor. Take your gun back. I've got it right here in my pocket."

"Why, thank you, honey," she drawled. "But I have plenty. And not one of them is registered. Why don't you just keep it?"

"I don't know."

"It comes in handy. And don't you worry about the address book. All that information is on my personal computer."

"Tell me, Pris, why did you start collecting firearms?"

She stretched out flat on her back to answer that one. Her breasts stuck up right into the air like the legs of a dead animal in rigor mortis.

"Years ago, when I was very young, I had a girl friend who worked as a hooker. There were always creepy men coming around demanding things and she was very tough with them but sweet with me, real sweet. In my youth I was a lazy lover, and she did everything. One night we were making love at her place. Her mouth was full of my breasts. She had such delicate bones, we were sitting together on a rocking chair. Suddenly, she stopped everything, right in the middle. I mean both of our faces were flushed red. When you're that turned on the air is sparking, everything could burn. So, her pause had this magical feeling. I understood perfectly not to say or do anything. She picked up her gun, naked, with those sunshine stretch marks girls get from making babies, those marks were gleaming like gold leaf in an old book. She pulled open the curtain and a man was standing there jerking off. His dick was flopping up and down in his hands, like a sausage. I remember the steel of her gun and the precious metal on her stomach. And I remember his expression, knowing she would blow his balls off. But she didn't. He was some old boyfriend of hers and she forgave him. He left her alone after that, knowing that the next time she'd kill him for sure.

" 'Get tough, cookie,' she told me. 'Get a gun.' "

"That's a great story, Pris. Do you know Coco Flores?"

"I've got a lot more," Pris said. "If we're ever in a car for a long drive with no radio, I'll tell you six or seven."

"Do you honestly think I need a gun?"

I was moving real slowly, not sure of what I'd be hearing or feeling next.

"Priscilla, what would you do if someone you loved, who had hurt you very badly, killed someone you loved who hadn't done anything bad to you at all?"

"I'd stay out of it," she said.

"What would you do if your old girl friend used you for a place to live and then dumped you for a yuppie with a loft in TriBeCa?"

"Keep the gun," she said. "You're gonna need it."

She dropped the accent and started washing up in the kitchen sink, putting on her plain clothes and looking like a normal girl again.

"I'm gonna give it to you straight. If you're nice people think you're a sap. Give it back! Show how much you hate them. It's the only thing they'll understand."

"Yeah, what you're saying works theoretically, but in real life, that's how people get killed."

"Oh, don't be such a pansy," she said, brushing her hair. She said it so carelessly that it tossed off her head with a stroke of the brush. I saw a fire inside her that cleansed her skin. It burned through her makeup.

Then I looked at the clock. The hands were dramatic. It was seven-thirty, almost time for Delores. I watched the second hand race round its face and I didn't have the stomach for hating her. I wanted, most of all, to believe in peace and love. I wanted to be romantic, read Chinese poems on a snowy day, watching a crow fly across a country sky. I wanted to sit with my lover in a big house in old sweaters, drinking tea and listening to Javanese music. I wanted to ride a horse and when it gallops, I start coming and when it stops, I keep coming. I wanted to be the horse

"You're sweet," she said, kissing me. "And this was fun. Maybe we'll do it again sometime. But not too soon."

"Peace and love, Pris," I said when I walked out the door. "Peace and love."

And oh God, I really meant it.

25

The basic obstacle to getting justice is that everything in life has its consequences. Of course, you could argue that *they* hurt *you* and *your* revenge is *their* consequence. But bullies see themselves as the status quo, and when a person is a reactive type, like myself, what you consider "getting even," they call "provocation." They actually expect you to sit back and take it. And once you learn that the consequences are coming, it gets harder to ever relax. For each pleasure I've enjoyed, I've had to pay back in sorrow. So now, every moment is shadowed by the evil one, waiting with a grin. Each emotion becomes, in that way, a parody of itself.

Outside it was nice and cool and clear. Every single person in the whole city was right there looking at each other. All the hidden craziness was blatantly dancing, blasting radios, making conversations, shrugging off responsibilities, flirting, fighting, leaving forever and turning over a new leaf. It was evening. It was beautiful. Then, across the street, I saw Sunshine.

I was a freight train. I didn't have to think. I ran right into her screaming. Not words, but a high-pitched shriek and she saw me coming and was surprised. I ran into her face and it had surprise on it because bitches like that think they can get away with anything. They think they can take your girl friend, rub your face in it, sic their goons on you and still be invincible. It was so sweet letting her know how wrong she was. I smashed her. I could smell her fear. I could smell her leather jacket, it was spanking new. I smashed her face and gritted my teeth and pulled her by her new shirt and smashed her again. I hit her so hard my hand broke. I could feel it go. Then she actually fell down and began to cry. You hit them and they fall down. It really works that way. Then some blood started dribbling out of her nose, like a school kid. It was the same color as Dino's blood but there was a lot less of it this time. Everyone on the street who had nothing to do kept looking at us and everyone else kept walking.

She didn't say anything. I felt great. I felt really good. I walked away with my hand swelling but I started to feel tense again, so I kicked her one more time, really hard, and then I felt fine. I was so happy. I was free. I was the freest bird.

There was only one thing left to take care of, Delores. I touched the gun. I could shoot her. Or better yet, I could smash her too. I could smash her ugly little face.

Then the weirdest thing happened. I remembered the way Delores used to say my name when she came in after work. I remembered how I was the only one who never took her money or broke her nose and who always took care of her, even when she was driving me crazy. I remembered the way we used to run into the water in our underwear in front of everyone at the beach because neither of us had bathing suits.

Oh shit, I thought. *Oh shit.* I can't smash Delores. I love her. Maybe we can talk things over. Maybe she can act like a reasonable human being. But we'd have to go away from here, far away from Sunshine and all those yuppie influences. Then she could get her own apartment and we could have a normal relationship. All she had to do was show in some little way that she really loved me.

When I got home the red light was blinking on the answering machine. Wow, my first message. I bet it was Delores. She probably thought the whole thing over and decided to come back home.

"Hello? This is Coco Flores. I want my eight dollars for the paint. Eight dollars."

She didn't even add "I know you're having a hard time right now and that I can't be there for you at this moment but I really am your friend." She just said, "Eight dollars." In fact, she said it twice.

I almost turned off the machine but there was a second message. Delores!

"I hope you fucking die," she said.

All my breath came out of me. I was very quiet. The city was quiet too. All I could hear was the buzz of the cassette inside the phone machine. It was spinning around and around. What would happen to all my anger now? Where could it possibly go? I walked into the kitchen and poured a drink. I didn't care what color it was anymore. Then I stood at the threshold of the bedroom, staring at the bed. Maybe I'd be able to sleep there in a couple of weeks. I went back into the living room and stared at the answering machine, sipping my drink. I listened to the hum as the tape rolled on empty, empty.

"I just want you to talk to me, Marianne."

It was a man's voice. A man's voice on the tape. A man's voice was inside my apartment. He was panting, out of breath, but from tension, not exercise. You could hear him sweating. I punched the button and rewound it back.

"I just want you to talk to me, Marianne. Talk to me or I'll kill you."

"I know who you are."

Oh God, it was Punkette's voice.

"I know who you are and you're in big trouble."

Right on, Punkette. What a doll. Look at the way she stood up to that bully. Who was it, Punkette? Who?

But the tape was finished.

All that was left of Punkette was her comeback.

Outside the church bells tolled eight. I could hear the noises again, the cars and the drug dealers and people saying all kinds of bullshit. I was shaking with the memory of Punkette and the voice of her killer. A killer who wasn't a dope-fiend actress. Charlotte was just a run-of-the-mill liar in a standard fucked-up relationship. She didn't murder women. She loved and hurt them. That's all. She didn't kill Punkette. It was a man. A man did it. Of that I was sure.

26

"Hi, Charlotte," I said, when she answered my knock on her door.

Something about seeing her again made me happy, like I was the person I was supposed to be because Charlotte was in the same place as me. I rocked back and forth on my heels, shyly like a little boy in short pants and suspenders. I was smiling, feeling peaceful because Charlotte was as close to innocent as she could be while still being Charlotte.

"I was wondering when I'd hear from you again."

She looked great. She was so beautiful. Just the way gay men look when they're on display walking down the street, cool and embraceable.

"You can come in, I guess."

We sat around the kitchen table. I could smell an overripe mango fermenting in the heat, mixing with the warm garbage, the perfume of Charlotte's refuse. She was quite fashionable and proper that day. Almost pristine, like the librarian in the old commercials. Once she washes with Breck, she becomes a showgirl. She was wearing those trendy, nerdy horn-rimmed glasses on the edge of her nose, complemented by a shock of black hair hanging over her forehead. Her eyes were dancing black things.

"What do you say, Charlotte?"

"I say what the Maharishi said. 'The purpose of life is the expansion of happiness.' That's all."

We sat there for a while in the quiet. I broke it.

"You know what I found out? I found out that you didn't kill the Punkette after all."

As soon as I said it I wasn't so sure.

"Right?"

"No I didn't."

Charlotte was my fantasy so I could make everything right.

"And you're not a dope fiend after all either. You just like a little taste now and again. Plus, you do so like me. You weren't just trying to intimidate or get information. That's right, isn't it?"

"Right."

"You're just a regular liar."

"I lie all the time," she said.

She took the mango in her right hand and bit into the skin. Then she pulled a strip off with her teeth. The whole world smelled of mango. It dripped on the table and when she wiped it up partway, she left sticky mango fingerprints for me to look at and admire.

"I'm always lying. If that's the truth then what I just said is a lie in itself, which makes it even more true than any regular fact could ever be."

"Thanks, Charlotte. I was scared to bring all that up but I had to clear the air. Now we can really be friends. Don't you think? Now that everything is out in the open."

"Yeah."

She was slurping the mango and untangling the

threads of fruit caught between her teeth and the huge, hairy pit.

"One more question." I took a breath because my heart was pounding over this one. It was the hardest question of all.

"Charlotte, whose house is this really? Punkette said it was yours and you say it's yours but Beatriz said it's hers. I mean really, whose is it?"

"It's mine," she said. "Beatriz has a place uptown."

Then she laughed but it wasn't happy. It was unusually stifled. She looked down at her fingernails and for the first time I could see that she was uncomfortable. She didn't know what to do next. I didn't want that at all. I liked her on top. It made her radiate. It made her special. Some women you have to break through to get through to but Charlotte was the kind to turn off if you got her number. It wouldn't be fun for her anymore. So, I tried to put a stop to the bad feeling. I wanted to take it back so she could have fun again, but another way of thinking was rumbling and growing inside me. It was taking over before I had a chance to hold it back. I started to feel very angry. I don't know why but for the first time I really wanted to hurt her.

"So you're not a killer or a drug addict, you're just evil and a liar and I love you anyway."

I wanted her to stop me. I wanted to be generous instead of vengeful. I wanted to say "I care about you" without trying to hurt her at the same time. I wanted to prove we were both better than Delores.

This is the place where the events passed very quickly. Time went so fast that even though there was a sequence, it was three-dimensional instead of chronological. Everything happened on top of each other at the same time. I'm not sure if it speeded up as I was speaking or right after I said "I love you anyway." But somewhere between the *way* of *anyway* and the period at the end of the sentence, Daniel came into the apartment and he was sweating. I had time to smell him before I actually noticed him, but I'm not sure precisely when. I do think that before he said "you cunt," I noticed that he was sweating and I noticed how much he looked like Beatriz.

"You cunt, you ripped me off."

He was holding a gun in his right hand, but I didn't see it at first because I was looking at Charlotte.

"This isn't a game," he said. "This is real."

She didn't have a chance to say much, but she did open her mouth. That I'm sure of. I saw her open her mouth but everything happened so fast that I don't know if she opened it to answer me or to answer him. I wasn't sure what moment she was in. Later on it did occur to me that she might not have been in my moment or Daniel's but maybe just in her own as usual. Maybe she was about to protest Daniel's accusation that she had dipped into his stash at the wrong time, or maybe she was turning away in shame when he said, "And what about that girl, Charlotte? Huh, what about that little girl?"

Maybe she was turning toward me to defend her, to tell Daniel it was a man who did it, the man on the phone machine. Or maybe it was to tell me to leave, or not to love her anymore. That it wasn't worth it. Maybe Charlotte only opened her mouth to stretch.

Daniel's bullet caught her in the process of opening her mouth. It grazed the side of her head, but that mouth stayed open and she looked both ways out of the two sides of her eyes, behind those brown eyeglasses. She made a classically comic gesture like I Love Lucy used to make when she was in trouble. The laugh track would go wild over that one. Then she put her face on the table next to the mango peels because she thought she had been shot in the head and her blood was on everything.

The most unusual element of my experience of this event was that I hadn't caught up with what had happened at all. So, right then I didn't have time to feel anything about blood from Charlotte's face, the third blood of the summer, the second blood I'd seen that week. I was still feeling the little seed of anger from our conversation and a bit of surprise that the way I expressed it was by saying "I love you anyway." It was that emotion, I swear, that made me reach into my pocket and pull out Priscilla's gun. I'd held it, caressed it and posed with it so many times that it felt natural, clasped between my fingers. Then I pointed it at Daniel's face. Of all the faces I had imagined at the other end of that gun, his was obviously the wrong one, but the turn of events had brought me to this place and there was no going back.

I felt a terrible explosion. Not huge, but compact and powerful. I tasted it in the air and then realized it hadn't come from me. It came from Beatriz, aiming at the sky. I knew I was able to kill someone, but only the right and most deserving person. I just had to figure out who that was.

Beatriz stepped through the bedroom doorway and slapped Daniel's hand, like he was seven. His gun fell to the floor, spinning, and we all watched it slide across the tiny room. My gun was still pointed at his face but Beatriz paid no attention. She held on to hers and picked his up off the floor. Then, with one in each hand, she fired them into the walls and ceiling until they couldn't be fired anymore and until the already cracked plaster fell off and you could see the rotting wood underneath that held the building together. Daniel was standing there surrounded by plaster. So was I. Charlotte was sitting, the collar of her shirt soaked through with blood. It was as though none of us could accept what had just happened, so we were all waiting for it to pass. But the room smelled bitter. It would never smell the same again.

I had begun the motions necessary to shooting Daniel in the face when, in the scheme of things, he wasn't clearly the most deserving. I had wanted to shoot him right in the middle of some thought that would have never been finished, had I been successful.

The face is everything. When you want to obliterate someone, you do it in the face. That's where all the lies come out. That's what you remember most about someone. No part of a person can be more cruel and stupid than their face.

Beatriz's face was stone with fury and had no room for surprise. Then she turned to Daniel and that all faded and transformed into the fear in every parent of burying their own children.

"I checked your arm for track marks every day," she said.

"Kids don't hit up that much anymore, Beatriz," I said. "They all smoke coke now."

"And you," she said, pointing to Charlotte, who was sitting in a pool of her own blood, unable to decide what she could possibly do about it. "You get out of my house and never come back."

"Your house?" Charlotte said, suddenly, as though she had nothing better to do than be indignant. "This is my house."

Oh God, they didn't know who lived there either.

27

It wasn't until the sun rose that I realized I'd been up all night walking around and then sitting down in different places. Sometime during all of that I got drunk and some other time it rained. That's what I remember best, the rain. First it started to land on me softly like kisses, and then it started to sing in an even, settling sort of way. It gave me something to do, which was listen to it, and a place to hide, which was inside it. Then there were thousands of drops coming at the same time and they started to roar, but I didn't want to leave, because it defined both parts of me: the outside part confronting the rain and the inside part that stayed warm and safe. I waited in the rain because it let me know that inside me there was still something alive that hadn't been ruined.

"Where the hell have you been?" Dino said through his teeth when I walked into Herbie's Coffee Shop and stood behind the counter.

"Huh?"

"You're a mess. Get over here."

He dragged me into the dishwashing section like I was a misbehaved schoolgirl and started running the water. "Shit, you got vomit all over your shirt. Where have you been? Never mind. Here."

He stuck my head under some warm water running out of those huge industrial faucets, and shoved a white T-shirt into my hands.

"Now, change your clothes and comb your hair. Here, use this." He handed me his red, green and black Afro pick. "Jesus, now sit down and drink a cup of coffee."

I threw my shirt in the garbage and sat there in Dino's large one, drinking the cup of black coffee he put in front of me. The lights were so bright you could see everything wrong and nauseating about the place.

"Do you realize that you have not shown up for work for a few days and you lost your goddamn job? Or are you in better shape than I think?"

A new waitress came whizzing by just then. She was old and had hair dyed silver and sprayed so hard it wasn't hardly hair at all.

"That's the Snitch," Dino said, chewing on a toothpick. "They hired her when you didn't show. She's always going over to Momma and saying, 'Dino threw out the crackers,' when I only did it because the mice chewed through the cellophane. Now you wait here until I get off and then I'm taking you to a meeting with me."

I sat in Herbie's for a couple of hours until Dino was ready. The Snitch kept coming by asking if I wanted anything, being snitty 'cause I was taking up a table. Every time I said no, she clucked.

"You just leave her alone," Dino told her. "That girl is my responsibility."

I watched Snitch all afternoon long. I never took my eyes off of her. She was a terrible waitress because she was rude to everyone she worked with. When she'd pass the

532

busboy, she'd never say "Excuse me," she'd only say "Watch your back." When the customers asked what kind of soup there was, she'd say "Read the menu." In between it all she'd be clucking all the time and occasionally squealing to Momma.

Dino and I walked uptown from work. We had never been next to each other outside of Herbie's before and it was funny to see him out of uniform. In the sunlight I would tell that Dino got into looking like a cool, older black man. He wore soft green pants, tight around the ass, double knits with a little flair at the bottom over his two-toned shoes. He wore a tan V-neck sweater, a little tan cap and lots of jewelry around his neck. He had a thin mustache that looked somewhat debonair, and a gold ring on his right hand.

"That drinking thing," he was saying, "all has to do with the twelve steps. It has to do with accepting a higher power no matter how you interpret it."

People looked at us once in a while as we walked. I guess we were an interracial couple.

"I am over sixty years old," he said. "I woke up one morning and I looked around and realized that America is the land of opportunity and a smart man like me should be able to make a good dollar. So, first, I stopped doping and drinking. Since then I got a mobile home in North Carolina, satellite dish, everything. I got a woman there and my son. I got another son in Detroit and I take care of him too."

He was smiling now, like he was on top of the world, like he knew the way and got joy just from telling me all about it.

"I do not take my worries home with me. I go to AA meetings, to AA dances, to the movies. But I make sure that when I hit that apartment alone at night, I don't bring any troubles in there with me or else they sneak up behind you and take over."

I saw Dino three times a week. I wasn't some girl he

could impress at a party. I saw how boring and hard his job was and how little he got paid. I saw him stumble out tired and frustrated, hanging around late sometimes like he had no other place to go.

"This is the meeting that I like the best," he said. "It's not near my house, but it's worth the extra trip."

The church basement in Chelsea was full. There were maybe a hundred and fifty people there and it wasn't even dinnertime yet. Many of them were black men.

"That's why I like this one," he said.

There was every kind of black man you could imagine. There were quiet gay men with skinny bodies, young turks with wild hair, old sophisticated intellectual types, businessmen, paunchy in their suits, younger artists trying to get straight and a whole contingent of street guys, smoking heavily around the coffee machine and asking each other for cigarettes. There was also a handful of Buppies in their dry cleaned blah, and dudes like Dino.

Someone was talking. When he finished there was a collective breath and then a lot of people raised their hands.

"My name is Tom and I'm an alcoholic and a drug addict," said one good-looking young man, with an actor's composure and booming vocal tones.

Then everyone else said "Hi, Tom" in a monotone unison and then he said "Hi."

Tom started to talk about how much he had wanted to cop that morning and how easy it would have been. When he finished everyone raised their hands again and another guy started to talk.

"My name is Jeff and I'm an alcoholic."

Jeff was a bloated, nerdy-looking guy with thick glasses and food stains on his shirt, a typical egghead.

"Hi, Jeff."

"Hi."

Jeff talked about what his wife said to him the day before that made him want to drink and how much pressure there was at his job. It all went like that, being lonely or under too much pressure or not having a place to sleep or a bad memory. Whatever it was, they were all saying it and saying their names and everyone said "Hi" and each one had some reason why they wanted to get wasted and why they did or didn't let it happen. But, after I realized how the whole operation functioned, I also realized what was different between them and me. They wanted to stop and I didn't. That got me off the hook real quick. So I stopped paying attention to the specificities of what each one of them was saying and got more into observing the atmosphere, like how each person talked as long as they needed to talk. Even if they started to ramble nobody stopped them. Sometimes it got really boring but no one looked bored. I kept shifting my eyes back and forth between the yuppies and the street people. I couldn't help feeling that the businessmen were part of the derelicts' problems. But there was no hostility between them. Everyone was concerned with their own personal thing. There they were, sitting in the same room talking about the same topic, except that the employed brought their coffee in little deli cups and the street people drank the coffee provided by AA.

I was leaning back, relaxing into the voices when a white guy behind me started to speak. I wasn't paying attention at first but I could tell from his voice that he was white. It was in his pronunciation and the little sounds he made between the words. He got more nervous as he talked, clearing his throat too much and mumbling. Then he must have leaned forward on his chair because his hard breathing was suddenly on the back of my neck and it felt wrong. Something in his voice made my stomach get tight before I could realize why. I think my stomach heard him before my head did.

He's been having problems with his woman, he said in between coughing and other distortions. She didn't want to see him anymore so she cut out with no note, nothing.

He knows where she's staying, though, and keeps trying to get in touch.

"I just want her to talk to me," he said. "Just talk to me."

It was the way he repeated the "talk to me" part that made my spine pull away from my back. He repeated it at AA exactly the way he had repeated it on the answering machine tape on my living room floor.

A kind of unfamiliar stillness came over me, the kind you read about in books when people reach the tops of mountains or hide from the soldiers or watch their lover leave forever. Sitting behind me was the same man who had put his hands around my Punkette's neck and broken it. It was the man who had carried her limp, light body through the projects and heard it splash into the slimy, shiny surface off the East River Drive. It was the man whose voice sat on a spool of cassette tape in a box in my apartment.

In my head was the sound of a waterfall that hit the rocks like a drum solo or a forty machine-gun salute. That's when I turned around and saw his long hair and David Crosby mustache, and his leather jacket with the worn-out fringes. It was the next-door neighbor from Charlotte's building. The cab driver with the electric shock on his door to keep the junkies away. It was the same man.

28

I went over to the coffee machine to get a better view. The killer had no neck. He was overdeveloped and sloppy. When he turned his head I could see that his mustache was red and filled with spit. Then I gave him a general once-over with a degree of disbelief because my search for this man had taken me much too far.

I poured a cup of coffee. It was bitter. I added two spoonfuls of nondairy creamer and three sugars. Some guy was hanging out by the coffee machine being quietly but distinctly out of it. He kept talking in low tones with no encouragement from me.

"I smoked some reefer and I got a headache," he said. "I've had a bad one since Saturday. I guess I'm out five dollars. A five-dollar headache."

I could see Dino checking me out from his seat. He

flashed me a big smile, convinced he had done his duty by turning me on to a really good thing.

"I've been smoking since 1964 and I ain't ever had no headache. It's them Trinidadians messing with the marijuana, putting in birdseed."

Dino waved at me. I smiled and waved back. David Crosby looked at the clock. His eyes were bright blue. He was a blue-eyed little boy.

"Used to be when it was in the hands of brothers, everywhere you'd go in Harlem the smoke was the same. No wacky bags then. No headaches."

Crosby was getting ready to go. He ran his large hands over his greasy hair and was out the door. I was right after him. I didn't say good-bye to Dino or anything.

Outside the sky was the kind of blue that only comes out when the sun goes down in early summer. There are days, now and then, when you're standing outside from the moment it starts until hours of beer and summertime conversation have moved the evening into night and that color into a midnight blue. Midnight blue has to be paid attention to softly if you want to see the blue. If you don't really look, it will seem black.

I followed him for three blocks before I noticed that at night I listen more and I also hear more as a result. During the day the eyes take priority over the ears for me. Only when it's dark does the music come through. He walked with his head down. I walked with my ears. We heard a carpet of machine roar, plush in horns. On top were the voices, and in between were radios. Then he got into the driver's seat of his cab. I walked into the street and flagged down one of my own.

"Excuse me. Do you see that cab in front? Could you follow him wherever he goes? Thank you."

"Okay," said the Israeli behind the wheel. He had a Playboy decal on the windshield.

The thing about a cab is that you sit back in the leather like a movie star and instead of being part of the street and the life of the city, you only watch it. You don't come into contact. The only sounds are the sirens and the shrill whistles that bike riders blow when you're in their way. Then David Crosby parked in front of his and Charlotte and Beatriz and Daniel's building and walked into the hall.

What had begun inside me as a private disaster had played itself out so thoroughly that everything around me was also in ruins. Confusion and violence defined the world in which I was living as well as the world that was living inside of me.

I took the pearl-handled gun out of my pocket and squeezed it between my hands. I pressed it against my heart and over my breasts, hard until my nipple was squashed flat against the bone. I passed it between my legs and in my mouth, in every secret part of me. I rubbed it over my face, pushing its nose into my cheeks, cleaning the trigger with my tongue. Then I was ready. Up the broken stairs, slowly, at first, and then fast with no fear, stomping, tripping, flying down the stinking hallway. I slammed against the door with my fists first, with my right hand already gone from Sunshine's face, then kicking until my feet gave way too. So, I threw my entire body against it over and over because I was the only person in this twisted city who wanted justice and was determined to get it.

I was fermenting in my own sweat. I was dancing in my own blood. I was panting, exhausted, looking for a solution in the limitations of my own body, when I saw his blue eye look out at me through the peephole. It was bloodshot and frightened, like he had been crying all the way home from AA. It was one eye with no context and no purpose. I put the nozzle of Priscilla Presley's pistol up through the eyepiece and then I fired. There was a nauseating whine, like a pig being slaughtered. Then the door began to shake. It began to tremble and I began to tremble from the shots of electric current. I was holding on to the gun. I couldn't let go. Electricity whipped through it and throughout my body, conquering me, making me part of the gun, part of the door, part of that rotting tenement building. The gun stuck in the door as I rattled and whined like the useless carcass of antiquated machinery. Like junk. That's when Beatriz came up behind me, pulled me away from the door and pried my hands off the gun, which clattered, like me, to the floor. I experienced a physical manifestation of who I had spiritually been for the past four months. It started with that snowy night in March when I got a weapon from a girl in drag, and degenerated into this hot vomit called late July when everything is putrid in New York City. It was the numbest pain. It was a dull wound caused by some foreign power stronger than myself, which could dominate me whenever it pleased. I looked at Beatriz but she was watching the first drops of his bloody slime seeping slowly out of the gash in the door and sliding past my face onto the floor.

"I got him," I said to Beatriz. But I didn't move from the floor. I was completely exhausted. His blood was on the collar of my shirt. "I got the guy who killed Punkette. I made everything right. I suffered but I never gave up and now I have a victory, do you hear me? I have a goddamn victory. I won."

"What are you talking about?" Beatriz said. "You weren't going through all of this to find some man. You are just a lonely person who had absolutely nothing better to do. Don't fool yourself."

"Don't fool myself? You should talk." Then I remembered what was really important. "Where's Charlotte?"

"Sleeping."

"Well, Charlotte is a goddamn liar, talking about fooling yourself. Everything she told me about you wasn't true."

"She did the right thing," Beatriz said. "Why should she tell you anything about us? That's private. Why should I tell you anything? I don't even know you."

I snapped my head back like she had kicked me in the

face and cracked my head against the bloody base of the door.

"Are you all right?" Beatriz said without thinking.

I didn't say a thing. I wasn't even there. I was a floating sensation. A sea.

"Forget it," Beatriz said, disgusted by her own show of tenderness. "I'm not going to take care of you. Now get out of here before the cops come and it will all be forgotten eventually." And she went back into her apartment.

29

I let myself sleep for three days. During that time no policeman came to my door to take me to prison. I had no bad dreams. No person called my house to ask me questions. There were no repercussions of any kind. A man went farther than the legitimate boundaries of human behavior and to the extent that anything can be avenged, his crime was now neutralized in the scheme of things because I had killed him. This solved one question—the death of Punkette. There were many, many questions that remained and which I had no energy or ability to continue to try and solve. I could only ignore them. I was not a satisfied woman. I was only quiet. And so, having gotten away with everything for the time being, I sat up on the fourth day and telephoned Herbie to ask for my waitressing job back. There didn't seem to be any alternative. By that time it was first thing Monday morning and he said to call him back Tuesday afternoon for the final answer. So, I walked to the park to wait.

As soon as I got there I saw Coco looking around. I had the feeling she was looking for me. So, I just stood there, not avoiding her, not running into her, until we ended up standing together staring at the graffiti on the bandshell, and the homeless guys who lived in front of it.

"Did you see the paper?" she said.

"No," I said. "Did the Yankees win yet?"

"No," she said. "They lost again."

"Figures," I said.

"Some guy on Third Street got shot in the face. His face got blown off."

We weren't looking at each other at all. We were both looking around.

"Yeah?"

"I had the feeling this might be important to you. I know you only read the papers when you're at work."

"It is important," I said. "Thanks."

Then we both waited.

"Listen," she said.

Coco very frequently began her conversational sentences with "look" or "listen."

"Look, I still like you. It's just that you've been too sad and it's hard to deal with that sometimes, okay?"

"Okay," I said. "I'll get you some new paints as soon as I start working."

I was quiet and Coco was kind of embarrassed so she said, "Listen, I gotta go now. I have a ten A.M. cut and dye. But I'll see you later. I have a new story about making love in the bathroom of the Waldorf-Astoria during a drag ball. Imagine how crowded the ladies' room must have been."

I watched her walk all the way out of the park and down the street. It was hard to lose her in the crowd because her hair that day was canary yellow with lime-green streaks. I stopped looking as she was about to go out of sight because if you watch someone leave until you can't see them anymore, they'll never come back. That's a super-stition but it might be true.

I walked over to the Polish newsstand across from the park and picked up a paper and a cup of coffee. Daniel was leaning on a parking meter wearing a baseball cap on backward and his name in big letters around his neck.

"Page eleven," he said.

"How are you doing?" I said.

"Same."

I started turning the pages.

"How's your mom?"

"Same."

"How's Charlotte?"

"Still there. It's family, you know?" he said flexing his biceps. I could see he was growing a mustache. "Family doesn't disappear," he said. "Family is forever."

"What does the paper say?" I asked, dumping it in the trash and sipping on my coffee.

"Well, that guy who got blown away?"

"Yeah?" I was watching him. We were so calm. We were both back in daily life.

"Turns out some girl went to the police a few months ago and tried to file a complaint against him. A dancer. He gave her a ride in his cab home from New Jersey one night and called her up the next day saying he would kill her. Turns out she ended up dead a couple of weeks after that but no one put it together."

He was so cool, he could have been talking about anybody. I could see that Daniel was becoming a man.

"How come nobody put it together?" I asked, playing his game now because I didn't have one of my own.

"Well, the paper says the cops wouldn't take the com-plaint. They asked her how she knew that the guy on the phone was the same as the guy driving the cab. They wanted to know how she could be sure. 'You talk to lots of men,' one of the cops remembered saying."

"What did she say?"

"I can't remember. Look in the paper."

I fished it back out of the garbage and turned to page eleven. I could tell Daniel was walking away, real slow. We didn't need to say good-bye.

"Men don't call me" is what she said to the police that night. "Men never call me." But the cops couldn't figure out what Punkette was talking about. They didn't get it.

I was so lonely at that moment, I have never been so lonely. I considered trying to remember every time in my life that I have needed comfort and someone was there to give it to me. But, instead I walked back into the park and sat down on a bench watching the old people with their old dogs and the young people with their young dogs. I watched two skinhead teen-agers trying to score and a man drinking wine out of a paper bag. An older woman was trying to explain something difficult to a younger woman and an older man and a younger man were in love. I saw art students in funky clothing smoking cigarettes and a straight couple having a fight. I saw everything because the sun was shining so brightly, the top of my head was cooking up a storm.

It made me cook up some very private things.

My moods swing like mad.

I feel close to people when I'm afraid of them.

Every person I've met I've used as a measure to see what relating to people is like, how much I want it and how often it disappoints me.

It's all over, I thought.

I remembered everything that had happened and all I had to show for it was Priscilla's gun. I took it out of my pocket, wiped it clean and wrapped it up in an old potato-chip bag sticking out of the garbage can. Then I tucked it under the bench, where someone who needed it could find it.

There wasn't anyone to be afraid of anymore.

At that moment I didn't miss any of it. I didn't miss

Priscilla and her polyester, not Charlotte and her power, not Beatriz and her desire. None of it was fascinating anymore. None of it was groovy. I didn't want to end up in any more go-go clubs or dirty theaters or smoke-filled bars or AA meetings. None of it meant anything to me. There was only one thing I really missed. I missed Delores.

SARAH SCHULMAN was born in New York City in 1958. She is the author of eight books: *The Sophie Horowitz Story* (1984), *Girls, Visions and Everything* (1986), *After Delores* (1988; American Library Association Lesbian/Gay Book Award), *People in Trouble* (1990; Gregory Kolovakos Memorial Prize for AIDS Fiction), *Empathy* (1992), *My American History: Lesbian and Gay Life During the Reagan/Bush Years* (1994; Gustavus Meyers Award on the Study of Human Rights), *Rat Bohemia* (1995; Ferro/Grumley Award for Lesbian Fiction), and *Shimmer* (1998). She has received a Fulbright Fellowship (1984; Judaic Studies), two New York Foundation for the Arts Fiction Fellowships (1987, 1991), a Revson Fellowship for the Future of New York City at Columbia University (1991), a Regents Fellowship at the University of California, Santa Cruz (Judaic Studies; 1996), and was a 1997 finalist for the Prix de Rome.

A playwright, journalist, and essayist, Schulman is currently at work on two books: *Stagestruck: Theater, AIDS and Marketing* and *Do Not Enter*, a novel. She is also adapting her novel *Shimmer* for the musical stage.